From Progressivism
to Prosperity

From Progressivism to Prosperity

World War I and American Society

Neil A. Wynn

HOLMES & MEIER
New York • London

First published in the United States of America 1986 by
Holmes & Meier Publishers, Inc.
30 Irving Place
New York, NY 10003

Great Britain:
Pindar Road, Hoddesdon
Hertfordshire EN11 0HF England

Library of Congress Cataloging-in-Publication Data

Wynn, Neil A.
    From progressivism to prosperity.

    Bibliography: p.
    Includes index.
    1. United States—History—1913–1921. 2. World
War, 1914–1918—United States. 3. Progressivism
(United States politics) 4. United States—Economic
conditions—1865–1918. 5. United States—Social
conditions—1865–1918. I. Title.
E780.W96 1986   940.3'73   86-19568
ISBN 0-8419-0767-6
ISBN 0-8419-1107-X (pbk.)

Manufactured in the United States of America

For Elspeth
and Sarah

and in memory of my father
Eddie Wynn
who died June 1, 1986

Contents

Acknowledgments

Like many historical works this study has taken much longer to write than the actual events it describes. That it was completed at all was due to the patience of my publisher, Max Holmes, who had more faith in the author than was perhaps justified, and, with many editors, persisted through many delays. The final product is intended primarily for undergraduates and is the result of several years teaching courses about war and social change in America. My attempts to present the significance of particular historical events within the context of broader general change benefited from the contributions of numerous final-year students who have suffered many bad jokes and challenged several ill-formed assumptions.

Many other people and institutions assisted the author. The Polytechnic of Wales provided leave of absence and some financial help to make possible my acceptance of a research fellowship from the American Council of Learned Societies in 1979. The ACLS fellowship enabled me to work unhindered in Washington, D.C., and Prof. Richard Downar of ACLS provided helpful guidance. The International Student House in Washington, D.C., provided a secure haven and a home base, which enabled me to become a student again, and the director, Paul Feys, Barbara Dirks, and the many "inmates" contributed to my education in the broadest possible sense. The Burtons, Murrays, and Rukeysers made my visits to Nashville, Buffalo, and Princeton possible—and enjoyable.

My stay in America would not have been possible but for the unpaid assistance of colleagues in Wales. The late Hugh Thomas was a dear friend and a source of encouragement who refused to let any obstacle stand in my way. James R. Burns also acted as my substitute and more than filled my shoes; Muriel Evans and Peter Brunsdon helped shoulder my teaching duties. My friend and colleague, Peter Mercer, not only took over some of my teaching, but tolerated all the agonies of gestation, read parts of the manuscript, and made endless cups of tea. For a medievalist he proved to have a sharp eye for relevant questions.

Other academics provided advice and suggestions: David Kennedy and Valerie Jean Conner were both incredibly generous in providing details of their own lines of inquiry; Arthur S. Link gave time, hospitality, and encouragement beyond anything I had hoped for; Jordan Schwartz made useful suggestions; and Arthur Marwick provided his usual mixture of encouragement and criticism on more than one occasion. Andreas Falke, Fletcher Burton, Pat Fuke, Jack McAndrew, and Sean Murray all listened and responded helpfully to my ideas in their early stages, while Ian Purchase read much of the text in draft, provided incisive comments and suggestions, and still urged me on. While I cannot thank these friends and scholars enough, I am sure they will be disappointed with the result, the product of my own usual obstinacy. The faults are all mine.

The research itself could only have been completed with the assistance and patience of librarians and archivists at the Library of Congress, National Archives, New York Public Library, Fisk University Library, and the Polytechnic of Wales. Mrs. Nicholson, Mrs. Roos, Mr. Kelly, Mr. Croker, and Mr. Kohn of the Library of Congress were especially helpful, as were Joe Howerton, Jerry Hess, James Walker, and W. Mahoney at the National Archives. Mary Jones got as much material for me as was possible in Wales.

Special thanks are also due to E. Samuel, who typed much of the manuscript and often made sense of what was barely legible or intelligible.

While I am indebted to all these people, many of whom had a greater influence than they might guess, my greatest thanks are to my long-suffering family—Elspeth, David, and Sarah. My wife, Elspeth, sacrificed her own time to free mine and gave endless encouragement. David and Sarah did their bit, but as David had the first, this is for the two women in my life with love—the next is for Bimbo!

Neil A. Wynn
The Polytechnic of Wales

Note on Sources

Much of this research was completed before the publication of the later volumes of the *Papers of Woodrow Wilson,* edited by Arthur S. Link et al. (Princeton University Press). Where possible these have been cited in the notes (thus: *Papers, 43,* 271, refers to volume 43, page 271), together with original citations of material in the Library of Congress.

Introduction

War, Reform, and Social Change—The First World War in American History

A British reviewer recently wrote that one of the major products of war in the twentieth century has been a mountain of written records, so much so that in the British case at least, it seems as if there has been as much writing as fighting. In fact, the reviewer could have gone further in his observation: the writing continued once the fighting had ceased as the professional historians began to endlessly examine, discuss, and debate the causes and effects of the conflicts so recently ended. In part this has been due to a desire to justify national policies, but it is also a recognition of the role war has had in shaping modern European institutions and cultures. Thus another British historian could conclude, sadly, that

> war has been not only one of the favourite collective occupations of the human race but also one of the most revealing. It has been a formative influence in the development of every society. . . . It has . . . reflected the characteristics of peoples engaged in it. . . . Thus to examine a nation's experience of war and its response to it is to learn something about its values, its social order and the way in which it has developed.[1]

This wider recognition of war's significance is now an established fact among British historians and scholars generally, in large part as a consequence of the work of historians such as Arthur Marwick, Alan Milward, Geoffrey Best, and others. "War and society" courses ranging from the Middle Ages to modern times have, in the last ten or fifteen years, become commonplace in colleges and universities, and numerous texts deal with topics including war and government, war and the economy, war and propaganda, war and labor (and Labour!), and war and women.[2] The same cannot be said of the United States, where such studies are still relatively few.

There still exists in America, despite considerable evidence to the contrary, a popular view of history and of twentieth-century history in particular that depicts the United States as having a peculiar ability to fight (and win) total war with little social effect or disturbance at home. The impression remains of a nation with such enormous resources and reserves of power that it is able to beat plowshares into swords and swords back into plowshares with considerable ease and few lasting consequences. This reflects both American optimism and the nation's actual experience of history. So, while military and diplomatic aspects of war might be fully explored, the domestic social, economic, and political effects tend to be overlooked: wars are regarded as temporary interruptions or deviations from the main thrust and development of American history. In 1971 Jim Heath, writing of World War II, "one of the cataclysmic events of recorded history," could truthfully say that historians "relegate the home front in America to a secondary place in the narrative."[3] Perhaps because of the consequences and "lessons" of Vietnam there has been some change since Heath's article appeared, and the American experience of World War II has now become the subject of some detailed study—by Richard Polenberg, John Morton Blum, Russell Buchanan, and others looking at particular aspects of society during the 1940s—labor, women, race. However, World War I, by comparison, still remains neglected despite one or two monographs on select topics and David Kennedy's welcome, but ultimately disappointing, study, *Over Here: The First World War and American Society.*[4]

The contrast between Britain and America on this subject (as in so many others!) is interesting and, as Maldwyn Jones suggested, revealing. That the Great War, as it was known, should exercise an "eternal fascination" for the British (and other Europeans) is hardly surprising. Both at the time and later, the war was seen as a watershed marking the end of an epoch and shaping everything that followed. "The shadow of the First World War hung over Europe for years afterwards."[5] All developments could be attributed to its effects: John Galsworthy has his fictional character, Soames Forsyte in *To Let* (1921) say, "Money was extraordinarily tight and morality extraordinarily loose: the war had done it." The cost of the war in human life alone was enough to explain this response. The British suffered almost one million war dead, the French almost one and a half million, the Germans over one and a half million, and the

Russians over two million. War memorials in villages and towns the length and breadth of the country testify to an effect of war that produced social and economic consequences and seared nations psychologically. When Europeans spoke of a "lost generation" they meant the war dead, not the scarred survivors. Such was the stress of war produced by these huge losses, high financial costs, economic strains, and military defeats, that four empires collapsed while the rest, even if victorious, were weakened by the outbreak of revolution or political and social instability that was not to be resolved finally until the 1940s.

For the United States, the experience of World War I *appeared* to be very different. Only directly involved in the conflict for nineteen months, America was under no direct threat of attack, and its losses (112,000 dead, 200,000 wounded), although horrific, were insignificant compared with those of other belligerents. In fact, more people were to die in America as a consequence of the influenza epidemic of 1918–19 than as a result of the war. In addition, America seemed to slip back easily into its old ways, to return to isolation, and move into a period of relative prosperity. However, it was not this apparently limited impact of the war that colored the early historical response. On the contrary: the war was seen as having considerable effect, but all of it negative.

In the revisionist writings of the 1920s and 1930s American entry into the war had been a mistake, the consequence of undue influence of either Allied propaganda or American arms manufacturers. The results of the conflict were seen as the nemesis of Wilson's New Freedom, the recovery of conservative interests, social division, and political repression. The war was seen as a futile aberration of American foreign policy that ended in diplomatic failure, divided the nation, betrayed American liberal promise, and resulted in a mood of disillusion and cynicism that "spread like a poison gas, to every part of the social body." This feeling was captured by a reviewer in *The New Republic* (a journal that had supported the war and Wilson's war aims in 1917), when, reviewing *All Quiet on the Western Front,* he described the First World War as one that "did no good to anybody. Those of its generation it did not kill, it crippled, wasted or used up."[6]

This perspective of disillusionment, encouraged no doubt by the writings of literary figures like Fitzgerald, Hemingway, Dos Passos, and e. e. cummings, dominated American historical texts through to the 1950s, and in doing so simplified the account, reducing the subject to a formula:

The trauma, frenzy, and repression generated by the war supposedly replaced political reform with reaction, social tolerance with prejudice, intellectual optimism with disillusionment, and overall public concern and engagement with retreat into privacy and apathy.[7]

The negative view, then, concentrated primarily on three aspects of the war: the growth of centralized authority in government, the federal attack on civil liberties, and the widespread popular hysteria that it produced, culminating in an end of optimism and the collapse of the Progressive reform movement. These topics have dominated all the studies of wartime America and continue even to the present; for Kennedy, the war years are "a sad story, a tale of death, broken hopes, frustrated dreams."[8]

The disillusionment evident in these historical views was a measure of the optimism and the high hopes with which America had entered the war. War was still regarded as "a great adventure, the greatest adventure in the world," and American entry was described as "America's glorious day." For some Americans, at least, there was the expectation that a "new civilization would emerge from the New Patriotism."[9] When such faith was proved unjustified, the victory parades were seen instead as funeral marches, and the peace settlement was depicted as a lost opportunity. "We had the most unique opportunity that ever came to any generation and we weren't wise enough to see it or big enough to take it."[10] Coupled with this sense of failure abroad was a realization that much had been sacrificed to the cause of war at home, and so domestic war measures were then seen in a new critical light.

A common element in the negative approach was a view that there had been excessive use of power in central government during the war. According to one contemporary, President Wilson

> became the dictator at home with unlimited control of the country's finances; the dictator of the press; the dictator of the farms; of all business, or nearly all; soon of the transportation; and dictator as to who of our youth should live or die—greater power by far than had ever been Abraham Lincoln's.[11]

Later writers were to agree, describing war measures as "the most remarkable laws ever enacted," which not only gave the president "dictatorial powers," but also resulted in an "authoritarian" or "socialized state."[12] Interestingly, the subject of the war administration has been one of the few to be singled out for examination by modern historians, but to be fully understood it should be integrated in the study of the rest of wartime society.

The shaping of public opinion, and the control of dissent, are also features of the growth of government that have clearly had a special fascination for historians. The subject of civil liberties during the war is still a matter of some debate. In what has been characterized as the "American Reign of Terror," one historian writing recently has seen "a deliberately planned program of federal suppression . . . , in the form of opinion moulding, Americanization, homogenization, the coercing of patriotic support, and the rooting out of disloyalty."[13] This program, implemented by the passage of the Espionage and Seditions Acts, led to control of the press and the suppression of dissent via two thousand prosecutions and one thousand convictions. According to one view, these actions were carried out by forces that resembled "the Russian police of the old regime." There is much to suggest that with these developments "democracy became a mob, ruled by mob psychology and injured by it,"[14] but too often this theme has been examined in isolation—out of the longer historical context and that of wider wartime change—ignoring the forces of general social and economic change that lay behind it, and placing too great an emphasis on central government.

The wartime propaganda campaign is also often seen in a narrow context, although in truth there are fewer studies of this subject. The few there are concentrate on the organization and structure of the Committee on Public Information headed by George Creel, and there is little real consideration of the propaganda itself or its impact. However, the total American propaganda effort, of all its government agencies, was significant and probably equaled anything in Europe in quantity, and probably surpassed it in the severity of its tone. While Oswald Villard could write of "the bitterest and most unscrupulous campaign of lies," the Beards suggested that

> never before in history had such a campaign of education been organized; never before had American citizens realized how thoroughly, how irresistibly a modern government could impose its ideas upon the whole nation and, under a barrage of publicity, stifle dissent with declarations, assertions, official versions, and re-iterations.

For Morison and Commager, writing slightly later, this "mass suggestion" was "one of the most appalling revelations of the entire war."[15]

Historians like the Beards, Morison, Commager, and many others saw one of the major consequences of the war as the end of the reformist era of the Progressives, and the beginning of the conservatism of the twenties. Just as later, following Vietnam, Americans might ask, "What happened to the radicalism of the sixties?" so too in the interwar years they asked, "What happened to progressivism in the twenties?" However, a number of later historians have argued for continuity, and so the question of the war's impact on progressivism is still a subject of debate. Put simply, the different positions are that the progressive thrust had ended before the war in either 1912 or by 1916; or that the war, with its enlargement of government for the national good and its recognition of minorities, adoption of Prohibition, and moves toward women's suffrage, was actually the high point of progressivism. On the other side, it is argued that the war diverted attention from domestic matters to foreign affairs and ended in failure, or that the attack on civil liberties and the rehabilitation of business disillusioned or discredited the reformers. Finally, some historians have argued that progressivism survived through the 1920s and reemerged in the 1930s when politicians drew upon war experiences to combat the depression.[16] What these different arguments reveal, is, of course, the diversity of the progressive movement itself. Never a coherent or easily definable body, the reformers reacted to their experience of war in different ways, and the variegated impact of the war on progressivism will be a major aspect of this study. However, one of the major problems with much of the debate so far is that it concentrates on what Arthur Marwick would call the "guided" changes: the actions and responses of the governors, rather than the "unguided" changes brought about as a consequence of the war itself and affecting the lives of ordinary people as much as, if not more than, political acts. Thus, whole sections of the community found their lives transformed by the war, as "hitherto socially and economically marginal individuals and groups . . . now became citizen workers, essential parts in the war machine."[17]

It is this broad social impact of the war that will be the main concern of this book. Groups which have been considered separately by different historians, when they have been dealt with at all, will now be drawn together against the background of both prewar changes and of the wartime developments already mentioned above. Groups such as labor have figured in excellent studies, but the best are still those that were written in the immediate postwar period. One excellent modern study, Valerie Jean Conner's *The National War Labor Board,* is of value but deals primarily with labor in relation to government and government policy—that is, "guided" shifts in social policy rather than "unguided" social change. Here I·shall consider those important administrative and bureaucratic aspects but also the impact of the war on wages, conditions, standards of living, and population movement—what *happened* to labor as well as what was done to it. Similarly, women and the war have figured in a number of monographs, but the emphasis in America, as in Britain, has been on one of two aspects of female war experience: either the political dimension and the effect of the war on the struggle for the franchise; or the economic impact and women's changing role in the work force. Thus two excellent recent books deal separately with these issues: *American Women's Activism in World War I* and *Women, War, and Work.*[18] My thesis will be that the two are intimately related, and I shall consider something of the totality of women's war experience, including the war's effects on the family and particularly children.

Finally, I wish to consider black Americans and the war. While labor and women have both often featured in early accounts, the same cannot be said of blacks. Frederic L. Paxson's three-volume *America at War,* for example, does not even mention blacks, and the same is largely true for Preston Slosson's volume in the *History of American Life*. More recent historians have divided the subject into discrete areas: some have looked at blacks and the military, others have considered the political trends, while most have concentrated on the "great migration" of blacks from South to North, and so subsumed the war under the heading of the rise of the ghetto.[19] Again, I wish to look at black life in all its dimensions and consider the way in which the First World War affected the pattern of black history between progressivism and the twenties.

To a considerable extent then, this book is a work of synthesis that draws upon a range of existing scholarship in order to provide an integrated study of American society in wartime. As Marwick, again, said in another context, too often writers have "addressed single topics in isolation, thus missing the complex interactions across a whole range of topics triggered by the experience of war".[20] While the synthesis itself may not be new, the particular emphasis on individuals and social groups drawn primarily from original sources should provide the special focus. While a comparative approach will be used to draw attention to the distinct character of the American experience, the real subjects of this book are the American men, women, and children, black and white, who, individually and severally, played a part in the war and whose lives were affected by it. For there can be little doubt that the war *did* bring change to the United States, some permanent, some temporary, but all of consequence. One observer writing shortly after the war had ended went as far as to claim that "the changes in the United States in a year and a half are as great as those of a century and a quarter preceding," and a number of commentators felt that the world and their particular society were being remade.[21]

It may well be, of course, that the war was merely accelerating developments already in progress. Undoubtedly, the fundamental pattern of American life and history had been established with the onset of industrialization and its consequences—a point made implicitly in the number of book titles which end in either 1914 or 1917[22]—but the processes of modernization, of urbanization, and of bureaucratization, once started, were going to continue. The war, with its emphasis on increased production, efficiency and standardization, conformity and uniformity, may only have been a speeding up of these processes. But the significance of the war was that it brought a host of such changes on a wide front and in an incredibly short space of time. In so doing, the war served to highlight the shift in social and economic relations that had occurred in the previous thirty or fifty years, and by compressing and emphasizing certain trends it made many Americans aware of just how far their country had come since the 1870s and 1880s.

Of course, all historians use periodization and begin and end their particular studies with one event or another, but the First World War was more than just an historical full stop marking the end of one period and the beginning of another: for America, as for other countries, the war was a complex affair that saw some pre-war developments brought to a conclusion, some come to a temporary halt, and others continue, colored by the peculiar nuances of wartime. The experience of war also brought new concerns, new emphases, new ideas, and new personalities to the fore, thus creating the sense and reality of change. So much was this to be the case that a digest of newspaper articles and editorials in 1918 found a widespread "unargued assumption that things will never be the same again as they were before the war."[23] Try as they might in the 1920s, Americans could not turn back the clock and deny the experience of the war years.

Notes

1. M. A. Jones, "American Wars," in Dennis Welland, ed., *The United States: A Companion to American Studies* (London, 1974), 153; the reviewer was David Englander, "An Age of Total War," *Times Higher Education Supplement,* 1 June 1984.
2. See Arthur Marwick, *War and Social Change in the Twentieth Century* (London, 1974); *Britain in the Century of Total War* (London, 1968); *The Deluge: British Society and the First World War* (London, 1965); and numerous journal articles and papers; Alan Milward, *The Economic Effects of the World Wars in Britain* (London, 1970); Geoffrey Best, *War and Society in Revolutionary Europe* (London, 1983), and editor of the Fontana History of European War and Society series. The Open University History course and television programs broadcast on BBC television entitled "War and Society" (led by Marwick) have been very influential in Britain. See for example, J. M. Winter, ed., *War and Economic Development* (Cambridge, England, 1975); B. Bond, ed., *War and Society: A Yearbook of Military History* (London, 1975); and, with I. Roy, vol. 2 (London, 1977).
3. Jim Heath, "Domestic America During World War II: Research Opportunities for Historians," *Journal of American History* 58 (September 1971): 384–414.
4. *Over Here: The First World War and American Society* (New York and Oxford, 1980), despite its title is not, as the author admits (p.v.) "a study of the impact of the war on American society," but only of certain aspects of it. Thus labor, women, and blacks are all dealt with in a single chapter, and the main focus of this ably written book is on traditional areas of interest. The central chapters deal with the military experience and its interpretation through literature. Two other studies, both "folksy"—almost to the point of nostalgia—are Edward Robb Ellis,

Echoes of Distant Thunder: Life in the United States, 1914–1918 (New York, 1975); and Steven Jantzen, *Hooray for Peace, Hurrah for War: The United States During World War I* (New York and Ontario, 1978).

5. A. J. P. Taylor, *From Sarajevo to Potsdam* (London, 1966), 59.
6. T. S. Matthews in *The New Republic*, 19 June 1929, 130; Samuel Eliot Morison and Henry Steele Commager, *The Growth of the American Republic* (New York, 1950), II, 549.
7. John M. Cooper, ed., *Causes and Consequences of World War I* (New York, 1972), 24–25.
8. Kennedy, *Over Here*, vii.
9. Mary Roberts Rinehart, "The Altar of Freedom," *Saturday Evening Post*, 21 April 1917; *Washington Post*, 19 April 1917; Carl Vrooman quoted in Ross E. Paulson, *Radicalism and Reform: The Vrooman Family and American Social Thought, 1837–1937* (Kentucky, 1968), 238.
10. Raymond B. Fosdick, *Chronicle of a Generation: An Autobiography* (New York, 1958), 212.
11. Oswald Garrison Villard, *Fighting Years: Memoirs of a Liberal Editor* (New York, 1938), 326.
12. Charles and Mary Beard, *The Rise of American Civilization: Vol. II: The Industrial Era* (New York, 1929), 635, 636; Morison and Commager, *The Growth of the American Republic*, 469–70.
13. Paul L. Murphy, *World War I and the Origins of Civil Liberties in the United States* (New York and London, 1979), 15; H. C. Peterson and Gilbert C. Fite, *Opponents of War, 1917–1918* (Seattle and London, 1968), 194. Other studies of civil liberties in wartime include: Zechariah Chafee, *Freedom of Speech* (London, 1920); Harry N. Scheiber, *The Wilson Administration and Civil Liberties, 1917–1921* (Ithaca, 1960); Joan M. Jensen, *The Price of Vigilance* (Chicago and New York, 1968).
14. Beard and Beard, *Rise of American Civilization*, 643; Frederic L. Paxson, *American Democracy and the World War: America at War, 1917–1918* (New York, 1939), 272.
15. Villard, *Fighting Years*, 327; Beard and Beard, *Rise of American Civilization*, 639–40; Morison and Commager, *The Growth of the American Republic*, 477. The two major studies of American propaganda are James R. Mock and Cedric Larson, *Words That Won the War: The Story of the Committee on Public Information 1917–1919* (New York, 1939); and Stephen Vaughn, *Holding Fast the Inner Lines: Democracy, Nationalism, and the Committee on Public Information* (Chapel Hill, 1980).
16. Contemporary views were expressed in *The New Republic*, 8 December 1920; *The Nation*, 2 November 1920 and 9 January 1924; *Survey*, 1 February 1926. The variety of historical viewpoints can be seen in Allen F. Davis, "Welfare, Reform and World War I," *American Quarterly* 19 (Fall 1967); Sidney Kaplan, "Social Engineers as Saviors: Effects of World War I on Some American Liberals," *Journal of the History of Ideas* 17 (June 1956); Arthur S. Link, "What Happened to the Progressive Movement in the 1920's?" *American Historical Review* 64 (July 1959); Stanley Shapiro, "The Great War and Reform: Liberals and Labor, 1917–1919," *Labor History* 12 (Summer 1971); Richard Hofstadter, *The Age of Reform: From Bryan to FDR* (London, 1968), 272–301; Stuart I. Rochester, *American Liberal Disillusionment in the Wake of World War I* (London, 1977); W. E. Leuchtenburg, "The New

Deal and the Analogue of War," in John Braeman et al., *Change and Continuity in Twentieth Century America* (New York, 1966).

17. Melvyn Dubofsky, *Industrialism and the American Worker, 1865–1920* (Arlington Heights, Ill., 1975), 114.

18. The best studies of labor and the war remain Alexander M. Bing, *Wartime Strikes and Their Adjustment* (New York, 1921); and Gordon S. Watkins, *Labor Problems and Labor Administration in the United States During the World War* (Urbana, Ill., 1919). Valerie Jean Conner's *National War Labor Board: Stability, Social Justice, and the Voluntary State in World War I* (Chapel Hill, 1983) is a valuable addition. On women and the war see Barbara J. Steinson, *American Women's Activism in World War I* (New York and London, 1982); Maurine W. Greenwald, *Women, War and Work: The Impact of World War I on Women Workers in the United States* (Westport, Conn. and London, 1980).

19. Paxson, *America at War;* Preston Slosson, *The Great Crusade and After 1914–1928* (New York, 1930); Florette Henri, *Black Migration: Movement North 1900–1920* (Garden City, N.Y., 1975); Alan Spear, *Black Chicago: The Making of a Negro Ghetto 1890–1920* (Chicago, 1967).

20. Arthur Marwick, "Total War and Social Change: Myths and Misunderstandings," "War and Society," Social History Conference, 4–6 January 1984, Sheffield.

21. Albert Bushnell Hart, "The New United States," *The Yale Review* 8, no. 1 (October 1918): 4; and see, for example, letters from Belle and Robert La Follette in *Robert M. La Follette* (New York, 1953), II, 924, 935; Newton D. Baker to Thos. Howells, 17 October 1914, Baker Papers, NYPL; Charles W. Wood, *The Great Change: New America as Seen by Leaders in American Government, Industry and Education . . .* (New York, 1918).

22. See for example: Henry F. May, *The End Of American Innocence: A Study of the First Years of Our Own Time 1912–1917* (Chicago, 1964); Samuel P. Hays, *The Response to Industrialism, 1885–1914* (Chicago and London, 1957); Harold U. Faulkner, *The Decline of Laissez Faire, 1897–1917* (New York, Evanston, Ill., and London, 1951); Arthur S. Link, *Woodrow Wilson and the Progressive Era, 1910–1917* (New York, 1963).

23. *New York Times,* 10 September 1918; and others in "Daily Digest," National War Labor Policy Board, NARG 1, Series 2, Box 43.

From Progressivism to Prosperity

1

The Progressive Era
American Society, 1900–1914

In much of the popular imagination the view of both European and American society before 1914 remains that of a "golden age"—a period of peace, prosperity, and optimism shattered only by the experience of war. However, the reality was far different. For most Western countries, the prewar years were marked by economic difficulties, social unrest, and political instability as nations grappled with the problems created by nineteenth-century industrialization and the liberal-democratic ideas of the American and French revolutions. In Czarist Russia workers' and peasants' grievances, heightened by defeats in the war with Japan and political ineptitude at home, erupted in the attempted revolution of 1905; in Germany growing industrial unrest was linked to the rising political challenge of the Social Democratic party, and both were countered with authoritarianism, militarism, and an increasingly more extreme nationalism; in France too, divisions between left and right became more pronounced and led to political paralysis, while strikes affected areas ranging from the civil service to the vineyards; in Britain constitutional crises were complicated by the issue of Irish Home Rule, a succession of national strikes, and the mounting violence of the women's suffrage campaign. As individuals and governments struggled to come to terms with change, and to resolve their internal conflicts, the European powers were simultaneously lurching toward international confrontation. Indeed, internal pressures were part of that process as each government tried to redirect its domestic tensions through nationalism or to find relief in diplomatic or military successes abroad. In part at least, it was the interconnectedness of domestic and foreign policies that led to the outbreak of war in Europe in 1914.

While America did not share the diplomatic and international involvement and conflicts of the European states, it did, nonetheless, face similar domestic issues in the years before the war. Writing in 1912, the young social commentator Walter Weyl could say of America:

> We are in a period of clamor, of bewilderment, of an almost tremulous unrest. We are hastily revising all our social conceptions. We are hastily testing all our political ideals. We are profoundly disenchanted with the fruits of a century of independence.[1]

Historians subsequently have written of "the decline of laissez-faire," "the search for order," "the loss of innocence," and the "air of crisis" that marked American society in the first decades of the twentieth century.[2]

In some ways the problems seemed more severe in America than in Europe because the contrasts between old and new, past and present, were more sharply evident and the pace of change appeared that much greater in the United States. On the one hand America was, by 1900, industrially advanced, the world's foremost producer of foodstuffs, raw materials, iron, steel, and coal, and in the next decade or so was to produce many of the features associated with modern life—the mass-production techniques of the moving assembly line, the cheap automobile, the spread of mass communication through telephone, radio, and the movies, the appeal to the consumer market through large-scale advertising, and so on; on the other hand, the nation was still relatively young, still growing, and still in the process of settlement. The rural frontier—officially only declared "closed" in 1890—was still very much part of American life and culture. Owen Wister's classic western, *The Virginian,* appeared in 1902, and the first western movie, *The Great Train Robbery,* was produced in 1903. The last western states, Arizona and New Mexico, were only admitted to the Union in 1912, and events in western history such as the Battle of the Little Big Horn (1876) or Wounded Knee (1890), were recent enough to be recalled by many Americans. While many could mourn the passing of the frontier and the loss of traditional values in the face of rapid industrialization, more than 50 percent of the population was still classed as rural in 1900, compared with only 25 percent in Great Britain. Despite the development of communication networks—railroads, cars, telegraphs, and telephones—the American population was still widely scattered, and physical distance, regional variation, and separation still made for a more diverse and less homogeneous society than European counterparts. That basic diversity was, paradoxically, increased by the economic and social changes that occurred in America in the latter part of the nineteenth century. Thus, while much of the old remained, much that was new had also come into existence, and the historian, journalist, and descendant of two presidents, Henry Adams, could rightly say, "My country in 1900 is something totally different from my country of 1860."[3]

The most obvious and striking development in post–Civil War America was industrial growth and its effects. Rapid technological and organizational innovation resulted in a huge expansion of the American economy and the transformation of its society. The value of manufactured goods rose from $1.9 billion in 1860 to $11.4 billion in 1900; railroad mileage increased from 30,000 to 250,000 miles; coal production rose from 10 million tons to 212 million; and steel output rose from less than 1 million tons to over 11 million. Between 1890 and 1900 alone, the national wealth doubled—but that wealth was not necessarily evenly distributed. One of the features that distinguished American economic growth from that of its foreign rivals was the absence of central state direction and the concentration of power in a few areas and in the hands of private industrialists. By 1900 the American economy was dominated by business monopolies or trusts, huge business empires that virtually controlled key sectors, and that in turn were under the authority of single men—Andrew Carnegie in steel (before he sold his interests in 1900 to the banker J. P. Morgan, for half a billion dollars over dinner), John D. Rockefeller in oil, Morgan in banking. There were trusts too in sugar, cotton, tobacco, meat, flour, and even whiskey. Almost all life's essentials were covered between 1887 and 1903 as the number of industrial combinations rose from 12 to 305 and as over twenty-six hundred smaller firms disappeared. By 1900 1 percent of all companies produced 40 percent of manufacturing output.[4] Such enormous economic power enabled the industrialists to dominate politics and government almost unchecked until well into the twentieth century.

If economic wealth and political power lay in the hands of a few, it was made possible only by the work of many. The late nineteenth-century industrial development of America was matched and fueled by a dramatic increase in population. Between 1860 and 1900 the population grew from 31 million to 76 million, and by 1914 totaled 99 million. The major factor in this growth was the wave of immigrants, 30 million in all, who entered the country between 1865 and 1900 in search of a better life. Another 9.5 million came between 1900 and 1914. These newcomers not only added to the population, but also changed its ethnic composition, for unlike the predominantly white, Anglo-Saxon Protestant arrivals of the pre–Civil War years, the "new" immigrants came increasingly from southern and southeastern Europe, Poland, Russia, the Austro-Hungarian Empire, Italy, and Greece, and were mostly Catholic, Jewish, or Greek or Russian

Orthodox in religion. Mainly of peasant background, most lacked capital or skills, and the great majority had little choice therefore but to join the unskilled industrial labor force. By 1900 60 percent of industrial workers were foreign-born, while in the population as a whole over one-third were either foreign-born or had at least one parent who was foreign-born.[5]

The ethnic and racial diversity of the population was further increased by the presence of a sizable black population, the legacy of slavery. Almost 10 percent of the American population was black, but over 90 percent of these blacks remained in the former slave states of the South, where most eked out a living as sharecroppers on the land. However, driven by economic deprivation, political discrimination, social segregation, and race violence, and attracted by opportunities in industry and a greater degree of political and social freedom, blacks, like the European peasants, were increasingly moving to cities in the North. Between 1890 and 1910 some two hundred thousand blacks left the South, and already before 1914, New York, Chicago, Philadelphia, and Washington, D.C., had sizable black populations crowding into Harlem, the South Side, and other ghetto areas.

This movement of the black population toward the cities was only a fraction of a larger trend, as America as a whole moved from being a rural, agricultural nation toward becoming an urban and industrial one. In 1860 only five million Americans lived in cities, but by 1900 this had risen to 25 million and was to reach 45 million by 1910. Chicago, New York, and Philadelphia trebled in size while other, lesser, centers doubled in the decades after 1865. Although "there were fourteen million more Americans living on the farm in 1910 than there were in 1860,"[6] and America was to remain a predominantly rural country until the 1920s, the number of industrial workers was more than twice the number in agriculture, and increasingly it was the industrial and urban work force that dominated life and politics. Already this fact was creating tensions between town and country, the old population and the new, for, while many of the new city-dwellers came from the American countryside, most were immigrants. Almost a quarter of the populations of Philadelphia and Boston, and over 80 percent of those in New York, Chicago, and Detroit, were either foreign-born or of immigrant parentage: by comparison, in London, England, 94 percent of the population came from either England or Wales.

Within the cities there were further divisions along ethnic and class lines as the different immigrant groups gathered together and as the middle classes, aided by the development of urban transportation, moved to the suburbs. Subways, elevated railways, and public transit systems all affected the growth of the city in the 1880s and 1890s, and the motorcar too was beginning to have an impact as annual production rose from 4,000 to 187,000 between 1900 and 1910. By 1915 there were 2.3 million private vehicles on the road. Clearly, although the car was still a luxury few could afford, it was becoming more accessible (particularly with Ford's Model T introduced in 1908 and the adoption of the moving assembly-line production method in 1913),[7] and enabled the wealthier to escape from the city centers where rapid, uncontrolled growth had led to conditions reminiscent of Dickens's England: crowded, filthy, and dangerous areas peopled by impoverished, ill-nourished, and unhealthy industrial workers. In 1900, over two-thirds of the population of New York City inhabited slums, 1.5 million people were crowded into forty-two thousand tenements in Manhattan, and the infant mortality rate was higher than it had been at the beginning of the nineteenth century.[8]

As in England, so too in America, these conditions were often best described by literary figures. In *The Jungle* (1906), Upton Sinclair portrayed the stockyard districts of Chicago as an area surrounded by "ugly and dirty little wooden buildings," blackened by "half a dozen columns of smoke, thick oily, and black as night," which reeked of an "elemental odor," and in which the inhabitants could constantly hear "the distant lowing of ten thousand cattle, and the distant grunting of ten thousand swine." Here Lithuanians, Poles, Slovaks, or Bohemians lived in wooden tenements, "some times thirteen or fourteen to one room, fifty or sixty to a flat."[9] Nevertheless, Chicago—"Hog Butcher, Tool Maker, Stacker of Wheat, Player with Railroads and Freight Handler of the Nation," as Carl Sandburg described it in his famous poem of 1914—offered work and more besides; as Theodore Dreiser wrote in *Sister Carrie* (1900), the city was "a giant magnet, drawing to itself from all quarters the hopeful and the hopeless." It was "a city with the ambition, the daring, the activity of a metropolis of a million" that could offer "wealth, fashion, ease" to the successful. New York likewise could be seen in terms of "the magnificent residences, the splendid equipages, the gilded shops, restaurants, resorts of all kinds." Many were, like Dreiser's Carrie, seduced by these symbols of success, but many more failed, and formed instead "the class that sits on the park benches during the endurable days and sleeps upon them during the summer nights," "the class which simply floats and drifts."[10]

As these authors suggest, American society was marked by enormous inequality, but it was more pronounced in the cities, where one could easily travel from the extremes of Fifth Avenue and Wall Street to those of Brooklyn and the Bowery. It was estimated that at the end of the century there were four thousand millionaires but ten million Americans living in poverty. In 1900 Andrew Carnegie had an income of $23 million while unskilled worker in his steel plants earned around ten dollars a toiling for twelve hours, six days a week. In 1905 it was esti was the minimum income required to keep a family, l of all wage workers earned less than $570. Of course better than others: the average banker's salary in 1910 was $7,726; the lawyer's, $4,169; and the professor's, $2,878. In January 1913 the *New York Times* reported average weekly wages of fifteen dollars for a clerk, thirty dollars for an accountant, and twenty-five dollars for a mechanical engineer, but the following year Henry Ford created an outcry from his fellow manufacturers, and a riot among aspiring workers outside his plant, when he introduced the five-dollar day.[11] Even those fortunate enough to earn such princely sums (and there were few of them, even in the Ford works), could be reduced to poverty by temporary or seasonal layoffs, which were a regular feature of working-class life. Even in periods of boom some workers could expect to be laid off for a short time, and during recessions unemployment and economic hardship became widespread. In the depression of 1894 one out of every five workers was unemployed; in 1908, 1914, and 1915, over 12 percent of the labor force was without work. As a rather sardonic song of 1905 expressed it, "Everybody works but father."[12]

For those in employment conditions were often at least hard, and at worst dangerous. Long hours and hazardous factory machinery could make a lethal combination, and the number of deaths and injuries sustained at work in America was appalling. Sinclair described scenes in the killing beds of the stockyards where it was "a wonder that there were not more men slaughtered than cattle," while workers in the steel mill could be crushed or burned.[13] These literary scenes were based upon hard reality: in 1910, one person died every hour on the railroads; in the mining industry in 1913 there were 2,785 fatalities in a year when the total number of deaths due to all industrial accidents was 25,000. Many of those injured were women or children. In 1910 1,820,570 women worked in manufacturing, many of them in the textile and clothing industries amid dangerous looms, frames, and sewing machines. The same was true of the 1.9 million children under the age of fifteen who were employed, twenty thousand of them in textile mills.[14] The sewing room depicted by Dreiser, in which Sister Carrie was to work for $4.50 a week, was not untypical: "Not the slightest provision had been made for the comfort of the employees . . . the whole atmosphere was one of hard contract."[15] It was in such a place in 1911 that 146 workers, mostly women or young girls, died when fire broke out in the Triangle Shirtwaist Company of New York City.

Not surprisingly, American workers, like workers faced with similar conditions elsewhere in the world, began to organize themselves. The latter part of the nineteenth century witnessed the growth of labor unions and an increase in strike activity. In 1904, the American Federation of Labor (AFL), the federation of craft unions founded in 1886, had a membership of 1,675,000 through its affiliated unions and was still growing in strength; by 1910, total union membership in the United States was 2.6

million.[16] This, however, represented little more than 10 percent of the work force, and the AFL policy of excluding all but skilled workers and craftsmen through its high dues limited its membership. These conservative policies, and the tone of the AFL, were set by its president for all but one year since its inception, Samuel Gompers. Gompers, after earlier toying with socialist ideas, disavowed radical actions, mass unionism, and involvement in politics. Concerned with practical, day-to-day economic issues, rather than proposals to change society, Gompers's aim was, he said, to make trade unionism a business.

Despite Gompers's attitude, strikes increased throughout the 1880s and 1890s. Between 1880 and 1900 there were over twenty-four thousand industrial disputes. However, the employers were determined to fight back, and they formed organizations of their own, such as the National Association of Manufacturers (1895) and its offshoot, the Citizens' Industrial Association (1903), in order to resist unionization and maintain the open shop as part of "the American Plan." As a consequence, industrial relations in America were marked by bitter violence on both sides. In the strike at Carnegie's Homestead Steel Plant in Pennsylvania in 1892, ten strikers and three of the company-employed Pinkerton agents were killed; the Pullman strike of 1894, which involved the use of federal troops and the intervention of the courts, still resulted in twelve deaths. Between 1902 and 1904 alone, 180 union men were killed, 1,600 were injured, and over 15,000 were arrested in the course of strikes. The workers were not saints either. Strikebreakers were intimidated, beaten, and shot at, and a series of bombings—notably at the mines of Cripple Creek, Colorado, 1903–4, and at the *Los Angeles Times* building in 1910—encouraged the belief in a national dynamite conspiracy. Growing fear of class warfare led to the setting up of the Commission on Industrial Relations in 1913, but that body was itself deeply divided between workers' and employers' representatives and was to produce three separate reports in 1915. They agreed on one thing—"their recognition of deep-rooted conflict . . . in American society." That view was confirmed in April 1914 when two women and eleven children were among those killed in an attack on the camp of strikers at Rockefeller's mines in Ludlow, Colorado.[17] Although such violence met with public condemnation, little was done. With the control of politicians, courts, and the press, the employers were in the strongest position in the prewar years.

Confronted by conservative unionism and obdurate employers, some workers clearly were prepared to take direct individual action. Others, however, sought solutions to their problems via organization. In 1905 representatives of the Western Miners' Federation, the Railway Workers, and a variety of socialist organizations met together in Chicago to form the Industrial Workers of the World (IWW). The Wobblies, as the IWW came to be known, concentrated on class rather than job differences and aimed to unite all workers, skilled and unskilled, in one big union. A policy of nondiscrimination and low contributions followed from this, and, advocating direct, mass action, the Wobblies recruited from among those excluded from AF of L locals: the unskilled, migrant work force of construction workers, lumbermen, farm laborers, fruit pickers, and miners. Their support came primarily from the itinerant work force of western and midwestern states, but, denied the right to hold open-air public meetings, the Wobblies attracted national attention with their free speech campaigns in the years from 1909 to 1914. Increasingly, they appeared to be winning members from among the new immigrant workers in eastern cities: in 1909 the IWW successfully led striking steel workers in McKees Rocks, Pennsylvania, and in 1912, amid great publicity, they headed the victorious textile strike in Lawrence, Massachusetts. However, the IWW strike in Paterson, New Jersey, the following year ended in humiliating defeat despite the support and efforts of middle-class radicals like John Reed and his friends from Greenwich Village, and it seemed unlikely that the organization would recover the lost ground. Even so, the Wobblies still had an estimated membership of forty thousand in 1916 and were to prove an active force during the war years.[18]

A number of workers looked for political answers to their economic problems rather than the industrial action of either the AFL or the IWW, and they joined a variety of radicals to form the Socialist Party of America (SPA) in 1901. Created primarily by a combination of the Social Democratic party, led by the head of the Railway Union, Eugene V. Debs, and the Socialist Labor party, led by the labor lawyer Morris Hillquit, the Socialist party appealed to a mixed assortment of people. A third of the party's membership was foreign-born, and it recruited particularly among the immigrant workers of northern industrial cities, especially Chicago and New York. However, it also found support among native white sharecroppers and tenant farmers in the Southwest and, increasingly, among the respectable middle classes in the East—there was even a Socialist Society at Harvard, led by Walter Lippmann, and the Inter-Collegiate Socialist Society formed by Upton Sinclair in 1905 had branches in sixty colleges by 1915. In 1912, the SPA had almost 118,000 members, and in the elections that year its presidential candidate, Debs, polled 897,000 votes, 6 percent of the total, while twelve hundred socialists were elected to office in over 340 cities across the country.[19]

Despite the apparent increase in their support, however, neither the Socialists nor the Wobblies were really able to win more than minority support. The situation in America was unlike that of Europe, where, for example, the British Labour party and the German Social Democratic party were both rapidly winning a considerable following among the working and middle classes and were providing a real political alternative to the established parties. Divided along racial and ethnic lines as much as along class ones, the American work force lacked the group consciousness of its European counterparts and rarely spoke with one voice. Most native-born Americans, other than a few intellectuals and writers, still regarded socialism and trade unionism with suspicion, something foreign that ran counter to good, old-fashioned American beliefs in individualism and self-reliance. At the same time, there was often resistance to such political movements among the immigrant communities themselves either because of religious or traditional influences, or because life in America, while hard, still offered better conditions and greater opportunities than had the mother country. One such difference, and another factor in the failure of left-wing movements in America, was the responsiveness of the existing political system and the growth of an indigenous reform movement in the form of progressivism, and its eventual incorporation into the two-party framework.

Just as the Liberals in Britain tried to head off radical challenges by introducing their own reform programs, so too the American reform movement was in part a response to the Socialists, Wobblies, and other, more extreme, groups. However, Progressivism's origins were much more complex than that. The first demands for change, and the questioning of the principles of laissez-faire, arose from the discontent of the American farmers in the 1870s and 1880s and resulted in the formation of the Populist party in 1892. Although populism declined after defeat in the 1896 election and the failure to achieve its immediate, short-term objectives, it did succeed in arousing concern and in initiating demands for government control and regulation of the railroads, banks, and industrial combinations, as well as for further democratization of American politics. Thus, while populism waned as the economic plight of the farmers eased in the 1890s, their demands for action were taken up by members of the urban community in response to the problems of the industrial cities. The awareness of those problems grew as a result of the protests and militance of industrial workers, and also because of the work of "muckraking" journalists such as Lincoln Steffens, Ida Tarbell, Ray Stannard Baker, and others, who, writing in magazines like *McClure's, Harper's, Collier's,* and *The Nation,* exposed the corruption of business and the squalor and poverty of the city. Such concerns were evident in the writings of Jacob Riis in *How the Other Half Lives* (1890), Robert Hunter's *Poverty* (1904), and Steffens's *The Shame of the Cities* (1904), and in the novels of Dreiser, Sinclair, Frank Norris, Jack London, and others. Behind the success of these magazines and writers was a growing literate and concerned middle-class audience whose members, motivated by a combination of anxiety and idealism, expressed a desire to improve American political and economic life.

American industrialization had resulted in the rapid growth of the professional and clerical classes (from 756,000 in 1870 to 5,600,000 in 1910), and it was these, the doctors, lawyers, teachers, managers, and office workers sandwiched between the entrepreneurs at the top and the laborers at the bottom, who seemed foremost in the demand for change. In a much-quoted, and subsequently much-debated, description, William Allen White, the Progressive newspaperman from Kansas, said the movement "was in its heart of hearts *petit bourgeois:* little businessmen, professional men, well-to-do farmers, skilled artisans from the upper brackets of organized labor."[20] However, the Progressive movement covered a wide political and social spectrum and encompassed a diversity of aims. (White was, after all, describing those who had mainly come from the Republican party led by Theodore Roosevelt.) As historians have pointed out, the movement varied from region to region, city to city. In some areas it was middle class; in others, it was almost upper class. Ranging from California to New York, through Wisconsin, Iowa, and Illinois, the Progressives had a diversity of aims. While some groups wished to prevent extremism and violence by reforming society and removing the root causes of strife and disorder through social justice, others were more concerned with social control and the preservation of existing institutions and beliefs. For some, concern with efficiency was seen in terms of human values and social welfare; for others it was seen in economic relations and political pragmatism. As a consequence, progressivism was to include social workers, town planners, urban managers, trade unionists, businessmen, church leaders, politicians, and representatives of both sexes. The one thing almost all had in common was the faith in society's ability to resolve major problems satisfactorily through political action. This belief led Progressives to look increasingly to government and resulted in the gradual spread of the movement from the state and local level up to the national level, culminating in the adoption of Progressive policies by both Republican and Democratic parties and their presidential candidates in the elections of 1912.

Whatever the problems about its motivation and composition, there is little doubt that progressivism began in the cities. It was concern for the plight of the urban poor that led to the formation of Charity Organization Societies, beginning in 1877, to oversee and coordinate the distribution of relief in order to maximize benefits and to minimize corruption and waste. Closely related to this was a sense of disquiet occasioned by the perception of a moral and religious decline in the cities, and a desire to bring moral uplift to the urban poor. The result was a religious revival in the shape of the Social Gospel movement and the development of the concept of Christian responsibility for the welfare of society. Both found expression in the growth of urban missionary work, the YMCA, and the Salvation Army: by 1900, for example, the Salvation Army had over three thousand officers and some seven hundred congregations, and the number of city mission houses had reached three thousand by 1920.[21] The Charity Organizations, while not so directly concerned with religious matters, were motivated by "the assumption that the urban poor had degenerated morally because the circumstances of city life had cut them off from the elevating influence of their moral betters."[22] Much of their work was, therefore, in the form of individual visits to the homes of the poor in an attempt to establish links between the lower classes and their so-called social betters.

To some extent these aims were shared by members of the Settlement House movement, which grew in late nineteenth-century America. However, the emphasis in the settlements was more on creating an environment in which the poor could achieve their own salvation, both in practical and moral terms, and in which social barriers could be broken down through the interaction of representatives of the different classes. This idea of a meeting point for different social groups in a mutually rewarding setting originated in England and was introduced to America in 1886. It spread rapidly across the country, and by 1916 there were some four hundred houses in different cities, the best-known being Jane Addams's Hull House in Chicago, Lillian Wald's Henry Street Settlement in New York, and Robert A. Woods's South End House in Boston.[23] The stress in these and other settlements was on awareness and education, but they also attempted to tackle basic problems facing the poorer city inhabitants. Thus they often provided accommodation and food for the needy, care for children of working mothers, health and civic education programs, plus classes in English as well as those on cultural or artistic topics. At the same time, of course, the settlements provided an opportunity for members of the middle classes to take part in worthwhile labor and to gain experience of the lives of the less fortunate sections of the community.

The social workers' efforts to improve local urban neighborhoods soon led them into other areas of concern. In order to achieve better city management, urban redevelopment, housing programs, and legislation to cover areas of social welfare, working conditions of women and children, and general labor matters, they began to call for political action. The desire for more responsive legislatures led in turn to demands for further democratization of the political system. At the municipal level this included the adoption of the referendum, the initiative, and the recall; at the state level it embraced direct primaries and the direct election of senators, and the extension of the franchise to include women. By 1916 more than twenty states had enacted the referendum, thirty-seven had direct primaries, and thirteen permitted women the vote. The direct election of senators was secured with the passage of the Seventeenth Amendment in 1913 and was implemented in the congressional elections of November 1914.[24]

Concern for democracy, efficiency, scientific and rational management, and a fairer and more humane order extended not just to the problems of the city, but also to the economic sphere. The Progressives' attack on corruption, exploitation, and suffering led them to challenge the power and influence of the industrial monopolies, and to call for government controls. However, not all Progressives could be labeled anti-business. Many accepted big business as the logical and natural outcome of beneficial economic developments, which had to be accepted as part of progress—if only in a modified form with governmental checks. Some businessmen were themselves party to the call for government regulation and rationalization in the industrial sector in order to bring stability and reduce unnecessary and harmful competition. However, like other groups involved in the Progressive movement, such businessmen were often divided on aims and methods, and along regional and ideological lines. The National Civic Federation (1900), representing corporate leaders, could be at odds with the smaller businessmen represented in the National Association of Manufacturers; eastern bankers could differ with those in the West and South; and western shippers could be sharply critical of eastern railroad men. Not even on the subject of labor relations was there unanimity of opinion among the industrialists: the National Civic Federation hoped to achieve stability through cooperation with labor and the adoption of programs of welfare capitalism, and to that end included labor leaders like Gompers among its members; the National Association of Manufacturers, on the other hand, steadfastly refused to contemplate union recognition.[25]

Labor's own position within the Progressive camp was itself ambiguous. The AFL traditionally concentrated on narrow economic objectives rather than on broad programs of political reform, and although the challenge from more radical organizations forced it into the political arena, the AFL resisted legislation that might undermine its authority in the economic sphere. Thus laws that strengthened the rights of workers were welcomed, but those that threatened government regulation of unions or that perhaps would make unions seem unnecessary, were not. Although Gompers and his colleagues supported some social welfare legislation, they still insisted that conditions could best be improved through collective bargaining on the shop floor rather than by political programs: increased wages and regular employment would enable individual workers to provide for the welfare of their families without government aid. The persistence of such attitudes was one reason for the division between the AFL and the Socialist party—unlike the situation in Britain, where a combination of unions and Socialists led to the formation of the Independent Labour party at the turn of the century. A more important difference, however, was that conservative, nativist strain within the AFL that reflected the division between the old-stock craftsmen and the un-skilled workers of "new" immigrant background. In order to protect and enhance the position of its members, the AFL was intent both on obtain-ing a greater share of the national wealth from the industrialists and ensuring that its workers' position was not undermined by immigrant labor. As a consequence, the AFL was one of a number of groups that, increasingly in the late nineteenth century, advocated immigration con-trols.

Many Americans, regardless of their political persuasion or social class, blamed the ills of urban society upon the "new" immigrants. This led some groups to initiate programs of Americanization, educational courses to aid assimilation such as that introduced by the North American Civic League for Immigrants in 1907:

> To change the unskilled inefficient immigrant into the skilled worker and efficient citizen, to strike at the cause of poverty, to improve the environ-ment and the spirit of America, the knowledge of America, and the love of America. . . .[26]

More basic was the lesson taught to Polish and other workers by the International Harvester Corporation.

> I hear the whistle. I must hurry.
> I hear the five minute whistle.
> It is time to go into the shop.
> I take my check from the gate board
> and hang it on the department board.
> I change my clothes and get ready to work.
> The starting whistle blows.
> I eat my lunch.
> It is forbidden to eat until then.
> The whistle blows at five minutes of starting time.
> I get ready to go to work.
> I work until the whistle blows to quit.
> I leave my place nice and clean.
> I put all my clothes in the locker.
> I must go home.[27]

All Americanization schemes to some extent demonstrated a continuing faith in the idea of America as a melting pot—an optimism best captured in the motto on the Statue of Liberty and in the Jewish immigrant Israel

Zangwill's play, *The Melting Pot* (1909), which described America as "God's crucible" in which the people of "fifty languages and histories," "fifty blood hatreds and rivalries," are turned into one people.[28] The more pessimistic view cast doubts on such hopes and argued for immigrant restriction, and even a reformer like Weyl could argue that "in the next decade or two our intensifying struggle for democracy will render a further restriction of immigration imperative."[29]

The revival of nativist sentiment began during the economic crises of the 1890s—years of depression, labor strife, and industrial violence. The anti-immigrant movement found expression first in the anti-Catholicism of the American Protective Association, which was formed in 1887 and which had a membership of five hundred thousand by 1894. Although the association declined following the end of the recession in 1897, the objection to immigrants continued and found support among all political groups. The foremost congressional spokesman of the anti-immigrant movement was the Republican senator for Massachusetts, Henry Cabot Lodge, leader of the Immigration Restriction League and an advocate of literacy testing to restrict immigration. The case for such controls was apparently strengthened by the Commission on Immigration, the Dillingham Commission, which suggested, in its report of 1907, that immigration lowered wages and increased unemployment among American workers. A number of bills to introduce the literacy test were passed by Congress in the years prior to World War I, but all were vetoed by presidents.

A "problem" often associated with immigration, and a concern of some Progressives, was that of drink. Prohibition, described by one historian as "the linch pin of modern reform," revealed the moralistic side of the reform movement—the wish to *make* people good if they could not control their own worst desires.[30] However, the Prohibitionists could not be characterized just as moral or religious bigots, nor as cranks: they had considerable public support, and, like nativism, Prohibition was a powerful force by the early 1900s. Initially, the Prohibitionist movements, the Women's Christian Temperance Union (1874) and the Anti-Saloon League (1893), both had their greatest following in southern and midwestern states, but they had some backing in eastern states, particularly the more rural type such as Vermont, Maine, and New Hampshire, and urban reformers often blamed drink for causing poverty and social decay in the cities. Nonetheless, the fight for Prohibition tended to be between rural and urban areas, and between native- and foreign-born Americans. In 1905 only Maine, Kansas, Nebraska, and North Dakota were "dry" states, but by 1914, following a state-by-state campaign led by the Anti-Saloon League, fourteen states had voted in favor of Prohibition.[31]

Like Prohibition, prostitution and vice were issues that revealed a mixture of influences among the reformers, ranging from a genuine concern for the poor, religious and moral outrage tinged with repressive puritanism, and anti-immigrant feeling. Prostitution clearly involved exploitation of the poorer classes, and it also posed a threat to public health; but for many it was indicative too of the physical and moral decline, and hypocrisy, of the cities and their new, foreign, populations. Muckraking exposés of prostitution and the white slave trade led to the setting up of investigatory vice commissions across the nation (over 100 between 1902 and 1916), the formation of organizations like the National Vigilance Society (1911) and the American Social Hygiene Association (1913), and the passage of the famous Mann Act in 1910, which made it a federal offense to cross state lines with a woman for immoral purposes.[32]

Prominent among all movements for reform, including those of prohibition and vice, were women. The Women's Christian Temperance Union was actively involved not just in the campaign against alcohol, but also in those for penal reform, labor legislation, and female suffrage. Leading settlement house workers like Jane Addams and Lillian Wald were described as "heroines in a new crusade against want, illiteracy, disease and crime," and they and others like Florence Kelley and Julia Lathrop were concerned with child welfare, regulation of women's work, peace organizations, and suffrage.[33] Florence Kelley, a former worker in Hull House, moved from Illinois's State Bureau of Labor Statistics to become secretary of the National Consumer League in 1899 and remained in that post for thirty-two years. With Lillian Wald, the director of the Henry Street Settlement in New York, Kelley helped to found the National Child Labor Committee in 1906, which led to the White House Conference on Children in 1909 and the establishment of the Children's Bureau in the Department of Labor in 1912. Julia Lathrop, another product of Hull House, became head of the Children's Bureau. Jane Addams and Hull House were clearly inspirations for many of the early social workers, women and men alike, and this was acknowledged in 1909 when Addams became the first woman president of the National Conference of Charities and Corrections (later to become the National Conference of Social Work). But as well as her welfare concerns, Jane Addams was also involved in the range of reform, from local politics through to the international peace movement and the women's suffrage campaign. In 1911, she became vice-president of the National American Women's Suffrage Association (NAWSA) and was involved in the struggle for suffrage until it was finally achieved in 1920.

Suffrage was an issue that united many women in the years before the war. The women's movement had its origins in the abolitionism and general reform ferment of the 1840s, but had languished after an internal rift following the Civil War. The coming together of the two sections, the Woman Suffrage Association and the National Woman's Suffrage Association, to form NAWSA in 1893 was the start of a revitalized campaign, which, like the British suffrage struggle, came to a peak from about 1910 to 1920. Led first by Anna Howard Shaw (1904–15) and then by Carrie Chapman Catt (and, as mentioned, with Jane Addams as vice-president from 1911), NAWSA increased its membership from one hundred thousand in 1915 to 2 million by 1917. By 1914, following a state-by-state battle, eleven states had granted women the right to vote. However, despite the inclusion of suffrage planks in the platforms of both major parties, Congress still failed to vote in favor of the suffrage amendment to the Constitution (the Susan B. Anthony Amendment, named after the suffrage campaigner, who died in 1906). Faced by strong resistance from southerners, who feared federal intervention in voting because of the racial question; from brewing interests because of female support for Prohibition; from businessmen, who opposed regulation of child and female labor; from machine politicians, who resisted the reforming impulse of women; and from those who generally resisted change, more militant and impatient women, led by Alice Paul, formed the Congressional Union in 1913, an organization modeled on the example of the Pankhursts' Social and Political Union in England. On the eve of the European war, American politicians, like their British counterparts, were increasingly confronted by women demanding recognition and the right to vote.[34]

The growth of the suffrage movement and the prominent part played by women in the Progressive movement as a whole, was a reflection of the changes that had occurred in women's position in society since the 1860s—changes that encouraged commentators to write of a "New Woman" as early as the 1890s. Changes in legal status, recognizing women's family rights and the right to own property, were matched by some economic progress. In 1870 less than 15 percent of women over the age of sixteen worked outside the home; by 1910 24 percent, or 8 million women, worked, and they constituted over 20 percent of the labor force.[35] The great majority, however, were employed either in domestic service or in "traditional" areas of female employment such as textiles, the garment trade, shoe manufacture, and food production—in other words, cooking, sewing, and making clothes. Nonetheless, the increase in employment of women did lead to some organization and the formation of the National Women's Trade Union League in 1903. But while the NWTUL was concerned with working conditions and wages and was involved in organizing the militant strikes in the textile industries of Baltimore, Chicago, Philadelphia, and New York in 1909 and 1913, the suffrage movement was to a large extent a separate campaign that drew its following primarily from the growing middle class of women, the college-educated and white-collar workers.

The number of women at college doubled between 1880 and 1900 as more and more colleges opened their doors to female students. Many of the female graduates then found employment as schoolteachers, and others, as we have seen, worked in the settlement houses. By 1890, 250,000 women were teaching, and some 70 percent of Settlement House residents were women.[36] Although these were often the only outlets for the talents of qualified women, new opportunities were increasingly opening up as industry grew and as jobs were created by the advent of the telegraph, telephone, and typewriter. In 1870 less than 3 percent of all clerical workers were women; by 1910 women accounted for almost 38 percent. The number of female telephone operators rose from 15,000 in 1900 to 88,000 in 1910, and by 1917 almost 99 percent of the 140,000 operators were women.[37]

Even with these changes, few married women worked outside of the home (only about 10 percent in 1910), and the midnineteenth-century image of the "ideal woman" concerned only with domestic matters still persisted. But even women confined to the home were becoming more active in society at large, and they found a voice through women's clubs and societies, which created the General Federation of Women's Clubs in 1889. By 1910 the federation had a membership of over one million, and it joined with other organizations in calling for child labor legislation, Prohibition, and women's suffrage. This involvement in politics, and the economic changes behind it, was reflected in William Allen White's observation concerning women at the Progressive convention in 1912—and at the same time perhaps reflected something of the persistence of a patronizing attitude among men.

. . . we invited women delegates and had plenty of them. They were our kind, too—women doctors, women lawyers, women teachers, college professors, middle-aged leaders of civic movements, or rich young girls who had gone in for settlement work.[38]

Whatever their social background or motivation, it is clear that women and their organizations not only shared many of the concerns of male reformers, but also did much to shape the movement that was to dominate national politics by 1912. In 1912 the Progressive influence was evident in both major parties and their platforms, and in the presence of Socialist and Prohibitionist presidential candidates. However, the clearest reflection of the reform impulse was in the formation of the separate Progressive party from among insurgent Republicans led first by Robert M. La Follette, and then by Theodore Roosevelt. But before that point was reached the Progressives had already achieved much at both the local and national level, and in doing so had created the base for a national political organization.

From about 1900 on, reformers took control in a number of city and state governments. La Follette was a leading example, turning Wisconsin into what Roosevelt described as a "laboratory of democracy," which was copied from Oregon and California through to Minnesota, Iowa, Ohio, New Jersey, New York, and many other states. As governor from 1900, and then as senator from 1906, La Follette could claim responsibility for the democratization of state politics in Wisconsin, the improvement of government and civil service organization, the reform of the education system, the introduction of child and female labor laws, and public health and pure food laws, the regulation and control of the railroads, and the implementation of income tax and inheritance tax. Similar programs were enacted elsewhere, and by 1914 over twenty-five states had some form of workmen's compensation provision, and over forty had child labor laws or laws regulating women's work. A number of states had pension schemes of one sort or another (although most mainly had widow's pensions), and, following the British example of 1911, consideration was being given to proposals for unemployment insurance in a number of states. Reform was not confined to state level—"Scarcely a major city in the nation escaped the municipal reform wave."[39] From San Francisco to Galveston, from Cleveland and Toledo to New York, city managers were introduced, civil service departments were shaken up and improved, and new departments were established to deal with urban developments, parks, police, fire, water, safety, and public hygiene. It was in eastern city government as an assemblyman and as police commissioner of New York City, that Theodore Roosevelt was to gain his political experience before becoming assistant secretary of the navy and then governor of New York in 1898.

Having established his reputation as a reformer in local government and become a popular hero leading his Rough Riders in the charge on San Juan Hill in Cuba during the war with Spain, Roosevelt was nominated as the vice-presidential candidate by Republican party managers in order to limit his influence. However, the gamble misfired, and, following the assassination of President McKinley by an anarchist in Buffalo, Roosevelt, "that damned cowboy," according to party organizer Mark Hanna, became president in 1901. Reelected in his own right with a landslide majority in 1904, Roosevelt was to provide the Progressive movement with a national leader and to begin the program of federal reform.

From the start, the ebullient Roosevelt made it clear that he would be an active president who intended to assert executive authority, particularly in the industrial and economic sphere. He was responsible for the revitalization of the Sherman Anti-trust Act of 1890, and in 1902 he encouraged his attorney general to file a suit against the newly formed combination of railroads owned by Morgan, Rockefeller, and others, the Northern Securities Company. As a result, the company was ordered to dissolve in 1904. This attack on excessive business monopoly continued with a further forty-three suits against other trusts, and, in a related act of

1903, Roosevelt established the Department of Commerce and Labor, with The Bureau of Corporations to investigate business organization and practice. The Elkins Act of 1903 and the Hepburn Act of 1906 forbade certain practices on the railroads, such as hidden rebates, and increased the power of the Interstate Commerce Commission to regulate charges. These various pieces of legislation, together with the Pure Food and Drug Act and the Meat Inspection Act of 1906 (the latter inspired in part by Sinclair's *The Jungle*), did much to create Roosevelt's "trust-busting," antibusiness reputation. In reality, however, these measures were not as far-reaching as some Progressives like La Follette would have wished. In most cases the final acts were compromises, with limitations in their administration, requirements, and penalties.[40] They were, though, important precedents, and they were indicative of a new approach to government and to business.

Equally important precedents were set in the area of land conservation and labor policy. Roosevelt, an avid naturalist and at heart a westerner, supported his chief forester, Gifford Pinchot, in withdrawing millions of acres from possible private use and exploitation in order to conserve and develop the nation's natural resources. Land reclamation and irrigation programs were introduced with the Newlands Act of 1904, and conservation was brought fully to the public's attention with the White House Conference of 1908. Once again, the achievements of Congress were few, but as a publicist Roosevelt directed attention and provided leadership in a vital aspect of the country's life. This was also the case with his intervention in the mining dispute of 1902 when, acting in the public interest as he saw it, Roosevelt intervened, as no previous president had ever done, to bring the conflict to a conclusion. In this case Roosevelt appeared sympathetic to the workers—the miners won a 10 percent raise—but this did not stop the mine owners and other employers denying union recognition, nor did it prevent the Supreme Court decisions in 1905 and 1908 that respectively invalidated maximum-hour laws and allowed the Sherman Anti-trust Act to be applied to unions. However, in his final annual address in 1908 Roosevelt pointed to these and other areas in which legislation was still required. He then went off to hunt lions in Africa. When he returned to the presidential campaign trail as the candidate of the Progressive party four years later, it was on a platform that included equal suffrage, legislation to prevent industrial accidents, to reduce working hours, prohibit child labor and women's night work, to provide for minimum wages, and to introduce social insurance, as well as further regulation of the corporations.[41]

Roosevelt's return to active political campaigning was a consequence of divisions within the Republican party and disillusionment among Progressive Republicans with Roosevelt's successor, William Howard Taft.

Although Taft had continued some of Roosevelt's policies, launching twice as many antitrust suits (including one against U.S. Steel, begun in 1911), extending the Civil Service, and creating a separate Department of Labor in 1913 and the Children's Bureau within that department, he failed to lower the tariff as promised, alienated Progressive Republicans such as La Follette, angered Roosevelt on a number of issues, and was cast as an anticonservationist as a consequence of his support for his secretary of the interior, Richard Achilles Ballinger, in his conflict with Gifford Pinchot. When, despite apparent widespread public support for Roosevelt, the Republican National Committee nominated Taft at the party convention, Roosevelt's supporters left to join other Republican insurgents in the Progressive party, and Teddy displaced La Follette as the new party's candidate.

The election of 1912 was remarkable because all parties could claim to be for some degree of reform, but the division in the Republican party ensured the election of the Democratic candidate, Woodrow Wilson. Although himself a "reformer" while governor of New Jersey, there were considerable differences between Wilson's brand of progressivism and that of Roosevelt. Roosevelt increasingly accepted business monopoly as a feature of modern life, but he stressed the positive role of a strong federal government acting as a regulating or countervailing force. Influenced by Herbert Croly's *Promise of American Life* (1909), Roosevelt described his philosophy as a "New Nationalism" of "government supervision . . . of all corporations," with the president acting as "the steward of the public welfare." In his campaign he clearly moved toward the idea of a protective welfare state. Woodrow Wilson's "New Freedom" was much more conservative. As a southerner, the new president was strongly influenced by states' rights; as a staunch Presbyterian he expected men to be governed by moral law. In principle, Wilson wished to restore the laissez-faire system in which men were free from *both* the domination of the trusts *and* from government controls, and in which all men were free to compete equally. He was, he said, for "the men who are on the make rather than the men who are already made."[42]

The first act of the New Freedom was the massive reduction of protective tariffs in 1913 and the replacement of lost revenue with the introduction of an income tax. The Federal Reserve Act the same year prevented the buildup of a bank trust and provided for federal regulation without a central national bank. The Farm Loan Act of 1916 provided long-term loans at low cost and met a long-held demand of the Populists to counter exploitive banking. Regulation of business continued too: more than eighty antitrust suits were launched, and the Clayton Anti-trust Act of 1914 specified those business practices regarded as unfair. The creation of the Federal Trade Commission in 1914 enabled the investigation of business and the examination of some two thousand malpractice complaints. However, the powers of the commission were limited by the appointment of weak officials, and fewer than four hundred cease-and-desist orders were issued as the body increasingly became "a counsellor and friend of the business world," rather than its adversary.[43] In 1916, to ensure Progressive support in an election year, Wilson moved left and began to implement some of the Progressive party's proposals for social reform. That year witnessed the passage, with presidential support, of the Child Labor Bill, the Workmen's Compensation Act (for federal civil servants), and the Adamson Eight Hour Act (establishing the eight-hour day for rail workers engaged in interstate commerce, and so averting a threatened national strike). According to leading historian, Arthur Link, Wilson and the Democrats had enacted every important plank of the Progressive platform of 1912 by the end of the year, and, as the president and American people became preoccupied with foreign affairs, the drive for reform came to a halt.[44]

Although "presidential progressivism" may have ended, the movement for reform was to continue for some time at the lower levels. Main concerns of progressivism—women's suffrage, Prohibition, immigration, the "problem" of the cities—were to find their resolution either during the war years or in their immediate aftermath, and new concerns and issues were also to arise. Nonetheless, for a variety of reasons the movement did change after 1917, and an assessment of its achievements before America entered the world war is in order.

Progressivism's prewar accomplishments are, of course, the subject of some historical debate.[45] Certainly, when compared with developments in Britain or Germany, where the foundations of modern welfare states had been laid in the form of national insurance plans, old-age pensions, educational reform, and progressive taxation schemes, then American reform had not gone very far. In fact, the legislation passed may have served to satisfy the popular demand for reform, but in reality it left basic social and economic patterns largely unchanged. Class relationships were hardly altered, the distribution of wealth remained uneven, workers' organizations were hardly more secure, nor had the power of business been much affected, as the Ludlow massacre of 1914 clearly revealed. The reasons for these shortcomings are not hard to find: the federal system of government and effects of different regional interests; the division of political authority given the checks and balances of the American system; the entrenched power of conservative political and economic elites in Congress and in the Supreme Court; the racial and ethnic divisions of the population; and above all, the persistence of values based on individualism and independence. In fairness, too, it must be said that the Europeans had hardly solved the problems facing them any more successfully than America, as events of the period were to show. Class conflict, poverty, squalor, disease, and suffering persisted everywhere.

Judged against that context, and in terms of the early twentieth century rather than more recent times, then progressivism was not necessarily a failure. Even the most deep-seated of American values had been modified to some extent. The tensions introduced by rapid industrial and urban development and the clear evidence of physical, economic, and social change had forced the American people to act in order to preserve traditional institutions and standards. The result was the revitalization of government at all levels and the acceptance of an enlarged role for central government, and particularly for the national executive, in an attempt to ensure a more efficient and equitable society. By 1916 Roosevelt and Wilson had both successively shifted the balance of political power in favor of the presidency and, emphasizing the paramount importance of the public rather than the individual good, had committed government to a positive interventionist policy. If the rich were not stripped of their wealth, they were at least made aware of the poor and forced to accept some responsibility for them; if industrialists could still combine to wield enormous power and influence, competition was now at least partially regulated, and the employers had to consider the rights and welfare of both their workers and consumers; if men still exercised all economic and political power, women now insisted on being heard and were accorded some recognition; if politics was still dominated by an elite, there were new groups to be reckoned with, and there was a greater public accountability and the opportunity for general political involvement. Although this might not add up to the revolution some historians have claimed took place in this period, it was by no means insignificant. Out of what one writer has described as "two decades of extraordinarily divisive political and social upheaval" there emerged a complex, "modern" industrial society committed to a mass consumer economy already using new production and marketing methods, with new economic and political organizations, and with an increasingly active, growing, central state bureaucracy.[46] Some groups, such as black Americans, remained largely untouched by these developments, and tensions and conflicts remained in American society. The involvement of the United States in the First World War revealed both how much had changed as well as how much was unchanged, and while it brought some prewar trends to a conclusion, the conflict also introduced new dilemmas and problems of its own. At the war's end Americans would remark upon the extent of these changes and describe again what seemed to be "the New United States."[47]

Notes

1. Walter Weyl, *The New Democracy* (New York, 1914), 1.
2. Harold U. Faulkner, *The Decline of Laissez Faire, 1897–1917* (Evanston, Ill., and London, 1951); Robert H. Wiebe, *The Search for Order, 1877–1920* (New York, 1967); Henry F. May, *The End of American Innocence: A Study of the First Years of Our Own Time, 1912–1917* (Chicago, 1964); Otis L. Graham, "America at the Turn of the Century," in Graham, ed., *Perspectives on Twentieth Century America* (New York and Toronto, 1973), 4; B. Lee and R. Reinders, "The Loss of Innocence: 1880–1914," in M. Bradbury and H. Temperley, eds., *Introduction to American Studies* (Harlow, Essex, 1981). May also described the period as "pre-revolutionary or early revolutionary."
3. Adams to Charles Milner Gaskell, 29 March 1900, in Worthington Chauncey Ford, ed., *Letters of Henry Adams (1892–1918)* (Boston and New York, 1938), 279.
4. Samuel P. Hays, *The Response to Industrialism* (Chicago and London, 1957), 50; J. A. Thompson, *Progressivism* (South Shields, England, 1979), 8.
5. For immigration figures see Maldwyn A. Jones, *Destination America* (London, 1976), 12, 16, 17.
6. Frederic L. Paxson, *American Democracy and the World War: Pre-war Years 1913-1917* (1936; New York, 1966), 59.
7. John B. Rae, *The American Automobile: A Brief History* (Chicago, 1965), 33; Keith Sward, *The Legend of Henry Ford* (1948, New York, 1972), 33.
8. John G. Clark et al., *Three Generations in Twentieth Century America: Family, Community, and Nation* (Homewood, Ill., 1977), 72–73; Charles N. Glabb and Theodore Brown, *A History of Urban America* (New York, 1967), 133.
9. Upton Sinclair, *The Jungle* (Middlesex, England, 1965), 32–33, 34.
10. Theodore Dreiser, *Sister Carrie* (Middlesex, England, 1981), 16, 23, 489; Carl Sandburg, "Chicago," *Poetry* 3 (March 1914).
11. Sward, *The Legend of Henry Ford*, 51–54; George E. Mowry, *The Era of Theodore Roosevelt, 1900–1912* (New York, 1962), 3; Clark, *Three Generations in Twentieth Century America*, 68; Alan Valentine, *1913: America between Two Worlds* (New York, 1962), 163.
12. Mark Sullivan, *Our Times: The United States 1900–1925: Volume III Prewar America* (New York and London, 1930), 342; Faulkner, *Decline of Laissez Faire*, 30–31; Clark, *Three Generations*, 68.
13. Sinclair, *The Jungle*, 98–99, 248–49.
14. Roland Berthoff, *An Unsettled People: Social Order and Disorder in American History* (New York, Evanston, Ill., and London, 1971), 398–99.
15. Dreiser, *Sister Carrie*, 39.
16. Leo Wolman, *The Growth of American Trade Unions, 1880–1923* (New York, 1924), 33–34.
17. The conclusions of the Commission on Industrial Relations are in Graham Adams, Jr., *Age of Industrial Violence 1910–15: The Activities and Findings of the United States Commission on Industrial Relations* (New York and London, 1966), 204–18; see also Rhodri Jeffreys-Jones, *Violence and Reform in American History* (New York and London,

1978). Other statistics are in Mowry, *The Era of Theodore Roosevelt*, 10–11; Edward Robb Ellis, *Echoes of Distant Thunder: Life in the United States 1914–1918* (New York, 1975), 65.

18. Melvyn Dubofsky, *We Shall Be All: A History of the I.W.W.* (Chicago, 1968, 349); Robert A. Rosenstone, *Romantic Revolutionary: A Biography of John Reed* (Harmondsworth, Middlesex, 1982), 118–32.

19. Alexander Trachtenberg, ed., *The American Labor Year Book, 1916* (New York, 1916), 94; K. McNaught, "Socialism and the Progressives," in Alfred F. Young, ed., *Dissent: Explorations in the History of American Radicalism* (Dekalb, Ill., 1968), 253–60; Wiebe, *The Search for Order*, 117–33.

20. White, *Autobiography of William Allen White* (New York, 1946), 482; Richard Hofstadter, *The Age of Reform: From Bryan to FDR* (New York, 1955), 131, 135; Mowry, *The Age of Theodore Roosevelt*, 85–105.

21. Paul Boyer, *Urban Masses and Moral Order in America, 1820–1920* (Cambridge, Mass., and London, 1978), 132–40.

22. Ibid., 149.

23. Allen F. Davis, *Spearheads for Reform: The Social Settlements and the Progressive Movement, 1890–1914* (New York, 1967).

24. Paxson, *Pre-War Years*, 55, 180.

25. Richard L. Watson, Jr., *The Development of National Power: The United States 1900–1919* (Boston, 1976), 12–15; James Weinstein, *The Corporate Ideal in the Liberal State, 1900–12* (Boston, 1968), 7–15.

26. Quoted in Edward George Hartmann, *The Movement to Americanize the Immigrant* (New York, 1967), 38.

27. *Harvester World* (1912), quoted in Gerd Korman, *Industrialization, Immigrants and Americanizers: The View From Milwaukee, 1866–1921* (Madison, 1967), 144–45.

28. Quoted in Ann Massa, *American Literature in Context, IV: 1900–1930* (London and New York, 1982), 40.

29. Weyl, *The New Democracy*, 346–47.

30. Berthoff, *An Unsettled People*, 430.

31. Ibid.; Paxson, *Pre-War Years*, 56–57.

32. Boyer, *Urban Masses and Moral Order*, 190–95.

33. Paxson, *Pre-War Years*, 53; Allen F. Davis, *American Heroine: The Life and Legend of Jane Addams* (New York, 1973), 75–80, 176.

34. On suffrage see Eleanor Flexner, *Century of Struggle: The Women's Rights Movement in the United States* (Cambridge, Mass., 1959); Lois W. Banner, *Women in Modern America: A Brief History* (New York, 1974); Paxson, *Pre-War Years*, 193.

35. Margaret Gibbons Wilson, *The American Woman in Transition: The Urban Influence 1870–1920* (Westport, Conn., and London, 1979), 8, 172–76; Banner, *Women in Modern America*, 6, 20, 45, 75.

36. James Leiby, *A History of Social Welfare and Social Work in the United States* (New York, 1978), 129.

37. For prewar employment patterns see Maurine Weiner Greenwald, *Women, War and Work: The Impact of World War I on Women Workers in the United States* (Westport, Conn., and London, 1980), 5–11; William L. O'Neill, *Everyone Was Brave: The Rise and Fall of Feminism in America* (Chicago, 1969), 148.

38. White, *The Autobiography of William Allen White*, 483; see also Barbara

Kuhn Campbell, *The "Liberated" Woman of 1914: Prominent Women in the Progressive Era* (New York, 1979), 151–53.

39. George E. Mowry, *The Progressive Era, 1900–20: The Reform Persuasion* (Washington, D.C., 1972), 16; Arthur A. Ekirch, Jr., *Progressivism in America: A Study of the Era from Theodore Roosevelt to Woodrow Wilson* (New York, 1974) chs. 6 and 7.

40. Otis L. Graham, Jr., *The Great Campaigns: Reform and War in America, 1900–1928* (Englewood Cliffs, N.J., 1971), 35–37.

41. Ibid., 41; Progressive party platform, 1912, in Henry Steele Commager, ed., *Documents of American History* (New York, 1962), II, 73–75.

42. Richard D. Heffner, *A Documentary History of the United States* (New York, 1952), 226–39.

43. Arthur S. Link, *Woodrow Wilson and the Progressive Era 1910–1917* (New York, 1963), 74.

44. Link, *Woodrow Wilson,* 229; Paxson, *Pre-War Years,* 240, 331; Wiebe, *The Search for Order,* 212.

45. Mowry, *The Progressive Era,* 29–36.

46. Wiebe, *The Search for Order,* 181; Mowry, *The Age of Theodore Roosevelt,* ix–x, 2; Ellis W. Hawley, *The Great War and the Search for a Modern Order: A History of the American People and Their Institutions 1917–1933* (New York, 1979), 1–15; David M. Kennedy, *Over Here: The First World War and American Society* (New York, 1980), 11.

47. Albert Bushnell Hart, "The New United States," *The Yale Review* 8, no. 1 (October 1918): 1–17.

2

From Peace to War

1914–1917

Among the many concerns of American Progressives was the cause of international peace. Between 1900 and 1914 some forty-five different peace organizations were established in America, and the membership embraced "an impressive number of the nation's political, business, religious, and academic leaders" including, among others, President Wilson, former President Taft, and both Andrew Carnegie, president of the New York Peace Society and founder of the Carnegie Endowment for International Peace, and Jane Addams, a leading officer in the American Peace Society. Indeed, as Roland Marchand has pointed out, the diversity of the campaign for peace was a reflection of the breadth of progressivism itself. The common factor was a "longing for order, for stability, for regularity" at home and abroad, and an optimistic belief that reason could triumph over irrationalism in order to achieve this goal. War was the very antithesis of reform: "the devil's answer to human progress."[1] Thus, the outbreak of war in Europe in August 1914 was greeted with a mixture of horror and disbelief. Jane Addams wrote of her "astonishment that such an archaic institution should be revived in modern Europe," and of "that basic sense of desolation, of suicide, of anachronism, which the first news of the war brought to thousands of men and women who had come to consider war as a throwback in the scientific sense." The *New York Times* went further and suggested that in failing to prevent war the Europeans had revealed their "backwardness," and in reverting to "the conditions of savage tribes" had shown that "their civilization is half a sham."[2] However, the force of events was to change many attitudes, and by the time President Wilson came to ask Congress for a declaration of war on Germany in April 1917, Progressives were divided on the issue, and voices like those of Jane Addams were in the minority.

Few Americans, if any, expected the European war. Over one hundred thousand were on the Continent when hostilities broke out, and for those still at home in America the news in the summer of 1914 was dominated by the business recession, reactions to the Ludlow massacre in April, and the death of President Wilson's wife on 6 August. The most immediate problem in international affairs was on America's doorstep in Mexico, where a series of revolutions and coups, and American interference, had brought a deterioration in relations to the point of armed conflict. Only prolonged negotiations from May to July 1914 averted an actual outbreak of war, and even then, friction between the two neighbors did not cease. In 1916 Pancho Villa's raid into New Mexico, and the killing of several American citizens, provoked a punitive American military expedition deep into Mexico, and again, all-out open conflict was only prevented by further negotiations from September 1916 to April 1917. By then, of course, relations between the two countries were seen in the context of European affairs and, indeed, were to play a part in bringing about America's entry into the war.

The American government's initial response to the European war in 1914 was to declare a policy of strict neutrality. Indeed, President Wilson called upon Americans to be impartial in thought as well as in action, and if that seemed unrealistic in expecting too much, it nonetheless reflected the desire of most Americans to remain free from involvement in the conflict. The traditional American policy of isolationism was reinforced by the large and diverse foreign-born population of the United States: with half the population of British or French descent, and one-fifth of German ancestry, not to mention those of Italian, Austrian, or Russian extraction, it was unlikely that any American government would openly side with one particular nation, or group of nations, unless its own interests were directly threatened. Neutrality was the most sensible course regardless of any moral considerations and despite the propaganda of both warring parties aimed at Americans of foreign origin.

Not surprisingly, the American population was bombarded with enormous quantities of propaganda from both the Allies and the Central Powers. After the war some historians suggested that this was a major cause of America's entry into the war, as a distorted image of the Germans and the events of 1914, arising from British propaganda, led to a move away from neutrality and impartiality. Certainly, the British had major advantages in the war of words. The common language and heritage was a bond, which was further exploited by British control of the transatlantic cables, and the fact that much of the American war news came from the western front via London made for built-in bias. Moreover, British claims about the atrocities committed by the Germans—looting, pillaging, raping, and killing innocent civilians, men, women, and children—seemed to be given credibility by the actions of the German forces themselves—the invasion of neutral Belgium, the razing of towns, the shooting of nurse Edith Cavell, and above all else, the submarine attacks on merchant ships and liners. German propaganda efforts were also undermined by the chance capture of documents on a New York subway in 1915 that revealed a rather heavy-handed approach that included German funding of peace organizations and even involvement in acts of sabotage in the United States. These revelations resulted in the sending home of the Austro-Hungarian ambassador and of the German military attaché and did nothing to improve German-American relations.

However, the British were not exactly saints either, and their interference with the rights of neutral shipping and the crushing of the Easter rising in Dublin in April 1916 did little to reduce anti-British sentiment among the Irish-Americans or those who opposed British colonialism. Clearly, both Britain and Germany had their American supporters, but in the end it seems that propaganda alone had little effect in shaping or altering opinion one way or the other before April 1917. It did, though, help to provide a basis for the virulent attacks on Germans *after* 1917. Ultimately, it was acts, not words, that brought America into the war.

The one effect all propaganda *did* have was to demonstrate the horror and monstrosity of war, and so strengthened the desire of some Americans to bring peace by persuasion or mediation. Such feelings were evident in the march down New York's Fifth Avenue of fifteen hundred women, clad in funereal black, on 29 August 1914. Out of this Women's Peace Parade there grew new peace organizations that were not to be without influence or importance. In September, following the parade a meeting of "influential liberals and social workers" met at the Henry Street Settlement in New York and formed the committee that was to evolve into a national organization under the title of American Union against Militarism by April 1916. The AUAM fought against intervention in Mexico and was the leading Progressive organization against the preparedness campaign of 1916. Although unsuccessful in preventing war, the AUAM continued in being after 1917 and concentrated on the protection of civil liberties, and the organization gradually evolved into the American Civil Liberties Union.[3]

Among the early members of the AUAM was the ubiquitous Jane Addams, and it was she, encouraged by the Hungarian pacifist Rosika

Schwimmer, British suffragist Emmeline Pethick-Lawrence, and American Carrie Chapman Catt, who called the meeting in Washington, D.C., in January 1915 that led to the formation of the Women's Peace party. Some three thousand women attended the first convention, and "hundreds were turned away." By 1917 the WPP had an estimated membership of between twenty-five and forty thousand, and its list of national officers read like a roll call of some of the most prominent American women of the day.[4] These women exerted considerable influence in support of a mediated settlement both in America and abroad. In April 1915 Jane Addams and another forty-six women delegates attended the International Peace Congress at The Hague and went on to meet statesmen from most belligerent nations. Addams subsequently met with Woodrow Wilson on her return, but found little practical support from the president or European leaders. Sadly, the WWP was to become a somewhat discredited force following an address Addams gave at Carnegie Hall in July 1915, in which she pointed out, correctly, that the warring armies provided their troops with alcoholic stimulants prior to launching an attack. Her charge was widely criticized as a slur against brave men, many of whom had died in action. Even more damaging was the subsequent linking of Addams and of the WWP with Henry Ford's campaign "to end the war by Christmas" by organizing a conference of neutral powers from a "peace ship," *Oscar II,* which the car manufacturer purchased. Ford's plan was subject to ridicule from the beginning, and by the time the ship sailed on 4 December a number of participants, including Addams, had withdrawn, leaving among the passengers sixty-four newsmen and a "group of very eccentric people [who] had attached themselves to the enterprise."[5] But the harm was done. The peace ship had no effect on the course of the war, but did damage the cause of peace. Ford himself came home early and was reputed to have remarked, "I didn't get much peace. I learned that Russia is going to be a great market for tractors." Having spent $465,000, he had gained a million dollars' worth of publicity and made his name known throughout Europe.[6]

Despite their declining support, the peace campaigners still had some influence. The idea of a settlement arrived at as a consequence of external mediation was not altogether dismissed in American political circles. Although noncommital in meetings with the peace campaigners and clearly reluctant to be publicly associated with the Women's Peace party or Ford's peace ship, Woodrow Wilson was himself engaged in attempts to bring peace. As early as January 1915 the president sent his adviser Col. Edward House to Europe to discuss the possibility of a negotiated settlement. Initial discussions with the governments in London and Berlin seemed hopeful but collapsed in the crisis that followed the sinking of the *Lusitania.* A second attempt to bring the opposing nations to the peace table was made by House in January 1916, but the British and French expected the American government to side with them, and, moreover, were only prepared to negotiate when they determined that the moment was in their favor. As the American government was at the same time seemingly reaching some accord with the Germans, these talks proved fruitless.

In December 1916 President Wilson appealed directly to the belligerents to state their terms for peace, and on 22 January 1917 he delivered his "peace without victory" message before Senate and the world. His speech, calling for a peace based upon the equality of sovereign nations and international cooperation, was widely applauded in liberal circles, but had little immediate effect abroad. On 31 January 1917 the German government implicitly rejected such proposals by announcing its intention to resume unrestricted submarine warfare. The actions that followed shortly afterward brought America into the war.

The First World War clearly demonstrated how difficult it had become for a major nation to maintain a neutral stance while other countries fought a total war. Given the patterns of world trade and American economic involvement overseas, it was impossible to remain unaffected, and British naval power and German submarines combined to make absolute neutrality sustainable only by enormous sacrifices of economic self-interest or moral principle. In any event, the United States government was prepared to do neither. The refusal of the Wilson administration to ban trade with the belligerent powers meant that, given the Allied blockade of Europe, commerce would assume a one-sided nature, and German retaliation would jeopardize its relations with the United States. Thus, the value of American trade with the Allies rose from $824 million in 1914 to over $3 billion by 1916; trade with the Central Powers dropped from $170 million to less than $1 million in the same period. In 1915, in order to enable this trade to continue, and the American economy to prosper, the United States government relaxed its restrictions on loans to warring powers. By 1917 loans to the Allies exceeded $2.5 billion; loans to the Central Powers were in the order of a mere $127 million. As far as Robert M. La Follete was concerned, America had "ceased to be neutral in fact as well as in name."[7]

America's economic links by themselves did not mean that it would necessarily enter the war on the Allied side, or even at all. American business benefited without entering the war: the recession that had affected the American economy since 1913 ceased by 1915, and many towns and cities were enjoying a boom as a result of war orders. Trade as a neutral meant all profit and few losses, and to join the war could destroy that situation. However, the pattern of trade, whether by accident or design, did amount to economic favoritism, and it tied the United States to the Allied cause with an implicit investment in its victory. When, in addition, the United States government insisted upon its unabridged freedom of the seas and the right of American citizens to travel freely without delay or hindrance, American shipping and American lives were put at risk, and the possibility, even probability, of confrontation with Germany increased.

The question of neutral shipping rights in time of war was not new to American experience. Conflicts arising from interference with American vessels had contributed to the coming of war with Britain in 1812, and Union actions against British ships had provoked angry diplomatic exchanges during the Civil War. Attempts to clarify the situation by international agreement had been made at the conference that produced the Declaration of London in 1909, but this had not been totally successful because the British, reliant upon their naval defenses, were unwilling to accept restriction of their use of sea power. It was Britain's refusal to accept international practices that first came to the fore in 1914 with its immediate declaration of a continental blockade and the mining of the North Sea. Insisting on the right to stop ships at sea and to search them, the British went further by extending the definition of "contraband" to include foodstuffs and raw materials. Such actions brought American protests, which reached a height in 1916 when the blockade was further tightened, and American companies and individuals deemed to have aided the enemy were placed on a British blacklist.

The differences with Britain were, however, mainly legal, and centered upon questions of definition, interpretation, and compensation. The issues raised by German acts posed questions of a more fundamental and emotive nature and concerned the morality of their behavior. With its own fleet bottled up and its war effort adversely affected by the British blockade, the German government responded in perhaps the only way it could: in February 1915 it announced that *all* enemy shipping in a war zone around the British Isles would be subject to surprise submarine attack from its U-boats. Neutral powers were warned that given the problems of identification, their vessels could be at risk in the proscribed area. The American government's response made clear that it would hold Germany strictly accountable for any loss of American ships or lives, and that such losses would be totally unacceptable. This was the position when a German U-boat sank the Cunard liner the *Lusitania,* off the south coast of Ireland on 7 May 1915.

The *Lusitania* sank in eighteen minutes, and 124 American citizens were among the 1,198 people who lost their lives. The American press reacted to the attack as an act of barbarity unworthy of a civilized nation, though the *Lusitania* was known to be carrying war materials, and passengers boarding her had been warned of the risk of attack. President Wilson described the sinking as an illegal and inhuman act, and in a strong exchange of notes with the German government, he warned that a repetition would be regarded as "deliberately unfriendly." Secretary of State William Jennings Bryan felt that the language was too strong and that America's actions were not those of a neutral power, and he resigned in order to campaign for a more peaceful approach. But while Bryan and others urged caution and compromise, some Americans, led chiefly by Theodore Roosevelt, were demanding tougher action. Few Americans, however, were prepared to contemplate war at this stage, and Woodrow Wilson found considerable support when, in a speech of 10 May, he could say, "There is such a thing as a man being too proud to fight. There is such a thing as a nation being so right that it does not need to convince others by force that it is right."[8] It was still clear, though, that future attacks would not be tolerated, and when the government reacted strongly to the deaths of two Americans on the sunken liner *Arabic* in August 1915, the German government hastily issued a pledge to halt attacks on liners without warning and to allow for the safety of passengers.

Although President Wilson could claim to be too proud to fight, the crisis of 1915 made many Americans, inside and outside of government, aware that their country was in fact in little position to defend its neutrality. Theodore Roosevelt, bellicose as ever, articulated a growing concern in certain circles when, as early as 1914, he criticized America's military weakness. This cry was taken up by the Navy League and the Army League, and by the newly formed National Security league. The view of America vulnerable to attack was also portrayed in the 1915 film *The Battle Cry of Peace,* based upon Hudson Maxim's (of machine-gun fame) book *Defenseless America.* The film showed America being overwhelmed and destroyed by an invading army, but the moral may not have been immediately obvious to its audience. Such films probably did as much to reinforce the general view of the horror of war and of the need for America to remain uninvolved. This was certainly the message of Thomas Ince's popular movie of 1916, *Civilization,* which showed Christ intervening to reveal the monstrosity of war to its originators, and to bring it to an end. Similar sentiments were expressed in D. W. Griffith's *Intolerance,* which also ended with divine intervention in the cause of peace.

Such was the success of Ince's film (described as "a million dollar extravaganza with forty thousand actors"—"The Picture that Should Stop the War") that President Wilson suggested it had contributed to his election victory in 1916, as public opinion still clearly favored peace and opposed militarism.[9] Two of the most popular songs of 1915 were "Don't Take My Darling Boy Away," and "I Didn't Raise My Boy to Be a Soldier." The chorus of the latter went:

I didn't raise my boy to be a soldier
I brought him up to be my pride and joy,
Who dares place a musket on his shoulder,
To shoot some other mother's darling boy?
Let nations arbitrate their future troubles,
It's time to lay the sword and gun away.
There'd be no war to-day,
If mothers all would say,
"I didn't raise my boy to be a soldier."[10]

These sentiments were echoed at the Democratic party convention in 1916, when delegates spontaneously took up the chorus, "He kept us out of war" during one speech, and so provided the catchphrase that, like it or not, became Wilson's election slogan and helped ensure his narrow victory over Republican Charles Evans Hughes. That victory was also made possible because of the support of the majority of the old Progressive party and the votes of many who had supported the Socialist candidate, Eugene Debs, in 1912.

Popular songs, movies, election slogans, and Progressive support notwithstanding, Wilson was himself aware of America's military weakness and was moving toward a position of "reasonable preparedness" in 1915 in order to deter the Germans and to win Republican votes. As Jane Addams wrote, by 1917 the president had "seized the leadership of the movement which had been started and pushed by his opponents."[11] The administration's proposals to double the size of the regular army and to replace the National Guard with the Continental Army of four hundred thousand under federal control were made public as early as November 1915, but these provoked considerable opposition from southern and western Democrats and Progressives, alarmed by the apparent threat to both states' rights and peace. Faced with such strong opposition from within his own party, Wilson moved toward compromise. He accepted the resignation of his antagonistic secretary of war, Lindley M. Garrison, and replaced him with Newton D. Baker, reform mayor of Cleveland and self-proclaimed pacifist. The plan for the Continental Army was dropped, and the size of the increase to the regular army strength reduced. Congress too made concessions, prompted by a further crisis with Germany and its use of submarines.

On 24 March 1916, a German U-boat torpedoed the unarmed French passenger ship, the *Sussex*. Not only was this a breach of the *Arabic* pledge, but among the passengers injured in the attack were four Americans. Woodrow Wilson declared the act "singularly tragical and unjustifiable," and on 19 April he announced that if the German government did not abandon "its present methods of warfare against passenger and freight carrying vessels this Government can have no choice but to sever diplomatic relations with the Government of the German Empire altogether."[12] Not prepared to risk such a breach at that stage, the German government issued its *Sussex* pledge on 4 May, promising that all vessels would be visited prior to attack. Although this marked a considerable victory for the peace advocates, the crisis was sufficient to persuade Congress to pass the Army Reorganization Act, which Wilson signed on 3 June 1916. The Act raised the size of the regular army to almost 220,000 and integrated the National Guard under federal control. Naval spending was also increased in a bill approved in August. While Progressives were divided on preparedness, with some arguing it would weaken America's neutrality and others seeing it as strengthening America's position, it did not in the long run, however, deter the German government from breaking the *Sussex* pledge when it felt that the force of circumstance demanded it.

On 31 January 1917, having decided against the possibility of a negotiated peace settlement in favor of a last decisive offensive against the Allies, the German government announced its intentions to resume unrestricted submarine warfare. Only one American ship a week would be allowed safe passage to England; all other vessels would be subject to attack. Given the earlier commitments, the American government had little choice but to break off diplomatic relations, which it did on 3 February, and on 26 February the president called upon Congress to approve the arming of American merchant ships for defensive purposes. Opposed by La Follette and a handful of other senators, whom Wilson described as a "little group of willful men" who had "rendered the great government of the United States helpless and contemptible," the measure was not passed. However, the president proceeded to use his executive authority to arm vessels under an antipiracy law of 1819.[13]

On 1 March 1917 Wilson made public the text of a telegram sent by the German foreign minister, Alfred Zimmermann, to the German ambassador in Mexico. The telegram, which had been intercepted and decoded by the British, proposed that in the event of war between Germany and the United States, Mexico might enter an alliance with Germany in order to regain territories lost in the Mexican-American war of 1846–48. Not surprisingly, the publication of the telegram's details provoked an outburst of anti-German sentiment in the United States and helped to swing opinion in favor of firm action. The sinking of seven American merchant ships by German submarines only increased feelings against Germany, and thousands took part in demonstrations in support of war in New York, Boston, Philadelphia, and other cities at the end of March. Finally, with public opinion aroused and his cabinet now unanimous, Woodrow Wilson called a joint session of Congress to ask for a declaration of war on 2 April 1917.

The president began his address at 8:40 on a rainy evening before a packed and silent assembly. He outlined the events leading up to that point and described the submarine campaign as "war against mankind" in which even armed neutrality was of little effect, and he called upon Congress to "accept the status of belligerent which has been thrust upon it," and to prepare the organization and mobilization necessary for war. "Neutrality," he said, "is no longer feasible or desirable where the peace of the world is involved and the freedom of its people." The war was not just to be about American shipping rights—in a ringing phrase he declared that "the world must be safe for democracy."[14] Throughout the president's speech Robert M. La Follette sat unmoved, silently chewing gum, his arms remaining folded while others around him applauded. In the course of the Senate debate on 4 April, La Follette was to speak for almost four hours in opposition to the declaration. He was supported by five others—Norris of Nebraska, Vardaman of Mississippi, Stone of Missouri, Gronna of North Dakota, and Lane of Oregon. All did so under considerable strain, and Norris was accused of "grazing treason" by his critics, while Lane, a broken man, died returning to Oregon in September 1917. Clearly in a minority, this small group was not able to prevent the passage of the war resolution, eighty-six votes to six.

There was opposition, too, in the House of Representatives, led by the Democratic floor leader, Claude Kitchin from North Carolina, a staunch opponent of preparedness. Also among the no votes was that of Jeanette Rankin of Montana, the first woman to sit in Congress. Obviously under tremendous pressure, she said, "I want to stand by my country, but I cannot vote for war," and tearfully voted against the motion.[15] She was to do the same in 1941. The majority in the House, however, like the Senate, supported the president, and the resolution passed 373 votes to 50. Shortly afterward it was signed by the president, and on 6 April 1917, America had entered the war.

In couching the call for war in terms of a crusade for democracy Wilson's "golden glowing words" (as Upton Sinclair was to describe them) articulated the view of a number of Progressives by 1917. America was not entering the war for selfish aims of self-aggrandizement, but in order to create a new liberal world order. *The New Republic* could declare on 14 April 1917 that

> for the first time in history a wholly independent nation has entered a great and costly war under the influence of ideas rather than immediate interests and without any expectation of gains, except those that can be shared with all liberal and inoffensive nations.

Rather than a negative force, the war was now seen as a positive one: in the words of Raymond Fosdick, "a high adventure, a crusade with a compelling purpose," which, said Walter Lippmann, "could be redeemed by the better world to follow."[16]

Many of the older peace organizations supported this view, calling for "Peace through Victory," "A War to End All Wars," and urging "Win the War for Permanent Peace." Having been unable to achieve these aims by mediation, war was seen as the only alternative, made necessary by German actions. In February 1917, in a meeting with a number of peace advocates, including Jane Addams, President Wilson suggested that participation in the war would ensure some say in the creation of the postwar world by allowing America a place at the peace table rather than having " 'to call through a crack in the door." But Jane Addams and her friends were not persuaded, and from that "time on we felt officially outlawed, and . . . left the White House in deep dejection."[17]

Not all reformers were dejected at the coming of war, nor was it just in the field of foreign affairs that some saw the American participation leading to gain: some now argued that entry into war would pave the way to greater social progress at home. A group of leading Progressives and Republicans, including Hiram Johnson, Harold Ickes, Gifford Pinchot, and William Allen White issued a statement of support for the administration's war policies and called for measures to bring universal military training, guaranteed farm prices, government control of the necessities of life, protection for wage earners, graduated income tax, a tax on war profits, and legislation to grant women equal political rights. In general they argued that "to perpetuate and advance democracy there should be assurance of common benefit, so that out of the sacrifice of war America may achieve broader democracy in Government, more equitable distribution of wealth, and greater national efficiency in raising the level of the general welfare." Such statements were broadly echoed in an editorial in the *General Federation of Women's Clubs Magazine* in June 1917, which said:

> We shall exchange our material thinking for something quite different, and we shall all be kin. We shall all be enfranchised, prohibition will prevail, many wrongs will be righted, vampires and grafters and slackers will be relegated to a class by themselves. . . ."[18]

Social welfare advocates could also view the war in positive terms. Speaking at the National Conference of Social Work in Pittsburgh in June 1917, the director of the New York School of Philanthropy, Edward Devine, suggested that war had demonstrated the shallowness of prewar achievements, but was also creating "a vast laboratory for the demonstration of the truths in which social work is based." The following year the conference president, Robert Woods, head of South End Settlement House in Boston, spoke of "the cleansing influence of the war" and asked, "Why not continue on into the years of peace the close, vast wholesome organism of service, of fellowship, of creative power?"[19] Collective action, patriotic sacrifice, and national and civic unity were to be the benefits of war as individuals worked for the common good rather than personal profit, mobilized and led in the cause of greater efficiency by a central government whose power was extended in response to the war's demands.

The radical reporter, John Reed, captured the reality of wartime involvement when he wrote of spending an evening in Washington, D.C., with four or five "clever youngsters a year or so out of college, now doing volunteer work on the Munitions Board, Hoover's Food Administration, or one of the innumerable sub-committees of the Council of National Defense."[20] Individuals who before 1917 might have gone into settlement or charity work now worked for the government; the Settlement Houses themselves now turned to war service, as they "were stirred to a new sense of responsibility for a more coherent loyalty."

While social work leaders like Lillian Wald, Florence Kelley, Julia Lathrop, and even Jane Addams became involved in war agencies and committees, and Hull House raised fifty thousand dollars among neighbors for Liberty Loans, other settlements were involved in Red Cross, food and fuel conservation, and Americanization programs.[21] Numerous Settlement House workers found openings in agencies like the Red Cross and the YMCA. The Red Cross grew in membership from 250,000 in 1917 to 21 million in 1919, and in the first year of the war some 75 percent of all Red Cross appointments came from Charity Organization Societies. Paul U. Kellogg, editor of *Survey,* had opposed the war before 1917, but once America had entered, wrote of it as "the opportunity of a generation," and he served in the Red Cross from September 1917 to 1918; Harold Ickes, the Chicago progressive and party administrator, desperately sought war service in the government or Red Cross before finally being appointed business secretary of the YMCA's National War Council in April 1918; Raymond Fosdick, former commissioner of New York City's accounts, became chairman of the Committee on Training Camp Activities, an agency to provide for soldiers' welfare and morale, and to protect their morals, by providing decent, wholesome, in-camp entertainments—over four hundred social workers were engaged in the War Camp Community Services in one form or another.[22]

For the editors of *The New Republic* the very "extension of government power during wartime was an opportunity to secure that radical reconstruction of American society which they had long advocated." While *The New Republic* became such a supporter of the war that it was virtually an organ of the administration (and its circulation rose from sixteen thousand in 1917 to forty-three thousand in 1919), two of its editors took posts in war agencies. Walter Weyl served for a year in the War Department, and Walter Lippmann acted as aide to the secretary of war and served on the army-navy labor relations board before joining a group of academics in the think tank known as "The Inquiry," to help plan the peace.[23] Among others in *The New Republic* circle enlisted in the war effort were Dean Frederick Keppel of Columbia University, who became assistant secretary of war, and Felix Frankfurter, the young lawyer and Harvard professor whom Secretary of War Baker invited to Washington for a weekend in 1917 to sort out problems in the clothing industry relating to the manufacture of uniforms. Frankfurter remained with the government until 1919, serving as secretary for the President's Mediation Commission, before being made chairman of the War Labor Policies Board. Frankfurter's involvement and enthusiasm was such that former President Taft described him as "the hot dog of war," and one biographer suggested that Frankfurter's reputation was shaped during the war years.[24] For men such as these, the war brought recognition and a share of the power of government. For the time being, at least, they became "the spokesmen for the status quo." Even the most radical could be affected by this wartime change: Scott Nearing quoted an old-time Socialist who said:

> All of my adult life I have been in opposition. I was a rebel, a radical, a socialist, an outcast. I could get no steady job, had no dependable income. Now I have changed all that. I have turned right-about-face and joined up with the right side. I am doing exactly what I am supposed to do, what everybody is doing. I'm part of a big powerful movement, headed by the President of the United States, with all the right people as members. I tell you it's great.[25]

It remained to be seen what effect the war would have on these optimists, and upon those who continued to oppose American involvement. Both groups agreed on one thing—that the war would bring change of one sort or another to the United States. As William Allen White said, "War will bring either a large forward jump or a large backward jump."[26]

Notes

1. William Allen White, *The Autobiography of William Allen White* (New York, 1946), 96; C. Roland Marchand, *The American Peace Movement and Social Reform, 1898–1918* (Princeton, 1972), ix–xi; also see Charles De Benedetti, *The Peace Reform in American History* (Bloomington, Ind., and London, 1980), 79–85.
2. Jane Addams, *Peace and Bread in Time of War* (1945; reprint New York, 1971), 1; Jane Addams, *The Second Twenty Years at Hull House* (New York, 1930), 119; W. E. Leuchtenburg, *The Perils of Prosperity 1914–32* (Chicago and London, 1958), 13.
3. Marchand, *The American Peace Movement*, 240–46; Donald Johnson,

The Challenge to American Freedoms: World War I and the Rise of the American Civil Liberties Union (Kentucky, 1963), 3–10.

4. Marchand, *The American Peace Movement,* 184–89; Barbara J. Steinson, *American Women's Activism in World War I* (New York and London, 1982), 16–35; Marie Louise Degen, *The History of the Woman's Peace Party* (Baltimore, 1939; reprint New York and London, 1972).

5. Jane Addams, *Peace and Bread,* 39.

6. Steinson, *American Women's Activism,* 79–88; Ford quoted in Mark Sullivan, *Our Times: The United States 1900–1925, Volume V, Over Here 1914–1918* (New York and London, 1933), 162.

7. La Follette, in Paxson, *American Democracy and the World War, Pre-War Years 1913–1917,* 292. Trade figures, Link, *Woodrow Wilson and the Progressive Era 1910–1917* (New York, 1963), 278–79.

8. Albert Bushnell Hart, ed., *Selected Addresses and Public Papers of Woodrow Wilson* (New York, 1918); "Address to Naturalized Citizens," Philadelphia, 88.

9. Michael T. Isenberg, *War on Film: The American Cinema and World War I, 1914–1941* (London and Toronto, 1981), 99–102; Mary Jean DeLozier, *Putnam County, Tennessee, 1850–1970* (Nashville, 1978), 160.

10. Steven Jantzen, *Hooray for Peace, Hurrah for War: The United States During World War I* (New York and Scarborough, Ontario, 1971), 107–8; Walter La Feber and Richard Polenberg, *The American Century: A History of the United States Since the 1890s* (New York and London, 1975), 67.

11. Jane Addams, *Peace and Bread,* 67.

12. "Ultimatum on Submarine Warfare," address To Congress, in Hart, ed., *Selected Addresses,* 111–16.

13. Link, *Woodrow Wilson and the Progressive Era,* 273–74.

14. "Necessity of War against Germany," address to Congress, 2 April 1917, in Hart, ed., *Selected Addresses,* 188–97.

15. Richard Lowitt, *George W. Norris: The Persistence of a Progressive 1913–1933* (Urbana, Ill., Chicago and London, 1971), 73–76; Edward Robb Ellis, *Echoes of Distant Thunder: Life in the United States, 1914–1918* (New York, 1975), 321–25.

16. R. Fosdick, *Chronicles of a Generation: An Autobiography* (New York, 1958), 157; Lippmann quoted in Ronald Steel, *Walter Lippmann and the American Century* (Boston and Toronto, 1980), 114; Stuart I. Rochester, *American Liberal Disillusionment in the Wake of World War I* (Philadelphia and London, 1977), 26–27; and J. A. Thompson, "American Progressive Publicists and the First World War, 1914–1917," *Journal of American History* 48, no. 2 (September 1917).

17. Addams, *Peace and Bread,* 64, 71; Steinson, *American Women's Activism,* 241–42.

18. GFWC *Magazine,* quoted in O. Graham, *The Great Campaigns: Reform and War in America 1900–1928,* (Englewood Cliffs, N.J.: 1971), 98; Progressive statement, *New York Times,* 23 April 1917: 4.

19. National Conference of Social Work, *Proceedings of 44th Annual Session, Pittsburgh, June 6–13, 1917* (Chicago, 1918), 46–50; *Proceedings of 45th Annual Session, Kansas City, May 15–22, 1918* (Chicago, 1919), 9.

20. John Reed, "This Unpopular War," *The Seven Arts* 2 (August 1917): 397–408.

21. Robert A. Woods and Albert J. Kennedy, *The Settlement Horizon: A National Estimate* (New York, 1922), 298–303.
22. Fosdick, *Chronicles of a Generation,* 143–57; Roy Lubove, *The Professional Altruist: The Emergence of Social Work as a Career, 1880–1930* (Cambridge, Mass., 1965), 178–92; John F. McClymer, *War and Welfare: Social Engineering in America, 1890–1925* (Westport, Conn., and London, 1980), 162–165, 181. Kellogg, quoted in McClymer, 157, and see Clarke A. Chambers, *Paul H. Kellogg and the Survey: Voices for Social Welfare and Social Justice* (Minneapolis, 1971), 62–65.
23. Steel, *Walter Lippmann and the American Century,* 75, 134–39; Charles Forcey, *The Crossroads of Liberalism: Croly, Weyl, Lippmann and the Progressive Era, 1901–1925* (London and Oxford, 1972), 278–90; Laurence Emerson Gelfand, *The Inquiry: American Preparation for Peace, 1917–1919* (New Haven, Conn., and London, 1963), 23–24, 38.
24. Michael E. Parrish, *Felix Frankfurter and His Times: The Reform Years* (New York and London, 1982), 80–85; Taft quoted in Valerie Jean Conner, *The National War Labor Board: Stability, Social Justice and the Voluntary State* (Chapel Hill, N.C., 1983), 33.
25. Scott Nearing, *The Making of a Radical: A Political Autobiography* (New York, 1972), 103; Robert H. Wiebe, *The Search for Order, 1877–1920* (New York, 1967), 292–3.
26. White quoted in John A. Thompson, "The First World War and the American Progressive Publicists," Ph.D. dissertation, Cambridge University, 1969, 303.

3

Mobilizing the Population for War

Propaganda and Civil Liberties

"Once lead this people into war," President Wilson is reported to have said on the eve of his war message, "and they'll forget there ever was such a thing as tolerance."

> To fight you must be brutal and ruthless, and the spirit of ruthless brutality will enter into the very fibre of our national life, infecting Congress, the courts, the policeman on the beat, the man in the street.[1]

Whether or not the president actually said these words to newsman Frank Cobb is a matter of some doubt, but they were nonetheless an accurate prediction of what the war was to bring. Almost immediately following American entry, the mood of the general public became one of warlike patriotism and an extreme nationalism—100 percent Americanism—that would tolerate no dissension. This public demand for conformity was matched and fueled by official rhetoric and by a mounting campaign at the state and federal level to silence opposition. As a result, America's participation in the world war brought new departures in the shaping and controlling of public opinion by government and posed a serious challenge to the principles of free speech and individual liberty enshrined in the Bill of Rights.

The wartime hysteria had its basis in prewar tensions and conflicts and reflected the insecurity endemic in a nation of immigrants. To that extent, the war merely continued or heightened the sentiments revealed in prewar nativism and the attempts to restrict immigration and Americanize the newcomers. The war only gave a focus and urgency to previously unspoken or generalized doubts about loyalty and national identity. As one writer subsequently pointed out, the American entry into the war emphasized the necessity for Americanization in very obvious ways, and he included the fact that 34 percent of alien males of military age were unable to understand military orders spoken in English, and that war industries were "largely dependent on alien labor."[2] However, while the demand for unity led to a general rejection of all foreign elements and hyphenates, it was the existence of a German-American population that caused most alarm.

The presence of 2.5 million people who were actually German-born, not to mention the 8 million or so of German descent plus those who had come from parts of the Austro-Hungarian Empire or even just from regions that were anti-British or anti-Russian, obviously encouraged fears of subversion. One senator, Lee Overman of North Carolina, could suggest that there were as many as a hundred thousand spies in America, and the Connecticut State Council of Defense issued leaflets warning, "Beware of Spies And Enemy Eavesdroppers!"; "The Kaiser's Agent May Be the Man or Woman You Least Suspect."[3] Such suspicions had been given some point even before America entered the war as a consequence of the activities of German agents, activities that, as captured documents indicated, had included espionage and sabotage. The documents, published in the *New York World* in August 1915, were given additional credence following a number of detonations on ships in American ports bound for destinations in Britain or France, and a series of explosions in munitions plants in New Jersey, Illinois, and New York. The dismissal of the Austro-Hungarian ambassador to America in September 1915, and of German military and naval attachés in December, made clear the American government's view of these activities.[4] If there was any doubt, the president cast it aside in his annual address to Congress on 7 December 1915, when he spoke of

> citizens of the United States . . . born under other flags . . . who have poured the poison of disloyalty into the very arteries of our national life. . . . They have formed plots to destroy property, they have entered into conspiracies against the neutrality of government, they have sought to pry into every confidential transaction of the government in order to serve interests alien to our own.

Once America had entered the war, the president reminded the nation of these charges, and in his Flag Day Address in Washington on 14 June 1917, he referred to the "insults and aggressions of the Imperial German

Government," which had "filled our unsuspecting communities with vicious spies and conspirators and sought to corrupt the opinion of our people in their own behalf." They had, he said, "sought by violence to destroy our industries and arrest our commerce."[5]

The president's charges were given further support by reports in the press of the arrests of large numbers of spies immediately following the declaration of war. The *New York Times,* for example, announced the arrest of sixty spies on 7 April, and an explosion at a munitions plant in Chester, Pennsylvania, in which 125 people died, was also attributed to saboteurs. On 30 April 1917, Secretary of War Newton D. Baker reported the breakdown of the big engine at the Springfield Armory as a result of emery being put into the bearings, but wrote that this was "the first instance of destruction in any of our Government arsenals which is obviously malicious."[6] However, the government clearly could not take chances, and a total of sixty-three hundred aliens were arrested, of whom twenty-three hundred were interned. Given the number of German- and Austrian-born in the United States, this does not seem excessively high, particularly when compared with the forty-five thousand interned in Britain. Nonetheless, the fear of aliens persisted in America and, indeed, was to grow during the war.

The possibility of divided loyalties among immigrant groups on grounds of nationality was not the sole cause of concern for the administration. Given the strength of the prewar peace movement, and the sudden change in American policy, there was, understandably, considerable uncertainty about the attitude of many native-born Americans to the war. However, once America had officially entered the conflict, most peace campaigners accepted the fact and joined the majority of the population in favor of patriotism and loyal support of their country. William Jennings Bryan, the former secretary of state who previously "spoke against war day and night" following his resignation in 1915, now threw himself behind the government and even volunteered for armed service— at the age of fifty-seven. David Starr Jordan, president of Stanford University, a director of the World Peace Foundation, and a leading peace campaigner, was addressing three thousand antiwar demonstrators on the day of Woodrow Wilson's war message, but subsequently declined further invitations to such meetings, "it being neither wise nor reasonable to oppose in any way the established policy of the nation," and he later spoke on behalf of the government's war policies.[7] The Women's Peace party (WPP) also ceased its demonstrations, and while many of its branches became involved in relief work and war-related programs, its leading officers, Kelley, Wald, and others, joined government committees to organize various aspects of the war effort. Carrie Chapman Catt left the WPP altogether in March 1917, having earlier volunteered the services of

NAWSA to the government, arguing "that wartime service would win more support for the woman suffrage cause than pacifism." She and Anna Howard Shaw became members of the Woman's Committee of the Council of National Defense. Even Jane Addams supported the war effort, albeit less conspicuously. While Hull House was used as registration center for the draft board and provided classes in Red Cross work, food conservation, and social hygiene, Addams herself toured the country for the Food Administration and also urged the purchase of Liberty Bonds for the Committee on Public Information, although she still found "some towns would consider me too pacifist to appear."[8]

But not all the former opponents of war followed the line of national duty. There still remained considerable opposition, sufficient to cause the government concern. According to Oswald Villard "the bulk of the people beyond the Alleghenies was not in favor of going to war," and Josephus Daniels wrote that as late as August 1917 one report estimated two-thirds of the nation to be against war. Despite these apparently widespread feelings, it was chiefly the Socialist Party of America that led organized opposition. Meeting at its annual convention in St. Louis on 7 April, the SPA, unlike its European counterparts, most of whom had become nationalists, reaffirmed "its allegiance to the principle of internationalism and working-class solidarity" and proclaimed "its unalterable opposition to the war," which it categorized as a capitalist conflict. For some members this was too much, and a number, mainly newer middle-class members, left the party to support their country. Among them were leading figures such as Upton Sinclair, who wrote to Woodrow Wilson "that the power of the Prussian military caste must be broken and that civilization waits until this job is done." Others included John Spargo, William Walling, J. G. Phelps Stokes, Charles Russell, and even the antiwar candidate of 1916, A. L. Benson. Russell later suggested that his former comrades should be driven out of the country, and Phelps Stokes proposed that they be shot. The majority of members, however, remained loyal to the party, and at the convention they voted three to one to continue active public opposition to the war.[9]

Large antiwar demonstrations were organized in Boston and later in Chicago and Evansville. The Boston parade in July was broken up by soldiers and sailors, while the police waited an hour and a half before intervening. The *New York Times* of 2 July recorded that "none of the soldiers and sailors who figured in the disturbance was arrested." However, the Socialist party was not without its support: it actually registered a rise in membership of almost twenty thousand between the beginning of the year and June, and in the elections of 1917 ten Socialists were elected to the New York assembly, the Socialist mayor of Milwaukee was reelected, and Socialist mayoralty candidates in New York, Chicago, and

Buffalo, though unsuccessful, polled 22 percent, 34 percent, and 25 percent of the vote respectively.[10] These results suggested that the antiwar position was not unanimously unpopular, and this was supported by other wartime developments.

Leading Socialists were active, with remnants of the WPP in New York and with other pacifist groups, in the creation of "the most important organization fighting for a quick peace," "a kind of popular front," called the People's Council of America for Peace and Democracy.[11] Formed at the end of May 1917, the People's Council called for a statement of American war aims and a negotiated settlement to the war. Following a large rally at Madison Square Garden, subsequent meetings were held in Chicago, Philadelphia, Seattle, and Los Angeles, but with increasing harassment from opponents and police. In the face of continued and growing opposition the council began to disintegrate and ceased to have much significance by the end of the year. Nonetheless, the government felt the council was a sufficient threat for it to create a rival organization in the form of the Alliance for Labor and Democracy.

Although the People's Council may not have attracted widespread support, and the bulk of the population clearly supported the declaration of war, there was some evidence of a reluctance to actually fight in a war beyond the shores of America. The number of volunteers for military service was such that in six weeks the forces had only increased by seventy-three thousand, a slower rate than for the Civil War or the Spanish-American War, and the New York Times commented that at the rate things were going it would be months before America could raise an army.[12] (In Britain, the first month of the war had brought 750,000 volunteers, and by 1916 2.5 million had enlisted.) However, when the administration introduced a bill to draft 2 million men on 5 April 1917, there was a considerable outcry in and out of Congress, and it was clear that many Americans had strong misgivings about conscription for armed service.

Traditionally, America had always relied upon volunteer forces, a citizen's army, organized at state rather than federal level, and the principle was even recognized in the Constitution. In addition, many immigrants had left Europe to avoid compulsory military service in their former country, and they associated conscription with autocracy. There was considerable feeling, too, against the resultant increase in the power of federal government. Before April even Josephus Daniels, the secretary of the navy, had resisted the idea, asking, "Why introduce Prussianism to fight Prussianism?" and the Speaker of the House echoed this thought when he declared that conscript and convict were synonymous terms. Senator James Reed of Missouri, alarmed at the racial implications of universal military service, warned that if the bill was passed "the streets of St. Louis would run red with blood." When the act was passed on 17 May, it was not by an overwhelming majority—199 for and 178 against, with 52 abstentions in the House; 65 for and 8 against, with 23 abstaining, in the Senate.[13]

Even after the passage of the Selective Service Act, there was still uncertainty about reactions to its implementation. The reformer and pacifist Lucille B. Milner could not believe "that our peace-loving nation would be changed overnight into a great war-machine with compulsory military service without serious difficulties." However, on registration day, 5 June, she reported that "the crowd on the street, to my surprise, was light-hearted and good humored. A holiday spirit seemed to prevail," and elsewhere the event was celebrated "with bands and festive crowds." The registration records themselves were impressive evidence of national support: on that one day 10 million men registered, and by the end of the war the total was to be 26 million out of a total male population of 54 million. Of this number only 340,000 failed to show up.[14]

Opposition to the draft did not, however, completely disappear. In certain parts of the country resistance continued. In one town in Pennsylvania 40 percent of those who registered gave fictitious addresses, and in a single Chicago district almost half the registrants failed to show up. In Butte, Montana, a crowd of over six hundred gathered shouting, "Down with war"; in Arizona Navajo Indians drove off the government agents; and in Colorado Ute Indians refused to register and took to the hills.[15] On 25 July a crowd of eight to ten thousand gathered in New Ulm, Minnesota (a state where one-fifth of the population were of German ancestry), to protest against sending men to Europe, and in Texas twenty-four men were arrested for draft resistance in Marin County, and fifty-five members of a Farmers and Laborers Protective Association were also arrested in West Texas. Perhaps the most serious, and yet pathetic, resistance occurred in Oklahoma in August when between eight hundred and one thousand members of a tenant farmers organization, the Working Class Union, prepared to march on the state capital and then on to Washington, armed with muskets and living on beef and green corn, in order to arrest "the Big Slick" (President Wilson), and end the war. This so-called Green Corn Rebellion was a fiasco and was crushed before it could begin. Some 450 men were arrested, 184 were indicted, and 150 were convicted, with the leaders being jailed for up to five years.[16]

As David Shannon has said, the Green Corn Rebellion was clearly "naive and altogether fantastic,"[17] but seen with all the other forms of war opposition, it was bound to cause the government alarm. To counter this situation the administration embarked on a two-pronged campaign: of propaganda to win over public opinion and to mobilize what Joseph Tumulty described as "the people's righteous wrath"; and repression to silence resisters. Only seven days after entering the war, the president, using his executive authority, established the Committee on Public Information to sell the war at home and to acquaint the American people with the government's war aims and objectives as well as carrying out a program of foreign propaganda to win over neutrals and undermine the morale of the enemy. The committee was to be one of the most significant agencies of the war and was to be a major force in shaping American public opinion—so much so that it was described as having "carried out what was perhaps the most effective job of large-scale propaganda which the world had ever witnessed."[18]

In theory, the Committee on Public Information (CPI) consisted of the secretaries of war, navy, and state, and a civilian executive, but in practice the Committee was soon dominated by the civilian chairman, George Creel. Opinion on Creel (and to some extent the CPI) is divided. The historians Mock and Larson said of the president's appointment that "it is hard to see how he could have made a better choice"; on the other hand, the *New York Times* of 16 April 1917 was "unable to discover in his turbulent career any evidence of the ability, the experience, or the judicial temperament required to gain the understanding and co-operation of the press." Yet another commentator thought "if he doesn't put everybody in the hole and get everything upset, it will be because his whole brain has been revolutionized."[19]

The forty-one-year-old Creel was a Missourian who had established a reputation as a journalist and reformer. He helped found the *Kansas City Independent* ("A Clean, Clever Paper for Intelligent People") before moving on to Denver, where he edited the *Denver Post* and the *Rocky Mountain News*. He was reform police commissioner of Denver from 1912 to 1913, and in 1916 he was responsible for the Democratic party's publicity, and he became a personal friend of the president's. He was, said Wilson, a man with "a passion for adjectives," and he had a tendency to oversimplify: according to journalist Mark Sullivan, Creel saw two types of men: "skunks" or "the greatest men who ever lived."[20] His views on propaganda were, if not this simplistic, optimistic and perhaps naive by modern standards.

Creel had outlined his views of the function of a propaganda agency as early as 28 March 1917 when, in a letter to Josephus Daniels, he said censorship "must be based on publicity, *not* suppression," and he urged the creation of a Bureau of Publicity, which would "issue the big, ringing statements that will arouse the patriotism of the nation." Later, Creel wrote that the emphasis of the CPI was on "expression, not repression," "for we had such confidence in our case as to feel that only fair presentation of the facts was needed."[21]

Initially, the main concern of the CPI was the handling of news stories, providing information for the press, distributing official news releases, coordinating news emanating from government departments, and trying to ensure that information useful to the enemy would not be printed. This type of role was not popular with the American press, jealous of its traditional independence and suspicious of government regulation, and the committee was accused of being petty in its restrictions and of giving "misinformation." An exaggerated story of a naval "battle" issued on 4 July 1917 helped to discredit the committee when it transpired that only one German submarine had been engaged. Similar criticisms were to be made about undue CPI optimism concerning figures of airplane production and in authenticating documents purporting to show that the Bolsheviks were German agents. The committee was also attacked in Congress for its partisan approach and for the stress it placed upon President Wilson's war aims, war messages, peace plans, and so on. The fact that the committee was an executive creation and that Creel was a presidential appointment did not help, and Creel only made matters worse when, asked to respond to congressional criticism, he declined on the grounds that "I do not like slumming." In an eight-column article on 19 March 1918 the *New York Times* listed fourteen of Creel's indiscretions, and this seems to reflect upon his standing generally.[22]

Partly because of criticisms, and partly because censorship was increasingly dealt with elsewhere, either by the Censorship Board or by the Postmaster General's office, the CPI gradually concentrated more and more on selling the war and promoting "a national ideology." It did this through a veritable bombardment of material—over 100 million pieces of literature ranging from leaflets, articles, and pamphlets, through to full, book-length studies on the causes, nature, and meaning of the war. In addition, the committee produced posters, slides, photographs, newspaper advertising, and held exhibitions. Enlisting an army of 150,000 people on its twenty-one separate committees, the CPI drew upon reporters and muckraking journalists such as S. S. McClure and Ida Tarbell, reformers such as Jane Addams, artists such as Charles Dana Gibson and Howard Chandler Christy (originators respectively of the "Gibson Girl" and the "Christy Girl"), and a host of historians headed by two of the most eminent of the day, Guy Stanton Ford and J. Franklin Jameson. The committee also utilized film, producing its own films such as *Labor's Part in Democracy's War, Woman's Part in the War, Our Colored Fighters,* and *Americans All.* In addition, it provided scenarios for film studios to use as in Paramount's *A Girl's a Man for A' That, I'll Help Every Willing Worker Find a Job,* and Pathé's *Feeding the Fighter*—titles that are revealing of the war's impact. Film stars also played a part in the committee's efforts, and Douglas Fairbanks, Sr., Charlie Chaplin, and Mary Pickford assisted in public meetings to sell the war and war savings bonds.

In addition to well-known public figures, ordinary citizens—as volunteer "Four Minute Men"—were also used by the CPI. These part-time propagandists addressed audiences prior to theater performances or movie shows along lines suggested in CPI leaflets. Some 75,000 different people took part in this exercise, and in Illinois alone 2,800 "Four Minute Men" were performing a week, while in Chicago 451 speakers gave a total of fifty thousand talks to an estimated overall audience of 25 million in the course of the war. There were even "Junior Four Minute Men" who competed as speakers to be selected in school Christmas roll calls, and children too were subjected to their own propaganda: while adults were told to "Save Food," "Buy Bonds," and "Enlist," children were urged, "Do Not Slide, Do Not Scuff Your Feet" in order to save leather, and were asked to buy Thrift Stamps to aid the national savings.[23]

It was largely the CPI that mobilized opposition to the People's Council of America for Peace and Democracy through the Alliance for Labor and Democracy, which was launched on 6 August 1917. Partly funded by the CPI and partly by its treasurer, millionaire former Socialist J. G. Phelps Stokes, the alliance was chaired by labor leader Samuel Gompers and was intended to counter Socialist propaganda and to mobilize the American labor movement behind the government. It established 150 branches in forty states, held two hundred mass meetings, and published 2 million pamphlets "in order to demonstrate the Administration's support of labor."[24]

If these efforts reflected the positive aspects of the CPI in stressing and trying to further national unity, the more negative side was its depiction of the enemy. In posters, advertisements, and leaflets, it resurrected the images used earlier in Allied propaganda and showed the Germans as Huns, bestial monsters beyond the pale of civilized nations. War posters showed burning cathedrals, Belgian children without hands, drowning victims of submarine attacks, and, in one instance, depicted the Kaiser as a crazed ape, clutching a club marked "cultur," carrying off a half-naked, swooning female. A now warlike Hollywood also took up these themes in films such as *The Kaiser—The Beast of Berlin,* and *To Hell with the Kaiser.* The actor Eric von Stroheim regularly played the evil Hun whose cruelty knew no bounds, brutalizing both women and children: in a scene in *The Heart of Humanity* he is shown as a German soldier, throwing a crying infant out of a window before turning to rape the child's nurse.[25] Little wonder that he became "the man you love to hate."

Given the nature of this propaganda, it was hardly surprising that many American people rejected all things German during the war, named sauerkraut "liberty cabbage," frankfurters "liberty sausage," and German shepherds Alsatians. Worse still, schools stopped teaching the German language, and orchestras forbade the playing of German music and in some cases dismissed conductors of German origin. Oswald Garrison

Villard, the editor of the *New York Post* and *The Nation*, a pacifist with a German father, suffered considerable personal harassment; his children were abused, and his dachshund puppy was stoned. He had grounds to remark that the war "was marked by a bitterness, a vindictiveness, a rage against all who opposed it."[26] But it was not just the war's opponents who suffered: in Collinsville, Illinois, in April 1918, a rather simple German youth, Robert Prager, who had in fact tried to enlist but was rejected because he had one glass eye, was seized and hanged by a drunken mob, which decided he was guilty of antiwar acts. His last request, apparently, was to be buried covered in the American flag.[27]

If the CPI contributed to the mood of hysteria that made such acts possible, it was not alone. The Espionage Act of 15 June 1917 provided penalties of imprisonment for up to twenty years and fines of up to ten thousand dollars for acts of sabotage, aiding the enemy, and inciting rebellion. It also empowered the postmaster general, Albert Burleson, to deny mailing rights to magazines and journals that, in his opinion, advocated treason, insurrection, or opposition to the war effort. This censorship power, although less than originally called for, was used by Burleson with considerable effect. One of the first victims of the act was Robert Goldstein, producer of a movie, *Spirit of '76*, which showed the British encouraging Indians to commit Hun-like atrocities in the War of Independence. The film was seized, and Goldstein was fined ten thousand dollars and sentenced to ten years in prison. This was commuted to three years, and he was released after two. Prewar films with a pacifist message, such as *Civilization* and *The Battle Cry of Peace*, now ceased to be shown.[28]

By May 1918 the postmaster had suspended mailing rights of forty-five newspapers under the Espionage Act. They included the anti-British *Bull*, the pro-Irish *Freeman's Journal*, *Catholic Register*, *Gaelic American*, and *Irish World*, and a number of Socialist journals: *American Socialist*, *Mother Earth*, *New York Call*, *Milwaukee Leader*, and *The Masses*. The *Masses* was first stopped in August 1917 for one issue, but was then denied further mailing rights because it had ceased to be a regular publication! An issue of the single-tax journal, *The Public*, was refused rights for criticizing the government's tax policy and calling for greater taxation! When a number of individuals protested to the president about these and other acts, Wilson declined to comment publicly, but in reply to Herbert Croly of *The New Republic*, he said that he believed the postmaster was "inclined to be most conservative in the exercise of these great and dangerous powers." In a reported conversation with Burleson, he said, "'Now Burleson, these are well-intentioned people. Let them blow off steam!'" but when the postmaster replied that this could mean violation of the Espionage Act, he was told "'go ahead and do your duty.' "[29] Villard was in fact fortunate because *The Nation* was saved from exclusion from the mails because of the intervention of friends in the cabinet, but clearly not all were that lucky.

In order to enforce other aspects of the Espionage Act the government had to increase its police and surveillance machinery. One feature of this was the federal loyalty program initiated on 7 April 1917, enabling heads of departments to remove any employee deemed a risk because of " 'conduct, sympathies, or utterance,' " and as a consequence some twenty-six hundred individuals were vetted. Outside of government Military Intelligence grew in strength from a staff of two officers in 1917 to three hundred officers with one thousand civilian assistants in 1918.[30] Civilian intelligence gathering was the responsibility of two departments, the Justice Department with its Bureau of Investigation created in 1908, and the Treasury Department with the Secret Service, which dated back to 1864. This duplication led to some rivalry, and in June 1917 the secretary of the treasury, William McAdoo, proposed the establishment of a single bureau in either the State Department (where there was already a section concerned with foreign espionage), or the Treasury Department. Naturally, Attorney General Thomas W. Gregory suggested that the department of Justice was more appropriate. In the end, the Justice Department appeared to win, and the Bureau of Investigation was to grow into the Federal Bureau of Investigation. However, McAdoo's concern increased during the war because the attorney general enlisted the aid of volunteers, who then acted as if they were government agents. McAdoo felt it "unfortunate that a miscellaneous horde of so-called Secret Service operatives be let loose upon the country," and he feared "harmful possibilities."[31]

There were, in fact, a number of voluntary, vigilante-style organizations formed after Attorney General Gregory had asked people to report any acts of disloyalty they witnessed. As a result of his request, his office was inundated with reports—one thousand a day in 1917, fifteen hundred a day in 1918—and assistance was needed. The most important group to help was the American Protective League, an organization established by a Chicago advertising executive, A. M. Briggs, which began, with Justice Department approval, by providing transportation for investigating officers but became much more significant. By 1918 there were 250,000 APL operatives in over six hundred towns and cities. Mainly bankers, businessmen, attorneys, or former policemen, they took part in a number of war-related activities, not all legal: their historian could boast, perhaps with exaggeration, of acts of burglary and wiretapping. Most of their activity, however, centered on investigations of disloyalty, breaking up antiwar meetings, and searching for draft evaders. They took part in the "slacker" raids of 1918, detaining ten thousand people of draft age in Chicago and eleven thousand in New York city in order to ascertain the reasons for their non-military status. In New York alone they were reputed to have taken part in 15,000 loyalty investigations and 29,680 draft evasion cases; nationally, they were involved in 3 million investigations.[32] When Woodrow Wilson raised the subject he wrote, "It seems to me that it would be very dangerous to have such an organization operating in the United States" and wondered "if there was any way which we could stop it," but the attorney general replied in the negative, and the matter was not pursued. At the end of the war Gregory could say that such voluntary bodies had "rendered very great assistance," and that the APL, "a most important auxillary and reserve force for the Bureau of Investigation," had "proved to be invaluable."[33]

One of the consequences of the government sanction for groups such as the APL was that private individuals were encouraged to take the law into their own hands to deal with those they considered to be disloyal or unpatriotic, and among the worst aspects of the wartime mood of repression was the widespread incidence of different forms of vigilante action. One of the most regular forms of punishment inflicted on individuals deemed to be of doubtful loyalty was public humiliation in the form of flag-kissing—"By 1918 flag-kissing had become so frequent that it was hardly first-rate news." Other victims of the patriots were tarred and feathered, shaved, ducked, given a coat of yellow paint, or just beaten up, or permutations of all of these. The American Civil Liberties Union recorded 164 cases of mob violence throughout the war, but it is clear that this was an underestimate.[34] Organizations thought to be disrupting the war effort or not clearly committed to supporting it were especially targets for such attacks, and in western states the Industrial Workers of the World provided just such a target.

Opposed to the war in general, the Wobblies also used the opportunity presented by labor scarcity to push their demands for better working conditions and pay. The movement grew in strength, with an increase of about forty to fifty thousand members between 1916 and 1917, and it was involved in a series of strikes in the mining and lumber industries in western and midwestern states in 1917. As a result, it was quickly singled out by its opponents and labeled as a subversive and unpatriotic organization, and it was subjected to increasing attacks upon its members. On 10 July 1917, sixty-seven striking coppermen in Jerome, Arizona, were rounded up by vigilantes and shipped across into California in cattle trucks. Two days later in Bisbee, Arizona, members of the Citizens Protective League, the Workmen's Loyalty League, local mining company officials, and sheriff Harry Wheeler rounded up 1,186 workers reputed to be Wobblies, placed them in twenty-three boxcars, and transported them into New Mexico, where they were abandoned without food or water at a remote desert station, from which they had to be rescued by the military.

Of the 1,186, 472 had registered for the draft, 250 had purchased liberty bonds, and only 426 were Wobblies. The Bisbee men were lucky to escape with their lives: in Butte, Montana, the IWW organizer Frank Little was involved in a strike of fifteen thousand miners. After making various inflammatory speeches about the war and the capitalist classes he was seized by vigilantes on 1 August 1917, dragged through the streets tied behind a car, and finally hanged from a railway bridge.[35]

Exploiting the mood of patriotic fervor, various western newspapers, politicians, and businessmen argued that the murders of men like Prager and Little were a consequence of the frustration and anger resulting from the government's failure to suppress opposition, and they called for tougher federal action. At the state level, a number of administrations had passed sedition and criminal syndicalist acts, but they too were calling for a greater federal initiative. In response to such demands, and in the hope that vigilantism would cease, the government passed the Sedition Act of May 1918, amending the Espionage Act, and providing fines of ten thousand dollars and up to twenty years imprisonment for

> uttering, printing, writing, or publishing any disloyal, profane, scurrilous, or abusive language intended to cause contempt, scorn, contumely, or disrepute as regards the . . . government . . . the Constitution . . . the flag . . . the uniform of the Army or Navy, or any language intended to incite resistance to the United States or to promote the cause of its enemies.[36]

This sweeping piece of legislation was followed with the Alien Act of 16 October 1918, which enabled the government to deport any alien in America subsequently discovered to have been, or be, a member of any revolutionary organization prior to their entry or since entering into the country. With such enormous powers as these it is hardly surprising that the attorney general could say that "never in its history has this country been so thoroughly policed." As Max Eastman, editor of *The Masses,* remarked, "You can't even collect your thoughts without being arrested for unlawful assembly."[37]

Whether such acts were necessary is hard to say because even before the passage of this additional legislation the government, clearly impressed by appeals from various quarters and concerned by the events of the summer of 1917, was in the process of silencing radical opposition to the war. As early as June 1917 the anarchists Emma Goldman and Alexander Berkman had been charged with conspiracy to oppose the draft, and in July both were sentenced to two years in prison. Following the events at Bisbee, the attack on radicals intensified, and in September 1917 raids were made on IWW offices in over sixty towns and cities, and over three hundred people were arrested. Eventually 184 Wobblies, mainly officials and organizers, were brought to trial in Chicago, Sacramento, and Wichita. The trials resulted in 101 convictions in Chicago, 46 in Sacramento, and 26 in Wichita. Among those was the Wobbly leader, Big Bill Haywood, who was fined thirty thousand dollars and sentenced to twenty years' imprisonment. Allowed out on bail pending appeal, he fled the country and went to Russia, where he died in 1928. Others were less fortunate, and the last of those convicted were released in 1923. In Omaha, Nebraska, another 64 Wobblies, arrested in November 1917, were held for almost a year without a trial, and some of them were held until 1919 before the case was dropped. But by then the organization, shorn of its leadership, membership reduced, and funds depleted, was of little significance.[38]

The Socialist party suffered much the same fate as the Wobblies, as its leading officials and spokesmen and women were arrested and jailed, and most of its newspapers and journals were excluded from the mails. A list of "the most important, typical cases" involving Socialists included over fifty individuals ranging from the state chairman of the party in South Dakota through to the national executive secretary in Chicago. Kate Richards O'Hare, former international secretary, was sentenced to five years in Missouri Penitentiary in December 1917. After various appeals had been dismissed, she entered the jail in April 1919 and served one year before release. In February 1918, following a raid on the Chicago offices the previous September, charges were brought against Victor Berger, the Austrian-born editor of the *Milwaukee Leader* who was a member of the national executive committee and a former congressman for Milwaukee. The national executive secretary, Adolph Germer, and J. Louis Engdahl, editor of the party's publications, plus two other office holders, were also charged. The trial finally began on 9 December 1918 and ended in January 1919 with a guilty verdict against all five. Each was sentenced to twenty years' imprisonment, but following a succession of appeals and dismissals, the case was dropped in 1923 with none of the five being jailed. In the meantime, Berger had run in the senatorial contest in Wisconsin and, although defeated, had attracted one hundred thousand votes. In 1918 he was elected to Congress again as a representative for Milwaukee but was denied his seat by the House. Reelected in 1919, he was again denied admittance. He was finally accepted in 1923.[39]

Further cases involving Socialists occurred in 1918 under the Espionage Act and its new amendment, and the party's million-dollar defense fund was clearly necessary. In April 1918, Max Eastman and his fellow editors of *The Masses* were charged with violating the espionage law, but the jury proved unable to arrive at a verdict. Another jury also failed to agree following a second trial in September, and the charges were finally dropped in 1919. In March 1918, Scott Nearing and the Rand School of Social Science, a center of socialism in New York City, were both indicted for respectively writing and publishing an antiwar pamphlet, "The Great Madness." The Rand School was found guilty and fined, but Nearing, paradoxically, was acquitted. Nonetheless, he later could write, "The guns shattered my career as completely as though I had been under an artillery barrage."[40]

Undoubtedly the most significant case of 1918 was that of the Socialist party leader and three-time presidential candidate, Eugene V. Debs. Until the summer of 1918 Debs had resisted making any provocative speeches, but, faced with the jailing of fellow party members, he finally felt obliged to speak out in protest and make clear his support for his comrades. On 16 June 1918, he addressed the state convention of the Ohio Socialist party in Canton. Knowing full well that federal agents were among the audience, he called for the maintenance of free speech, attacked "Wall Street Junkers," and defended Socialists and Wobblies then on trial for opposition to the war. He was indicted on 29 June, and his trial began on 9 September in Cleveland. On 14 September he was sentenced to ten years in prison, and in his final address to the court he affirmed his basic principles, saying, "While there is a lower class, I am in it; while there is a criminal element, I am of it; while there is a soul in prison, I am not free." He went on to give an emotional and ringing criticism of a society in which "money is still so much more important than human life." When all appeals had failed, he went to jail, aged sixty-four, on 13 April 1919. The president refused to commute his sentence, despite pleas from a number of Americans and recommendations of clemency from the attorney general. " 'This man was a traitor to his country,' " Wilson said, " 'and he will never be pardoned during my administration.' " Debs was finally released by President Harding on Christmas Day 1921.[41]

Debs ran as a presidential candidate from jail in 1920 and was still able to secure more votes (919,800) than he had in 1912, and considerably more than the candidate in 1916, A. L. Benson, Although the percentage of voters overall was small (3.4 percent of the vote as opposed to 6 percent in 1912), the number still revealed support and sympathy for the Socialist party, even though it was 1932 before there was another Socialist candidate for the presidency. However, the Socialist party *did* survive the war. It declined in rural areas—in Oklahoma, membership dropped from ten thousand to thirty-five hundred—and became a more predominantly city-based movement with a higher proportion of foreign-born among its remaining members than had previously been the case. Something of the fluctuating performance of the party was revealed in New York City, where the number of assemblymen fell from the ten of 1917 to two in 1918 and rose to five in 1919. According to one historian the war actually strengthened the party by creating unity: "At no time in the history of the American Socialist movement were Socialists as unified."[42]

It is fairly clear that in the case of both the Socialists and Wobblies, the federal government was following the lead of the states in taking a tough line, and that at a local level there were groups that wished to use the war to attack radical movements. This was certainly true in the Midwest, where established interests mobilized to attack a farmers' organization, the Non-Partisan League. Although only formed in 1915 by former Socialist party member Arthur C. Townley, the league had quickly spread from North Dakota into neighboring states. Primarily an organization of wheat growers, it echoed many of the demands of the Populists in calling for the end of exploitation and the exclusion of middlemen through public ownership of marketing facilities, terminal elevators, flour mills, packing houses, banks, and railroads. The league's membership, estimated at 25,000 in 1916, was said to be over 188,000 in 1918.[43] Townley supported the war but called for greater government control and taxation of the rich in order to finance the war effort. Such policies inevitably attracted the opposition of certain conservatives, but the league invited still greater criticism when it identified with Robert M. La Follette and had the senator address a league meeting in St. Paul, Minnesota, in September 1917. To make matters worse, La Follette was then misquoted as having said that the United States had *no* grievances against the German government, and a considerable outcry against the senator and the league followed. However, the league had its supporters, and no less a person than George Creel could still defend it and report to the president that the attack on it was "fundamentally the fight of machine politicians." Having seen Townley personally, Creel wrote, in February 1918, that the league leader was "backing the war and backing Hoover," but that "politicians hate this League and are trying to destroy it."[44]

Despite the CPI chairman's defense, Townley was indicted for antiwar activities on 28 February 1918, following complaints from the county attorney; President Wilson wrote to Creel that Townley and his colleagues "are certainly getting in bad with the communities in which they are most active," and suggested "that we had better pull away from them."[45] Although the first charges against Townley were rejected, he was subsequently tried for violation of the state sedition act in 1919, found guilty, and sentenced to ninety days in prison. He was finally jailed in November 1921. Despite the election of two hundred of the league's supporters to state legislatures in the 1918 elections, the league was a discredited force by the end of the war and began to decline. This process was accelerated by the postwar agricultural depression, and although remnants survived in Dakota, it ceased to have influence in other states.

In all, a total of 2,168 cases were brought to trial under the Espionage and Sedition acts, and by 1921 there had been 1,055 convictions, 181 acquittals, and 790 cases that were either quashed, dismissed, or discontinued.[46] One other group to suffer because of its attitudes to the war was not a political organization at all but a varied collection of individuals who objected to military service on grounds of conscience. America had a tradition recognizing religious objection to military service that went back to the War of Independence, and in the nineteenth century the practice of substitution or commutation had been developed to accommodate those who wished to avoid military duty, for whatever reason. Prior to 1917 the problem had always been a local one, dealt with at the state level, but with Selective Service everything changed: "conscription became, personal, universal, and absolute; there was no provision whatsoever for the hiring of a substitute or the paying of a commutation fee," and the matter became a federal one. Section Four of the Selective Service Act recognized the right to conscientious objection for those members of "well-recognized religious sects or organizations whose creed forbids participation," and Secretary of War Baker extended this in December 1917 to include those who objected on grounds of "personal scruples."[47] However, all individuals were to be subject to the draft, and those exempted from armed service were, nonetheless, expected to accept noncombatant duties. Furthermore, conscientious objectors were to be dealt with by the military at regular army camps, alongside, but segregated from, other troops, and subject to military discipline and military persuasion.

Secretary Baker explained this policy to the president when he wrote:

> I am pretty sure that no harm will come in allowing these people to stay at the camps, separated from the life of the camp but close enough gradually to come to understand. The effect of that I think quite certainly would be that a substantial number of them would withdraw their objections and make fairly good soldiers.[48]

In one respect at least, Baker was correct, and a considerable number of objectors did change their minds in the camps. Out of the 20 million men registered for armed service, 65,000 claimed c.o. status; 20,813 of these were actually inducted into the services. Of these, 16,000 gave up their claims at the camps, another 1,300 accepted noncombatant service in the quartermaster, engineers, or medical services, 1,200 were furloughed out to farms and industries, 99 assisted with Quaker relief, and only 1,390 absolutists remained opposed to any service at all. That the policy was successful to this extent suggests powerful methods of persuasion, and although commanding officers had been ordered to treat c.o.s. "with kindly consideration," this was not always the practice. In some camps the objectors were forced to run the gauntlet, given repeated cold showers, beaten, or merely subjected to ridicule and insult; in a few cases the victims actually died as a consequence of their maltreatment, and rather than endure this ordeal, one or two objectors committed suicide.[49]

For those men who refused to accept military discipline or alternatives to armed service, the penalty was court-martial. A number of individuals were sentenced by civil courts for refusing to register for the draft or for violating the law prior to induction, and about fifty were court-martialed between April 1917 and April 1918. After April 1918 Secretary Baker ordered that any objector whose sincerity was questionable or who was sullen and defiant should be court-martialed. On 1 June 1918, The Board of Inquiry was established in order to determine the sincerity of those men remaining in the camps, and although it found the vast majority to be "sincere," a number were judged to be "insincere." Altogether 450 men were court-martialed, and sentences ranged from the death penalty in seventeen cases to terms of imprisonment lasting from ten to thirty years. None of the death penalties were carried out, but the objectors were to suffer considerable hardship in prison, whether in the military prisons such as Leavenworth, or civil penitentiaries such as Alcatraz.[50]

Secretary Baker ordered that the objectors in prison should be treated just like any ordinary prisoners, "and recalcitrancy on their part should be punished in the same manner and to the same degree as in others." Elsewhere he spoke of the "curative and helpful discipline of the prison," but whether this included what many objectors suffered—the solitary confinements, bread-and-water diets, or the manacling of prisoners' arms to cell windows to maintain a standing position for hours—is not clear. However, once the war had ended Baker wrote that "the time has now come to quite definitely dispose of this whole subject," and he proposed a program of staggered releases and paroles according to conduct. The president gave his assent on 1 August 1919, and on 23 November Baker ordered the release of the last thirty-three objectors so they could be home for Thanksgiving. In 1933 Franklin Roosevelt gave all conscientious objectors a full and free pardon, and this sad episode was officially concluded.[51]

However harsh the World War I treatment of conscientious objectors may now seem, it was viewed at the time as a successful policy that compared favorably with that of other countries. In his account to President Wilson, Secretary Baker pointed out that almost six thousand British conscientious objectors were imprisoned, and that while forty-five hundred of these were released to work outside prison, fifteen hundred absolutists remained in jail. In fact, such was the treatment of these men that ten died and thirty-one went insane.[52] It is worth bearing in mind, too, that many more American conscientious objectors were to be jailed during the Second World War than during the first, and seen in that light perhaps Baker's satisfaction can be justified. Certainly, he does not appear to have been especially vindictive, and in other respects his actions were marked by humane and sympathetic considerations. He did, for instance, resist

General Pershing's requests to be allowed the power to authorize summary executions in court-martial cases, as was the British and French custom, and moreover interceded on a number of occasions to have death sentences commuted by the president. In the case of two boys sentenced to death for sleeping on duty, Baker subsequently reported that "both made good soldiers"—one died in battle, the other was twice wounded.[53] However, that said, there is little doubt either that Wilson, Baker, and others in government accepted that some restrictions on civil liberties in wartime were inevitable, and in doing so they had much in common with men like Lloyd George in Britain, whose liberal reputation also suffered accordingly.

It is tempting to see in the events of the war years the invidious consequences of the growth of big government and deliberate use of the war emergency by those in power to crush opposition. However, politicians on both sides of the Atlantic were to some extent at least responding to popular pressures, and on balance it seems that although the president spoke of the "firm hand of stern repression" in his war message to Congress, the Wilson administration followed the public mood as much as it led it. No matter how severe or repressive the government's measures were to be, local politicians, newspapers, and businessmen called for more extreme action. In Oklahoma the war emergency encouraged attacks on the Socialists and the Farmers' Union by their opponents; in Arizona, it enabled mine owners and managers to reassert their control; and in Minnesota a nonstop campaign was waged against the Non-Partisan League. While western papers could advocate direct, violent, action against the IWW, even a staid journal like the *Saturday Evening Post* could condemn pacifists as "traitors [who] take the Kaiser's dirty dollar," and urge, "When you find a disloyal neighbor whom you can't send to jail, send him to Coventry. Shun him as if he had small pox," and Judge McGee, chairman of the Minnesota Public Safety Committee, advocated the use of military discipline and the firing squad in matters of "sedition."[54] These extreme attitudes were apparent when eleven of the leaders of the mob responsible for the murder of Robert Prager were acquitted. Then President Wilson was forced to speak out, and he denounced lynching as a "disgraceful evil" that served to discredit democracy and America's war aims.

Although perhaps slow to speak out in this instance, Wilson did urge restraint in other areas: he declined to take drastic action against the Peace party, preferring to "let them show their own impotence"; he opposed the bill to introduce courts-martial for civil offenses, which was proposed by Senator Chamberlain of Oregon; expressed misgivings about the APL; and counseled moderation in censorship. Having suggested in reference to one paper that government could not go after all daft fools, he wrote of another, "We must act with the utmost caution and liberality." In the case of the *Milwaukee Leader* he said, "Doubt ought always to be resolved in favor of the utmost freedom of speech," and on several occasions the president asked Postmaster General Burleson to look again at the case against *The Masses*. In any event, however, the president accepted that normally innocent statements could be seen as "very dangerous to public welfare" during wartime, and he left the final decisions in such cases to Burleson, and *he* took a much tougher line. Although the editors of *The Masses* were not convicted (despite two trials), the journal was denied mailing rights on grounds of irregular publication; the *Leader* was banned from the mails on grounds of content until 1921.[55]

The president was, of course, ultimately responsible for the actions of his subordinates, and he can be faulted for allowing men like Burleson, Creel, and Gregory an almost free hand. But while Burleson and Gregory might still be seen as reactionary in their attitudes (and there is some doubt about this in the case of Attorney General Gregory, who was often more restrained than local attorneys), George Creel may be seen more sympathetically than has often been the case. It is only in more modern times that the "manipulation" of public opinion is fully appreciated and that the word *propaganda* has assumed pejorative connotations; Creel and his colleagues, "liberal, reform-minded journalists and intellectuals—some of the most forward looking members of American society," thought not in terms of propaganda as such, but of education and the creation of a national ideology, a sense of common identity and purpose. Indeed, the CPI was criticized by its opponents during the war for not being extreme enough, and one critic in Congress described the CPI workers not as reactionaries, but as "socialistic, muckraking misfits."[56]

However, while it may fairly be argued that wartime repression "was a natural outgrowth of progressivism,"[57] the idea that government agencies were run solely by reformers is clearly just as misleading. Among the countless volunteers who worked for the CPI, the Food Administration, the various state councils of national defense, or more ominously, of public safety, were representatives of conservative interests. The Four Minute Men, the American Protective League, and most of the councils of national defense were dominated by the middle classes, and the nationalism that the CPI did so much to encourage also enabled these elements to impose order and uniformity and to resist challenges to their authority. Thus the mood of intolerance that swept America during the war was a reflection of prewar political and ethnic divisions, exacerbated by wartime fears and tensions. As the work of David M. Rabban has made abundantly clear, the precedents for both the attack on free speech and the judicial decisions sustaining it lay in the prewar era. But where the earlier suppression of First Amendment rights was localized, intermittent, and varying in its subject (ranging from political and religious matters to those of obscenity), during the war it became a widespread, national campaign focused on the issue of loyalty.[58] While this reflected the insecurity of a nation of immigrants, it was also a response to the disruption and change brought by the war itself; in the words of historian Charles Hirschfeld, the violence of the reaction was "an indication of the extent and intensity of the wartime departure from traditionial American norms." To some degree, the CPI and other agencies concerned with shaping public opinion were only part of a much greater change which affected American society—a "process of change that was destroying the old order, its ideals and values."[59]

Notes

1. Wilson to Cobb, quoted by Jerold S. Auerbach, "Woodrow Wilson's 'Prediction' to Frank Cobb: Words Historians Should Doubt Ever Got Spoken," *Journal of American History* 44, no. 3 (December 1967): 615–17; see also Arthur S. Link, *Woodrow Wilson and the Progressive Era 1910–1917* (New York, 1963), 277.
2. Howard C. Hill, "The Americanization Movement," *American Journal of Sociology* 24, no. 6 (May 1919): 612.
3. Overman quoted in John F. McClymer, *War and Welfare: Social Engineering in America, 1890–1925* (Westport, Conn., and London, 1980), 114; Connecticut State Council of Defense Papers, LC.
4. Edward Robb Ellis, *Echoes of Distant Thunder: Life in the United States 1914–1918* (New York, 1975), 180–90.
5. Ellis, *Echoes of Distant Thunder,* 190; Albert Bushnell Hart, ed., *Selected Addresses and Public Papers of Woodrow Wilson* (New York, 1918), 211.
6. *New York Times,* 7, 8, 11 April 1917; Baker to Wilson, 30 April 1917, Newton D. Baker Papers, LC, Reel 2.
7. Steven Jantzen, *Hooray for Peace, Hurrah for War: The United States During World War I* (New York and Scarborough, Ontario, 1971), 150; David Starr Jordan, *The Days of Man: Being Memories of a Naturalist Teacher and Minor Prophet of Democracy* (New York, 1922), II, 730–31, 734, 748–49.
8. Barbara J. Steinson, *American Women's Activism in World War I* (New York and London, 1982), 237; Marie Louise Degen, *The History of the Woman's Peace Party,* (Baltimore, 1939; reprinted New York and London, 1972), 10–11; Jane Addams, *Second Twenty Years at Hull House* (New York, 1930), 144–46.
9. David A. Shannon, *The Socialist Party of America* (New York, 1955), 97–101; Norman Bindler, "American Socialism and the First World War," Ph.D. dissertation, New York University, 1970, 109–23; Oswald Garrison Villard, *Fighting Years: Memoirs of a Liberal Editor* (New York, 1939), 327; Daniels Diary in *Papers, 44,* 49.

10. Shannon, *The Socialist Party of America*, 104; Bindler, "American Socialism," 101; James Weinstein, "Anti-War Sentiment and the Socialist Party, 1917–1918," in John M. Cooper, ed., *Causes and Consequences of World War I* (New York, 1972), 241–46.
11. C. Roland Marchand, *The American Peace Movement and Social Reform, 1898–1918* (Princeton, 1972), 266; Alexander Trachtenberg, ed., *The American Labor Year Book, 1919–1920* (New York, 1920), III, 80–83.
12. *New York Times*, 22 April 1917; Frederick Palmer, *Newton D. Baker: America at War* (New York, 1931), I, 145.
13. Robert W. Dubay, "The Opposition to Selective Service, 1916–1918," *The Southern Quarterly* 7, no. 3 (April 1969): 308; Peyton C. March, *The Nation at War* (Garden City, New York, 1932), 233.
14. Lucille B. Milner, *Education of an American Liberal: An Autobiography* (New York, 1954), 62; U.S. Provost Marshal General, *Final Report* (Washington, D.C., 1920), 12.
15. *New York Times*, 1 and 6 June 1917; H. C. Peterson and Gilbert C. Fite, *Opponents of War, 1917–1918* (Seattle and London, 1971), 38–39.
16. James R. Green, *Grass-Roots Socialism: Radical Movements in the South West, 1895–1943* (Baton Rouge, La.; and London, 1978), 358–60; Weinstein, "Anti-War Sentiment and the Socialist Party."
17. Shannon, *Socialist Party of America*, 106.
18. Harold J. Tobin and Percy W. Bidwell, *Mobilizing Civilian America* (New York, 1940), 76.
19. H. H. Tammen of the *Denver Post* to William McAdoo, 17 April 1917, McAdoo Papers, Box 178, LC. *New York Times*, 16 April 1917; James R. Mock and Cedric Lawson, *Words That Won the War: The Story of the Committee on Public Information, 1917–1919* (New York, 1939), 51, 53–59.
20. Mark Sullivan, "Creel-Censor," *Colliers*, 10 November 1917; Wilson quoted in Stephen Vaughn, *Holding Fast the Inner Lines: Democracy, Nationalism, and the Committee on Public Information* (Chapel Hill, N.C., 1980), 21.
21. Creel to Daniels, 28 March 1917, Josephus Daniel Papers, Box 73, LC; *Complete Report of the Chairman of the Committee on Public Information: 1917: 1918: 1919* (Washington, D.C., 1920), 1.
22. Walton E. Bean, "George Creel and His Critics: A Study of the Attacks on the Committee on Public Information, 1917–1919," Ph.D. dissertation, University of California, 1941.
23. Lewis Paul Todd, *Wartime Relations of the Federal Government and the Public Schools 1917–1918* (New York, 1945), 6–7; Papers of Connecticut State Council of Defense, Case 1, LC; Vaughn, *Holding Fast the Inner Line*, 116–22.
24. Vaughn, *Holding Fast the Inner Lines*, 29; Frank L. Grubbs, *The Struggle for Labor Loyalty: Gompers, the A.F. of L., and the Pacifists, 1917–1920* (Durham, N.C., 1968), 40–43.
25. "Hollywood Goes to War," London Television.
26. Oswald Garrison Villard, *Fighting Years: Previews of a Liberal Editor* (New York, 1938), 326; Michael Wreszin, *Oswald Garrison Villard: Pacifist at War* (Bloomington, Ind., 1965), 77.
27. Peterson and Fite, *Opponents of War, 1917–1918*, 202–3.
28. Kevin Brownlow, *The War, The West and the Wilderness* (London, 1979), 80–81.

29. Croly to Wilson, 19 October 1917; Wilson to Croly, 22 October 1917, *Papers, 44,* 408–10, 420 (Wilson Papers CF4244, Reel 364 LC); Ray Stannard Baker, *Woodrow Wilson: Life and Letters, Vol. VII: War Leader April 6 1917–February 28, 1918* (New York, 1968), 165.
30. Harold H. Hyman, *To Try Men's Souls: Loyalty Test in American History* (Berkeley and Los Angeles, 1959), 271–72; Paul L. Murphy, *World War I and the Origin of Civil Liberties in the United States* (New York and London, 1979), 74.
31. McAdoo to Gregory, 5 May 1917; McAdoo to Wilson, 15 May 1917; McAdoo to Gregory, 2 June 1917; in McAdoo Papers, Boxes 178, 179, 180, and McAdoo to Wilson, 15 May 1917, 2 June 1917, Box 522, L.C.
32. Hyman, *To Try Men's Souls,* 272–80; Emerson Hough, *The Web: The Authorized History of the American Protective League: A Revelation in Patriotism* (Chicago, 1919), 185; Joan M. Jensen, *The Price of Vigilance* (Chicago and New York, 1968), 217.
33. *Annual Report of the Attorney General of the United States for the Year 1917* (Washington, D.C., 1917), 83; Wilson quoted in Peterson and Fite, *Opponents of War,* 19.
34. American Civil Liberties Union, *War-Time Persecution and Mob Violence* (New York, March 1919), 3; Peterson and Fite, *Opponents of War,* 196–207; Murphy, *World War I and the Origins of Civil Liberties,* 128–32.
35. Peterson and Fite, *Opponents of War,* 57–60; James W. Byrkit, *Forging the Copper Collar: Arizona's Labor-Management War of 1901–1921* (Tuscon, Ariz., 1982).
36. H. S. Commager, ed., *Documents of American History* (New York, 1962), 145.
37. Eastman quoted in Ronald Steel, *Walter Lippmann and the American Century* (Boston and Toronto, 1980), 124; *Annual Report of the Attorney General . . . 1918* (Washington, D.C., 1918).
38. Melvyn Dubofsky, *We Shall Be All: A History of the I.W.W.* (Chicago, 1969), 383, 406–10, 434–42; Philip Taft, "The Federal Trials of the IWW," *Labor History* 3, no. 1 (1962).
39. Trachtenberg, *The American Labor Year Book 1919–1920,* III, 92–109; Bindler, "American Socialism and the First World War," 149–54.
40. Nearing, *The Making of a Radical,* 121.
41. Ray Ginger, *The Bending Cross: A Biography of Eugene Victor Debs* (New York, 1919), 371–76, 405.
42. Bindler, "American Socialism," 165; James R. Green, *Grass-Roots Socialism,* 377–82.
43. Robert L. Morlan, *Political Prairie Fire: The Nonpartisan League, 1915–1922* (Minneapolis, 1950), 87; Trachtenberg, *The American Labor Year Book 1919–1920,* 285.
44. Creel to Wilson, 29 January, 19 February 1918; George Creel Papers, vol. 1, LC.
45. Wilson to Creel, 1 April 1918, Creel Papers, vol. 2, LC, also in *Papers, 47,* 215–16, and see 87–88, 177–78, 193–94.
46. Harry N. Scheiber, *The Wilson Administration and Civil Liberties 1917–1921* (Ithaca, New York, 1960), 47.
47. U.S. Selective Service System, *Conscientious Objection,* Special Monographs no. 11, 2 vols. (Washington, D.C., 1950), 49–56.
48. Baker to Wilson, 1 October 1917, Newton D. Baker Papers, Reel 3, LC.
49. Norman Thomas, *The Conscientious Objector in America* (New York,

1923), 15; Peterson and Fite, *Opponents of War,* 121–31.

50. Peterson and Fite, *Opponents of War,* 259–64.
51. Baker To Col. Sedgewick Rice, Fort Leavenworth, 21 May 1919, Baker Papers Reel 8; Reply of Secretary of War to delegation from Socialist Convention, n.d., n.p., Baker Papers, Speeches and Writings 1918–1919, File, Box 251; Baker to Wilson, 1 July 1919, Baker Papers, Reel 9, LC.
52. Baker to Wilson, 1 July 1919; Mulford Q. Sibley and Philip E. Jacob, *Conscription of a Conscience: The American State and the Conscientious Objector, 1940–1947* (Ithaca, 1952), 2–3.
53. Baker to Wilson, 1 and 11 May 1918, Reel 6, and 19 August 1919, Reel 9, Baker Papers, LC.
54. McGee quoted in Morlan, *Political Prairie Fire,* 179–82; also see Michael Johnson, "The I.W.W. and Wilsonian Democracy," *Science and Society* 28, no. 3 (1964): 258–74; *Saturday Evening Post,* "The War in Your Town," 8 December 1917; Peterson and Fite, *Opponents of War,* 172–80.
55. "Lynching Is Unpatriotic," public address, 26 July 1918, *Papers, 49,* 97–98; Wilson to Burleson, 13 July 1917, 11, 13 October 1917, and to Max Eastman, 18 September 1917, *Papers, 43, 164* and *44,* 371, 210–11; and Daniels Diaries in *Papers 43,* 389, 512. Also Burleson Papers vol. 19, 3026.
56. George T. Blakey, *Historians on the Homefront: American Propagandists for the Great War* (Lexington, 1970), 128; Vaughn, *Holding Fast the Inner Lines,* 37, 236; also see CPI, *Complete Report,* 1.
57. David M. Rabban, "The Emergence of Modern First Amendment Doctrine," *The University of Chicago Law Review* 50, no. 4 (Fall 1983): 1214.
58. Rabban, "The Emergence of the Modern First Amendment Doctrine," and "The First Amendment in Its Forgotten Years," *The Yale Law Journal* 90, no. 514 (1981): 522–95.
59. Charles Hirschfeld, "The Transformation of American Life," in Jack J. Roth, ed., *World War I: A Turning Point in Modern History,* (New York, 1967) 78, 79.

4

Organizing for War
Government, Business, and the Economy

Among the most important of all the changes affecting the American people during the First World War was the growth in size and influence of the national government. So great was this change that the postwar commentator and historian Mark Sullivan could write that of all the effects of the war "by far the most fundamental was our submission to autocracy in government." This view has been echoed repeatedly by other writers, who have described wartime developments in terms of "war socialism," "dictatorial powers," and so on.[1] More recently, however, historians have suggested that, while the war might have brought an "unparalleled expansion of the State," the changes were not quite as dramatic nor as effective as earlier observers had thought. Instead, modifications in government are now seen as haphazard, confused, chaotic, and with little permanent alteration in basic principles or approaches. What emerges instead is a picture of compromise between traditional laissez-faire beliefs and minimal government activity, and an enlarged federal administration following interventionist policies that exceeded anything imagined by Progressives. To some extent, this compromise was "planning without bureaucracy, regulation without coercion, co-operation without dictation,"[2] and while it often built upon precedents and ideas of the Progressive era, it also provided a basis for many postwar developments.

Despite the achievements of the Progressives and the increase in the size of the federal bureaucracy, which had occurred before 1914, it was probably true to say that the national government still had little impact on the lives of most ordinary Americans, and that it was the war that made Washington, D.C., the center of the nation. Until then, the most likely point of contact between the average citizen and government was the post office, although for a small number (337,000 in 1915) a more painful relationship had been established with the introduction of the income tax in 1913. Indirectly, of course, all Americans were affected by the increased federal regulation of trade and commerce, laws regulating the food and drug industries, and taxation in the form of excise duties, but the central government remained small. In 1901 the Federal Civil Service numbered 239,000 employees; ten years later it had risen to 396,000. (In Britain, with a much smaller population, the Civil Service numbered 135,721 in 1911.) For the majority of people Washington, D.C., was a distant place, and state and local capitals were more important. Even at state level, however, government was often dwarfed by business; in Massachusetts, for instance, one railroad company alone employed a work force of eighteen thousand and had gross receipts of $40 million in one year, while the state employed six thousand and spent about $7 million.[3] Despite progressivism and the beginnings of the regulatory state, business still had considerable power and independence, and besides, both government and people remained committed to the basic principles of the free-market economy—progressivism was, after all, largely an attempt to restore free and equal economic competition, not destroy it.

Apart from the power of business and popular attitudes toward the state, the other limitations on the role of the American government were structural and could be traced to the Constitution. The separation of powers, the system of checks and balances, and especially the relationship between Congress and the president made quick organization and speedy decision making difficult. This was particularly so because party politics continued throughout the war, and whereas the British prime minister worked *within* Parliament and, after the various crises of 1915, *with* his former political opponents in a coalition government, President Wilson had to contend with the problem of steering legislation through Congress from the other end of Pennsylvania Avenue and in the face of opposition from political rivals. Although the Democrats had maintained their majority in the Senate in 1916, they had lost it in the House, and the two parties remained evenly balanced. However, the president met resistance to war measures throughout the conflict. When in October 1918 Wilson made his conduct of the war a political issue and asked for the return of Democratic majorities, he suffered overwhelming defeat, and as a consequence the control of key congressional committees passed to the political opposition.[4]

With all these constraints on its power, the administration faced enormous problems from the beginning of the war. Not only did it have to organize and supply an army of its own, it still had to supply Allies desperate for war materials and meet the continuing needs of the American civilian population. If these were not complications enough, the separate branches of the American forces competed for supplies among themselves, each bidding independently in the open market. Within the army alone there were ten different procurement agencies ranging from the quartermasters, engineers, and ordnance through to the medical and signal corps. This multiplication of demand led to escalating prices, shortages of materials, duplication of effort, and general chaos.

Some of these problems had been anticipated during the period of preparedness, and as early as May 1915 the Naval Consulting Board headed by the inventor Thomas Edison had been established to consider industrial and technological developments relevant to the navy. In August 1915 this became the Committee on Industrial Preparedness chaired by Howard Coffin, vice-president of the Hudson Motor Company and, as president of the Society of Automobile Engineers, one of the leading prewar advocates of efficiency and standardization in industry. The committee began to compile an inventory of industrial plants capable of producing munitions, and by 1916 had data on twenty thousand of them. That such information was necessary became evident when the army inquired "where they could buy some machine guns right away" for possible use in the campaigns in Mexico.[5] The urgency of such planning increased during the mounting crisis with Germany and was recognized in the National Defense Act of June 1916, which empowered the president to place obligatory orders with manufacturers capable of producing war materials. The secretary of war was authorized to take a census of industrial plants in order to provide the president with the necessary information. More significant to the mobilization of the American war effort in the long run was the Council of National Defense (CND) established under the Army Appropriations Act of 1916.

The Council of National Defense consisted of the secretaries of war, the navy, the interior, agriculture, commerce, and labor, and was authorized to "supervise and direct investigations and make recommendations" relating to the railroads, the mobilization of military and naval resources, domestic industrial production, and "the creation of relations which will render possible in time of need the immediate concentration and utilization of the resources of the Nation." It was, said historian Frederick Paxson, "to bridge the gap between what the armies needed and the civilians possessed." To do this the council would work through an advisory commission of seven individuals with "special knowledge of some industry, public utility or the development of some natural resource, or be otherwise specially qualified."[6] The seven appointed were Howard Coffin, who assumed responsibility for the subcommittee on munitions; Daniel Willard, president of the Baltimore and Ohio Railroad, who became chairman and was responsible for transportation; Hollis Godfrey, the head of the Drexel Institute, responsible for engineering; Dr. Franklin Martin, physician and director of the College of Surgeons, responsible for medicine; Julius Rosenwald, president of Sears Roebuck, responsible for supplies; Bernard Baruch, a Wall Street speculator and financier responsible for war materials; and Samuel Gompers of the AFL, responsible for labor. The director of the Advisory Commission was to be Walter Gifford, a statistician from the American Telephone and Telegraph Company. As President Wilson said, announcing their appointments, the recruitment of such men "marks the entrance of the non-partisan engineer and professional man into American governmental affairs on a wider scale than ever before."[7] In utilizing such technical experts on a voluntary basis, the Council of National Defense was to set an example that was to be followed throughout the war.

Once America entered the war the Council of National Defense, through the Advisory Commission and its many different offshoots, assumed the major responsibility for coordination and organizing the economic war effort. As early as February 1917 the council could be said to touch "the life of the nation at practically every point." However, there were still major obstacles to the efficient mobilization of industry and the armed forces, and it was only after severe crises that these blocks were removed. The central problem was the control and coordination of the demand for war goods, as the CND and Advisory Commission had control only over supply. An attempt had been made to rationalize demand with the creation of the Munitions Standards Board in February 1917, chaired by the Cleveland instrument manufacturer Frank A. Scott. Scott's main concern was the standardization of munitions specifications, but he was hampered by not knowing what the different branches of the military required. In order to resolve that problem the Munitions Standards Board was replaced in April 1917 by yet another body, the General Munitions Board, which was intended to coordinate army and navy purchases. This, of course, then overlapped with the functions of the Advisory Commission of the Council of National Defense (ACCND) and its offshoots, and rather than achieving centralized control there was instead "a hot house growth of committees and councils with little co-ordination."[8]

The pattern of development of the government's war organization was well described by Herbert Hoover, a man who was himself to play a considerable part in the war administration. According to Hoover, each problem produced "a rash of boards, commissions, and committees."

When one of these boards fell sick from conflicting policies and ambitions, the administration had several standard cures. The favorite included changing the membership, changing the name or appointing another board, committee or commission with the same powers as the ailing one. . . .9

This was the case in 1917, and it continued to be so until August, when after much pressure from various concerned and interested individuals, and in the face of rapidly increasing prices, President Wilson finally established the War Industries Board (WIB) to act as a clearinghouse, to control prices and limit war profits, and yet ensure the industrialist a fair return—and so encourage production. The War Industries Board, superseding the General Munitions Board and absorbing the ACCND, consisted of Frank Scott, Bernard Baruch, Hugh Frayne of the AFL, Robert Lovett, chairman of the Union Pacific Railroad, Robert Brookings, millionaire and university president (and founder of the Brookings Institute), and two military representatives. Unlike its predecessors, the WIB was to survive and develop and eventually became the most important of the war agencies.

With other bodies established during the conflict, the WIB was a major innovation in the regulatory power of the federal government. While the WIB concerned itself with industrial mobilization, additional agencies were established to direct other aspects of the war economy. The best known of these was the Food Administration, which was established to organize the supply of foodstuffs and regulate food and agricultural prices. The agricultural situation in 1917 was dire; poor harvests that year, and in 1916, coupled with the enormous demand from overseas, created shortages and caused prices to spiral upward. Particularly badly affected were wheat, sugar, and pork. The price of wheat had risen from $1.39 a bushel in 1915 to $2.58 in July 1917; the price of hogs had risen from $7.28 per hundred pounds to $15.46; and food prices in general had risen 82 percent between 1914 and 1917.10 In an attempt to control this situation the administration presented Congress with the Lever Food and Fuel Bill, but when Congress—resistant to an increase in presidential authority and concerned about any undue interference with the economy—delayed, the president used his powers under the Army Appropriations Act to appoint a food administrator in May 1917. The man appointed was again an engineer, a millionaire, former head of the Belgian relief agency and future president, Herbert Hoover. Hoover was to become one of the best-known figures of the war administration, acting first as a one-man subcommittee of the Council of National Defense, and then as the official head of the Food Administration following the eventual passage of the Food and Fuel Bill on 10 August 1917. According to the *New York Tribune* of 9 August, the act marked "the longest step toward socialism ever taken by the American Congress." This was obviously an exaggeration, but nonetheless revealed something of the reaction to wartime departures.

The Food and Fuel Act empowered the president "to establish and maintain governmental control" of foods, feeds, fuel, and to "prevent . . . scarcity, monopolization, hoarding, injurious speculation, manipulation . . . and private controls."[11] However, while Hoover felt his authority should cover every aspect of food production, "from the soil to the stomach," he stopped short of total control. Prices of certain commodities such as wheat, sugar, hogs, beans, and peas were fixed by purchasing entire crops at agreed levels, and sold through dealers who were licensed by the Food Administration. But, despite the wishes of America's allies, Hoover refused to impose mandatory rationing and argued that it was essential that America demonstrate "our ability to defend ourselves without being Prussianized."[12] Instead, the Food Administrator relied upon patriotism, exhortation, and voluntary controls. Like Creel in the CPI, he directly involved ordinary Americans: with only 1,400 paid workers, the Food Administration mobilized an army of 750,000 volunteers, mainly women, in local committees and organizations, distributed posters and fair-price lists by using 25,000 traveling salesmen, and issued forty-three thousand posters and two thousand press releases that urged people to save food, utilize scraps, and use substitutes for scarce produce. One leaflet, for example, listed all the possible alternatives to wheat flour and provided recipes for different breads: buckwheat bread, potato bread, and, of course, corn bread, which the war did much to popularize. The population was urged to observe "Wheatless Mondays, Meatless Tuesdays, Porkless Thursdays and Saturdays," and over twenty million pledged to do so, no doubt inspired by Hoover's call to "go back to simple food, simple clothes, simple pleasures. Pray hard, work hard, sleep hard and play hard. Do it all courageously and cheerfully. We have a victory to win."[13]

That such appeals got through to the public was evident in the jokes about "eatless days" and the very knowledge of the name Hoover; there was even a Hoover Valentine:

> I can Hooverize on Dinners
> And on lights and fuel too,
> But I'll never learn to Hooverize
> when it comes to loving you.[14]

Indeed, there could be too much exhortation—the *Hartford Courant* commented, having received a government pamphlet called "Five Ways to Save Fuel": "We can name a sixth: burn the documents the Government keeps sending to your office." But the success of Hoover's program could be seen in the fall in consumption of sugar and wheat, and even in the amount of waste: the volume of garbage collected in Chicago, for instance, fell from 12,862 tons in June 1916 to 8,386 tons in June 1917. More telling was the increase in food exports from over 12 million tons to almost 19 million tons—an achievement that helped to sustain the Allied war effort.[15] It was little wonder that Hoover was a household name and one that was to feature in the postwar years and beyond.

Almost as well known as Hoover was the man who took over the railroads during the war, the secretary of the Treasury and the president's son-in-law, William Gibbs McAdoo. Unlike Hoover, McAdoo did not acquire his wartime responsibility immediately. Initially, the nearly seven hundred railroad presidents had agreed to run their different lines as though they constituted a single system, and they established the five-man Railroads War Board. However, it proved impossible for them to secure full cooperation in the thirty-two different systems, and by December 1917, with a growing shortage of railcars in some areas while cars stood empty and idle elsewhere, the president was forced to act. On 26 December 1917, using his powers under the Army Appropriations Act, and while Congress was in recess, he announced the temporary takeover and administration of the rail system, effective two days later—"the most drastic step yet taken in the history of railroading on the American continent" according to the *Washington Post*. Finding the railroad system "anaemic, undernourished, and subject to alarming attacks of heart failure," McAdoo was to divide the railways into three principle regions, consolidate timetables, standardize rolling stock, and build several thousand additional railcars.[16] However, this program was to take time to enact, and as far as transportation was concerned, things were to get worse before they got better.

During the winter of 1917–18 the problems of organizing the economy, coordinating supply with demand, and establishing the means of transportation were compounded by exceptionally bad weather. The winter was the worst in twenty years, and a blizzard on 28 December was the most severe in over forty years. In cities like Cleveland shops, factories, and schools were closed down through December and January; New York City was described in January as "deserted: heatless, wheatless, meatless, sweetless," while in Boston the shops were closed at 5:00 P.M. and the theaters at 10:00. On 6 February 1918, Secretary of the Navy Josephus Daniels recorded the situation in his diary following a "depressing meeting of the Council of National Defense":

> Hoover could not get food to our allies for lack of cars, Garfield could not get coal for lack of transportation, Hurley could not build ships because of the cold weather, Houston troubled about wheat. Transportation fallen down. Weather made it worse.[17]

Central in this crisis was fuel and the problem of providing adequate coal supplies for industry, the railways, and the domestic consumer. Like food, fuel had been under central administration since August 1917 when college president Harry A. Garfield, son of President James A. Garfield and a friend of President Wilson, was appointed fuel administrator. Garfield, who was not such a public man as either Hoover or McAdoo, was instrumental in stabilizing coal prices and improving labor relations, and the war years have been seen as "something of a golden age in the industry's history."[18] However, coal production did not rise significantly during the war, and the bad weather that increased demand also made transportation difficult. In order to break the deadlock Garfield took drastic action. In January 1918 he closed all industry east of the Mississippi for a week, and then every Monday for the next nine weeks. While this relieved the pressure on coal stocks, helped to free needed railcars, and broke the economic deadlock, it created political uproar and led to widespread criticism of the Wilson government. It was only following these crises that the administration finally accepted the need for, and then established, a more centralized control of the war economy.

The lack of an overall Democratic majority in Congress guaranteed that the president would face considerable criticism of his handling of the war. Moreover, some Democrats, particularly those from the South, were as likely to resist increased executive authority as were Wilson's Republican opponents, and suggestions that Congress might be entirely eliminated during the war were guaranteed to encourage bipartisan insistence on the maintenance of its traditional role. Thus Congress constantly acted to slow the passage of legislation and to question the government's actions—encouraged in many instances by critics outside the political arena, such as Theodore Roosevelt. By December 1917, various committees in the House and Senate were attacking the Food Administration, the Shipping Board, the Fuel Administration, and the Department of War. Secretary of War Baker seemed particularly to provoke attack, for in addition to the problems relating to coal supply and transportation, Congress was investigating military supply, especially shortages in the production of machine guns and airplanes, and the conditions of soldiers in the training camps. When the harsh winter brought a spate of deaths due to pneumonia, this was blamed upon an inadequate building program and the lack of sufficient blankets and warm clothing for the troops.

The charges of incompetence and maladministration in the War Department forced Baker to confront his critics, and from 10 to 12 January he appeared before the Senate Committee on Military Affairs. Calmly smoking his cigars, the pint-sized secretary provided a full account of the army's preparations and demonstrated that the health of the army was better than in any previous conflict. However, criticism continued unabated. On 19 January, George E. Chamberlain, the Democratic chairman of the Military Affairs Committee, announced there was "inefficiency in every bureau and in every department of the Government of the United States."[19] Two days later the Chamberlain Committee reported favorably on a bill (proposed by the chairman) to establish a war cabinet with supreme responsibility for the direction of the war effort.

Faced with such a challenge, the government was bound to act. Firstly, army procurement was reorganized and made more efficient under the new quartermaster general, George W. Goethals, and the Chiefs of Staff was strengthened with the appointment of Peyton C. March. Secretary Baker appeared before the Military Affairs Committee again on 28 January and after a five-hour session appeared to have silenced, if not won over, his critics. On 6 February Senator Lee Overman introduced the administration's answer to the Chamberlain bill: a proposal instead to extend the power of the president "to make such redistribution of functions among executive agencies as he may deem necessary." According to the *Washington Post* of 8 February, this concentration of power was "an astonishing suggestion," but "a logical development of the war," and, having called for stronger measures, Congress could hardly resist. Passed in May 1918, in the view of one senator the only thing lacking from the Overman act was a clause stating "if any power, constitutional or not, has been inadvertently omitted from this bill, it is hereby granted in full."[20] In addition, beginning in March 1918, an unofficial war cabinet consisting of the secretaries of state, war, the navy, and the Treasury, plus the heads of the chief war agencies, met every Wednesday to discuss war matters. The main Cabinet, meanwhile, became virtually inactive with meetings consisting of almost nothing but "telling stories." The final significant development to emerge from the winter crisis was the appointment of Bernard Baruch to head the War Industries Board.

By the end of January 1918 some change in the War Industries Board was inevitable. Frank Scott, the original chairman, retired exhausted and in ill health the previous October, and was succeeded by Daniel Willard. Willard, too, resigned in January 1918 in order to return to the Baltimore and Ohio Railroad. For a time the WIB existed without a leader, and it was not until March that Wilson finally appointed Baruch. Part of the delay was due to Baruch himself, who insisted that to be effective the WIB had to be strengthened and the new chairman be given greater authority than his predecessors. The president accepted these principles and granted the board much greater powers to determine and direct prices and priorities in supply and production rather than just coordinate. According to one view, with the appointment of Baruch "the stage of 'dictators' had been reached in the development of the great war machine."[21]

The WIB as established in March 1918 marked the final stage in the evolution of the war administration that had begun in 1916, and with Baruch at its head it was to be the most important of all the boards. However, it was in practice far from dictatorial in its use of power. As its leading historian has said, the WIB was "a bundle of paradoxes" trying to resolve competing tendencies such as the traditional American impulse toward decentralization and individualism, and the centralization demanded by the war. The board was also motivated by a vision of American industry as "corporate capitalism led by socially responsible men" and in doing so it reflected the view of Baruch himself. He was not an industrialist as such, but a speculator or financier (he described himself as a banker), and he made money by forecasting the entrepreneurial success of other men (he had contributed an estimated thirty-five thousand dollars to the Wilson campaign in 1916). Thus he was involved in, but separate from, industry as such, and while his wealth freed him from ordinary cares and concerns, he was also free from commitments to any one sector of the economy. His personal success ensured the respect of the business world while he in turn saw businessmen as like himself, rational men motivated by a desire to serve the public interest. As a consequence, the WIB operated by involving businessmen in the decision-making process, encouraging discussion and cooperation in order to arrive at agreements on a voluntary basis. The result was, as Robert Cuff and David Kennedy have pointed out, the integration of business and government interests.[22]

In practice, the WIB consisted of a vast number of committees, each dealing with particular materials, products or commodities, and each made up largely of the representatives of the leading industries in those areas. This system was really a continuation of that established by the Advisory Commission to the Council of National Defense, now revamped under the auspices of the U.S. Chamber of Commerce, and known as the War Service Committees. By the end of the war there were over three thousand War Service Committees working not just with the WIB, but also with the Food Administration and other war boards, and ranging from the Steel Committee (dominated by U.S. Steel and Bethlehem Steel), the Sheet Plate Committee, the Committee on Bolts, Nuts, and Rivets, through to committees on Canned Goods, Alimentary Pastes (Macaroni and Noodles), Wrapping Paper, and Chalks and Crayons.[23]

The main function of the WIB and its committees was to agree on priorities and to fix prices, and between 6 April 1917 and 1 June 1919 the WIB handled three hundred thousand contracts worth $14.5 billion with various businesses. Often the WIB acted to restrict nonessential production to ensure supplies for necessary war industries. Baruch recalled a famous example in his autobiography:

Thus, when steel was in short supply we refused to permit the building of a theatre in St. Louis, saved over 2,000 tons by reducing bicycle designs, and garnered enough metal for two warships by taking the stays out of women's corsets.[24]

This last act, presumably the work of the Brassiere War Service Committee, was an indication both of the liberating effects of the war and the lengths gone to in order to support the war effort. Savings were also effected by standardization of products. Not only were the number of bicycle designs reduced, but so also were the number of auto tire sizes (from 287 to 9), the number of types of plows (from 326 to 76), and the size of typewriter spools (from 150 to 5), in order to save needed metals. Other materials were saved by limiting the production of bathing caps, shortening the length of coats, standardizing knitwear colors, and limiting the choice of shoe colors to three—black, brown, or white. As an ad in the *Saturday Evening Post* put it, "The Government orders American Footwear to be Simplified, Economized, and Standardized."[25]

In nearly all cases, these changes and restrictions were carried out with the agreement of the manufacturers following negotiations in the appropriate War Service Committees. However, the WIB did have powers to enforce decisions and, if necessary, fix prices—the system was "voluntary co-operation with the big stick in the cupboard." In two cases Baruch threatened to bring the big stick out: firstly, when Henry Ford refused to limit private car production, and secondly, when Elbert Gary of U.S. Steel refused to accept the government's price of steel. Faced with this opposition Baruch warned that he would instruct the military to take over the plants. The industrialists both backed down.[26] These cases demonstrated that, whatever its limitations, the WIB clearly had authority and was prepared to use it.

As a consequence of the growth of the WIB and the myriad of other war agencies, Washington, D.C., was transformed. Not only was it a war boomtown, it had also become the "business capital as well as the political capital": "the center of the nation," with even the "newspapers . . . edited from here." "Everyone in the world," said Ray Stannard Baker, "is at Washington," a fact reflected in the growth in the number of employees in the executive branch of the federal government, from 482,721 in 1914 to 691,116 in 1920.[27] By the end of the war ordinary Americans were affected by decisions made in Washington to an unprecedented degree. Not only were the prices and supplies of food, clothing, fuel, and raw materials now determined to a considerable extent by federal agencies, but individual citizens were, in addition, exhorted to eat less, burn less, drive less, travel less, and work more. While all Americans were urged to use rail travel only for essential purposes, and free travel for state officials was suspended, the Fuel Administrator also urged auto drivers to observe "gas-less" Sundays from 1 September 1918. Earlier that year Congress had approved the adoption of daylight saving time, and the changing of the clocks by an hour was estimated to have resulted in the saving of over 1.25 million tons of fuel.[28] That government could alter even the time of day was a very real indication of the increase in its power, although like all other measures this was to be temporary.

The most obvious and direct form of wartime contact between government and citizens was, of course, Selective Service. The registration of 26 million males and subsequent induction of 4 million into the forces required considerable central organization. One of the most striking features of the exercise was the enormous amount of information now collected and stored by the government. As the provost marshal said, "Never in the history of this or any other nation had a more valuable and comprehensive accumulation of data been assembled upon the physical, economic, industrial, and racial composition of a people."[29] While this was, given the U.S. census conducted every ten years, something of an exaggeration, the different nature and focus of the information gathered through the draft was significant, and it was to reveal much that could be used by planners and by politicians in calling for legislative action.

However, even with Selective Service, there were, as with the WIB, limits to centralized control. All American wartime organizations operated within traditional constraints, as was evidenced by the reliance on voluntarism in agencies ranging from the WIB and Food Administration through to the CPI. Even the Selective Service system was to operate with assistance of willing volunteers. Moreover, these agencies each relied upon the cooperation and involvement of individual state governments and vested much of their authority with local politicians. Of the more than 192,000 workers involved in the administration of the draft, only 429 were federal employees in the office of the provost marshal general, the rest being engaged by, and in, the 4,650 state and local boards established by the government precisely to counter charges of overcentralization and "Prussianism." The appointments to these various boards were determined by local and congressional politicians, and the actual process of selection, the administration of deferments, and so on, was carried out within the local communities.[30]

Like the Selective Service System, the WIB also operated through state councils of defense as well as the War Service Committees. By the end of the war each state had a council appointed by individual governors and involving over one million people in their activities. In addition to the state councils there were over 184,000 county, city, and town bodies: in Arkansas, for example, there was a state council, a council for each of the seventy-five counties, and almost five thousand additional community councils. Such organizations varied enormously. Some states, such as Massachusetts, Pennsylvania, and Michigan, spent in excess of $2 million dollars each, while Ohio managed on less than $500,000, and the total expenditure of North Carolina's defense council came to $5,420.[31] In most cases the various councils were just existing state legislatures, or committees drawn from them under another name, and their activities reflected the concerns of local government: public health, law, transportation, highways, and the like. However, they were now important channels of communication for the federal government and assisted with the efficient mobilization of the armed forces and industrial labor, food and fuel conservation, and propaganda. Inevitably, given the pressures on manpower during the war, they drew upon volunteers, and particularly women.

The Women's Committee of the National Council of Defense was established in April 1917 to "co-ordinate and centralize the organized and unorganized forces of women throughout the country" and "to provide a new and direct channel of communication between American women and their Government."[32] The national committee had its counterparts at the local level, and, judging from the records, these committees were among the most active of all. In Missouri, the women drew up a register of women available for employment; in Georgia they were concerned with the Red Cross, Liberty bond drives, food conservation, and provision of additional clothing for troops; and in Illinois, California, and elsewhere, they were involved in child welfare provision. These activities all served to strengthen the demand for the political recognition of women and demonstrated that wartime relationships could be a two-way thing, pointing up the dual nature of the obligations of citizens and government. This reform aspect of war government was not missed by the Progressives. For Louis Brandeis such organization represented "laboratories in which exciting experiments in war government are being conducted," and the very idea of mobilizing the entire community for war service was one that appealed to those of a liberal persuasion.[33] However, the councils also had a conservative tone. Chief among their functions was to "endeavor to increase the number of loyal American citizens," and their membership reflected establishment interests. Not only were they dominated by politicians, lawyers, and businessmen, but also, according to President Wilson, they were primarily Republican.[34]

While the validity of the president's statement about the state of councils might be doubted, there is no question that the war brought an enormous increase in the participation of industrialists, businessmen, or their representatives, at every level of government. So much was this so that the war could be, and has been, seen as reversing the thrust of prewar government-business relations. According to the conservative *Saturday Evening Post* in 1914, "We have a government at war with business, not merely taxing and regulating but enforcing its own ideas as to how business should be organized"; "persons who know nothing about business are saying how business should be conducted." If this was a bit extreme, in the view of one historian there could be said to be "no close co-operation and no effective mingling of the national power with the industrial power" prior to 1917.[35] Of course, more recent writers have shown this view to be an oversimplification, and the idea that progressivism was simply anti-business is now not accepted. Businessmen, in bodies like the National Civic Federation, consented to the idea of a new corporate order and were themselves often involved in drawing up reform legislation. While antitrust suits gave the impression of external control and of antagonism between government and industrialists, this only applied in extreme cases, and the Wilson administration was already moving toward accommodation and "self-regulation" before 1917. As Arthur Link has shown, the Federal Trade Commission, established in 1915 to prevent unfair methods of competition, became a counselor and friend to business rather than an enemy.[36] At the same time, bodies like the FTC and the acts regulating railroads and the industry generally provided some precedents for wartime measures.

Nonetheless, the war did bring a change in both the relationship between government and business, and the public perception of that relationship. The greater need for efficient management and organization of the economy during the war was bound to lead to greater regulation. When it became clear that the government lacked the personnel and expertise required, the administration turned to the organizational and technical experts, to professionals rather than to politicians. It was engineers and managers who staffed the war agencies, and the war enabled the "dollar-a-year men" to demonstrate their morality and their patriotism and show that cooperation between business and government was to the nation's benefit. In so doing, they gained in public esteem. The *Baltimore News* described the alliance between government and industry as "an unprecedented development" that "does honor to the men who are freely giving their expert advice." Other news headlines referred to such items as "Many Patriotic Men of Business," "Businessmen Running the War," and "Businessmen Work for the Country."[37] Significantly, the public figures to emerge from the war were not the military heroes, but the managers of the domestic effort—Hoover, William Gibbs McAdoo, and Baruch.

Prosecutions under the antitrust laws virtually ceased during the war. The Federal Trade Commission investigated cases of profiteering, and advised other agencies on prices and costs, but clearly, the pressure of war encouraged practices in restraint of free trade and competition. The price-fixing, standardizing, and coordinating activities of the various War Service Committees and the WIB marked a move toward "working oligopoly." Indeed, now government agencies actually encouraged mergers; when Josephus Daniels expressed concern to Bernard Baruch that small businesses were not getting their share of government contracts, the WIB chairman replied that the board had "been trying . . . to get a number of firms to consolidate, or to take the work as a unit and distribute among themselves."[38] Here, in voluntary cooperation and combination for greater efficiency in the national interest, was the pattern that was to be followed, particularly by Hoover as secretary of commerce, in the postwar era. Not surprisingly, the war years have been seen as providing "the model, the precedent, and the inspiration for state corporate capitalism for the remainder of the twentieth century," and as marking "the triumph of business in the most emphatic manner possible."[39] While one might wish to qualify such a statement by pointing out that business too had changed and was adopting new methods, and that the age of the robber barons had gone—and had been even before the war—the force of the argument remains.

One aspect of the war's impact upon business about which there can be little disagreement, and one that also helped to restore businessmen in the eyes of the public, was the economic boom. Above all else, the war brought business expansion and encouraged the optimism that was to continue, after just a brief hesitation, into the twenties. This could not be seen in 1914, for the initial impact of the European war was to further the recession already being experienced in America. The drop in the export trade and falling prices that followed the outbreak of hostilities led to an 18 percent decline in American industrial production. However, this trend was soon reversed as Allied war orders began to pour in, and by 1915 a number of towns were experiencing a war boom as U.S. exports rose from a low of $110 million in August 1914 to $613 million by January 1917. Expansion quickened and became more widespread after 1917 as American industry responded to the demands of its own armed forces and of its allies. The American army, for instance, placed orders for 19 million blankets, 89 million socks, and 70 million pairs of drawers—the latter on the assumption that its troops' underwear would not be laundered, but destroyed after an (extended) period of wear. The army also required one hundred thousand trucks and eighteen thousand cars. Henry Ford, who in 1915 during his pacifist phase, had sworn never to accept war orders, was by mid-1917 producing twenty thousand tractors, sixteen thousand tanks and twelve hundred submarine chasers for the military. The Ford work force grew from thirty-two thousand in 1916 to forty-eight thousand in 1918, and the General Motors work force, also building trucks and airplane engines, rose from ten thousand to fifty thousand. More plant was needed to meet this demand, and Ford opened the world's largest single plant at River Rouge, Detroit. Total capital expenditure in the United

States leaped from $600 million in 1915 to $2.5 billion in 1918, and the total number of manufacturing establishments rose by 5 percent. More significant, however, was the greater application of modern technology in production: by 1919 the number of leading industries using electric power was 16.3 million—almost double the 1914 figure.[40]

The search for great efficiency and maximum production during the war encouraged not just the increased use of electric power, but also the techniques of mass production pioneered by Ford. These included the moving assembly line and the breakdown of production processes into a number of simple and routine jobs. Not only did such methods speed ordinary production, they also enabled the use of new, unskilled workers to replace craftsmen who had gone to the war. As a consequence of these developments attention to worker efficiency increased and encouraged the spread of the ideas of Frederick Taylor, the founder of "scientific management" or work study. Concern for shop floor organization, worker motivation, and job analysis led in turn to the creation of departments of personnel management and industrial welfare schemes, like those already run by Ford. The increase in business paternalism was a step toward the welfare capitalism of the twenties. By the end of the war modern industrial methods had become widely established, and America was well on her way to becoming an organizational and managerial society.[41]

Industrial growth brought a number of benefits, but one was more obvious than others. As Morison and Commager put it, the war produced "not only efficiency but profits." Figures for overall profit, below $4 billion in 1914, were over $10 billion in 1917. The average annual prewar profit for U.S. Steel was $76 million; in 1917 it was $478 million. These figures could also translate into personal wealth: in 1914 the number of people with taxable incomes in the fifty- to one-hundred-thousand-dollar range was five thousand, by 1918 it was thirteen thousand, and there were estimated to be forty-two thousand millionaires.[42]

An automatic consequence of this wartime prosperity was that more people were liable to income tax. However, in order to cover the costs of the war the government further extended income tax in the Revenue Acts of 1917 and 1918, lowering exemptions and increasing taxes on profits and excess profits. Indeed the pattern of taxation in America shifted during the war as taxes on incomes and profits displaced excise and customs as the main source of revenue. This fact, coupled with the increase in number of those paying tax (from a mere 437,000 in 1916 to 4,425,000 in 1918), and the higher rates, which placed 74 percent of the tax burden on richer individuals and industrial corporations, have led some commentators to write of a "fiscal revolution" and the "Triumph of a Democratic Tax Policy." However, only one-third of the cost of the war was met by taxation, the other two-thirds being raised by loans, and wartime taxation of the rich never satisfied the demands of Progressives like La Follette, Norris, or Borah.[43] Nonetheless, here again was the extension of a Progressive measure—even if nowadays few people would see income tax in terms of reform.

Manufacturing was not the only sector of the economy to be affected by the war. The demand for foodstuffs gave an enormous impetus to expansion in farming, and the war years provided a boom period in agriculture. The value of farm produce rose from $9.8 billion in 1914 to $21.3 billion in 1918, and farm production increased overall by between 20 and 30 percent. This was achieved, despite a 10 percent decline in farm labor, as a consequence of increased investment in farm machinery and by extending farm acreage. Thus, while farm income rose, from $4.5 billion in 1914 to $9.6 billion in 1918, so too did farm debts, from $4.7 billion in 1914 to $8.4 billion in 1918.[44] Once agricultural prices began to drop after 1918, farmers in America would begin to suffer. Unlike manufacturers, they could not lay off workers, nor was there to be an upsurge in consumer demand, and so many farmers would fall victim of foreclosures. In this respect, if in no other, the war contributed to the economic problems of the postwar years, although again, it should be remembered that the problems of the farming industry were not new.

Although the long-term effects of the war varied from one sector to another, the single feature common to government, industry, and agriculture was growth, and industry and government at least were also increasingly interrelated in this expansion. Observers at the time saw these developments as remarkable—even, in some instances, alarming. However, with hindsight we can, of course, see that these wartime changes were not unprecedented, nor that revolutionary. While there was undoubtedly an increase in the size and importance of the national government and its use of "professionals," this was not "war socialism" of the European type. Rather it consistently involved the states, local communities, and private individuals in one national purpose, and throughout depended upon voluntarism and self-regulation, cooperation, persuasion, and the force of public opinion shaped by official propaganda. In the process it brought industrial managers back into government and, in enabling the rehabilitation of business, provided evidence that businessmen were reformed and that excessive control and regulation by government was unnecessary. Planning and coordination were acceptable for efficiency and the greater good of all, but some aspects of wartime change were clearly viewed as temporary. As the *Saturday Evening Post* editorialized, "All this government activity will be called to account and re-examined in due time," and "Government management at present predicates nothing for normal conditions."[45] The fact that war mobilization was carried out through specially created agencies separate from cabinet departments itself signified the special, and temporary, nature of these developments. Nonetheless such changes were remarkable, and as departures from the norm they raised expectations and created their own tensions.

Something of the contradictory nature of wartime change and of the tensions left unresolved were captured by Woodrow Wilson in a comment to his secretary.

> The war by revealing the close relationship between the individual and the state has taught us many things we did not previously know about national economy and efficiency at the same time stimulating the opportunities for individual achievement and development.

The president went on to identify one of the chief areas of conflict still remaining when he said "measures of co-ordination as between capital and labor can no longer be evaded,"[46] for labor, like business, had grown during the war and was now a force with which to be reckoned. It remained to be seen whether the state would continue wartime policies and intervene to provide the necessary coordination between these opposing forces in the postwar period or revert to a more traditional position of laissez-faire.

Notes

1. Mark Sullivan, *Our Times: The United States 1900–1925* (New York and London, 1933), V, 489; Charles and Mary Beard, *The Rise of American Civilization* (New York, 1929), III, 636; Samuel Morison and Henry Steele Commager, *The Growth of the American Republic* (New York, 1950), 469–71.
2. George Soule, *Prosperity Decade: A Chapter from American Economic History 1917–1929* (London: 1947), 4; Robert D. Cuff, *The War Industries Board: Business-Government Relations During World War I* (Baltimore and London, 1973), 1, 5–9, 149, 265; and Robert D. Cuff, "Herbert Hoover, the Ideology of Voluntarism and War Organization during the Great War," *Journal of American History* (September 1977):358.
3. Edward Berkowitz and Kim McQuaid, *Creating the Welfare State: The Political Economy of Twentieth Century Reform* (New York, 1980), 25–26; Cuff, *The War Industries Board*, 9; Richard L. Watson, *The Development of National Power: The United States 1900–1919* (Boston, 1976), 23.
4. Seward W. Livermore, *Politics Is Adjourned: Woodrow Wilson and the War Congress, 1916–18* (Middletown, Conn., 1966).
5. Watson, *The Development of National Power*, 221.
6. Frederick Paxson, *American Democracy and the World War, II: America at War 1917–1918* (New York, 1939), 20; Army Appropriations Act in Grosvenor B. Clarkson, *Industrial America in the World War: The Strategy behind the Line 1917–1918* (Boston and New York, 1923), 491–92.

7. President's statement announcing appointment of the Advisory Commission, 11 October 1916, in Papers of Thomas James Walsh, LC, Box 166.
8. James L. Tyson, "The War Industries Board, 1917–18," *Fortune* (September 1940): Supplement, 5; Cuff, *The War Industries Board*, 56.
9. Herbert Hoover, *Memoirs: Years of Adventure, 1874–1920* (London, 1952), 261.
10. Harold J. Tobin and Percy W. Bidwell, *Mobilizing Civilian America* (New York, 1940), 168.
11. Lever Act in Henry Steele Commager, *Documents of American History*, Vol. II (New York, 1968), 132.
12. Hoover, *Memoirs*, 252.
13. Hoover, *Memoirs*, 250; Craig Lloyd, *Aggressive Introvert: A Study of Herbert Hoover and Public Relations Management 1912–1932* (Columbus, Ohio, 1972), 50; William C. Mullendore, *History of the United States Food Administration 1917–1919* (Stanford, Calif., 1941), 8.
14. Joan Hoff Wilson, *Herbert Hoover: Forgotten Progressive* (Boston, 1975), 60.
15. Preston W. Slosson, *The Great Crusade and After, 1914–1928* (New York, 1930), 59.
16. William G. McAdoo, *Crowded Years: The Reminiscences of William G. McAdoo* (Boston, 1931), 463; John F. Stover, *American Railroads* (Chicago, 1961), 185–92; *Washington Post*, 25 November 1917.
17. Josephus Daniels, *The Cabinet Diaries, 1913–21*, edited by David E. Cronon (Lincoln, Nebraska, 1963), 276; R. S. Baker, *Diaries and Notebooks*, LC, vol. 15, 21, 30 January 1918.
18. Robert Cuff, "Harry Garfield, the Fuel Administration, and the Search for a Cooperative Order During World War I," *American Quarterly* 30 (Spring 1978):47.
19. Livermore, *Politics Is Adjourned*, 91; Paxson, *American Democracy and the World War*, 216.
20. Paxson, *American Democracy and the World War*, 226.
21. Peyton C. March, *The Nation at War* (Garden City, New York, 1932), 174.
22. Cuff, *War Industries Board*, 149–50; David M. Kennedy, *Over Here: The First World War and American Society* (Oxford and New York, 1980), 141; Jordan A. Schwarz, *The Speculator: Bernard M. Baruch in Washington, 1917–1965* (Chapel Hill, N.C., 1981), 47; U.S. War Industries Board, *American Industry in the War: A Report of the War Industries Board (March 1921)* (New York, 1941), 15–16.
23. Paxson, *American Democracy and the World War*, 124; Burl Noggle, *Into the Twenties: The United States from Armistice to Normalcy* (Urbana, Ill., Chicago, and London, 1974), 55.
24. Bernard Baruch, *The Public Years* (New York, 1960), 59; Noggle, *Into the Twenties*, 63.
25. *Saturday Evening Post*, 23 November 1918; Slosson, *The Great Crusade*, 55; WIB, *American Industry in the War*, 67–71.
26. Baruch, *The Public Years*, 62–71.
27. U.S. Dept. of Commerce, Bureau of the Census, *Historical Statistics of the United States 1789–1945: A Supplement to the Statistical Abstract* (Washington, D.C., 1949), 249; *Saturday Evening Post*, 2 March 1918; Franklin K. Lane, *The Letters of Franklin K. Lane: Personal and Politi-*

cal (Boston and New York, 1922), 274; Baker Diaries, vol. 15, 19 February 1918.

28. *Saturday, Evening Post,* 9 March 1918; U.S. Food Administration, *Fuel Facts* (Washington, D.C., 1 August 1918), in Records of Council of National Defense, RG62, Committee on Women's Defense Work, 13A–DA, Box 572, NA.

29. U.S. Provost Marshal General, *Final Report . . . on the Operations of the Selective Service System to July 15, 1919* (Washington, D.C., 1920), 9.

30. Jane P. Clarke, *The Rise of a New Federalism* (New York, 1938), 91.

31. U.S. Council of National Defense, *First, Second, Third Annual Report* (Washington, D.C., 1917, 1918, 1919); Arizona Council of Defense, *The Arizona Council of Defense* (Phoenix, 1917); Alabama State Council of Defense, *Proceedings . . .* (Montgomery, 1917); Missouri Council of Defense, *Final Report,* 1919; Ohio State Council of Defense, *A History of the Activities . . .* (Columbus, 1919); Georgia Council of Defense, *Final Report of Women's Committee, Georgia Division, April 1917–July 1919* (Atlanta, 1919); Illinois State Council of Defense, *Final Report . . .* (Chicago, 1919); Women's Committee of State of California Council of Defense, *Report* (Los Angeles, 1919); Wisconsin State Council of Defense, *Report* (Madison, 1919); Milwaukee County Council of Defense, *Report on Twenty Months of War-time Service* (Milwaukee, 1919); Connecticut State Council of Defense, Papers, LC.

32. U.S. Council of National Defense, *First Annual Report,* 46.

33. Gerald Senn, "Molders of Thought, Directors of Action: The Arkansas Council of Defense, 1917–1918," *The Arkansas Historical Quarterly* 36, no. 3 (1977):290; William J. Breen, "The North Carolina Council of Defense during World War I, 1917–1918," *The North Carolina Historical Review* 50, no. 1 (January 1973):2–23.

34. Wilson to Newton D. Baker, 16 November 1918, Baker Papers, LC, Reel 6; Edward L. Burchard, *Organization of the Community Councils of Defense by the Federal Government* (Washington, D.C., 1942?), 14, a file of papers, clippings, etc., in LC. In Connecticut the CND was "run by Republican businessmen of Yankee ancestry," and much the same was true of Oklahoma. See Herbert F. Jannick, *A Diverse People: Connecticut to the Present* (Chester, Conn., 1975), 9; and James R. Scales and Danney Goble, *Oklahoma Politics: A History* (Norman, 1982), 87.

35. *Saturday Evening Post,* 9, 30 May 1914.

36. Arthur S. Link, *Woodrow Wilson and the Progressive Era, 1910–1917* (New York, 1963), 70–74.

37. *Baltimore News,* 24 July 1917; *Grand Rapids News,* 24 July 1917; and see *San Francisco Bulletin, Louisville Herald, San Francisco Quarterly,* 21 July 1917, all in Council of National Defense, RG62 Directors Officer, Clippings 2-E1, Box 143, 144, N.A.

38. Daniels to Baruch, 27 April 1918, Baruch to Daniels, 3 May 1918, Josephus Daniels Papers, Box 65 LC.

39. Murray N. Rothbard, "War Collectivism in World War I," in Ronald Radosh and Murray N. Rothbard, *A New History of Leviathan: Essays on the Rise of the American Corporate State* (New York, 1972), 66; Gabriel Kolko, *The Triumph of Conservatism: A Reinterpretation of American History* (Glencoe, Ill., 1963), 304–5; Stephen Skowronek, *Building a New American State: The Expansion of National Admin-*

istrative Capacities, 1877–1920 (Cambridge, London, and New York, 1982), 236.
40. U.S. Dept. of Commerce, Bureau of the Census, *Abstract of the Fourteenth Census, 1920* (Washington, D.C., 1923), 1034–35; John G. Clark, et al., *Three Generations in Twentieth Century America; Family, Community and Nation* (Homewood, Ill., 1977), 144; Benedict Crowell and Robert Forest Wilson, *How America Went to War: The Armies of Industry* (New Haven, Conn., 1921), 638, 672.
41. Ellis W. Hawley, *The Great War and the Search for a Modern Order, A History of the American People and their Institutions 1917–1933* (New York, 1979), 81–82; Barry D. Karl, *The Uneasy State: The United States from 1915 to 1945* (Chicago, 1983), 31–32; Berkowitz and McQuaid, *Creating the Welfare State,* 44–47; Irving Bernstein, *The Lean Years: A History of the American Worker, 1920–1933* (Boston, 1960), 174–87.
42. Morison and Commager, *The Growth of the American Republic,* 516; Rexford Tugwell, "America's Wartime Socialism," *The Nation,* 6 April 1927, in Keith Nelson, ed., *The Impact of War on American Life: The Twentieth Century Experience* (New York, 1971), 18; George Soule, *Prosperity Decade: A Chapter from American Economic History, 1917–1929* (London, 1947), 48, 78–80.
43. Charles Gilbert, *American Financing of World War I* (Westport, Conn., and London, 1970), 76; Kennedy, *Over Here,* 112.
44. *Historical Statistics of the United States,* 99–111; John Maurice Clark, *The Costs of the World War to the American People* (New Haven, Conn., 1931), 227–35.
45. *Saturday Evening Post,* 7 September 1918.
46. Wilson to Tumulty, 11 May 1918, in Burleson Papers, vol. 20, 3212, LC.

5

Labor and the War

The changes that affected business and industry during the war automatically affected labor. A labor historian described the war situation when he wrote:

> It immediately became apparent to our government that production of materials must be stimulated and even new sources of supply created; . . . To attain these ends, moreover, it was clear that there must be unprecedented reorganization of industry, seeming if not actual violation of cherished constitutional rights and guaranties [sic], and the abandonment of our traditional policy of *laissez-faire*.

As a consequence, the writer suggested that for labor, "it is much easier to think of the period of the World War in terms of revolution rather than evolution."[1] As we shall see, the word *revolution* may be too easily used here: changes in government labor policy, as in so many others, took time in coming and were not always "revolutionary" in their approach. But the wartime change did not stop with government policy or industrial organization: the "unguided" changes brought about by the pressures of war themselves affected the workers' bargaining position, working conditions, and wage levels; they also altered conditions outside of the workplace in terms of the workers' physical situation, housing, and general welfare. Even the composition and distribution of the labor force was changed, as "hitherto socially and economically marginal individuals and groups, people whose main function had been to form a reserve labor army, now became citizen-workers, essential parts in the national war machine."[2] Thus the war could be seen in terms of a continuation of advances in government labor policy, as "developments only barely visible in the Progressive period" came "to full flower during the war years."[3] On the other hand, the enormous economic demands of the war brought new social situations, new problems, and new tensions, which together created a degree of disruption at a crucial moment in the nation's history and so led to new departures for management, labor, and government.

Unions, Government, and Labor Relations

The position of labor in America had been changing even before the outbreak of war, but the picture was mixed. After a succession of setbacks and defeats, compounded by the effects of the depression in the 1890s, organized labor had grown in strength as total union membership rose from less than five hundred thousand in 1897 to over 2 million by 1904. However, this was largely under the leadership of the conservative, craft-based American Federation of Labor, led by Samuel Gompers, and the majority of unskilled workers were still to be unionized. Nonetheless, labor organizations were now at least established and seemed to have more future than had the earlier National Labor Union or Knights of Labor. Equally significant was the apparent change in attitudes toward labor, particularly in government circles, that occurred in the early twentieth century.

Perhaps the first indication of the changed climate in labor affairs was the action of Theodore Roosevelt during the 1902 Pennsylvania anthracite mining strike. Given a state of growing national emergency, Roosevelt did not use federal troops to force the miners back to work as might previously have been the case, but urged arbitration on both sides. When the employers proved unwilling to negotiate or compromise, he privately threatened *them* with a possible takeover of the mines. As a result, the owners conceded and accepted the rulings of a presidential commission. Although the miners did not win union recognition, they did secure a pay raise and some reduction in hours. More important was the precedent of sympathetic presidential involvement where the public interest was concerned. The president's position was not specifically prolabor: Roosevelt did not identify himself as a representative of working-class interests any more than he did with those of employers, but he offered what he was to call a "square deal" to all sides. The same was also true of Woodrow Wilson, who in 1916 specifically disavowed narrow class interest when he said he had "tried . . . to get rid of any class division" and "of any class consciousness and feeling."[4]

The spirit of detached concern for the well-being and harmony of the nation as a whole lay behind much of the Progressive movement. However, the plight of working people and of the poor was a major issue for the reformers, and labor was clearly to benefit from the general program of remedial legislation even though the attitude of many Progressives toward unions, and of unions toward Progressives, was ambiguous. Settlement House workers and charity organizations reflected and articulated a consideration for the condition of the industrial work force, which manifested itself in municipal reform, city planning, housing development, and parks programs. More directly, reform politicians were responsible for the passage of workmen's compensation legislation, regulation of working hours and conditions, and controls on child and female labor. By 1915 thirty-five states had some form of workmen's compensation, twenty-eight had established maximum hours of work for women, and twenty-five had also limited the work hours of men.[5]

Recognition both of the strength and importance of unions, and a concern for the human problems of labor, coupled with a desire to increase efficiency, and hence production, encouraged some employers to join with reformers in working for improved industrial relations and to support a policy of co-operation between management and work force. A leading instrument in this area was the National Civic Federation, an organization of corporate and labor leaders, which encouraged the growth of factory welfare and worker representation schemes and encouraged belief in a unity of purpose rather than a class division of interest. By 1914 over twenty-five hundred companies, including such names as Ford, Procter and Gamble, Eastman Kodak, and General Electric, had some form of welfare or betterment scheme, and Ford of course was famous for the reduction of hours coupled with increased rates of pay, which began in 1914.[6]

However, such programs only affected a tiny minority of workers, and for most employment continued to be hard, dangerous, poorly paid, and uncertain in its regularity. Despite the signs of progress in union affairs, average real wages of unskilled workers were actually in decline from about 1898 until just before the war. One estimate of the real annual per capita earnings in all industries for 1904 put the figure at $582; in 1914 it was $576. Obviously there were variations, and some groups measured gains in their purchasing power—providing they remained fully employed. With unemployment running at around 12 percent in 1914, that was no certainty.[7]

It was not just the economic climate that adversely qualified labor's gains in the Progressive era. Many employers remained unmoved by the appeals of Progressives or the advice of the National Civic Federation, and instead fought concessions to labor and resisted the growth of trade unionism. Some went further and launched their own counteroffensive. In 1903 the National Association of Manufacturers (NAM) unanimously adopted a declaration of principles opposing unions and collective bargaining. In his conference address that year NAM President David Parry summed up the extreme attitude when he described the AFL as a "fountainhead of inspiration which breeds boycotters, picketers and Socialists." Elsewhere he spoke of unions in general as a "mob knowing no master."[8] Encouraged by the NAM, various employers' organizations fought their workers in a series of bitter strikes, which were often marred by violence on both sides. The employers were aided by the courts, and in the cases of the stove polishers (1906) and the Danbury hatters (1908) the Supreme Court ruled that strikes and boycotts could be classed as restraints of trade under the Sherman Anti-trust Act. As a consequence of these different factors, union growth slowed after 1904, and total union membership had only reached 2.7 million in 1914.

Faced with the frontal assaults of employers on one side, and the breakaway of disaffected elements to the more radical IWW or the Socialist party on the other, the AFL and Gompers began to move from "pure and simple" trade unionism toward the political arena. When the Democratic party accepted a plank in its 1908 platform supporting the exclusion of labor from the Sherman Act, the AFL threw its support behind the party and continued to do so again in 1912 and 1916. This process continued during the course of the war as Gompers became a spokesman for the administration, and Woodrow Wilson became "involved in the cause of the American labor movement as no other President before him."[9]

The administration's war labor policies marked the culmination of a succession of prolabor acts. The president's appointment of secretary to the newly established independent Department of Labor in the person of William B. Wilson was itself widely approved by labor. *This* Wilson was a former miner and organizer and secretary of the United Mineworkers union, and he was to be instrumental in seeing the new department become a voice for working men and a force for mediation in industrial disputes. The trade unions were even more delighted when Congress passed the Clayton Anti-trust Act in 1914, amending the Sherman Act. The famous Section Six of the new act declared that "the labor of a human being is not a commodity or article of commerce," so partly exempting unions from the antitrust laws. Samuel Gompers greeted this as labor's Magna Charta [sic], although subsequently the act proved to be less supportive of labor than he had imagined. Nonetheless, it encouraged a closer relationship between the AFL and the government, and periodic meetings between representatives of both sides in 1916 climaxed with the presence of the president and members of his cabinet at the dedication of the new AFL building in Washington, D.C. Later that year Gompers was appointed to the Advisory Commission of the Council of National Defense (where he became affectionately known as "the Chief"—he was also described by Newton Baker as "This little man with his big head, this statesman of labor and warrior for labor"[10]), and the administration had supported the Keating-Owen Child Labor bill and pushed through the Adamson Act, which averted a railway strike and introduced the eight-hour day for some rail workers involved in interstate transport. Thus, when America entered the world war in 1917, the labor movement was in a better position to press the claims of working men, and the country was led by a president more sympathetic to that cause, than at any previous time. It remained to be seen whether the war would further advance that concern or detract from it.

The most obvious effect of the conflict as far as the working people of America were concerned was the expansion of the American economy, full employment, and a growing labor shortage. That situation did not arise immediately; the initial impact of war in 1914 was to disrupt trade, reduce American exports, and increase unemployment. However, that was short-lived as a war boom soon hit the United States and continued apace after 1917. Ironically, as war growth brought an increased demand for labor, it also cut off the traditional supply of additional workers, namely immigration. The flow of immigrants dropped from 1.2 million in 1914 to 110,000 in 1918, and American employers were forced to seek additional labor within the United States or from her nearby neighbors. To make matters worse, at the same time workers were being removed from the job market by Uncle Sam himself in the guise of the draft boards. The mobilization of 4.8 million men was the equivalent of removing 16 percent of the labor force. The effect of this was further compounded by the fact that military service also increased demand for industrial production, as each single soldier required six to ten people working in industry to equip and maintain him in the field.[11] The combined effect of these forces was to place labor at a premium, but they also created problems for those responsible for the efficient production of war goods.

The resultant high demand for labor during the war led to a rapid turnover of workers. In some areas labor turnover was reported at 100 percent *per week,* where it had previously been 200 to 300 percent *per annum.* In some cities the wartime turnover of labor was estimated to be as high as 3,000 percent.[12] The consequences were obvious; shortages of labor were reported in numerous government surveys. In Canton, Ohio, the shortages were coupled with "a constant demand for increased wages." The situation in a cotton mill in Charlotte, North Carolina, was described thus:

> There is a general shortage of labor in all lines of industry, and this has created a very keen competition for labor so that employers are constantly bidding for each others' labor. This has created a much larger than usual moving element, and there are a great many employees who have worked in many different mills during the past year.

The American Tool Works in Cincinnati, where 99 percent of work was war work, reported delays in production due to the "loss of many of our skilled employees through voluntary enlistment and the draft, also through their being enticed away by companies having 'cost plus' contracts with which the sky seems to be the only limit as to the wages paid." Yet another company in Cincinnati spoke of "the existing unrest and migratory spirit of employees."[13] By July 1918, thirty-four states "faced a serious shortage of unskilled workers," and a government official predicted that between three and four million additional workers would be required in war industry in the coming year.[14]

These shortages, and their related problems, forced both employers and government to recognize that manpower was as vital and scarce a resource as any raw material, and one that, like raw materials and other commodities, needed careful husbanding with some central control to determine priorities. The free market again could not be allowed to operate without some modification. As the secretary of labor wrote to President Wilson, "We can no longer leave our labor supply to the unregulated forces of competition nor even the patriotic efforts of diverse agencies of the Government unrelated to a comprehensive policy and unified direction."[15] One form of direction was, of course, operated through the draft and the system of deferments granted to those in necessary industries such as arsenals and shipyards. Over half a million agricultural workers also received lower classifications. However, selective service deferments alone could not provide sufficient direction, particularly as the draft had itself to be further extended during the war, making the problem of labor even more acute. Early on in 1917 a number of employers demanded the conscription of labor, a call that was echoed in Congress, as was the proposal for an agricultural army under military control. Indeed, some states did pass "antiloafing" laws, and in May 1918 the federal government finally issued a "work or fight order," amending the Selective Service Act to require men in nonessential work to find other employment or be immediately drafted. Over 120,000 men appeared before their draft boards, and half changed their jobs. So serious had the situation become that later in 1918 Secretary of War Baker announced that all baseball players must find essential work or go to war after 1 September—a statement that itself revealed how lenient the government had been until that point.[16]

Given the limitations of the draft as a force for labor control and the growing magnitude of the problem the government was forced, somewhat reluctantly, to take further steps to ensure the desirable distribution of workers. That responsibility increasingly fell to the United States Employment Service (USES), which, in January 1918, was detached from the Bureau of Immigration and established as an independent unit within the Labor Department. In June 1918 the president requested that all employers engaged in war work recruit their unskilled labor exclusively through the USES, a move welcomed as a great step in some quarters: *The American Lumberman* suggested that the USES was "destined to revolutionize the employment situation in this country. The private employment agency, with its graft, its encouragement to labor turnover, and its specialization in bum and hobo labor, is at the end of its career."[17]

In the event, the USES did not measure up to these high hopes, but was instead a temporary advance, "a great and futile effort to lessen class antagonism in the United States." Nonetheless, the agency was a substantial move toward an orderly labor policy, and of some significance. Growing from a body of less than one hundred, by August 1918 the Employment Service had five hundred officers, a staff of over twenty thousand operating through state boards, and placed ten thousand workers a day. Between January and November 1918 the USES had registered 3.6 million job applicants and placed 2.6 million. However, the employers were seeking over 7.8 million, and the USES was never able to find those numbers nor to overcome the opposition of employers.[18]

Clearly, no employment agency, no matter how efficient, could find workers where there were none readily available, nor could men be shifted from one area of the economy to another without replacements being found. A number of methods were used to overcome these difficulties. The U.S. Public Service Reserve, a body organized within the Labor Department in 1917, was established in order to deal with those men already in employment but ready to change "in the interests of national welfare." By June 1918, the agency had placed between six and seven thousand skilled men in government service.[19] Freeing agricultural workers for deployment elsewhere was a major task of the USES, which recruited unskilled workers from Mexico for this purpose by agreement with the Mexican government. Although the 1917 Immigration Act had specifically banned the importation of contract or illiterate workers, these provisions were suspended for the duration of the war, and some thirty-five thousand Mexicans entered the United States under the provisions of the agreement between governments. All told seventy two thousand Mexicans crossed the border between 1917 and 1921. Many were reported "lost" at the war's end, and by the end of 1921, while almost thirty-five thousand workers had returned and fifteen thousand were still with their importers, more than twenty-one thousand had disappeared. This was not to the liking of American labor leaders, although Samuel Gompers's protest against the importation of "illiterate Mexicans for agricultural purposes" was clearly to no avail.[20]

Protests of a different nature were raised concerning the 110,000 Puerto Rican workers brought into America to help build army camps during the war. Unlike the Mexicans, they appear to have been mainly kept in camps (although some Mexicans in California were said to be kept actual prisoners in padlocked stockades, patrolled by armed guards[21]). The treatment of the Puerto Ricans was such that the Puerto Rican Association was moved to complain about their "terrible and deplorable condition" in places like Fort Bragg, North Carolina, where seventeen hundred were kept in a situation like that of prisoners of war. These complaints were investigated, and the reports on Fort Bragg were confirmed: "there had been very real mismanagement." At other camps in South Carolina, Georgia, Arkansas, and New Orleans, the workers were said to be "well cared for and contented." What happened to them after 1918 is not clear, but it is probable that they were returned from whence they came.[22]

Another source of labor used during the war was also behind bars—prison labor. Again, legislation had been passed in the Progressive era to restrict the use of convict workers in certain forms of employment for fear they undercut the wages of free workers. But the war saw the suspension of this legislation following pressures from both employers and prisoners themselves. The appeals of some inmates could be quite moving; one wrote to Felix Frankfurter from Leavenworth that "the boys are more than anxious to do their bit," and he pointed out that they had already "been purchasing Liberty Bonds, War Savings and Thrift Stamps." "We are," he said, "very anxious to get out and do our bit." The writer tapped a common theme when he suggested that the war provided an opportunity for prisoners not just to escape, but to redeem themselves. A writer from San Quentin said, "Never were the chances for the rehabilitation of the fallen brother greater than right now." In another letter to Frankfurter a prisoner asked: "Will you not give us a chance to do our bit by working in the ship yards, so that when in later years our children ask us what we did in the great war, we will not have to confess we were slackers by being in prison."[23] The prohibition of prison labor was suspended by executive order on 16 September 1918, too late to have much effect. However, various states had commuted sentences to allow prisoners out to do war work or to join the forces, and at least fifteen thousand former convicts were engaged in war industries.[24]

There was considerable pressure to suspend legislation in another area too during the war, namely that of child labor, but the Child Labor Law of 1916 limiting the employment of children under the age of sixteen had been a hard-won victory for the Progressives, and the reformers were determined to preserve it. However, many employers used the war emergency to press for its suspension (as they did the restriction on other forms of labor). One cotton company, for example, argued that as the family was still the basic unit in the work force of southern mills, the prohibition of child labor could bring a reduction of 20 to 35 percent in the labor force, as families were forced to quit.[25] The government resisted such demands, and even when the Supreme Court ruled the Child Labor Law unconstitutional in 1918 clauses prohibiting child labor were still inserted in federal war contracts.

More important than foreign workers, prison inmates, or children in providing additional labor were the twin reserve armies of labor of female and black workers who moved into industrial occupations during the war. Both these groups will be considered in detail elsewhere, and it is sufficient only to point out here that one million additional women joined the work force and half a million blacks entered industry. Women also formed the Land Army to replace agricultural workers. In both cases there was some direction and encouragement from government, but much of this move was the result of private initiatives or the spontaneous response of women and blacks themselves to the demands of war or market forces. For them the war provided an opportunity not to be missed. As a consequence, both groups were to be affected by the war, and the changes in their economic situation had social and political repercussions.

Whatever group was involved, and however their wartime role came about, the position of organized labor was involved. Unlike other resources, labor was not a passive element to be moved around and redistributed at will; it was instead an active agent that had to be recognized and incorporated into the decision-making process—particularly in a nation claiming to be fighting to uphold democracy. As in Britain, the control, direction, and "dilution" of labor could only successfully take place with the agreement and cooperation of the unions and spokesmen of the workers, and just as in Britain leaders of the Labour party and the unions were involved in wartime decisions and in government itself, so too in the United States the war brought the participation of labor leaders at the highest levels.

Even before 1917 it was clear that the conflict would affect the position of labor not just in Europe, but also in America. In 1914 Samuel

Gompers spoke of "the general reorganization" that would follow the war and suggested that "the workers must have voice and influence." As the possibility of American entry into the war increased, the labor leader, like many other people of his generation (including three of his fellow members on the Advisory Commission) abandoned his earlier pacifist position in favor of preparedness and nationalism in response to what he described as the challenge of "autocracy." As early as 1916 Gompers promised his organization's support for the government in the event of war, and, facing the imminent prospect of war in March 1917 the Executive Council of the AFL issued the following statement:

> we . . . offer our services to our country in every field of activity to defend, safeguard and preserve the Republic of the United States of America . . . and we call upon our fellow workers and fellow citizens . . . to devotedly and patriotically give like service.[26]

But at the same time the labor leaders argued that "whether planning for peace or war the government must recognize the organized labor movement through which it must co-operate with wage earners." Gompers's appointment to the Advisory Commission of the Council of National Defense was an indication that the government recognized this fact. It was through the Advisory Commission that labor's position was declared on 8 April 1917 when it was announced "that neither employers nor employees shall endeavor to take advantage of the country's necessities to change existing standards." However, this statement met some opposition, and the term *existing standards* required further amplification and qualification. A later release of 25 April pointed out that this referred to hours and wages and said that "employers and employees in private industries should not attempt to take advantage of the existing abnormal conditions to change standards which they were unable to change under normal conditions." Moreover, "no arbitary change in wages should be sought at this time . . . through the process of strikes or lockouts without at least giving the established agencies of the Government . . . an opportunity to adjust the difficulties without a stoppage of work occurring."[27] Thus, labor loyalty appeared guaranteed, but with the maintenance of the status quo on both sides of industry.

In the event such early agreements proved impossible to keep. The economic and social consequences of the war were such that there were bound to be demands for change from the workers and resistance from employers, both using the war to justify their respective positions. At its convention in November 1917 the AFL could again reiterate its position of unreserved loyalty: "A people unwilling to make the supreme sacrifice in support of the government . . . are undeserving to live and enjoy the privileges of free, democratic government."[28] But if sacrifice was acceptable, exploitation was not. The convention recognized that the war offered an opportunity "that would either be used by the wage-earners in furtherance of human welfare and progress or would be seized by the agents of reaction and for the entrenchment of the privileges of wealth." It was clear which the workers' representatives would prefer. As Gompers said before the United Mineworkers in January 1918, labor would make "any sacrifice which may be necessary to make our triumph sure, but we are not going to make any sacrifices that shall fill the coffers of the rich beyond the plethoric conditions in which they even now are."[29]

In a later speech the labor leader could emphasize the concern for standards when he called for what, in World War II, black Americans would describe as a war on two fronts: "one to win the war for freedom, and second . . . to maintain the standards of American life at home." The AFL president had the support in this of Woodrow Wilson, who in 1917, in the first-ever personal address by the nation's president at an AFL convention, underlined the importance of labor and agreed that "while we are fighting for freedom we must see . . . that labor is free" and ensure "that the conditions of labor are not rendered more onerous by the war." The prolabor position of the president was further evident when he told the convention that in industrial disputes "you are reasonable in a larger number of cases than the capitalists."[30]

In fact, of course, the president's message was a tacit acknowledgment of mounting labor unrest and was a call to use processes of conciliation and voluntary cooperation in the cause of the war. The AFL was seen as the best means of co-opting the entire labor movement, and by making Gompers the spokesman for all American workers it was hoped that he would be able to control the labor force and enlist its support. Thus while the AFL now received recognition and official sanction, other, more militant, elements of the labor movement were to be resisted. Although opposing mob action against radical groups, the president nonetheless noted that there were "some organizations in this country whose object is anarchy and the destruction of law." Samuel Gompers agreed with the president's position, gave his support to the campaign against more radical labor elements, and was at the forefront in the formation of the American Alliance for Labor and Democracy, which was established to counter the antiwar People's Council for Peace and Democracy. In a number of speeches around the country he attacked antiwar groups, such as, by implication, the Industrial Workers of the World, and time and time again referred to socialism as a "German virus" and the Socialist Party of America as un-American, "simply an adjunct of the German Socialist Party and German propaganda."[31] But his very speeches and the president's own remarks testified to the fact that many Americans still needed to be convinced about the justice of the war and the sacrifices they were making. Despite the many promises about preserving standards most American workers were feeling the effects of mounting wartime inflation and the consequent drop in real wages.

In common with workers elsewhere during the war, Americans were increasingly disillusioned with their leaders in government and the unions, and with the deterioration in their conditions. Using the one weapon they had, particularly in a period of labor scarcity, they struck. The largest number of strikes in the nation's history up until that point broke out in 1917 when more than one million workers took part in over 4,200 strikes. The numbers had already been increasing—there had been only 979 strikes in 1914, but there were almost 1,500 in 1915 and over 3,600 in 1916. The number did not drop after America entered the war. Over three-quarters of the 1917 work stoppages occurred after 6 April; by the end of the war there had been over 6,000 reported strikes. In the vast majority of cases wages, or wages and related factors, were the cause. By 1917 prices were already 60 percent above prewar levels, and April brought the biggest single jump of the year. Suggestions of war profiteering among businessmen, and a rumored increase in the number of millionaires, only contributed further to the wave of industrial discontent.[32]

Areas west of the Mississippi seemed particularly badly affected by strikes, and these were often attributed to the influences of the IWW. In part this was because it suited the Wobblies', and labor's, opponents to accuse them. As one observer said in September 1917, "The identification of all recalcitrant labor with IWW is encouraged by employers and employers' associations who are opposed to labor unions in general." Moreover, given that strikes were, de facto, damaging to the war effort, the IWW was an easy scapegoat because of its known opposition to the war. There was little doubt, too, that IWW strength *had* grown during the war with the swelling of the labor force and the pressure on wages and conditions. Wobbly membership was estimated to have risen from forty thousand to one hundred thousand between 1916 and 1917, and was traditionally strongest in the West.[33] The industries most affected were vital to the war effort—copper, lumber, and communications. A miners' strike that centered on Arizona, the world's largest copper-producing area, threatened the production of shells, bullets, detonators, and cable, while strikes in the forests of Washington, Oregon, and California halted the supply of spruce essential for aircraft manufacture. Strikes in various oilfields reduced fuel supplies, and disputes in the Chicago meat-packing industry held up the canning of food for the army. Equally, the suppression of strikes by violent or vigilante action was damaging to morale and harmful to claims of democratic unity. The deportations from Jerome, Bisbee, and other towns in the summer of 1917, and the brutal lynching of Frank Little in Butte in August, together with the threat to war production, indicated that voluntarism had failed and that more direct government intervention was necessary. In response to these pressures and the urging of a number of advisers, including Gompers, the president established the Mediation Commission in September 1917 to visit the strike-ridden states, bring a settlement to disputes, and further "the development of a better understanding between laborers and employers."[34]

The president's commission was chaired by the secretary of labor, William B. Wilson, and consisted of two business representatives—J. L. Spangler, a coal operator and banker from Pennsylvania, and V. Z. Reed, "a capitalist engaged in metal and petroleum mining, manufacturing, and ranching"—and two labor men—J. H. Walker from the Illinois Federation of Labor, and E. P. Marsh of the Washington Federation of Labor. The secretary and driving force of the commission was to be "the hot dog of war," Felix Frankfurter, the Harvard professor of law, friend and associate of the editors of *The New Republic,* and very much a Progressive who had already become involved in labor problems on behalf of the army, drawing up contracts in the clothing industry for the production of uniforms. The commission set out from Washington, D.C., at the end of September and toured the various affected states, meeting local politicians, employers, and employees, and conducting hearings. In a period of five weeks the commission had dealt with some 250 different disputes, and in general had found that "the overwhelming mass of the laboring population is in no sense disloyal." What was lacking was "a healthy basis of relationship between management and men" and a failure to accept collective bargaining, which resulted in a contrast between the nation's "democratic purposes" and "the autocratic conduct of some of those guiding industry at home."[35]

The commission found different specific causes in separate disputes, each with its own particular emphasis. The problems in copper mining were identified as distant ownership, poor management, high labor turnover, and a polyglot work force. Although the president of the Phelps Dodge mining company (whose profits had increased 216% percent in 1916) could describe the action of the unions as "unpatriotic and treasonable," the president's commission found "neither sinister influences nor the I.W.W. can account for these strikes."[36] On the contrary, arguing that the "trade union movement is the most promising unifying spirit among the workers," the commissioners established local district administrators and grievance committees and gave miners the right to organize. By October 1918 it could be said of Arizona that the commission had "laid the foundation for the possibility of Industrial Peace for the duration of the world war."[37] Similarly, in California the commission found the causes of unrest to be low wage rates, the high cost of living, nonrecognition of unions, and the problems of a migratory labor force, which in some cases numbered between seventy-five and eighty thousand. In a brief for the presidential body, the California State Commission on Immigration pointed out that in a number of cases strikes were "erroneously attributed to the I.W.W.," and was at pains to indicate where wage levels and conditions were at the root of conflict.[38] In Chicago, too, disputes had arisen from low wages and long hours, and a failure to meet union representatives on the part of the employers. The commission's settlement included arbitration and negotiating procedures and rights to union membership.

The one area in which the Mediation Commission was not as successful as others was in the logging industry of the Pacific Northwest. Here again, the workers were migratory and living in camps of varying quality, mostly very poor. As "disintegrating forces in society," the lumber workers were denied the "unifying and stabilizing" force of a union, and "this uncompromising attitude on the part of the employers has reaped for them an organization of destructive rather than constructive radicalism."[39] It was easy for employers to resist strikers by branding them as unpatriotic and influenced by the Wobblies. The Lumbermen's Protective League, for example, claimed:

> the I.W.W. have preached sedition, disrespect and disloyalty to the government to such extent that in some instances it has been only by the most insistent efforts of employers that patriotic, loyal employes [sic], who have freely subscribed to the Liberty Loan Bond issues, have been restrained from destroying I.W.W. headquarters and by brute force driving them out of the mills and camps.[40]

Other reports, however, suggested that in the lumber camps of Montana the Wobblies were "taking pains to see laws are NOT violated," and, in a situation where men slept in double bunks on rotten hay, "It is against the bunk house situation that most of the striking I.W.W.s are complaining." Agent provocateurs were also blamed.[41]

Whatever the perspective, it was clear that the IWW were influential among the lumbermen and had found support there: one estimate put membership of the organization in the northwestern forests at thirty thousand and men were now striking "on the job"—leaving after eight hours or actually damaging equipment or just being plain awkward.[42] The number of strikes had risen from 44 in 1916 to 295 in 1917, and so serious was the situation and its effect on aircraft production that there had been some suggestion that the military be used or a "regiment of foresters" be created to produce the needed spruce. Secretary Baker had resisted this suggestion "in the interests of the whole labor situation."[43] However, when the Mediation Commission's proposals of improved conditions, shorter hours, and an officially recognized workers' organization proved unacceptable more drastic measures were necessary. In October 1917 Col. Brice Disque of the Spruce Division of the Signal Corps created the Loyal Legion of Loggers and Lumbermen, an organization of employers and employees, including some enlisted soldiers with experience in the forests. The Four L's, as it was known, was in fact a compulsory company union, and combined with the program of suppression unleashed against the IWW across the nation plus localized arrests among lumbermen, it grew in strength. By the end of 1918 the Loyal Legion had over 125,000 members; the Wobblies had dropped to 20,000. Apart from coercion, the other reasons for the success of the legion were its introduction of the eight-hour day in the industry in March 1918 and attempts to improve sanitary conditions in camps by establishing basic minimum standards. To some extent, then, the Loyal Legion enacted the Mediation Commission's recommendations, and the number of strikes had fallen to 74 in 1918.[44]

The Mediation Commission, particularly Frankfurter, was involved in one other matter on the West Coast involving labor but not an industrial dispute. This was the case of Thomas H. Mooney, a labor organizer who had been convicted of murder in California in February 1917, and sentenced to death. Mooney had been found guilty of causing the explosion that killed six people during a Preparedness Day March in San Francisco in July 1916. The evidence against Mooney seemed flimsy, and labor organizations reacted angrily to the verdict and the sentence. Moved by the harmful effect on labor relations and the negative image of America the trial created in the international arena, President Wilson asked Frankfurter to look at the case. The commission's report of 16 January 1918 questioned the original verdict and called for a retrial, and the president requested the Governor of California to accept these recommendations. In April 1918 the secretary of labor could report to Samuel Gompers that the president was "doing all he possibly can with the governor of California to induce him to pardon or commute the sentence of Mooney so that he can have a new trial," but to no great effect. Mooney's life was spared, but his conviction stood, and his sentence was reduced to life imprisonment. He was not to be released until 1939.[45]

If the Mediation Commission was not overwhelmingly successful, it was still of considerable significance. As well as settling a number of major disputes, it marked yet another move away from voluntarism toward a centralized labor policy, and its decisions were often to labor's advantage. As one historian has suggested:

> In many respects the Commission's work is an important landmark in the history of American industrial relations. It brought peace to large segments of American industries at a critical time; it added support to

the movement for the eight-hour day; it introduced the principle of collective bargaining . . . in many industries which had known it only in theory, and it recommended a unified labor administration.[46]

This last suggestion was also being made elsewhere, as it became increasingly obvious that the government needed a coherent labor policy for the war. While the Mediation Commission had gone from one dispute to another on a purely *ad hoc* basis, various government departments and agencies were themselves entering into separate labor agreements in 1917 without any overall guidelines to follow other than the statements of April that year.

The fact that government bodies were negotiating with unions was itself remarkable—"the first time in our history that the United States Government entered into agreement with labor unions"[47]—but as various boards, from the Emergency Construction Wage Commission to the Shipbuilding Labor Adjustment Board through to the Ordnance Department and Fuel and Food Administration, reached their independent settlements with labor, chaos mounted. The Council of National Defense's earlier rejection of a proposal for a central labor administration now had to be reconsidered, and an interdepartmental committee was established under the chairmanship of the thirty-five-year-old Assistant Secretary of the Navy Franklin D. Roosevelt. In its report of 20 December 1917 Roosevelt's committee called for a federal policy administered by three bodies responsible respectively for the adjustment of disputes, the settling of basic standards, and oversight of housing and transportation of workers. Further discussion of these proposals led to the formation of the twelve-man War Labor Conference Board representing employers, workers, and the public, and headed by former President Taft and Frank P. Walsh, the chairman of the prewar Commission on Industrial Relations. On 29 March 1918 the Labor Conference Board endorsed the earlier proposals and called for the creation of a War Labor Board. Almost exactly one year after America had entered the war, on 9 April 1918, the president set up the National War Labor Board with Taft, Walsh, and the other participants in the Conference Board as its members.[48]

If the Mediation Commission was an important departure in labor history, the National War Labor Board (NWLB) was even more so. The significance of the board for the war years (and, with hindsight, as a precedent for the future) was captured by co-chairman Walsh when he said the NWLB would bring "a new deal for American labor." As the writer of the most comprehensive study of this war agency has said:

Never before had the federal government authorized pervasive policies to govern working conditions in American industries. Never before had representatives of organized labor shared equally with businessmen in determining federal labor policy.[49]

Although, as Conner rightly points out, the NWLB had antecedents in progressive aims and policies, it was the war emergency that made the application of such ideas possible on a national level under federal direction. Thus the significance of the board was twofold: first as a further step away from "spontaneous adaptation and free inter-play" and laissez-faire ideas in government; and second, in the principles it applied and established as the basis for its policies and decisions.[50]

The immediate object of the NWLB was to prevent disruption of the war effort—"to settle by mediation and conciliation controversies arising between employers and workers in fields of production *necessary for the effective conduct of the war*" [italics mine]. This was to be done following certain general principles which had emerged in the course of the war— that there should be no strikes or lockouts for the rest of the war emergency, a policy supported by the AFL executive committee which proposed at the 1918 convention that "no strikes be inaugurated which cannot be justified to the man risking his life on the firing line." In return for this pledge, the NWLB recognized the right of workers to organize, to bargain collectively, and to join trade unions, though existing negotiating procedures were to continue where they existed. The eight-hour day was recognized "in all cases in which existing law requires it. In all other cases the question of hours of labor shall be settled with due regard to governmental necessities and the welfare, health, and proper comfort of the workers." Wages, hours, and conditions were to be determined in line with local circumstances, but there should be equal pay for equal work by women, and the right to a living wage for all with a minimum level based on subsistence.[51]

In order to carry out these last proposals the Cost of Living Section was established within the Labor Department to decide what constituted a "living wage." The section determined that in order to subsist a family of five in New York City needed an annual income of around fifteen hundred dollars in 1918—to live in comfort required more like eighteen hundred dollars. On this basis the minimum hourly rate of pay would have been fifty-five cents, a figure that was felt to be impossible for employers to meet. As a compromise the NWLB was to apply a figure of forty cents an hour for unskilled labor, gradually rising to forty-five cents before the end of the war. In a number of disputes in which the NWLB acted as adjudicator, workers striking for lesser amounts were awarded the board's minimum figures. Thus one group of machine workers in Waynesboro, Pennsylvania, paid twenty-two cents per hour and striking for thirty, were awarded forty—although only after considerable disagreement within the NWLB.[52]

A large number of cases in the summer of 1918 involved streetcar workers who demanded raises to match the increased cost of living, but whose companies claimed *they* did not have the income to pay. The NWLB ruled in over 100 such cases, and applying the principle of the living wage, increased wages on 110 different lines, affecting 78,730 workers, and putting the burden on the public by forcing the companies to increase fares. In practice this meant that companies should pay decent wages or go bust, and, as Conner suggests, the NWLB in 1918 had "virtually set an unofficial minimum wage, and in that year common laborers earned a higher real wage than ever before." Of course, this was as much due to the general shortage of labor as the work of the NWLB, but there can be little doubt that the board assisted in this upward movement of wages.[53]

Besides encouraging the introduction of better basic rates of pay, the NWLB also did much to further the acceptance of the eight-hour day, one of labor's primary aims in the prewar years. The board granted the eight-hour day in 151 cases, and altogether

from June 1917 until July 1918, about 600,000 more workers from shipyards and packing houses to lumber mills and harness factories earned the basic or actual eight-hour day through the efforts of cabinet members, private manufacturers, federal arbitrators, governmental adjustment boards, and powerful labor leaders.[54]

That the board was actually following a pattern already set was clear in that over one million workers had achieved the goal of eight hours between 1915 and 1917, but the board's additional support was still important. By 1919 almost 49 percent of American workers were employed on eight-hour rates.[55]

The NWLB's support for collective bargaining and trade union membership was also of some significance, and between 250,000 to 300,000 of the 1 million additional union members came as a result of board decisions. On the street railcars alone the board was estimated to have increased unionization by one hundred thousand. The board did not always insist on unionization. Outside of the streetcars one of the most important cases was that involving Bethlehem Steel, where it was reported "that the dissatisfaction among the employees . . . is having a seriously detrimental effect upon the production of war materials absolutely necessary to the success of the American Expeditionary Forces." The board's omnibus ruling scrapped the complicated bonus system, established the eight-hour day, revised hourly rates, and granted the right to bargain collectively.[56] However, it required considerable pressure to persuade Bethlehem Steel to accept these rulings, and the company did not concede as much as labor leaders wished. Like many other companies, the steel firm was prepared to accept employee representation, but not outside interference in the form of union representatives. In this case as in a number of others the NWLB provided "an impetus toward company unionism," and in 125 cases it ordered the formation of shop committees. Influenced by wartime trends, a number of large companies, including International Harvester and Goodyear Tires, introduced such schemes voluntarily, and by 1919 more than 225 companies had "industrial plans" involving worker representation.[57]

The resistance encountered during the Bethlehem Steel dispute indicated some of the limits to the NWLB's powers. Never approved by Congress, the board had little real authority and could only rely on the force of publicity and persuasion. In three instances, however, these proved insufficient, and the board had to look to the president for tougher action. When Western Union refused to accept unionization and sacked eight hundred union members in April 1918 the NWLB was called in. The board proposed some form of worker representation scheme, but Newcomb Carlton, head of Western Union, refused to agree, and the workers threatened to strike in July. Faced with this situation, the administration invoked its war powers and took over the company through Postmaster General Albert Burleson. Ironically, Burleson himself was anti-union. In a similar case involving the Smith and Wesson Company in Springfield, Massachusetts, the War Department took over the plant in September 1918 when the company refused to reinstate sacked union members and accept collective bargaining.[58]

The third case demonstrated that intransigent workers who refused to accept board rulings could find the force of government directed at them. This involved the workers at the Remington Plant in Bridgeport, Connecticut, who, having won the eight-hour day and the right to collective bargaining in July 1918, failed to win a new minimum-wage scale and raises for skilled workers. Faced with considerable dilution of labor with the employment of women and inexperienced men, the skilled machinists struck to preserve differentials and their status on the shop floor. As the NWLB itself could not force the strikers back to work, it fell to President Wilson to warn in a public message on 13 September 1918 that the strikers could be barred from employment in any war industry and have exemptions from the draft rescinded. The strike soon ended.[59] The president had made his position clear in an earlier dispute between members of the Carpenters Union and the Shipbuilding Wage Adjustment Board when he said:

No body of men have the moral right in the present circumstances of the nation to strike until every method of abitration has been tried to the limit. If you do not act upon this principle you are undoubtedly giving aid and comfort to the enemy . . .[60]

These comments were sufficient to send the carpenters back to work; the president's action in Bridgeport showed that he meant what he said.

Whatever the limitations to its power and its success, great claims could still be made for the NWLB. As the secretary of labor acknowledged in his report of 1918, the board "during the brief period of its existence . . . has been one of the most effective instruments of the Department in producing historic and desirable changes in the relations of employers and wage earners in the United States." According to another observer, the board appeared

> to have accomplished something lasting in accustoming the public to certain concepts of industrial justice, such as the living wage, equal pay, and collective bargaining. If war time labor conditions were continued indefinitely there could be no doubt but that the labor organizations would achieve vastly increased power as a result of the Board's work.[61]

It remained to be seen whether this policy could be sustained once the pressure of war had gone.

Of course, it was not just the NWLB that influenced and shaped attitudes toward labor—it was, after all, in existence for less than half the war's duration. The Mediation Commission was undoubtedly significant, and the visible presence of Gompers and other union leaders on war boards was also important. In addition numerous government agencies made agreements with unions and workers that embodied Progressive policies. Indeed, one of the earliest statements of policy, and the basis of much that followed subsequently, came from the Office of the Chief of Ordnance in November 1917 in the form of General Order Thirteen. Drawn up by two reformers working for the Army, Morris L. Cooke, a leading member of the Taylor Group of work efficiency advocates, and Mary Van Kleeck, a member of the Russell Sage Foundation and lecturer at the New York School of Social Philanthropy, these orders stated that "industrial history proves that reasonable housing, fair working conditions, and a proper wage scale are essential to high production," and went on to lay down guidelines on hours, overtime, holidays, workroom standards, wage levels, the employment of women and children, and so on. The orders also supported labor in arguing that "during the war every attempt should be made to conserve in every possible way all our achievements in the way of social betterment."[62]

General Order Thirteen was to be used as a model by a number of other government offices including, notably, the Women in Industry Service of the Department of Labor. Perhaps the most important body to be influenced, though, was the War Labor Policies Board established in May 1918 and headed by Felix Frankfurter. Where the NWLB was a "supreme court of labor," the final arbitrator in industrial disputes, the War Labor

Policies Board was an administrative agency coordinating and shaping the government's own labor policy and representing the government as an employer. Its chief function then, was to unify the standards applied by the different government bodies in their dealings with labor, and, at the same time, to bring some stability to wage levels. There was some confusion as to the Policies Board's relationship with the NWLB. In fact quite naturally there was rivalry between different board members, and some fear of Frankfurter's ambition. However, Frankfurter accepted NWLB principles, and the Policies Board incorporated the earlier body's guidelines in federal contracts for war production.

Before the war ended the War Labor Policies Board, through its chairman, became more concerned with general standard relating to labor and was examining matters such as housing, transportation, and workers' welfare, areas that, as we shall see, became a subject of some concern during the war. As far as Frankfurter was concerned, the board "ought to furnish a medium for dealing with the problems that loom beyond," and he saw the war as an opportunity: "a fringe benefit of the war was making the industrial world safer for industrial democracy."[63] Not all labor groups were necessarily appreciative of this concern, fearing that excessive government intervention might undermine union strength and seeing the best safeguards for workers' welfare in decent wages and working conditions. Perhaps too they resented the implicit paternalism behind aspects of government labor policy, although Frankfurter was clearly sympathetic to their cause. Commenting on the strikes of 1917, he wrote that "in each case it comes down to a basic viewpoint as to men wanting to be prepared to have a share in the ordering of their working hours which are the substance of their lives."[64]

In the event labor need not have feared because the War Labor Policies Board was not able to accomplish a great deal before its demise in May 1919, other than contributing to the reputation of Frankfurter himself. Nonetheless, the board was significant as an attempt by Progressives to advance government labor policy and again was to be important in later years—among the members of the Labor Policies Board was Franklin Roosevelt, and not only could his friendship with Frankfurter be traced back to the war years, but so also could the labor policies of the New Deal.[65]

Like the War Labor Policies Board, other war labor agencies disappeared in 1918–19. Although the War Labor Board was to continue until June 1919, it was increasingly ineffective. The divisions between employers' and employees' representatives that had always existed within the board increased once the unifying force of the war had gone. It had always been clear too that the NWLB was only to be a war board and would not replace existing conciliation bodies, which had continued in existence within the Department of Labor. As the secretary of labor said, the NWLB was designed for the war emergency only, and "there is not the remotest likelihood that it will be continued after the readjustment period growing out of the war has passed."[66] Besides, the new boards had met with opposition, and many employers were of course resistant to wartime changes in labor relations. One writer suggested that industrialists "are not only antagonistic but hostile toward the National War Labor Board and the Department of Labor." The *Open Shop Review* blamed government policy for the "epidemic of strikes"—"The adoption of socialistic ideas due to the stress of war has stimulated the demands of labor politicians for more of the same sort and the legislators weakly yield." According to this writer, disputes were not settled by those involved but "taken to the favorable atmosphere of Washington and adjusted to satisfy the political labor leaders."[67] Even the more moderate Chamber of Commerce, while accepting that government involvement had been necessary during the war and that "some administrative control must be continued even after the war so long as it remains evident that an abrupt return to the policy of free contract is dangerous to the future prosperity and peace of the country," could reaffirm that "the principle of self-government by industries themselves . . . should prevail in this democratic country." Some concessions were to be accepted as a way of preventing government intervention: worker representation schemes, profit sharing, the living wage, and employer-employee cooperation could minimize the necessity for "state control or interference."[68] Thus the war provided further, if negative, support for the ideas of prewar groups such as the National Civic Federation, the Taylorites, or such individuals as Henry Ford in that it encouraged the spread of welfare capitalism as a means to combat both the growth of trade unions and government controls. It was also recognized that such programs could bring greater efficiency and higher output.

Despite these rather negative reactions there were undoubted gains for labor from wartime developments in government policy. The Department of Labor estimated that between 1917 and 1919 nearly five million men and women were affected directly or indirectly by the mediation, arbitration, or adjustment of one government board or another, and it is clear that in most cases those interventions were to labor's advantage. As a consequence of both government policy and the favorable labor situation, those unions seen as legitimate and given official sanction grew in strength and prestige. Membership figures for all American unions rose from 2.7 million in 1914 to over 5 million in 1920, and the percentage growth between 1915 and 1920 was 96 percent.[69] On the basis of this power, and with government support, labor was able to make considerable advances, most notably in the area of hours. In 1910 only 8 percent of the labor force enjoyed a forty-eight-hour week, and 70 percent worked fifty-four hours. In 1919 48 percent worked forty-eight hours, and 26 percent worked fifty-four. In Muncie, Indiana, the famous Middletown studied by the Lynds in the twenties, 73 percent of the work force worked an average of sixty hours per week before the war, but this had dropped to 33 percent in 1919, and the eight-hour day had become the norm. In addition, of course, there were increases in earnings, and on average real wages rose 20 percent during the war.[70]

Clearly wartime government initiative and leadership contributed to these advances for labor, and there is much to suggest that the war years provided a "second New Freedom" as far as labor was concerned. At the same time the desire to achieve harmonious labor relations forced the government to look beyond the confines of the work place and employee-employer relations to consider social conditions and general welfare, and to announce a commitment to "the maintenance of proper standards of living—such standards as are appropriate to American citizens devoting their energies to the successful prosecution of a righteous war."[71] In doing so the government was responding not just to the demands of organized labor, but also to the problems and difficulties arising spontaneously from wartime social change, which often lay at the root of labor troubles. This wider concern was to lead to new departures in government policy, and while this may be seen as a further extension of progressivism, in reality it was more innovatory and precedent-setting.

Wartime Standards of Living

As every historian knows, determining standards of living for any period is notoriously difficult and can be a controversial business. Nonetheless, there is quite a lot of evidence to suggest that during the First World War many Americans, including members of the working classes, became better off financially. Indeed, so much was this so that one contributor to the *Saturday Evening Post* could write sardonically of "labor Plutocrats," "six-cylinder, seven-seater types."[72] While it obviously suited some individuals to argue that workers were earning high wages, and the implicit criticism of labor in the *Post* piece causes reservation, the idea of a more affluent working class was substantiated elsewhere. Julius Rosenwald of Sears Roebuck wrote that

> If it is possible to speak of classes in our democratic country, it would seem that economy is being practiced by our middle and upper classes, while the lower classes are more than offsetting this economy by extravagance brought about by the sudden increase in wages.

His assertion was supported by M. B. Wild of the Retail Bureau of the Merchants and Manufacturers Association, who wrote that "the increase in business comes from a different class of the community." Thus, while sales were generally down by as much as 20 to 50 percent, there were interesting variations. Men's clothing sales, according to Rosenwald, were down 17 percent in 1918 compared with 1917, but the sale of work clothes was up 48 percent. Rosenwald also noted that "watches are in great demand, especially wrist watches, which have been enormously popularized by the war."[73] Car sales and production were certainly up: as early as 1916 it was reported that four times the amount had been spent on cars as in the previous year, and the production of passenger cars in 1917 exceeded 1.7 million. Although reduced by WIB restrictions, the number was still 925,000 in 1918, and by 1920 there were more than 8 million passenger cars registered in the United States compared with the 2.3 million of 1915. Another indication of consumer wealth was the spread of the chain stores or supermarkets: A & P (The Atlantic and Pacific Tea Company) opened 2,200 new stores between 1914 and 1917 alone, and by 1922 had 5,000 different outlets. J. C. Penney had only 14 stores in 1910 with sales just over $662,000; in 1918 there were 197 stores with sales of more than $31.3 million.[74]

All of these statistics indicate that America was already moving into the affluence and consumerism associated with the twenties well before the war ended. However, such figures can be misleading—like all generalizations they cover a multitude of exceptions. There were enormous variations in earnings according to geographic region, occupation, race, gender, and individual circumstance. Some indication of the pattern of earnings can be gathered from the enormous amount of detailed information collected by different government agencies during the war (a fact itself indicative of the government's concern). Despite all the evidence of increased wealth there was much to suggest that, even in boom conditions, many workers struggled to achieve the subsistence income, and few earned enough to live in comfort. Bearing in mind the fact the NWLB found that nationally an average family of five required $1,380 and $1,500 in New York City to subsist in 1918 (and $1,750 to live in comfort), and that the board had set a compromise figure of $960 per annum as a norm (i.e., forty cents an hour for a forty-eight-hour week), the following selection of information reveals some of the limits to wartime gains.

Among the lowest-paid workers were farm laborers, whose rates of pay varied from around $250 per annum in the South to $550 in the West, although board was provided in addition. In the South wages generally were low. In Atlanta, Georgia, where males in war work (i.e., the better-paid jobs) could expect to earn between $10 and $25 per week, one survey found in 1918 that one-quarter of male workers earned $10 to $15, one-quarter earned around $15 to $20, and one-sixth were on $20 to $25 per week—that is, on or above the NWLB guide of $960. For black men, and white women, earnings were more often in the $6 to $10 weekly range. Further north earnings improved: while a streetcar conductor in Atlanta was paid an annual income of $1,060, his counterpart in Pittsburgh received $1,554. Even a janitor in Pittsburgh could report an annual income of $900, while a laborer in the Carnegie Steel plant reported $25 per week ($1,250 per annum). Another steel mill laborer earned $40 per week, and his apprentice son, $20. Their combined annual income was $3,120.[75]

Skilled men were on considerably higher rates than those of laborers—a machinist in Pittsburgh had weekly earnings of $46 and an annual income of $2,400. Machinists generally were well paid: in the American Tool Works in Cincinnati, Ohio, of the 1,320 all-white male workers 520 earned between $15 and $20; 280 between $20 and $25; 168, $25 to $30; 78, $30 to $35; 60, $35 to $40, and twenty, $40 to $45. The women (46), all were below $15 per week. In the Cincinnati Bickford Tool Co., 55 percent of workers earned $20 to $25 per week, and the same was true in the Acme Machine Tool Co. In Bisbee, Arizona, at the end of 1918, a mining powderman could earn $35 per week, a pipefitter, $33, and a sawmill boss, $46 per week. Following a pay award in 1918 some half a million coal miners were earning an average of $30 per week. Whether these figures included overtime is not clear, but according to one commentator, "Large numbers of men are earning from $75 to $100 per week" with overtime, a fact which, he claimed, "frequently resulted in foolish extravagence and sometimes in intemperance."[76]

The extent of such supposed excesses is impossible to judge. Indeed it seems unlikely that many workers were able to indulge in such behavior, given that a family of four or five might spend anything between $400 and $700 per year on food, $300 to $400 on housing, and $200 to $300 on clothing. Not too many families in the government surveys had much to spare once such bills were met, although a few were able to invest. A number of families bought War Savings Stamps or Liberty Bonds—while some families spent nothing or as little as $20 in War Savings, others had $100, $200, or even $600 in Liberty Bonds. Occasionally the worker had little choice but to contribute to the war effort: U.S. Steel deducted a day's wages from workers every two weeks for the Red Cross.[77]

Overall, the war brought "unskilled earnings to the highest point in thirty five years," and earnings of skilled workers rose by as much as 50 to 100 percent in certain industries such as the railways or steel. However, set against this was the fact that such gains were often restoring the position that had applied at the end of the nineteenth century: 1914 figures were misleading for comparison because of the recession that year, and estimated *real* per capita earnings for all industries were not much higher in 1919 than they had been in 1909. Against all wage gains one had to offset the increases in cost of living. While some sources suggested that these had risen during the period 1914–18 by as little as 28 percent in places and 50 percent elsewhere, others suggested figures of over 80 percent. Average figures for the four-year period were put at between 55 and 65 percent. Thus the average increase in real wages was around 20 percent. Those who made such gains could consider themselves fortunate—for some workers, particularly those in white-collar or professional occupations on fixed salaries with limited opportunity for overtime, wages either stood still, declined, or were eroded by wartime inflation.[78]

For all workers, regardless of occupation, the standard of living involved more than money incomes, a fact the government was itself to realize. Wartime change affected the very quality of life, bringing not just economic losses or gains, but also social disruption, emotional strain, and, of course, personal loss. The tensions, conflicts, and problems evident in the Progressive era did not disappear but were, if anything, exacerbated as the war boom and Selective Service created new situations, encouraged internal movements of population to industrial centers creating problems in housing and transportation, and affecting the very health and welfare of the American people. This factor is recognized as significant in black history, and the "Great Migration" of blacks during the war is often a focus of attention. However, the movement of whites and its consequences in social problems and their contributions to labor unrest is rarely acknowledged.

The white migration during the war clearly exceeded that of blacks, but was not as novel or as noticeable. While blacks moved South to North, whites continued to move westward. While northeastern, north-central, and southern states all suffered a net loss in white population, the West gained almost 3 million. However, the other dominant demographic feature of the war years, for whites and blacks, was the increase in urbanization as the movement from the country to the city continued apace. Between 1910 and 1920 the urban population of America grew by 80 percent, the rural by 12 percent. Thus between 1910 and 1920 New York City grew by 800,000 (740,000 white) Chicago by 500,000 (435,000 white) and Philadelphia by 300,000 (250,000 white).[79] But the pattern was by no means uniform. In fact, the rate of increase for many larger cities either slowed or remained constant during the second decade of the century compared with the first, while smaller cities suffered much greater percentage increases. So, as movement to New York fell by 600,000, Chicago grew by almost the same amount as 1900–1910, Detroit's population more than doubled, Akron, Ohio, trebled in size, and Gary, Indiana almost quadrupled. (See table.)

Although these figures are problematical in that their focus is wider than the war years and so give no accurate picure of movement between 1914 and 1918 (and so, for example, obscure the *decline* in population that occurred in places like Bridgeport between 1918 and 1920), they do give some impression of the extent and variation of prewar and wartime growth. For some cities rapid growth had already taken place before the war, and now slowed, while others grew with the demands of the war and the effects of new, growth industries. Thus while growth in New York slowed, reflecting probably the decline in immigration and the slackening in garment manufacture, Chicago, with meat packing, remained attractive to labor. Detroit and Akron were already boomtowns because of the automobile industry and would have continued to grow but probably at a slower rate; Gary and Bethlehem both reflect the growth in steel, although Gary was something of an oddity, having only been established in 1906, but its

POPULATION OF SELECTED CITIES 1900–20
(in order of size)

	1900	% Increase	1910	% Increase	1920
New York	3,400,000	39%	4,800,000	18%	5,600,000
Chicago	1,700,000	29%	2,200,000	23%	2,700,000
Philadelphia	1,300,000	20%	1,500,000	18%	1,800,000
Detroit	285,704	63%	465,766	113%	993,678
Los Angeles	102,479	211%	319,198	81%	576,673
Washington, D.C.	278,718	19%	331,669	32%	437,571
Seattle	80,671	194%	237,194	33%	315,312
Akron (Ohio)	42,728	62%	69,067	202%	208,435
Bridgeport (Conn.)	70,996	44%	102,054	41%	143,555
Des Moines (Iowa)	62,139	28%	86,368	46%	126,468
East St. Louis	29,655	49%	58,547	14%	66,767
Chester (Pa.)	33,988	13%	38,537	51%	58,030
Gary (Ind.)	—	—	16,802	229%	55,378
Bethlehem (Pa.)	23,999	37%	32,810	53%	50,358

Overall National Population Increase: 1900–10 = 21%
1910–20 = 15%

Source: U.S. Dept. of Commerce, Bureau of the Census, *Abstract of the Fourteenth Census of the United States, 1920* Washington, D.C., 1923).

expansion was enormously accelerated by wartime demand. What the war did, then, was to add to, widen, and make people aware of, problems that in many cases had already existed, but if anything, it was the smaller centers of production that suffered most during the war, as they were less accustomed to rapid growth, ill prepared, and limited in their facilities. Housing shortages quickly arose, recreational resources proved insufficient, transportation was often inadequate, and relations between established residents and newcomers were often strained. In that situation of flux and uncertainty it is not surprising that there should have been an increase in labor unrest, outbreaks of racial violence, nor indeed the display of patriotic hysteria that affected so many communities.

The most obvious and immediate problem arising from these shifts in population was housing, and the experience of Bridgeport, Connecticut, was typical of that faced by the smaller war boom community. The commercial capital of Connecticut before 1914, Bridgeport was "the center of the corset trade in America," and also had a few light industries such as the Singer plant, the American Gramophone Co., and American Tube and Stamping Co. With an improved harbor and an industrial base in metalworking, by 1915 Bridgeport was "one of the greatest war order cities in America," shipping two-thirds of all small arms to the Allies. Following the building of a $12 million factory for the Remington Arms Co. employing eighteen thousand workers, the city became known as "the Essen of America." By 1917 the Remington plant employed thirty-six thousand, and the Union Metallic Cartridge company employed eleven thousand. But as a consequence of this rapid expansion the city's population grew by 50,000 in less than a year and jumped from 102,000 in 1910 to 175,000 in 1917. In 1914 the town had two thousand empty houses, but a few months later there was not one vacant house. By 1917 the number of families had grown by twelve thousand, but available housing stock had only increased by six thousand. By the end of 1917 the housing problem had "assumed dangerous and alarming proportions," and one observer wrote that "the conditions under which men and women are living here are dangerous to health, morals, and efficiency."[80]

The situation in Bridgeport was repeated elsewhere. In Akron, Ohio, the tire center of America, dominated by the Goodyear Company, whose work force increased from fifteen thousand in 1915 to thirty-three thousand in 1918, the total population grew by sixty thousand. Living conditions were said to be "exceptionally bad," and by July 1917 there was reported to be "Standing Room Only." In the summer of 1916 some families had lived in tents, and at the end of the war there were still twelve thousand more families in the city than there were homes. Other, larger cities faced similar problems: Buffalo, New York, needed forty-two thousand homes, Chicago required a colossal 288,135, and Philadelphia was suffering "the most critical housing situation in its history." Nationally it was estimated that 1 million new homes were needed.[81]

The results of these shortages are not hard to imagine: chronic congestion became endemic in certain cities, with individuals sleeping three, four, or five to a room, and in some cases even two, three, or four to a bed. In Chester, Pennsylvania, two or three men per bed was said to be common, and also to exist in Philadelphia, and in Gary, Indiana, thirty men were found in one attic sharing thirteen beds between them.[82] Insanitary conditions soon followed. In a housing area near shipyards in Quincy, Massachusetts, inspectors reported that in thirteen lodging houses 241 people were sleeping "in rooms unfit for such purposes on account of overcrowding, unsanitary conditions, and poor ventilation." The report went on:

> In one place we found a boy of 14 years sleeping in the kitchen with his clothes on; in another two men, one woman, and a baby in one room. In another, a man and wife and six children surrounded by filth. The stench that emanated from almost every room upon opening the door was unbearable, so much so that one inspector was compelled to discontinue the work.[83]

More alarming even than this, in Alton, Illinois, in a slum area known as "Dog Town," there was an epidemic of smallpox with over one thousand reported cases.[84]

The area in and around Philadelphia was particularly badly affected, nowhere more so than nearby Chester, where a new locomotive plant and the factories for Remington, Eddystone, and Westinghouse plus shipbuilding, attracted first black and then white workers in large numbers, swelling the population from thirty-eight thousand to an estimated eighty thousand in 1918. The rapid increase in population, its floating character, and inadequate housing produced the results that might be expected. Dwellings that previously had housed four or six people now housed ten to eighteen. One six-room house was given as the address of fifty-four men when they registered for the draft, and a report in September 1918 stated that "overcrowding and congestion of people in small houses has absolutely reached the limit." Many of the black population was said to occupy houses "that had no water and no toilets, whose roofs leaked and whose cellars were flooded," but one investigator found in 1918 that conditions "common in the colored district" were "almost as bad in districts occupied by foreign born people.[85] In Philadelphia poor housing was seen as causing a mounting death rate and increasing infant mortality, and not surprisingly these conditions generally were thought to have done much to encourage the spread of the influenza epidemic that killed five hundred thousand Americans at the end of the war.[86]

As well as causing ill health, which itself could disrupt war work, the housing shortages were at least in part responsible for absenteeism and the high turnover of labor during the war. In Chester, for example, turnover was reported at 15 to 50 percent per month, and the nearby Eddystone plant took on 5,500 additional workers and suffered 5,382 departures in a single month in 1918. In Washington, D.C., "the entire war program" was said to be "suffering from the housing situation," and the shortage was such that the recruiting operations of the government were threatened. An entire file consisted of complaints, mainly from the many new women workers in government, listing cases of overpricing, poor conditions, and overcrowding, and according to one report the War Department was losing workers as quickly as it gained them, with 309 departures and 374 starts in a single week because of housing difficulties.[87] In Bridgeport the situation was so severe by 1917 that a new factory could not be opened for lack of accommodation "except by taking men out of existing plants already working below capacity," and the War Department annnounced that war orders would be reduced in sixty cities because of serious congestion.[88]

Not everywhere was affected by housing problems: a few cities reported more favorable conditions, although with some interesting comments. In Raleigh, North Carolina, there was no congestion to report, nor in Seattle, where (perhaps surprisingly for the home of Skid Row) the mayor could boast "there are no slum conditions here." In San Francisco such crowding as existed was seen as of a different intensity from that of other cities. In Richmond, Virginia, there was no overall congestion, but, said the reporter, "where it does exist here is found chiefly among the negroes, which constitute . . . about 25 or 30 per cent of the city's population. However, that race is gregarious by nature and I doubt if they consider themselves overcongested." A similar comment was made in a report by the Columbus Real Estate Board.

> Aside from the congestion in the colored quarters of the city, industrial labor has never been duly hampered by living conditions, nor is it now contemplated that any additional housing would be required for the influx of 2,000 to 3,000 new workers, should the industrial expansion of the city bring in this most cordially invited addenda to the industrial army of the City of Columbus.

Intent on giving Columbus a good image, the Real Estate Board described the city as one "of homes, agricultural and rural happiness at the doors of a teeming commercial and vocational beehive."[89]

The racial comments made of Richmond and Columbus were revealing both of an obvious problem and of complacent and prejudiced white attitudes. Elsewhere, housing was often a root cause of racial competition and violence. In East St. Louis, scene of a major race riot in 1917, housing conditions "were almost indescribable." A report of 1918 said blacks inhabited "the poorest kind of housing" and described one area as "all unpainted shacks with no sewerage, no walks, no gardens, no lawns." The same kind of comment was made of black areas in Chicago, the chief destination for many of the black migrants, and, following numerous clashes over housing, the scene of the worst of a wave of riots in 1919.[90]

Besides adding to mounting racial problems in the United States, housing, if only because of cost, was a cause of general discontent and dissatisfaction among workers and most certainly a contributory factor to the outbreak of industrial unrest in 1917. In Bridgeport for instance, population had clearly overrun resources—"Recreation facilities are swamped. Lawbreaking and drunkenness are on the increase. Traffic problems are suddenly acute, and the school authorities don't know what to do with the children." Coupled with this was the fact that Bridgeport, formerly a conservative, nonunion town, now witnessed the growth of organized labor intent on winning better working conditions and higher wages to enable their members to improve their home situations. The dilution of labor and the attack on the position of skilled machinists on the shop floor to increase efficiency only added fuel to an already enflamed situation, creating "a seething cauldron," which manifested itself in the wave of strikes that affected the city from 1915 through to the final wartime confrontation of 1918. While the employers blamed agitators and un-patriotic elements, labor argued that conditions were "so bad that the workers would stand them no longer." Whatever the real cause, in one two-and-a-half-month period alone in 1917, there were fifty-five separate strikes. The last major dispute, from Easter to July 1918, finally culminated in the presidential letter ordering the strikers back to work.[91]

Directly or indirectly housing was acknowledged as vital to the war effort. At the close of the war a government committee could record that "the war has demonstrated in both Europe and America that the living conditions of industrial workers are a potent factor in production." The governor of New York agreed. Appointing a housing commission in 1919, he said, "The war made apparent how fundamental adequate housing is in relation to labor supply."[92] This new awareness was one of the positive consequences of the war. As a housing expert said, "The war has put housing 'on the map' in this country," and another suggested in 1918 that "the housing problem in the United States has been moved up at least a generation. Where yesterday it was with many industrial organizations a matter of sentiment or casual experiment, it is today a problem of grim necessity. . . ."[93] As this statement suggests, housing had been among Progressive concerns, and the problems of the city slums had led to tenement laws and the development of Garden City plans in a number of areas. Now, however, as the writer testified, the problem of housing had moved beyond the concern of state and municipal authorities or industrial organizations, and had become a matter for central government itself.

Initially, however, as in so many other cases, the federal government was not involved at all, but preferred to leave the matter to local authorities and private industries to solve. Thus in Bridgeport there was at first little or no action on the housing front, but finally the Remington Arms Company was forced to act. It established its own real estate department and built several hundred units of family housing and fourteen dormitories, including accommodation for four thousand women workers. When it became apparent that even greater effort was required a group of manufacturers formed the Bridgeport Housing Corporation in 1917 to build tenements and housing. The first family apartments and the first of 140 tenements were completed in August 1917, and by October the corporation had built houses for almost five hundred families. All told, the corporation provided a thousand new units in different city locations.[94]

The Bridgeport Housing Corporation was an example for other towns, and similar groups were established in cities such as Cleveland, Ohio, and Kenosha, Wisconsin. Various manufacturers also moved into the accommodation business. In Akron, Firestone built homes; in Duluth the Minnesota Steel Company did; while Du Pont, the big explosives manufacturer, representing "the new order of benevolently autocratic employers," built entire workers' villages in Penns Grove, New Jersey, Wilmington, Delaware, and Hopewell, Virginia. As one reporter pointed out, such "villages" could be of variable quality, and this was true of much of the housing provided by employers. The Chester Shipbuilding Company, for instance, housed 140 men in a garage and another seventy-eight in a single old building, seven or eight to a room.[95]

Such efforts made it apparent that neither local state nor municipal authorities nor private companies were able or willing to cope with the additional burdens placed upon war centers by the influx of new workers. The Bridgeport Chamber of Commerce pointed this out in September 1917 and suggested "that the government should offer financial assistance to help this situation in such industrial centers as Bridgeport, Wilmington, Flint, Akron, etc." Charles Harris Whitaker, editor of the *Journal of the American Institute of Architects,* in a letter to the *New York Times* argued that "no adequate means of relief is possible unless government funds are made available," and in a detailed outline to the government he proposed that the federal government should follow the British example and take over unoccupied properies, fix rents and prices, buy land, and build homes. "Industrial organization," he wrote, "is the key to the duration of the war. The key to industrial organization is proper living conditions."[96]

Once more British war experience provided a pertinent example for America, and one that was not lost upon reformers in the United States. Although a much greater precedent for state involvement in housing already existed in Britain, the war "marked a turning point both in the importance attached to housing as an instrument of social policy and in the scale of housing provision by the state."[97] Pressures similar to those experienced in America led the Ministry of Munitions to allocate 4.3 million pounds for housing between 1915 and 1918, and while much of this was temporary accommodation some ten thousand permanent homes were built on best garden city lines.

Such developments clearly were an inspiration for Progressive housing reformers across the Atlantic in 1917, but by then the first steps toward government involvement in housing had already been taken. A housing section had been established within the subcommittee on welfare of the Committee of Labor on the Council of National Defense as early as May 1917. Its first task was the gathering of information (one might say ammunition), and its chairman, Philip Hiss, an architect, sent questionnaires to more than one hundred cities in August requesting information on their housing needs. At the end of August he organized an informal conference of housing, planning, and architectural experts, which agreed on the need for federal intervention. In October the Committee of National Defense established a committee on housing chaired by Otto M. Eidlitz, a civil engineer, housing reformer, and head of a New York building company. This body again reported that housing shortages threatened war production and called for federal funds to alleviate the situation. Still there was no action. The administration remained reluctant to become involved in an area traditionally outside of its concern, and it was besides hampered by the adjournment of Congress, which made the passage of required legislation impossible. In January 1918 Philip Hiss wrote to the President, quoting the British example in war housing, and suggested that Wilson had "the chance to weld capital and labor together into an irresistible industrial machine" by means of a housing program. Finally, in March 1918, while legislation was pending, the president provided funds for the initial organization to begin, and in May Congress authorized an appropriation of $60 million, subsequently raised to $100 million, to establish the United States Housing Corporation. That this was a major departure was clear; as one observer remarked, Congress "would not for a moment have dreamed of considering favorably this project of the government going into the housing business, which some of them term 'state socialism' except as a means of winning the war." "But," as another commentator on housing wrote, "war changes everything."[98]

The government was, however, already in the "housing business" through the U.S. Shipping Board Emergency Fleet Corporation, which had been providing funds itself for the building of homes for shipyard workers since the Hiss subcommittee findings of 1917. By the end of the war the Emergency Fleet Corporation had spent approximately $64 million improving transportation and building over nine thousand homes and one thousand apartments accommodating some thirty thousand people in twenty-three cities. The Housing Corporation was actually to build rather fewer than this with six thousand homes and a number of dormitories in eighty cities including, of course, Bridgeport, Chester, Philadelphia, and Washington, D.C. The corporation also provided a home registration service listing vacant accommodation and helping to place individuals and families. More building projects might have been completed but for the sudden end to the war and but for the fact that the corporation opted to build substantial, permanent homes of a high standard rather than quickly built but temporary dwellings. Indeed, one of the criticisms made of the program by an always skeptical Congress was their "unnecessary excellence." This was often attributed to the presence in the corporation of reformers such as Otto M. Eidlitz, I. N. Phelps Stokes of New York, and Lawrence Veiller, a leading prewar housing reform advocate and director of the National Housing Association—" 'College professors and alleged experts,' " as one committee described them.[99]

Peace brought an abrupt end to the housing program, and completed projects were sold off in the postwar years. The last property was sold in June 1945, and the Housing Corporation was finally liquidated in the 1950s. Yet despite its brief history, the corporation was of some significance. As a contemporary writer observed:

> for the first time in our national history an effort has been made to deal with industrial community life in accordance with a carefully planned and liberal-minded policy. True, any general social purposes . . . were largely subordinated to the object in view—the prosecution of the war; but it is this very fact that gives the government's policy its real significance. The war has emphasized as never before the vital relation of decent living conditions to production. . . .

According to a more recent expert in the field, the wartime federal housing program "inspired a generation of architects and planners" and established "a precedent for the more elaborate and continuous federal housing program of the 1930s."[100]

Housing was not the only matter to become a subject of concern during the war—a number of related issues affecting the health and welfare of the American people arose as a consequence of wartime conditions and pressures. The shortage of labor, and the emphasis on maximum production with the most efficient use of all resources, human as well as material, encouraged a concern for the protection or conservation of the health of the population. "At no time," said the Assistant Surgeon General J. C. Perry, "has the efficiency of labor been of such paramount importance," and he argued that "it is as vital to maintain the health of our army of workers as it is that of our military forces." His point was given added force by revelations of the draft boards, which found that 30 percent of all registrants were unfit for armed service. These findings startled and shocked many Americans and strengthened demands that health be seen as a vital "factor in national efficiency."[101] National efficiency was clearly affected by overcrowding and congestion in centers of war production, and in August 1918 the Commission on Living Conditions of War Workers was approved by the War Labor Policies Board and established from Housing Corporation funds "to centralize and co-ordinate all efforts, both public and private, to secure proper living conditions and recreational opportunities for war workers." The committee had barely had time to come into being before the war ended, and the same was true of plans within the Public Health Service "to survey conditions in all war industry towns and to provide health administration where necessary." Proposals to provide medical examinations of all war workers also came to nothing.[102]

Individual states were spurred into action by Selective Service health findings, either providing data for the Public Health Service or, in some cases, giving free treatment to men rejected for military service on medical grounds. But the demand for greater federal involvement in public health continued. If the need for health conservation was accepted, ran one argument, then this could only be achieved by action at a national level. Another argument was that the nation should reward the workers' loyal participation "by giving health to labor," and that a step in that direction would be the creation of a separate and independent Public Health Service.[103] Senator Owen of Oklahoma, a longtime advocate of such a measure, suggested that the president use his authority under the Overman Act to do just this; another writer urged the president to heed the lessons of the war and to use the opportunity presented by the influenza epidemic to take action. President Wilson was not persuaded. "I should feel that this was an inopportune time to suggest to Congress the expenses and elaboration of such an instrumentality," he replied.[104]

The president was not, however, totally opposed to federal action in the area of health, and he supported the Children's Bureau in what was probably the most significant wartime action to improve health standards, a campaign to reduce infant mortality. Like other groups of reformers, members of the Children's Bureau used the war situation to argue for greater care for children, the citizens (and soldiers) of the future. The war emphasized the waste of human resources in civilian America—pointing out that the "number of children under a year old who die each year in the United States is greater than the total number of United States soldiers killed in France," the bureau suggested that the "cradle was more fatal than the trench."[105] Spurred on by the example of other warring nations and funded with $150,000 from the President's Defense Appropriation, the bureau launched a national program of health education entitled "Children's Year" on the anniversary of American entry into the war, 6 April 1918. Repeated the following year, the campaign provided information on the feeding and care of babies for their mothers and involved the weighing and measuring of some six million infants. The effects of this campaign were not temporary. A number of states established child hygiene divisions in their public health departments, and California alone set up twenty-two permanent child health centers as a consequence of the bureau's initiative. Perhaps influenced by the suggestion that children's health centers would be fitting memorials to soldiers, 132 were established in twenty-four states. This program did not, like so many others, end with the coming of peace, but led to the passage in 1921 of the Maternity and Infancy Care Act (the Sheppard-Towner Act), which provided federal funds on a matching basis for the development of state maternal and child health care centers. By 1929 some three thousand such centers had been established in forty-five states, and the number of general public health centers, a mere twelve in 1917, had risen to four hundred in 1920 and one thousand in 1927. In part at least as a consequence of these developments there was "a substantial decrease in infant mortality" between 1915 and 1921, and this continued in the postwar period as infant mortality declined from seventy-five to sixty-eight per thousand live births between 1921 and 1929.[106]

The one other group in the American population to benefit in terms of health care during the war was, paradoxically, that most at risk—the men in the armed forces. One of the many issues raised by the opponents of Selective Service had been the possible harmful effects of military services on the physical and moral well-being of American boys. This was a reflection both of the traditionally low opinion most Americans had of their armies and servicemen, and of past experiences—the Civil War and the Spanish-American War were notorious for the high death rates due to disease and poor medical attention. Not surprisingly then, once Selective Service was in operation propaganda was needed to overcome such prejudices. One recruiting poster claimed "The United States Army Builds *MEN*," and behind the figure of an upright soldier were images representing character, physique, and crafts. A CPI advertisement also suggested that "He Will Come Back a Better Man!" and said "that boy of yours" would return "strong in body, quick and sure in action, alert and keen in mind, firm and resolute in character, calm and even-tempered."[107] The fact that he might return dead or disabled was not considered.

However innocent, the propaganda had some justification. One contemporary historian wrote that "it took war to give comfort and sufficiency to millions who had not known them. Most of the soldiers were better clothed, better fed, and better housed than when at home, and their health was much better." Although this might sound like "war is a good thing," the claim was substantiated by other writers who alleged that the American soldier was said to have weighed twelve pounds more in 1918 than he did before the war began.[108] Certainly officials at the time boasted of the fact that disease caused fewer deaths than battle for the first time in American history and reflected with some pride upon the large number (forty-two thousand) of doctors in the army. If such sources might be questioned, they were supported by the soldiers themselves who sang of some of the merits of military service (including the minimum rate of pay):

> Oh, the army, the army, the democratic army,
> They clothe you and feed you because the army needs you
> Hash for breakfast, beans for dinner, stew for suppertime,
> Thirty dollars every month, deducting twenty-nine.
> Oh, the army, the army, the democratic army,
> The Jews, the Wops, and the Dutch and Irish Cops,
> They're all in the army now![109]

As well as physical health, the moral well-being of young men removed from the protective (and, implicitly, female) environment of home to an all-masculine society was a concern of the army. Again, one can detect strong overtones of the Progressive morality here and a sense that war was seen by some as an opportunity to enact reform. The manifestation of this was a campaign to educate servicemen about the risks involved in sexual liaisons, coupled with an attempt to prevent such encounters from occurring. Sections Twelve and Thirteen of the Selective Service Act prohibited the sale of alcohol to men in uniform and outlawed prostitution in areas around military camps. Combined with these restrictions was a positive program that would, according to Secretary of the Navy Josephus Daniels, "surround the men in service with an environment not only clean and wholesome, but also positively inspiring."

This program was organized through the Commission on Training Camp Activities under the direction of Raymond Fosdick, a young lawyer and reformer from the Settlement Houses, and a friend of both Newton Baker and Woodrow Wilson. The commission was, under Fosdick's leadership, responsible for the closure of over one hundred red-light districts, and he could claim that "through the efforts of this Commission" such areas had "practically ceased to be a feature of American life." Instead of temptation, troops in military camps were provided with organized programs of sports, recreation, and entertainment, which were described as "unique," and "perhaps the largest social program ever undertaken."[110] Assisted by the united efforts of the YMCA, YWCA, National Catholic War Council, Jewish Welfare Board, Salvation Army, and American Library Association, which together had raised $203 million by November 1918, the commission catered for the soldiers' social and spiritual needs, providing post exchanges, hostess houses, libraries, and educational material. Social problems were also dealt with through the War Camp Community Service with a staff of over four hundred social workers, and by the Red Cross Home Service, which involved over seven thousand social workers in ten thousand communities.[111]

At the end of the war much of this work ended, but Fosdick's commission had some lasting success. Venereal disease in the army was reduced by over 300 percent in the eighteen months of war, and public awareness of the problem rose. The number of free, public clinics for treatment increased from 25 in 1918 to 260 in 1919, and at the end of the war there began "a Nation-wide movement to conquer" sexually transmitted disease. The *New York World* reported that "more than thirty thousand professionally immoral women already have been taken in hand by the War Department, the Navy Department, and the Public Health Service and treated for contagious ailments," and Congress provided an appropriation of $4 million over two years for research to be carried out by the newly created Venereal Disease Division of the Public Health Service, which took over activities in this area from the War Training Camp Activities Commission.[112]

A more lasting, and significant, legacy of the war for servicemen was that resulting from "one of the most remarkable and interesting pieces of social legislation produced by the war"—the War Risk Insurance Act as amended in October 1917. Originally introduced in 1914 to cover American shipping, War Risk Insurance was extended first to merchant seamen and then to all American servicemen, with federal government indemnification rather than that of private insurance companies for whom the problem was too big. The scheme was enthusiastically supported by Secretary of the Treasury McAdoo, who saw it as a way for "this great progressive Nation" to "set the example," and as a means "to popularize the war."[113] The insurance provided monthly allotments for dependent families and compensation for death or disability. By 1942 the government was paying almost $300 million annually in disability pensions and $65 million in death benefits through what had become "the largest life insurance company in the world" and which was administered through the Veterans' Bureau, created in 1921.[114]

Perhaps not surprisingly the War Risk Insurance plan was drawn up by people with a reform background—Judge Mack of Cook County Juvenile Court and Julia Lathrop of the Children's Bureau, for instance. Moreover, the passage of the act encouraged demands for the extension of social insurance generally. While workmen's compensation laws continued to be enacted at state level, various schemes for health insurance were also under consideration during, and at the end of, the war. However, such proposals were opposed by private insurance companies and the American Medical Association, which described such ideas as "made in Germany" or, after 1918, "made in Russia."[115] Insurance schemes were also victims of the general reaction of 1919 and the conservatism that followed. Rather than government intervention in this area, it was the industrialists who offered protection schemes, or alternatively the individual worker took care of his own—or did without. For most Americans, the best form of insurance was still seen as regular work with a decent wage. For both returning servicemen and war workers it remained to be seen whether they would be able to achieve that goal; for organized labor it remained to be seen if it would maintain its wartime gains; for the often congested centers of war production it remained to be seen whether their problems would be solved or disappear in the postwar era.

Notes

Unions, Government, and Labor Relations

1. Gordon S. Watkins, *Labor Problems and Labor Administration in the United States During the World War* (Urbana, Ill., 1919), 18.
2. Melvyn Dubofsky, *Industrialism and the American Worker, 1865–1920* (Arlington Heights, Ill., 1975), 114.
3. Ibid., 108.
4. "The Right Hand to Labor," 18 November 1916, in Albert Bushnell Hart, ed., *Selected Addresses and Public Papers of Woodrow Wilson* (New York, 1918) 166.
5. Arthur S. Link and William B. Catton, *American Epoch: A History of the United States Since the 1890s* (New York, 1963), Vol 1., 72; David A. Shannon, *The Progressive Era* (Chicago, 1974), 107–8.
6. See chapter 1, p. 6 and Howard Berkowitz and Kirk McQuaid, *Creating the Welfare State: The Political Economy of Twentieth Century Reform* (New York, 1950), 20.
7. U.S. Dept. of Commerce, Bureau of the Census, *Earnings of Factory*

Workers 1899 to 1927: An Analysis of Payroll Statistics (Washington, D.C., 1929), 45.

8. Albert K. Steigerwalt, *The National Association of Manufacturers 1895–1914: A Study in Business Leadership,* Michigan Business Studies 16, no. 2 (Grand Rapids, 1964): 109–13; David Brody, *Workers in Industrial America: Essays on the 20th Century Struggle* (New York and Oxford, 1980), 26.

9. John S. Smith, "Organized Labor and Government in the Wilson Era; 1913–1921: Some Conclusions," *Labor History* 3, no. 3 (Fall 1962): 265.

10. Franklin H. Martin, *Digest of the Proceedings of the Council of National Defense . . . ,* 73d U.S. Congress, Senate, 2d Session, Doc. 193, 1934, 249–53; Frederick Palmer, *Newton D. Baker: America at War* (New York, 1931), 260.

11. Harold J. Tobin and Percy W. Bidwell, *Mobilizing Civilian America* (New York, 1940), 115, 117. In Britain 38 percent of male workers were in the forces, and in Germany an amazing 82 percent of draft age.

12. Watkins, *Labor Problems,* 59–60.

13. Department of Labor, Bureau of Labor Statistics Industrial Service Division Survey, in U.S. Housing Corporation, NARG 3, Series 75, Surveys and Statistics Division, Boxes 348, 350.

14. Watkins, *Labor Problems,* 56–57.

15. W. B. Wilson to Woodrow Wilson, 15 June 1918, in Dept. of Labor, NARG 174, 2, Box 208, File 19/16.

16. Tobin and Bidwell, *Mobilizing Civilian America,* 125; William Ganson Rose, *Cleveland: The Making of a City* (Cleveland and New York, 1950), 762; also see file called "Industrial Conscription in Agriculture," Dept. of Labor, NARG 174, Series 4, Box 208, File 20/16.

17. 20 July 1918, in "Daily Digest," National War Labor Policies Board (NWLPB), NARG 1, Series 2, Box 43.

18. Darrell Hevenor Smith, *The United States Employment Service: Its History, Activities and Organization* (Baltimore, 1923), 61; Alexander L. Trachtenberg, ed., *American Labor Year Book, 1919–20* (New York, 1920), 70.

19. NWLPB, NARG 1, 2, "Public Service Reserve File," Box 29, "History of The Public Service Reserve," 11 June 1918.

20. Smith, *The U.S. Employment Service,* 14; Wilson to Burleson, 26 January 1920, and Gompers to Wilson, 3 August 1917, in Dept. of Labor, Office of Secretary, NARG 174, Box 209.

21. "Brief on Labor Situation and Problems in California," 1917, Felix Frankfurter Papers, Box 150, LC.

22. Pedro Rodriguez to Section of Labor, 31 October, 1918, "Puerto Rican Complaints File," WLPB, NARG 1, 2, Box 10; "Report of Activities of the Commission on Living Conditions of War Workers" and "Report on Investigation of Living Conditions of Puerto Ricans Employed on Army Construction Projects," U.S. Housing Corp., Office of the President, General Records, Commission on Living Conditions, NARG 3, Box 5 and Box 10.

23. "Prison Labor File," WLPB, NARG 1, 2, Box 29.

24. *New York Times,* 5, 11 August 1918: U.S. Congress, House of Representatives, Committee on Labor, *Hearings To Employ Convict Labor*

for the Production of War Supplies, 65th Congress, 2d Sess., H.R. 7353, 18 January 1918.

25. American Spinning Company, Greenville, South Carolina, August 1918, quoted in memo to F. Frankfurter 1 August 1918, WLPB, NARG I, *2*, Box 9.
26. "Labor and the War," 7 September 1914, "American Labor's Position in Peace or in War," 12 March 1917, in Gompers, *American Labor and the War* (New York, 1919), 29, 295.
27. Press releases, 5, 25 April 1917, Walsh papers, LC, Box 166.
28. AFL, *Report of the Proceedings of the Thirty-Seventh Annual Convention, Buffalo, New York, 1917* (Washington, D.C., 1917), 67.
29. Gompers, "Always the Fight for Freedom," 23 January 1918, in *American Labor and the War*, 165.
30. Gompers, "The Double Duty of Americans," Milwaukee, 6 June 1918, *American Labor*, 207; Wilson, "Labor and the War," 12 November 1917, in Hart, *Selected Addresses*, 229–30.
31. See Gompers, *American Labor*, 115, 186, 262.
32. Alexander Bing, *Wartime Strikes and Their Adjustment* (New York, 1921), 292–93; Watkins, *Labor Problems*, 83; War Industries Board, *History of Prices During the War* (Washington, D.C., 1919), 41.
33. Melvyn Dubofsky, *We Shall Be All: A History of the I.W.W.* (Chicago, 1969), 349; Felix Frankfurter, "Plan for Dealing with so-called I.W.W. strikes and western labor troubles," 4 September 1917, in *Papers 44*, 161.
34. Memo, Woodrow Wilson to W. B. Wilson, 19 September 1917, Dept. of Labor, NARG 174, Box 82, 20.
35. Michael E. Parrish, *Felix Frankfurter and His Times: The Reform Years* (New York and London, 1982), 85, 87–95; W. B. Wilson to Woodrow Wilson, 31 August 1917, Dept. of Labor, NARG 174, Box 82, 20/473; President's Mediation Commission, *Report to the President of the United States* (Washington, D.C. 1918), 6.
36. James W. Byrkit, *Forging the Copper Collar: Arizona's Labor-Management War of 1901–1921* (Tucson, 1982), 69; Walter Douglas to Franklin K. Lane, 8 June 1917, Dept. of Labor, NARG 174, Box 205, 13/82; Mediation Commission, *Report*, 6.
37. Letter to Hugh L. Kerwin, Assistant Secretary of Labor, from Hywel Davies, 21 October 1918, Dept. of Labor, NARG 174, Box 84, 20/473. Mediation Commission, *Report*, 5.
38. "Brief on Labor Situation and Problems in California," prepared by State Commission on Immigration and Housing, 1917, Frankfurter Papers, Box 150, LC.
39. Mediation Commission, *Report*, 14.
40. Submission to Mediation Commission, Lumbermen's Protective League, n.d., Dept. of Labor, RG 174, *2*, Mediation Commission Files.
41. T. H. MacDonald, County Attorney, Flathead, Montana, to Attorney General, Thomas W. Gregory, 21 August 1917; and Wade R. Parks, Attorney, Thompson Falls, Montana, to Gregory, 29 August 1917, Walsh Papers, Box 191, LC.
42. Trachtenberg, *American Labor Year Book, 1919–20*, 191.
43. Newton Baker to Woodrow Wilson, 20 September, 1917, Department of Labor, NARG 174, Series I, Box 18, 8/102G.

44. Dubofsky, *We Shall Be All*, 412–13; Trachtenberg, *American Labor Year Book*, 195.
45. W. B. Wilson to Gompers, 5 April 1918, "Report on the Mooney Dynamite Cases in San Francisco Submitted by President Wilson's Mediation Commission, January 16, 1981," Dept. of Labor, Chief Clerk's File, NARG 174, Box 50, 16/510; John Lombardi, *Labor's Voice in the Cabinet: A History of the Department of Labor* (New York, 1942), 223–27.
46. Lombardi, *Labor's Voice*, 221.
47. Bing, *Wartime Strikes*, 15.
48. See Valerie Jean Conner, *The National War Labor Board; Stability, Social Justice, and the Voluntary State in World War I* (Chapel Hill, N.C.), 1983.
49. Ibid., ix.
50. Louis B. Wehle, "Labor Problems in the United States During the War," *Quarterly Journal of Economics*, 31 (February 1918): 334.
51. U.S. Dept. of Labor, National War Labor Board, *Report of the Secretary of the National War Labor Board* (Washington, D.C., 1920); AFL executive committee, in Marc Karson, *American Labor Unions and Politics 1900–1918* (Carbondale, Ill., 1958), 100–101.
52. Trachtenberg, *American Labor Year Book*, 49; Bing, *Wartime Strikes* 191; see NWLB, "Awards and Findings," NWLPB NARG 1, Box 27.
53. NWLPB, "Awards and Findings;" Conner, *National War Labor Board*, 67.
54. Conner, *National War Labor Board*, 90.
55. David Montgomery, *Workers' Control in America: Studies in the history of work, technology, and labor struggles* (Cambridge [England], London, and New York, 1981), 96.
56. NWLB Docket 22, "Machinists and Electrical Workers . . . vs Bethlehem Steel," findings, 31 July 1918, in Dept. of Labor, Women in Industry Service, NARG 86, Box 4; *New York Times*, 13 August 1918.
57. David Brody, *Workers in Industrial America: Essays on the Twentieth Century Struggle* (New York and Oxford, 1980), 55; J. R. Commons, Selig Perlman, Philip Taft, *History of Labor in the United States, 1896–1932: Labour Movements* (New York, 1935), IV, 408–9; Stuart D. Brandes, *American Welfare Capitalism 1880–1940* (Chicago and London, 1976), 126–28.
58. Bing, *Wartime Strikes*, 107–8; Conner, *National War Labor Board*, 131–33; Edward Berman, *Labor Disputes and the President of the United States; Studies in History, Economics and Public Law* 111, no. 2 (New York, 1924): 142–149.
59. Montgomery, *Workers' Control*, 127–33; Bing, *Wartime Strikes*, 73–79; Albert Shaw, ed., *Messages and Papers of Woodrow Wilson* (New York, 1924), 515–16; see also *Papers 45*, 95–6, 234; Wilson Papers CF 4341, Reel 366 LC.
60. Wilson to William L. Hutcheson, President, Brotherhood of Carpenters, 17 February 1918, in Wilson Papers and *Papers 46*, 377.
61. Trachtenberg, *American Labor Year Book*, 51, 53; U.S. Secretary of Labor, *Sixth Annual Report*, 107.
62. General Orders No. 13, Office of Chief of Ordnance, Washington, D.C., 15 November 1917, in *Quarterly Journal of Economics* (February 1918): 387–90, and *Official Bulletin*, 15 November 1918.

63. Liva Baker, *Felix Frankfurter* (New York, 1969), 78.
64. Frankfurter to Stanley King, 25 October 1917, Department of Labor, NARG 174, Series 2, Box 193; Parrish, *Felix Frankfurter and His Times*, 108–10.
65. See Gerald D. Nash, "Franklin Roosevelt and Labor: The World War I Origins of Early New Deal Policy," *Labor History* 1 (Winter 1960): 39–52.
66. W. B. Wilson to Joseph Valentine, President of the Molders' Union, 16 May 1919, Dept. of Labor, NARG 174, Box 208, File 19/19; and Memo, same file, "The Present Status of the National War Labor Board."
67. "Politics and Labor: A Serious Attack on the Modern Drift," *Open Shop Review*, 1918 in cuttings, files Hugh L. Kerwin, Assistant Secretary of Labor, NARG 174, 8–453, and letter, William C. Liller, to Kerwin, 30 October 1918.
68. Chamber of Commerce, Committee on Industrial Relations, "Report to Board of Directors," 15 November 1918, in WLPB, NARG 1, 2, Box 8.
69. Leo Wolman, *The Growth of American Trade Unions 1880–1923* (New York, 1924), 33–4.
70. R. S. and H. M. Lynd, *Middletown: A Study in Modern American Culture* (Chicago, 1929), 53–54; Montgomery, *Workers' Control*, 96: Tobin and Bidwell, *Mobilizing Civilian America*, 118; Preston W. Slosson, *The Great Crusade and After, 1914–1928* (New York, 1930), 172.
71. Bing, *Wartime Strikes*, 131; Smith, "Organized Labor and Government in the Wilson Era," 269.

Wartime Standards of Living

72. "Our Labor Plutocrats," *Saturday Evening Post*, 5 January 1918.
73. Rosenwald to W. S. Gifford, CND, 22 June 1918; Wild to Gifford, 22 June 1918; and letter from Conservation Division, WIB, 10 June 1918, Chief Clerk's file, Dept. of Labor, NARG 174, Series I, Box 58, 15–86.
74. Godfrey M. Lebhar, *Chain Stores in America, 1859–1950* (New York, 1952), 13; Slosson, *The Great Crusade*, 184; John B. Rae, *The American Automobile—A Brief History* (Chicago, 1965), 70–71; Herbert F. Janick, *A Diverse People: Connecticut to the Present* (Chester, Conn., 1975), 4–5.
75. "Schedules Cost of Living 1918–19," Dept. of Labor, Bureau of Labor Statistics, NARG 257, Boxes 610–13, 665; Watkins, *Labor Problems*, 101.
76. Bing, *Wartime Strikes*, 185; Watkins, *Labor Problems*, 101; Conner, *National War Labor Board*, 59; Dept. of Labor, "Schedules Cost of Living," Pittsburgh: U.S. Housing Corporation, NARG 3, Series 75, Surveys and Statistics Division, Box 350.
77. James B. Lane, *City of the Century: A History of Gary, Indiana* (Bloomington, Ind., and London, 1978), 88; Dept. of Labor "Schedules, Cost of Living."
78. Tobin and Bidwell, *Mobilizing Civilian America*, 118; Whitney Coombs, *The Wages of Unskilled Labor in Manufacturing Industries . . . 1890–1924* (New York, 1926), 119–20; U.S. Dept. of Commerce, Bureau of the Census, *Earnings of Factory Workers, 1899–1927* (Washington, D.C., 1929), 45; Trachtenberg, *American Labor Year Book 1919–20*, 256–58;

Jurgen Kocka, *White Collar Workers in America 1890–1940: A Social Political History* (London, 1980), 155–56.

79. See U.S. Dept. of Commerce, Bureau of the Census, *Abstract of the Fourteenth Census 1920* (Washington, D.C. 1923) and U.S. Dept. of Commerce, Bureau of Census, *Historical Statistics of the United States, 1789–1945* (Washington, D.C. 1949), 30–31.

80. Janick, *A Diverse People*, 4–5; Zenas L. Potter, "War-Boom Towns: Bridgeport," *The Survey* 35, 4 December 1915; "The War-Boom Town in America," *Living Age* 290, September 1916; *Bridgeport Telegraph*, 20 October 1917; letter, Bridgeport Chamber of Commerce to Philip Hiss, 4 September 1917, USHC, Office of President, NARG 3, Series I, Box 1.

81. Telegram, Carl Wyatt to Frank Morrison, AFL, 2 October 1917, in USHC, files, Box 1; "Akron: Standing Room Only!" *McClure's*, 49, no. 3 (July 1917); Francis C. Wickware, ed., *The American Year Book: A Record of Events and Progress 1919* (New York and London, 1920), 247–49; New York State Reconstruction Commission, *Housing Conditions: Report of the Housing Committee of Reconstruction Commission of the State of New York* (Albany, March 1920), 6. "Program of Disposition of War Housing and Transportation Properties of the United States Government . . .," 30 June 1919, USHC, Office of President, NARG 3, Box 5, 12; U.S. Dept. of Commerce, Bureau of Census, *Fourteenth Census, 1920: Population* (Washington, D.C., 1921), 1046.

82. "Report of Preliminary Survey of Housing Needs in the Tacony, Philadelphia, Conshohocken, and Chester Districts, July 15th to 23rd 1918," in USHC, Surveys and Statistics Division, NARG 3, Series 75, Box 374; *Housing Betterment* 6, no. 4 (December 1917): 17.

83. Letter, W. N. Buchan, Chairman Dept. of Health, to Mayor, Quincy, Mass., 26 March 1918, in U.S. Dept. of Labor, Bureau of Industrial Housing and Transportation, *Report of the United States Housing Corporation: War Emergency Construction (Housing War Workers)* (Washington, D.C., 1920), 8.

84. Dept. of Labor, *Report of the U.S. Housing Corporation*, 4.

85. "Report of Preliminary Survey of Housing Needs in the Tacony, Philadelphia, Conshohocken, and Chester Districts, July 15th–23rd 1918"; "Report of Housing and Sanitary Conditions in Chester, September 30, 1918", Box 5; John Ihlder, "How War Came to Chester," *The Survey* (1 June 1918): 243–46.

86. *Philadelphia Public Ledger*, 27 October 1918; Ihlder, "How War Came to Chester," 245.

87. "Washington Housing," USHC, Office of the President, Commission on Living Conditions, NARG 3, Box 13; John McIlhenny, et al. to President, 16 September 1918, WLPB, NARG I, Series 2, Box 7; "Report of Preliminary Survey . . . Chester," "Report of Investigation of Needs of Women in the Eddystone District," November 1st–6th 1918, USHC, Surveys and Statistics Division, NARG 3, Series 75, Box 374; *Housing Betterment* 7, no. 3 (October 1918): 41–42.

88. *Housing Betterment* 7, no. 3 (October 1918): 44; National Housing Association to President Wilson, 30 November 1917, in *Housing Betterment* 6, no. 4 (December 1917): 4–5.

89. Letters to Philip Hiss in response to inquiry of August 1917, in U.S. Housing Corp., Office of President, NARG 3, Series I, Box 2; "Report

City of Columbus, Ohio," 8 October 1918, USHC, Surveys and Statistics Division NARG 3, Series 75, Box 363.

90. Chicago Commission on Race Relations, *The Negro in Chicago: A Study of Race Relations and a Race Riot* (Chicago, 1922), 3, 152; Memo, W. E. Holmes to F. C. Butler, Community Organization Branch, Industrial Service Section, Ordnance Dept., 22 June 1918, in WLPB, NARG I, Series 2, Box 10; J. N. Fining, East St. Louis Chamber of Commerce to Philip Hiss, 20 August 1917, USHC, Office of President, NARG 3, Series I, Box 1.

91. The labor conflict in Bridgeport is examined by Cecelia Bucki, "Dilution and Craft Tradition: Bridgeport, Connecticut, Munitions Workers, 1915–19," *Social Science History* 4, (Winter 1980): 105–25; and in Montgomery, *Workers' Control,* 127–33. See also Potter, "War-Boom Towns," 237, 270, 270–72.

92. Memo, Commission on Living Conditions of War Workers to W. B. Wilson, 10 December 1918, WLPB, NARG 1, Series 2, Box 9; New York State Reconstruction Commission, *Housing Conditions,* 1.

93. Noble Foster Hoggson, "The Challenge of the Housing Problem," *The Hoggson Magazine* 4, no. 2 (March 1918); Robert D. Kohn, "Housing in a Reconstruction Program," *The Survey,* 31 May 1919.

94. Potter, "War-Boom Towns," 240; M. Proctor and B. Matuszeski, *Gritty Cities: A Second Look at Allentown, Bethlehem, Bridgeport . . .* (Philadelphia, 1978), 74; Bridgeport Housing Corp. to P. Hiss, 22 August 1917, USHC, Office of President, NARG 3, I, Box 1.

95. Potter, "War-Boom Towns in America," 752–53; Ihlder, "How War Came to Chester," 249; "How Bridgeport Went at Great Housing Problems Similar to This City," *Neward Star-Eagle,* 11 October 1917; File on Cleveland, and letter, P. Hiss to J. O. Betelle, Board of Trade, Newark, 19 November 1917 in USHC, Office of President, NARG 3, Series 4, Box 3.

96. *New York Times,* 6 October 1917; "Outline of a Tentative Program for Dealing with the Housing Shortage in Connection with Government Plants and Industrial Plants Making War Necessaries," 20 September 1917, USHC, Office of President, NARG 3, Series 4, Box 3.

97. Mark Swenarton, *Homes Fit for Heroes: The Politics and Architecture of Early State Housing in Britain* (London, 1981), 27, 51.

98. Lawrence Veiller, "The Housing of the Mobilized Population," *Annals of the American Academy of Political and Social Science* 78, no. 167 (July 1918): 23; "The Government's Standards on Housing," *Housing Betterment* 7, no. 2 (May 1918); P. Hiss to Wilson, 25 January 1918, Wilson Papers, LC, CF484B, Reel 279. For the genesis of the USHC, see Katherine H. Davidson, *Records of the United States Housing Corporation,* Preliminary Inventory No. 140 (Washington, D.C., 1962); and Council of National Defense, *Second Annual Report* (Washington, D.C., 1918), 84–85.

99. U.S. Congress, Senate, *Report of Committee on Public Buildings and Grounds,* 66th Cong., 2d Sess., Report No. 336, 18 December 1919, 7. See also Roy Lubove, "Homes and 'A Few Well-Placed Fruit Trees': An Object Lesson in Federal Housing," *Social Research* 27, no. 4 (Winter 1960): 477–78, 485.

100. Curtice N. Hitchcock, "The Housing Program and the Future," *Journal*

of Political Economy 27, no. 4 (April 1919): 241; Lubove, "Homes and 'A Few Well-Placed Fruit Trees' " 476, and Roy Lubove, *Community Planning in the 1920s: The Contribution of the Regional Planning Association of America* (Pittsburgh, 1963), 17.

101.   J. C. Perry, "Military Health Dependent on Civil Health," and John B. Andrews, "National Effectiveness and Health Insurance," in *Annals of the American Academy of Political and Social Science* 78, no. 167 (July 1918): 37–39, 50–56; see also Esther Lovejoy, "Democracy and Health," in F. A. Cleveland and J. Schafer, eds., *Democracy in Reconstruction* (Boston, New York, and Chicago, 1919), 165; and press release, American Public Health Association, Washington, D.C., 1917, Children's Bureau, NARG 102, Box 43, 14–16–0.

102.   "Report of Committee on Condition of Living," 20 August 1918; "Report of the Commission on Living Conditions of War Workers to Chairman of War Labor Policies Board," 19 November 1918; all in WLPB, NARG 1, Series 2, Box 9 "Condition of Living"; "Medical Examinations Card," file, and "Desirable Activities of the U.S. Public Health Service in the Field of the Hygiene Sanitation of Industries During War," in Council of National Defense, NARG 62, Committee on Labor Reports 10A–C3, Boxes 363, 364.

103.   Arthur W. Macmahon, "Health Activities of State Councils of Defense," *Annals*, 79, no. 168 (September 1918): 239–45. *The Survey,* 19 October 1918; Irving Fisher, "Health and War," *American Labor Legislation Review* 8 (March 1918): 3–4.

104.   Owen to Wilson, 3 June 1918; Irving Fisher to Wilson, 15 November 1918; Wilson to Fisher, 18 November, in WW CF 254 Reed 246, LC.

105.   U.S. Dept. of Labor, Children's Bureau, *Seventh Annual Report of the Chief, Children's Bureau* (Washington, D.C., 1919), 10–11; Paper, "Infant Welfare Work in War Time," 9 June 1917; Press releases, "Saving Human Capital," "Babies and War," "Children in Wartime"; article "Children's Year—And After," December 1918, all in Children's Bureau, NARG 102, Box 43 4–16–2; Box 69 8–2–1–10, and 8–2–1–11.

106.   Nancy Pottisham Weiss, "Save the Children: A History of the Children's Bureau, 1903–1918," Ph.D. dissertation, UCLA, 1974, 292; President's Research Committee on Social Trends, *Recent Social Trends in the United States* (New York and London, 1933), II, 763, 1079; J. Stanley Lemons, "The Sheppard-Towner Act: Progressivism in the 1920s," *Journal of American History* 55 (March 1969): 776–87; see file on "Children's Year," Children's Bureau, Box 69, 8–2–1–11.

107.   George Theofiles, *American Posters of World War I* (New York, n.d.), 129; Stephen Vaughn, *Holding Fast the Inner Lines: Democracy, Nationalism and the CPI* (Chapel Hill, N.C., 1980), 178.

108.   Grosvenor B. Clarkson, *Industrial America in the World War* (Boston and New York, 1923), 218–19; Benedict Crowell and Robert Wilson, *How America Went to War: The Armies of Industry* (New Haven, 1921), 587.

109.   John G. Clark, et al., *Three Generations in Twentieth Century America: Family, Community and Nation,* (Homewood, Ill., 1977), 137; Clarence H. Cramer, *Newton D. Baker: A Biography* (Cleveland and New York, 1961), 98–99.

110.   Fosdick, "The War and Navy Departments' Commissions on Training

Camp Activities," *Annals* 79, no. 168 (September 1918): 130–31; Fosdick, *Chronicle of a Generation: An Autobiography* (New York, 1958), 136–57; David Beaver, *Newton D. Baker and the American War Effort* (Lincoln, Nebraska, 1966), 220–22; Josephus Daniels, *The Wilson Era: Years of War and After 1917–1923* (Raleigh, 1946), 187.

111. Roy Lubove, *The Professional Altruist: The Emergence of Social Work as a Career, 1880—1930* (Cambridge, Mass., 1965), 191–92; John F. McClymer, *War and Welfare: Social Engineering in America, 1850–1925* (Westport, Conn., and London, 1980), 162–81.

112. Beaver, *Newton D. Baker*, 222; *New York World*, 23 March 1919; Wickware, *The American Year Book . . . 1919*, 422.

113. McAdoo to Wilson, 23 June, 3 July, 1917, McAdoo Papers, Box 522, LC; William Franklin Willoughby, *Government Organization in War Time and After: A Survey . . .* (New York and London, 1920), 339.

114. Trachtenberg, *The American Labor Year Book, 1919–20*, 26; Waldo G. Leland and Newton D. Mereness, *Introduction to the Official Sources for the Economic and Social History of the World War* (New Haven, Conn., 1926), 37–38.

115. Frank J. Bruno, *Trends in Social Work 1874–1956: A History Based on The Proceedings of the National Conference of Social Work* (New York, 1957), 265; Clarke A. Chambers, *Seedtime of Reform: American Social Services and Social Action 1918–1933*, (Minneapolis, 1963), 221–24.

6

War, Women, and the Family

In 1914–18, and until recently, war was generally thought to be a particularly male preserve of little concern to women. However, the social and economic consequences of total war know no discrimination, and American women were affected by wartime social change just as much as men were. At the same time, regardless of their class, race, or ethnic origin, whether in the workplace or the home, women often felt the impact of war in different ways from men precisely because of gender. Thus women were involved indirectly as mothers, wives, and sisters, for instance, but also directly as independent individuals—yet in a society that placed them in a subordinate and secondary position. In fact, so great was the force of the war that it challenged the sexist assumptions of the day and brought a combination of economic, social, and political change culminating in heightened expectations and political recognition for women.

The subject of the First World War and women has suffered from easy periodization and oversimplification. Traditionally, 1920 was seen as marking a clear divide in the chronology of women's affairs: the passage of the Nineteenth Amendment giving women the vote ended years of struggle, and with the "liberation" of the war, which destroyed old stereotypes, led on to the "New Woman" of the 1920s. However, subsequent writers questioned the idea of the "New Woman" and the extent of "liberation," and thus automatically reexamined the impact of the war. The revisionist view was that the war brought little lasting economic change and probably had little effect on the campaign for the vote. More recent studies combine both approaches, recognizing the limits of wartime change, but seeing the event nonetheless as one of some significance and complexity, one not simply reduced to glib generalization.[1] To understand the subject fully, it must be seen in the context both of the longer view and the changes affecting the rest of American society.

Work and Suffrage

Clearly, the situation of American women, in common with those of most other industrial states, was changing long before the war began, and those changes had brought women and women's issues to a prominent place in the Progressive era and among Progressive concerns. Increasingly since the 1870s women of all classes sought waged work outside the home, and by 1910 8 million, or 24 percent, of all women worked, and they constituted just over 20 percent of the labor force. While the largest single area of employment in 1910 was still domestic service (1.5 million), the proportion of working women in that category had declined from 60 percent in 1870 to 25 percent. Equally striking was the increased number of women in manufacturing and in white-collar occupations. By the end of the nineteenth century 360 of the 369 industries listed by the census employed women, and 1.2 million worked in the textiles industry alone in 1910. Outside of the factory five hundred thousand women were teachers, another nine hundred thousand were employed in clerical and sales occupations, and the revolution of typewriter, telephone, and cash register had created new stereotypes of female employment before the war began.[2]

While new technologies opened up employment opportunities, they also affected life in the home. Domestic servants either left to find more lucrative work in the factory or were displaced by modern machinery or methods, as domestic chores were made simpler by electric and gas lighting, indoor plumbing, new food technology, mass-produced canned goods, iceboxes, and even just modern housing. Increased urbanization and affluence also encouraged a decline in family size, which together with other factors gave middle-class women at least more leisure. One response to this was the increase in educational opportunity for women: by 1900 eighty-five thousand women attended college, and 80 percent of all colleges accepted female students. When these educated women sought outlets for their knowledge and training and found them limited in a male-dominated world, they found some satisfaction in new areas of professional work—the number of nurses increased sevenfold between 1900 and

1910, and the number of qualified female social workers rose from one thousand in 1890 to thirty thousand in 1920. Without women it is doubtful whether settlement houses could have existed.[3]

Women not in wage or voluntary work outside the home often looked for avenues for communication and expression in the growing number of clubs and organizations formed in the late nineteenth century, many of which were grouped together in the General Federation of Women's Clubs. Others became involved in the myriad of reform agencies and movements, ranging from the YWCA, the National Consumer League, and the Settlement Houses, through to individual bodies concerned with education, child labor, law enforcement, and moral reform. While such activities were indicative of the changes that had affected women, they also revealed something of the limitations to progress. Although more active and more conspicuous in society, women were by no means seen as equals. In America as much, if not more, than in western Europe women were still expected to remain in their separate spheres with their own peculiar concerns. New jobs were women's jobs, few married women worked, and women's employment patterns and social organizations reflected traditional female concerns—home, food, clothing, and the care and welfare of children.

Most women, including active reformers, accepted this segregation and the implicit view of gender difference. Women were the "mother half of humanity," the gentler, fairer, and more moral sex. This view cut both ways: for instance, while suffragists argued that the participation of women would bring an injection of decency and morality into politics, their opponents countered that the hard, brutal political arena was no place for innocent women. Others, of course, feared the effects of giving women the vote for reasons relating to Prohibition, industrial regulation, or questions of race but could use imagined gender differences to justify their position. Nonetheless, between 1910 and 1914 the suffrage campaign, spearheaded by the National American Woman's Suffrage Association (NAWSA), was growing in support and achieving some success. When suffragists marched in protest down Fifth Avenue, New York, in 1910, this was seen, even by women, as a radical gesture, and only a few hundred took part. In 1911 three thousand marched; in 1912, fifteen thousand; and by 1917 NAWSA had an estimated membership of two million.[4] While state-by-state campaigns for the vote had been largely unsuccessful between 1870 and 1910, with only two states, Colorado and Idaho, joining Wyoming and Utah as equal-suffrage states, a series of victories was achieved during and after 1910: Washington (1910); California (1911); Oregon, Kansas, Arizona (1912); Illinois (1913); and Montana and Nevada (1914). There were, however, still defeats in North and South Dakota, Nebraska, Missouri, and in both houses of Congress. Significantly, too, no eastern state had conceded women the vote, and campaigns in New York, Massachusetts, Pennsylvania, and New Jersey all ended in defeat in 1915. Still, the tide seemed to be turning. All parties in 1916 included commitments to female suffrage in their platforms, and that year Carrie Chapman Catt could predict that women would have the vote by 1922. In any event, success came two years earlier, and as Catt herself was to acknowledge, this was at least in part due to the war.[5]

As we have already seen in chapter 2, many of the women's activists before 1917 campaigned for peace and hoped to keep America out of the war, which, they argued, was a consequence of the cruelty, barbarity, and ultimate failure of male governments. The Woman's Peace party, formed in 1915, had twenty-five thousand members in 1917 including some of the most prominent women of the day. However, as the likelihood of American entry into the conflict increased, some of these women had second thoughts. In 1916 Catt and others in NAWSA withdrew from the Peace party, motivated by concern for American security and their opponents' charges that they were unpatriotic. They were also increasingly aware from the experience of women in warring countries of the emancipating possibilities of war. In 1916 Catt pointed to the example of Canadian provinces that had given women the vote in recognition of war service, and the American press generally carried numerous accounts of the wartime roles and activities of British women. These lessons were not lost on American suffragists, and in February 1917 NAWSA established departments of food production, food conservation, women's work, and Americanization and offered its services to the government in the event of war. When America joined the conflict the following month the majority of the suffragists were determined to participate.[6]

It was not just the suffragists who sought roles in war service. Their conservative opponents also looked to demonstrate their patriotism and to win recognition. Women were almost as active, if not as prominent, in the preparedness campaigns as they were in the peace movement. The Women's Section of the Navy League was formed in 1915, and various different groups established military training camps for women in 1916. As war approached more realistic steps were taken, influenced again by the experience of British women. After visiting Britain in 1916, Grace Parker, secretary of the National Camp Fire Girls, spoke at a National Security League conference in New York in January 1917 in favor of an organization to coordinate women's national service. A subsequent meeting led to the formation of the National League for Woman's Service with Maude Wetmore of the National Civic Federation as president. The league began to compile a register of women for voluntary service in February 1917, and by the time America declared war the league had branches in thirty-one states and a membership of 50,000; by the end of the year membership had grown to 250,000, and in October 1917 the Labor Department took over the organization's recruiting and information service and incorporated it within the U.S. Employment Service.[7]

If the National League for Woman's Service did not become the *one* central coordinating body its members had hoped for, that was because it had been superseded by other groups, particularly the Woman's Committee of the Council of National Defense established on 21 April 1917 with the assistance of Samuel Gompers. The Woman's Committee included representatives of a number of different organizations but was dominated by members of NAWSA. The chairperson was the former NAWSA president, Anna Howard Shaw, and the committee also included the NAWSA vice-president, Katherine McCormick, legislative leader Antoinette Funk, and Carrie Chapman Catt. Other prominent women involved in the activities of Council of National Defense and other government agencies were Florence Kelley, who resigned from the WPP to become secretary of the Board of Control of Army Contracts and to chair the industrialization mobilization committee of the Woman's Committee, and Lillian Wald, who chaired the committee on public health and child welfare.[8]

In actual practice, the Woman's Committee did not accomplish a great deal other than give added prominence to the women's cause. Once established, the Council of National Defense did not know quite what to do with it, and most other government agencies simply ignored it. Even when involved in a cooperative venture such as the food campaign of 1917, the committee members were angered and frustrated by the treatment they received from male bureaucrats, so much so that Anna Howard Shaw contemplated resignation but finally remained to the end. She and others felt that the Woman's Committee was a symbolic gesture on the part of the government and not much more. According to Carrie Catt, it was little more than a concession: "It did not cost much and it certainly did not do much."[9] The women's frustration increased as female representatives were omitted from other major war boards, such as the National War Labor Board, and in May 1918 the Woman's Committee held a conference, which passed a resolution stating:

WHEREAS, we believe that we can fulfill our obligations as women citizens of the United States to do our utmost to win the war *only* [italics mine] if we are given the opportunity to serve in such direct co-operation with the Government as has made possible the magnificent war work of British women. . . .

The resolution also called for the inclusion of women on all boards affecting their interests.[10]

However, the women's leaders underestimated their role, and that of their lesser-known counterparts in the states. Through publications and newsletters, the Council of National Defense was an important means of communication for women, and at the state level thousands of women were involved in a variety of different war-related activities ranging from food conservation, child welfare and community work, through to Liberty bond and loyalty drives. In Illinois, for example, twenty thousand women gave regular volunteer service and another three hundred thousand worked part-time in the Illinois State Council of Defense effort.[11] At the federal and local levels the importance of women in the Food Administration and its programs could not be denied. According to an article entitled "Women Behind Government's Food Administration" in the *Washington Sunday Star* of 15 July 1917, "It is like taking a sightseeing tour of celebrities just to walk through the offices of the food conservation department of Herbert C. Hoover's food administration." Equally important in the food program was the contribution of the voluntary Women's Land Army founded in 1917. By 1918 the Land Army had 258,300 full- or part-time workers and had been taken over by the Department of Agriculture.[12]

The most obvious evidence of the importance of women to the war effort was, of course, the many war posters aimed at them by the government agencies. Women were described as "Our Second Line of Defense," "The Girl Behind the Man Behind the Gun," and were urged to become nurses or war workers—"For Every Fighter a Woman Worker." Many Food Administration posters were aimed at women; others exhorted women to contribute to Liberty Loans or in more directly practical ways: "Our Boys Need Sox, Knit Your Bit."[13] However, the role of women in the Land Army, state councils of defense, and other agencies suggested that women did not need much direction to serve. Indeed, the government organization of most lasting significance for women arose not as an initiating force, but in response to spontaneous, and largely unguided, changes taking place during the war. The organization was the Women in Industry Service in the Department of Labor, later to become the Women's Bureau, and the changes that produced it developed out of "recognition of the great importance to the Nation of the work of women in industry, and the urgent necessity for a *national policy* in determining the condition of their employment"[14] [italics mine].

The labor shortage that affected work patterns for all social groups in America during the war "opened to women a host of new job opportunities at higher wages than women had been earning before the war" and created "a whirl of job changes." There was some encouragement for women to seek work outside the home—besides national propaganda various states aimed to overcome labor shortages by recruiting female labor. In Connecticut this involved leafleting from the air as well as door-to-door campaigns. In that state alone eight thousand additional women entered the work force, and with or without inducement this pattern was repeated elsewhere. In Massachusetts eight to ten thousand more women were employed than had been before the war; in Pennsylvania the number was estimated at fifty thousand, and even in a western non-industrial state like Oregon there was an increase of two thousand. A survey of 690 plants in Cincinnati, Ohio, found there was a 22.7 percent increase in the number of females employed between 1917 and 1918, compared with a 1.6 percent increase among men, and women accounted for 14,553 of the 60,000 work force. In Bridgeport, Connecticut, while women made up one-quarter of the labor force in the Remington plant, they constituted over 30 percent of the entire city work force. In Washington, D.C., presumably because of the many clerical and office posts, women accounted for almost 50 percent of those in gainful occupations in 1920.[15]

All told, one million additional women entered wage labor during the war, and within the female work force there was a considerable shift as women already in employment moved into better-paying, industrial occupations. Particularly evident was the decline in domestic and personal service as the number of female servants dropped by 253,000, or 20 percent, between 1910 and 1920. The number of dressmakers fell by 47 percent, and laundresses by 25 percent. The gains were in clerical work, where numbers leapt by 344,000, or a colossal 288 percent; semiskilled operatives in manufacturing, 319,000 (33 percent); stenographers and typists, 171,000 (92 percent); and a range of other occupations from teachers to bookkeepers, actresses, and show women.[16]

Not surprisingly, most gains were in war industries. Of the 9.4 million war workers 2.25 million were women, 1.25 million of whom were in manufacturing—the total number of female laborers in manufacturing industries generally rose by eighty thousand, or 100 percent between 1910 and 1920. Large numbers of these women were employed directly or indirectly by the government: one hundred thousand worked in munitions plants, and in one grenade factory nineteen out of every twenty workers were women. More than half the workers in plants manufacturing shells were women, and one gas mask plant alone employed eighty-five hundred women in a workforce of twelve thousand.[17] In addition to women in the Land Army, some twenty-four thousand served in the Army and Navy Nursing Corps, and over eight thousand worked in army and National Guard camps. A major departure was the use of women in the uniformed branches of the forces—11,000 "Yeomanettes" and 269 "Marinettes" worked for the navy. This was not as many as in Britain, where 40,000 served in the Women's Army Auxiliary Corps and a considerable number of these went to the front. Some impression of the importance attached to the roles of the American women was given by the secretary of the navy, whose only comment was, "The uniforms which were adopted were so beautiful that afterwards they were copied by women all over the country."[18]

Despite such patronizing remarks, women in uniform were symbolic of the impact of the war and also served to make many people aware for the first time of the long-term changes in female employment. Thus particular notice was given to the employment of six women in the New York city police force, and the use of female traffic cops elsewhere. Much publicity was given, too, to the rise in employment of women in the railway industry (from 31,000 to 101,785), and the *New York Times* of 1 May 1917 could report that "those who bought tickets in the ferry stations of the Lackawanna Railroad in New Jersey yesterday were surprised to see women on duty in the ticket booths." Most women in the rail companies were in fact employed in clerical capacities or ticket offices. Fewer than six thousand worked as laborers in 1920, and of these more than 50 percent were black or foreign-born.

Undue attention was also given to the women who became conductors and operators on streetcars. No woman had worked in such a capacity before the war, and it was only in a dozen or so towns that they were taken on during the conflict. In some cases the women appointed were relatives of carmen who had gone into military service, and they could be clearly seen as keeping jobs open for male family members. Other women, however, saw the positions as permanent jobs held in their own right. Although few in number (only in the hundreds), women streetcar workers became a subject of debate because of the public nature of their jobs and because of the opposition they faced from members of the Amalgamated Association of Street and Electric Railway Employees of America in certain towns. In Cleveland and Detroit this opposition led to strike action and the intervention of the National War Labor Board.[20] To that extent this minority area of employment revealed the limits of progress in women's employment and the measure of entrenched prejudice among males.

However, some women too had their doubts about their sisters' employment in certain capacities. Florence Kelley, the longtime campaigner to protect women at work, regarded the enlistment of women in "the utterly unfitting occupation of car conductor," as an "outrage," and other reform-minded persons agreed, arguing at the end of the war that "women should disappear as quickly as possible from such tasks . . . for which conditions of life and their physique render them unfit." The unions resisting women's employment on the streetcars of Detroit and Cleveland presented similar arguments at the War Labor Board hearings in 1919. The women concerned in the case disagreed. Their attorney argued that conditions on streetcars were superior to those experienced by the women in other previous occupations, and, besides, such considerations were out-weighed by the increased earnings. The Labor Board found in favor of the women and ordered their reinstatement, but by then the war was over and the board lacked the power to enforce its rulings and could be ignored by the companies. In 1920 the total number of women employed on the streetcars in America was 253; in 1930 it was 17.[21]

Despite the obvious limitations and setbacks to women's economic opportunities, it is clear that many new, if less publicized, positions did open to them during the war. Most were in traditional areas or those already becoming "women's jobs"—cooking, cleaning, and clerical work—but there were others. Help wanted ads revealed something of the range of employment available. In one Cleveland paper, for example, women were sought in an airplane plant as nurses, typists, and clerks—but "Also Women for sweeping." Other vacancies listed included book-keepers, cashiers, elevator operators, chocolate dippers, and sewing ma-chine operators. The Ohio Telephone Company wanted girls with a grammar-school education to take their place on "the Firing Line" and serve their community as telephone operators; the Cleveland Heater Com-pany offered factory experience and "Man's Pay When Competent"; and the National Carbon Company wanted women for soldering, benchwork, and inspecting.[22] Time and again government surveys revealed increasing numbers of women in a range of industries, many of which had not employed women previously. In an article titled "Present Economic Status of Women" in the *New York Times* on 6 October 1918, machine trades "hitherto thought alien" were said to be "far in the lead" of new occupa-tions open to women. Elsewhere there were reports from satisfied employ-ers. As early as January 1917 the *Saturday Evening Post* quoted a production executive as saying, "Women are wonderful workers along mechanical lines," and in 1918 a motor company classed inspectors as a "woman's job" because they had found women to be more efficient and accurate than men. There were other considerations too: "Sterling Motor Company prefer women to men because they have discovered that women can do the work and will work for a smaller wage."[23]

It was in response to this increased range of female employment and its different effects on the wages and working conditions of both men and women that the government began to establish guidelines on employment policy through its various agencies. It was to coordinate and centralize such direction that the Women in Industry Service was established. The origins of the WIS were in the Women's Section of the Ordnance Depart-ment, which had been created in January 1918 to facilitate the use of female workers in ordnance and munitions plants. In charge of the opera-tion was Mary Van Kleeck, former director of the Committee on Women's Work in the Russell Sage Foundation, a philanthropic organization in New

York, where she also lectured on industrial sociology. She was assisted by Mary Anderson, one of the leading women trade unionists, an organizer for the Women's Trade Union League, and a member of the Council of National Defense's Woman's Committee who had become dissatisfied with that body's lack of power. Van Keeck had already been instrumental in drawing up Ordnance Department Order No. 13 (see chapter 5, page 105), which contained the section "Standards for Employment of Women." These included a limit of eight hours' work a day even where the law permitted nine or ten, the prohibition of night work and dangerous or heavy work, the provision of rest periods, meal breaks, restrooms, and eating facilities. Significantly, the orders also proposed that "standards of wages hitherto prevailing for men . . . should not be lowered where women render equivalent service."[24]

Mary Anderson was later to express doubts concerning the success in having the standards applied given difficulties in gaining access to, or influencing the running of war plants. At the end of the war Van Kleeck wrote that "if the war had gone on, the indications were that these provisions would have been more and more comprehensive." As it was, she reported that the enforcement of standards was far from uniform. Nonetheless, concern to achieve some uniformity in the standards applied to female labor increased among government officials if for no other reason than to lessen labor unrest as "dilution" continued through the war, and with the formation of the War Labor Policies Board Felix Frankfurter turned to Van Kleeck and Anderson for guidance. He was instrumental in securing their transfer in June 1918 to the Women in Industry Service created in the Department of Labor, a move Anderson described as "the culmination of many years of work and agitation on the part of women and women's organizations."[25]

The Women in Industry Service, in consultation with other government departments, provided advice and guidance to employers on the utilization of female labor and formulated general standards to be applied. "Standards for the Employment of Women" was an extension and elaboration of the principles in General Order No. 13 and repeated the commitments to the eight-hour day, forty-eight-hour week, the prohibition of night work, equal pay for equal work, and a minimum wage. These were adopted by the War Labor Policies Board in October 1918 and finally issued in December. Although seemingly too late to have much influence, the publication of "Standards" was still significant. As Mary Anderson was to write

> It was the first time the federal government had taken a practical stand on conditions of employment for women, and although the standards were only recommendations and had no legal force, they were a very

important statement of policy and were widely used in all parts of the country.

Moreover, the pamphlet continued to be used after the war and was widely circulated. Over one hundred thousand copies were issued, and the standards

> were accepted as a goal by almost every group working to improve conditions for women. They were incorporated to a great extent in legislation, and they were adopted by many employers voluntarily. They were indeed the most important thing the Women in Industry did and their influence cannot be over emphasized.[26]

Nonetheless, the question of standards to be applied in the employment of women remained a thorny issue in government agencies and among those of a reform persuasion, even among women themselves. As already stated, most Americans viewed women as essentially different from men, and this notion of gender difference applied to the workplace as well as to the home or politics. Even if women were thought able to perform the same occupational tasks as men (and few believed it possible), not many Americans thought it desirable. Thus one of the main thrusts of prewar reform had been to discriminate between the sexes and to pass protective legislation in favor of women: shortening hours, limiting the type of work done, and so on. Reformers such as Florence Kelley were anxious that the war should not lead to any relaxation of laws applying to female labor, and one of the aims of the War Labor Policies Board was to prevent industrial exploitation of women as a consequence of the war emergency. The board made it clear that it saw certain places as "clearly unfit for women"—bars, saloons, poolrooms, mines, and quarries—and others, such as streetcar and other transportation services, as unsuitable for young women. Frankfurter wished to list the industries in which it was felt appropriate for women to be employed, but Van Kleeck and Anderson objected to such restrictions.[27]

Other women resented the limitations applied to their sex. As some of the female streetcar workers had made clear, they wanted economic equality. It was not just militant feminists who demanded equal treatment: one woman, a widow living in Wisconsin, wrote complaining of the ten-hour restriction on female labor that prevented her from being hired on the railroad and of being limited to "so-called 'woman's jobs.'" She went on:

> It is my belief that a woman can do everything that a man can do that is within her strength. Hundreds and hundreds of women might work and release men for war or war work, could they, the women, be employed on the railroads, etc. . . .

Industrialists, too, used the war emergency to ask for the lifting of restrictions, in one case asking for "authority to work our female labor on twelve hour basis," and in some cases the WLPB did approve the waiving of standards where it felt conditions were appropriate.[28]

The subject of night work for women was one in which the federal officials were prepared to make concessions if war production demanded it and if conditions were thought to be suitable. Time and time again, the disadvantages of employing women at night were pointed out. As one observer noted, drawing again on the English experience, "The cost is excessive and outweighs the advantage to be gained." A statement of regulations controlling night work of women in plants manufacturing war goods for the government claimed that "continuous and unregulated night work for women is harmful because of the bad effect on health, morals, and family life and the welfare of children." Nonetheless, if the circumstances required it, temporary certification could be granted to permit night work. Following inspection by the Woman in Industry Service, such permission was granted in a number of cases including Bethlehem Steel, Westinghouse, Tacony Ordnance, Sterling Motor Co., the DuPont de Nemours Brandywine plant, and the Worthington Pump and Machinery Company in Hazleton, Pennsylvania, which had a dispensary and hospital and five trained nurses.[29]

Clearly, the policymakers were prepared to compromise, in part because there were differences over some principles, and confusion over others. Nowhere was this more apparent than the principle of "equal pay for equal work," which the National War Labor Board upheld in theory, but from which it was prepared to deviate in practice. First, of course, the introduction of rest periods and shorter hours could change jobs and make them unequal, but even without this, the board differentiated between men and women and clearly saw their working roles as different. While the board calculated that a living wage for a single man was twenty-one dollars per week, it accepted that for a single woman fifteen was sufficient, and in a number of cases awarded women lower raises than men. However, the board did make some awards on the basis of equal pay, and although inconsistent the board has been seen as generally sympathetic to women workers.[30]

If government policy was at times contradictory, actual conditions for women in work were equally mixed. Inspectors for the government boards, and especially the WIS, reported on a wide spectrum of war plants and found that, regardless of government recommendations, women were employed for long hours in hard, and sometimes dangerous, occupations. One survey of factories, railway yards, and car barns in New York state counted 2,812 women who had replaced men between September 1917 and May 1918. The prejudices of the inspector were obvious when she pointed out that these laborers were "robust Polish and Italian women." A similar point was made of three hundred women employed at the Atlantic Refining Company in Philadelphia. Far from receiving favorable discrimination, these workers were given "the dirtiest, most disagreeable, and some of the hardest jobs first"—"building roads, mixing cement, unloading coal and coke cars, digging ditches, wheeling heavy wheelbarrow loads"—but again these were "large, strong, healthy foreign women who are able to do work which American women cannot and will not do." The report went on, "There is practically no laborers' job in this plant which these women are not doing, and they receive the same pay as the men—43 cents an hour."[31]

Two ice plants in Philadelphia also employed women, one "choosing the Russians and Polacks because they appeared to be the strongest and the neatest, also for the reason that they had come from countries of long winters." Paradoxically, the other company employed black women, as "Negro women would . . . be stronger than white women, not having undergone the enervating influences of civilization."[32]

The ethnic and racial references are important reminders of distinctions made by Americans between different groups in the labor force, and the fact that women of foreign origin or parentage were predominant in industrial occupations. Still, the number of native-born Americans employed in such capacities increased with the decline in immigration, although to some extent the gap was filled by blacks—men or women. Whatever their origin, women often suffered because of their sex. In one motor factory in Oakland, Michigan, eighteen women worked among five hundred men. Facilities were poor. The toilets were described as "shocking," and working conditions were "extremely dirty" with "no discipline in the shop." Even worse, there "was a great deal of jollying among men and girls on the floor." Even management took advantage of its position and dismissed girls who refused or failed to keep dates.[33] There is little reason to suppose that these were isolated cases. Maurine Greenwald details a number of instances of sexual harassment in the railway industry alone. Elsewhere, management could use fairly crude methods to discipline female workers. In a plant in Chester the monotony of the work was said to encourage idleness.

To keep the girls from idling too much, all the doors had been taken from the toilet rooms as it was found that the girls having no other place to go, would spend time here to avoid work.[34]

The demands made of women at work were obviously hard, and there is much to suggest that little allowance was made for their sex. Despite government strictures to use labor resources efficiently by limiting the hours worked, there is considerable evidence of women working hours regarded as excessive even by the standards of the time. In Indiana, for example, one of six states without legal limits on women's hours, women in 30 percent of establishments worked a regular ten-hour day. Some, however, worked sixty-five hours a week, and others were working seventy or even eighty hours. However, wartime policies and inspection could bring a change. A company in Waterbury, Massachusetts, reduced the hours of the eight-hundred-strong female work force from sixty to fifty-five following the intervention of the WIS, and while in general the ten-hour norm established before the war seemed to hold, the trend was downward in line with the WIS "Standards."[35]

Regardless of their hours, most women suffered discrimination when it came to pay. The many government surveys found that women's average earnings were half those of men. Thus the milling companies in Cincinnati, where men were earning $15 to $20 per week, paid most women between $6 and $10. In Grand Rapids, Michigan, the average daily rate among five thousand women workers was $1.98; for the twenty-three men, it was $3.16. In Bridgeport, following War Labor Board hearings in May 1918, the minimum hourly rate for men was set at 42 cents, for women, 32 cents. In September, Mary Van Kleeck recommended this be raised to 39 cents. In Atlanta, where the number of women in industry had doubled, and the number in war work in 1918 was over twenty-seven hundred, the average wage was between $10 and $15 a week, but one-quarter earned less than $15, and 30 percent less than $10. Some women elsewhere were less fortunate: cleaners and others were reported to be paid as little as $5 to $8 in some places. On the other hand, a conductress could be paid 43 cents an hour, $75 to $80 per month; railway office workers might earn between $87 and $100 per month, and even office cleaners $70 to $80. These were probably among the better paid, for it seems that not too many women were paid the minimum $16.50 set by the NWLB. Nonetheless, the *New York Times* in 1918 showed women's wages to have doubled during the war and quoted Marie Obenauer of the War Labor Board, who estimated average increases to be between 80 and 100 percent.[36]

But even with increased employment opportunities or higher wages women did not necessarily find life easy. Many discovered that accommodation was scarce and that prices quickly canceled out wage gains. One reporter in Chester was paid $17.70 a week by the Midvale Steel company. This seemed "a large wage," but the "cost of living in Chester was exorbitant," and accommodation was limited. The woman eventually found a cot in a YWCA dormitory, but had to rise at 5.30 A.M. to get to work. With no permanent home, she and others had to eat out, and "although the girls patronized one of the most reasonable restaurants, they found their week's expenses amounting to exactly $11.70, far in excess of value received." Girls on piecework could earn much more—$25 to $40 per week—but they showed signs of "excessive nervous strain." And regardless of earnings, there was little to do in towns like Chester, and young women suffered from loneliness and boredom and often spent their leisure hours walking the streets or staying to see the same movie two or three times a night.[37]

Women, then, like men, suffered all the disruptive consequences of the war, and were just as subject to the wartime stresses and strains but with the additional burdens of lower rates of pay and a working existence in a male world. Even worse, many of their jobs were either temporary in their very nature or viewed as temporary by male counterparts. At the end of the war women were expected to give up their jobs. In December 1918 the president of the Photo Engravers and Printers Union, Matthew Woll, could suggest:

> The same patriotic appeals which have so largely attracted women into industries during the war period, should be continued after the war to secure re-employment of soldiers and sailors in positions filled by women workers during the war.[38]

Woll was not alone in this view, but what he and others overlooked was the fact that women workers were not motivated just by patriotic appeals but by economic necessity or even the desire to fulfill themselves through work. Many women wished to continue in work but were to find it difficult in the postwar layoffs. While thirty-eight out of every hundred men lost their jobs at the end of the war, the rate for women was fifty-seven per hundred. Even women judges were forced to resign, and the percentage of the labor force that was female in 1920 was almost identical to that of 1910. However, that figure was apparently artificially low as a consequence of the actual form of question asked in the census (which excluded some farm workers and covered a slightly shorter period than that covered in the 1910 census), and the Women's Bureau, the successor to the Women in Industry Service, produced a pamphlet in 1920 significantly entitled *The New Position of Women in American Industry*. This report pointed out that "all the factors combined . . . did not exert sufficient influence to reduce the proportion of women in the new industries to prewar levels." Moreover, as Maurine Greenwald later wrote, "Participation in the war effort heightened the consciousness of women workers, male co-workers, managers, and government officials alike. . . ."[39]

The most tangible result of this awareness was the setting up of the Women's Bureau itself by act of Congress in 1920. With Mary Anderson as its head, the bureau became a permanent part of the Department of Labor and was to continue the program of education and investigation begun by the Women in Industry Service through the postwar period. Other evidence of the recognition of women's wartime contribution could be seen in the numerous press articles and comments such as:

"Woman and War Work," *The Survey*, 19 May 1917
"The Mobilization of Women," *Good Housekeeping*, June 1917
"Mobilizing Women's Service," *Independent*, 16 June 1917
"Organized Womanpower," *Delaware Gazette*, 17 August 1917
"Doing Her 'Bit' Making Munitions," *Washington Times*, 5 December 1917
"Women in War Industries," *The New Republic*, 15 December 1917
"Woman's Work for the War," *New York Evening Post*, 6 March 1918
"Women Helping to Win War By Working in Places of Men," *Washington Star*, 14 February 1918

This is merely a sample of the publicity given women's wartime contribution. During a conference on industrial safety in 1918 (a conference that devoted two evenings to discussing women in industry), it was noted that "wherever you go you hear discussed what has been done by women in the war. The conversation invariably turns upon women in industry."[40]

Such comments had wider implications, and regardless of postwar economic setbacks the lessons of the war and their significance in women's affairs could not be gainsaid. As Carrie Chapman Catt wrote, "Woman can never be accounted a negligible factor in the community again. Her economic value has been substantiated."[41] For Catt and her suffragist colleagues this was additional ammunition for their cause, and there can be little doubt that women's war work and participation in the war administration had some influence in the suffrage campaigns and contributed to their ultimate victory.

The significance of the war in the fight for the woman's vote has often been overlooked by historians who conclude that the battle was already won by 1917. However, the suffragists themselves were aware of the war's importance. For Carrie Catt, "The greatest thing to come out of the war was the emancipation of women," and she suggested that the war had "a tremendous effect on woman suffrage by revolutionizing the whole sphere of women." Jane Addams agreed. According to the veteran campaigner, the Nineteenth Amendment was accepted "so soon after the war that it must be accounted as the direct result of war psychology."[42] To an extent this was contrary to many expectations when the war first began. For some Americans, war reinforced the arguments for excluding women from politics, confirming the harsh and brutal nature of the world beyond the home, and antisuffrage supporters could argue anyway that wartime was not the moment to consider social legislation. There were also people who prophesied that the war would set back the woman's cause, but, as one observer noted:

> Exactly the reverse seems to have happened. Women's essential contribution to the country's war needs apparently has emphasized their claim to political recognition, and the year 1917 has recorded the greatest actual gains in the history of the American suffrage movement.[43]

Not only was it not clear at first that the war would have this effect, but there was also some doubt among the suffragists concerning their most appropriate line of action during the conflict. While some thought the suffrage campaign should be put aside for the duration, the militant Congressional Union, which joined with the Woman's party in 1917, continued its policy of public protests and maintained a silent vigil outside the White House even after April. NAWSA's position was to dissociate itself from the picketing, to support the government, to seek every opportunity to serve in the war effort, and to push its claims for recognition at the same time. Thus Catt and others urged the Congressional Union to withdraw the pickets and did not demur when a number of the women outside the White House were arrested and jailed in June. The more moderate position adopted by NAWSA probably helped to persuade the president to grant an immediate amnesty to the jailed women (although he also felt the arrests had been unjustified in the first place), and also helped to win him over to the suffrage cause. The other vital factor in his conversion was the evident tide in favor of woman's suffrage, and particularly the first victory in the East.

Although NAWSA disavowed militant tactics during the war, they nevertheless continued both their state-by-state drive for the vote through referenda and the demand for congressional action and an amendment to the Constitution. The wisdom of this was demonstrated in 1917 when a major victory was achieved in New York. This was a crucial turnabout: in 1915 the women had been defeated by over two hundred thousand votes; now they won with a majority of one hundred thousand. The influence of the war was readily apparent—"the New York Woman Suffrage Party had been conspicuous in women's war service activities in the months before the state election," and as the *Saturday Evening Post* noted, "the victory in New York . . . shows that suffrage for women is being won by the part that women are playing in the war."[44]

Perhaps the voters of New York were also influenced by President Wilson's growing public support for woman's suffrage. He expressed "a very deep interest" in the campaign and hoped that the White House pickets would not have an adverse effect upon it. He was, he wrote, "very anxious to see the great State of New York set a great example in this matter," a view he reiterated in his reply to a delegation from the New

York State Woman Suffrage party on 25 October. Again he pointed to the impact of the war and said he thought "the whole country has appreciated the way in which the women have risen to this great occasion."[45]

There can be little doubt that the war contributed something to the president's position, for he had changed his stance in a very short space of time. Formerly an opponent of equal suffrage, he had become a supporter some time around 1915, influenced by his second wife, political considerations, and events overseas. Initially, however, as a states' rights supporter and a Democratic president dependent upon southern congressional backing, he was not in favor of federal action but preferred the decision to be taken by the respective states. In September 1916 he addressed the NAWSA convention in Atlantic City and pointed out to his audience the rapid growth in support for their cause. Moreover, he said, "We feel the tide; we rejoice in the strength of it; and we shall not quarrel in the long run as to the method of it."[46] His concession here toward federal action was important, and the election of 1916 only emphasized further the political gain to be had in supporting suffrage, as it was evident that women's votes could be crucial. However, with the coming of war the president wrote to Carrie Catt, "I candidly do not think that this is the opportune time to press the claims of our women upon Congress."[47] Just over a year later he was to appear in person before the Senate to put the women's case. That he did so was a consequence of a number of factors, not least the work of the suffragists.

Mrs. Catt did not accept that war should postpone the women's struggle. She and her colleagues in NAWSA began to demand an amendment as a war measure, arguing that such an act would strengthen the American war effort and demonstrate that the United States was indeed fighting for democracy. This was the case the women made when they presented the amendment to Congress again in January, and in their representations to congressional committees the suffragists pointed to the role of women in the war effort and the lessons of foreign nations. Much was made particularly of the British example, in which women played a major part in the war machine and in which notable opponents to suffrage, such as Asquith and Northcliffe, had been converted. Anna Howard Shaw could tell a House committee that to fail to ask for an amendment "at this time . . . would be treason to the fundamental cause for which we as a nation have entered the war."[48]

Others close to the president endorsed the women's position. George Creel, for example, wrote to Wilson in September 1918:

I feel deeply that the passage of this Amendment is a war necessity for it will release the minds and energies of thousands of women for war work and war enthusiasm. I feel deeply also that it is necessary to have the

Administration receive full credit for its consistently courageous and friendly attitude.

Creel pointed to the political significance of the issue of the vote with the approach of congressional elections that November and suggested that the Republicans could make it a campaign issue.[49]

These considerations certainly weighed with the president, who urged all his party members to support the amendment, and in letters and telegrams to those in doubt he pointed out the international and domestic importance of the subject. Finally, on 30 September 1918 he appeared before the Senate to urge passage of the amendment as "vitally essential to the successful prosecution of the great war" and went on to suggest:

This war could not have been fought . . . if it had not been for the services of the women . . . not merely in the fields of effort in which we have been accustomed to see them work, but wherever men have worked and upon the very skirts and edges of the battle itself.

He repeated this in his annual address to Congress, whom he asked to make women "the equals of men in political rights as they have proved themselves their equals in every field of practical work they have entered."[50]

The role of women in the war had clearly influenced the president, but members of the Senate still required persuasion, and a two-thirds majority was not finally achieved until 4 June 1919. Nonetheless, a change in women's favor could be detected during the war years. In 1914 the vote in the Senate was almost equally divided, with thirty-five yeas and thirty-four nays. The House, in the vote of 1915, was opposed, 204 to 174. By 1918 only two votes were lacking in the Senate, with sixty-two for, and thirty-four against, while in the House there had been a total reversal with 274 yeas and 136 nays. The Senate finally approved the amendment in June 1919, but it was not ratified by the required number of states until August 1920—just in time to enable women to vote in the presidential elections that year.[51]

In the end, the vote was achieved through the combined effects of the continuous and effective campaigning of women's organizations at all levels; the victories in the states, particularly New York, and the progress in other countries; the demise of Prohibition as an issue during the war; the political struggle of the two major parties; and the influence of the president—all interwoven with the effects of women's war service and of the war itself. One suffragist neatly summed these all up when she referred to "the general fluidity of conditions" in which "the old moorings were all lose, everything had been broken up by the war."[52]

With the winning of the vote American women had achieved the goal of years of struggle, and perhaps earlier than some had expected. However, political recognition did not automatically alter perceptions about women any more than did their increased employment, and the fact that the Nineteenth Amendment was not followed by revolution was a source of some surprise and relief for many men and of disappointment for some women. Indeed, the lack of drastic change has led a few historians to see the enfranchisement of women as a hollow victory and to deny the significance of the war years in terms of both political and economic change. However, this is rather like denying the importance of the Thirteenth Amendment ending slavery. The war may not have been the "turning point" or "watershed" in women's history any more than for other groups, but it still brought recognizable change if only in the form of two steps forward followed by one step back. If wartime gains did not continue, neither did they completely disappear. Important aspects persisted as the importance of women in the marketplace as workers and consumers was recognized. The role of women in the war effort and their being acknowledged as an economic force clearly contributed to the suffrage debate and eventual passage of the amendment. If women subsequently chose not to vote collectively in order to effect change as women, that was their prerogative—one that they had not previously enjoyed. At the ballot box at least, American women demonstrated that they were little different from men.

Family, Children, Education, and the State

Despite the apparently liberating effects of the war, for most women the fundamental features of their lives remained unchanged. The place, and subordination, of women within the family continued, and in many ways the war served to reinforce stereotypes and to confirm women in their traditional and limited roles as housewives and mothers. Three important qualifications about employment opportunities that point up this fact must be made. First, as already stated, most of the changes took place among women *already* in work as they moved from one occupation to another. Second, the greatest *permanent* advances were made in precisely those areas that had been expanding before the war—the white-collar occupations of telephonist, clerk, typist, and saleswoman. Finally, the proportion of *married* women in wage work outside the home hardly changed, although the number increased by 350,000 between 1910 and 1920. In 1920 less than one-quarter of the 8 million paid women workers were married.[53] Now, for many Americans, including women themselves, this was how things should be. Thus, in October 1918, the notable reformer and head of the Children's Bureau, Julia Lathrop, could write to Alda Armstrong of the

Children's Aid Society that "mothers share the prevailing feeling of un-rest," and the attraction of high wages and demands of war "all tend to make them forget the home duties." She advised Armstrong that "the best service you could render the nation now would be to educate the mothers to the importance of remaining in the home to safeguard the health and morals of their children at this critical time." Elsewhere, motherhood was described as "the fundamental military service."[54]

Although a few war posters showed women in new wartime occupa-tions, most of the American propaganda stressed the role of women as housewives and mothers, using the images of hearth and home or, as in the case of Howard Chandler Christy's famous illustrations, merely using femininity as a vehicle for expression. Nonetheless, the war undoubtedly had an effect on American families and on the role of women within them. While the extensive propaganda urging food savings and conservation was primarily directed at the housewife, it did indicate the importance of their position and demonstrate that women were vital to the war effort even if still at home. For many women, too, the war brought added responsibility as they became the temporary, or in some cases, sadly, the permanent head of the family. This was not always necessarily due to war deaths. The war created a certain amount of instability by leading to separation, creating new situations, providing economic opportunities, and, perhaps, encouraging a new sense of freedom among some women (and men), which may have contributed to the rise in divorce that was registered during and after the war.

The statistics on divorce are, like many others, fraught with diffi-culties both in their estimation and their interpretation. The number of divorces had risen sharply in America during the latter part of the nine-teenth century, and, as William O'Neill has pointed out, was a matter of concern and debate in the Progressive era. Indeed, O'Neill sees the critical period as far as attitudes toward divorce went as being around 1912. Be that as it may, the figures suggest a dramatic rise during the war period.

	Number of divorces per 1000 existing marriages	Actual number of divorces	% increase
1880	2.2	19,663	
1890	3.0	33,461	70
1900	4.0	55,751	66
1910	4.5	83,045	49
1920	7.7	167,105	101

Figures compiled from Census material quoted in Margaret Gibbons Wilson, *The American Woman's Transition: The Urban Influence 1870–1920* (Westport, Conn., and London, 1979), 187–91.

The problem here is determining the causes of change, and particularly, given the ten-year spread, the influence of the war years alone. The Lynds in their study of Muncie gave more precise figures: in 1909 there were twenty-five divorces for each hundred marriage licenses issued; in 1918, fifty-four. Although the rates declined in comparison with marriages, the number of recorded divorces rose by 622 percent between 1921 and 1924. This points up the uneven and contradictory pattern. In America, as in other countries, the war also brought an upsurge in marriage. In 1914 there were 10.3 marriages per thousand of the population; in 1917, 11.1; a decline to 9.7 in 1918 (presumably brought about by the absence of young men and the uncertainty of war); and a rise to 11 in 1919 and 12 in 1920 as soldiers and peace returned. Birthrates too, having dropped during the war, rose once it ended, "the mobilization and demobilization of a large army being chiefly responsible for the changes."[55]

In the long run, of course, the war did not seriously alter the existing trends. While it may have resulted in a baby boom in the twenties, the move toward a smaller average family size and slower population growth continued—the median family size in 1900 was 4.7, in 1910 4.5, and in 1920 4.3. But there were signs of wartime disturbance in the family, particularly affecting children. Again, the picture is neither clear nor consistent, but there was evidence to suggest that the war brought a rise in juvenile delinquency. So concerned was Julia Lathrop over this issue that she called for reports from juvenile courts in ten cities—New York, Chicago, Philadelphia, Buffalo, Denver, Minneapolis, St. Louis, Birmingham, Jacksonville, and Richmond. All but two (Birmingham and Minneapolis) reported increases in juvenile crime. The percentage increase varied from around 20 percent in Denver and New York City to almost 30 percent in Jacksonville, but higher rises were noted in other cities—54 percent in Columbus, Ohio, and 50 per cent in Detroit.[56]

There were, however, exceptions—in New York state the number of juveniles in corrective institutions was below normal in 1918 and had been for about two years previously. This was thought to be due "to good industrial conditions which have lessened neglect and poverty, and second to the increasing effects of probation work and other preventive measures." In fact one explanation offered for the rise of juvenile arrests was said to be "the increased vigilance of social agencies."[57] Certainly, as Julia Lathrop reported, it was difficult to estimate the extent to which war conditions were responsible for the increases in particular areas, and the judge from New York City pointed out that while the 1917 figures were higher than those of 1916, they were in fact lower than 1913, 1914, or 1915. Nonetheless, certain aspects of the juvenile crime figures could be attributed to the war: the increase in larceny among the young was said to be "almost entirely the result of the unsettled social and economic conditions of the times" and "the social unrest that is everywhere manifest." The scarcity of fuel and food was explanation for the stealing of coal from the railyards and the increase in shoplifting, while the "increase in stealing in general" was, rather paradoxically, "attributed largely to the high wages paid child workers and the resulting tendency to extravagance." "War influences" were also suggested as an explanation "for the greater number of arrests for carrying concealed weapons."[58]

One aspect of juvenile crime that caused particular alarm and was seen as a definite consequence of the war was the apparent rise in immorality among young girls. This, said one observer, was a consequence of "the adoration in which young girls hold soldiers and sailors." Girls were reported to be flocking to "our camp towns attracted by the khaki, as well as by stories of the need for workers and the fabulous salaries paid them."[59] The admiration for servicemen could be articulated by the youngsters concerned in almost patriotic terms—one girl "said that she had never sold herself to a civilian but she felt she was doing her bit when she had been with eight soldiers in a night."[60] It was not just military towns that experienced these problems: in a war center like Chester there were accounts of "school girls who stand on street corners and ask passersby to treat them to dinner."[61]

The attraction of men in uniform was clearly only part of the explanation for such behavior, which probably had the same underlying causes as other juvenile crimes. The disturbance of family life and the absence of the restraining influence of fathers, brothers, or of mothers, coupled with the general disruption of normal life by the war, affected both girls and boys alike. The very violence of war itself and the sense of nervousness and excitement may well have encouraged antisocial behavior among the young, who were excluded from much of the war effort and relegated to the position of passive onlookers even though affected directly and indirectly by the conflict. For some youngsters actions classed as delinquent may well have been attempts to gain attention, to prove their maturity, demonstrate their virility, or merely a release for wartime anxieties. Whatever the cause, little could be done to prevent it although the war had clearly increased awareness of such social problems and of the changing place of the young in society. As early as 1920 articles were written entitled "The Uprising of Youth" and "The Revolt of Youth," and the conduct of teenagers, often seen as misbehavior, was viewed as symptomatic of a general breakdown in society following the war.[62]

The more conspicuous position of young people in society was, to some extent at least, a natural consequence of the war (and, probably, all wars. Similar tendencies were to be reported in Britain in World War I and again in America and the U.K. in World War II). Military service placed emphasis on youth, and an automatic response to war was to think of the welfare of future generations. Concern for juvenile crime was just one aspect of this, as was the continued attempt to control child labor. The move to limit the employment of children had been a major Progressive concern, and reformers were determined to resist pressure to reduce standards in this area. Where child labor was accepted, even encouraged as official government policy, it was under the aegis of various branches of the Department of Labor in programs that normally entailed work in healthy, outdoor activities during holiday or leisure hours. Such schemes could be justified as both aiding the war effort and being good for the child without lowering the wage rates of adult workers. Thus, some 1.5 million boys and girls in 1918 and 2 million in 1919 were active in the U.S. Garden Army, which produced vegetables worth $48 million. In greater Cleveland alone, it was estimated that war gardens provided sufficient food to sustain a country the size of Belgium for several weeks.[63]

While the Garden Army produced valuable foodstuffs, the U.S. Boy's Working Reserve enabled the maintenance of agricultural production during the war by replacing the farm laborers who went into the army or into war industry. The Boy's Reserve began in May 1917, the idea of William E. Hall, president of the Association of Boy's Clubs of America and director of the U.S. Public Service Reserve. Forming a kind of "agricultural army," the reserve recruited over two hundred thousand lads between the ages of sixteen and twenty, and from central farm camps sent them on to six hundred smaller "liberty camps" across the nation. As one writer said, "From the canning factories of Alaska to the cotton fields of the South and the sugar plantations of far Hawaii these sturdy boys of the Reserve have taken the places of men," and elsewhere the reserve was credited "with saving the sugar-beet crop in Michigan, the apple crop in Georgia, [and] the berry crop in Oregon."[64] In this way children and juveniles were able to play a part in the war yet in circumstances that were controlled and not harmful in their nature. Moreover, at the end of the war the children were urged to return to school:

Boys and Girls
The School Is Your Training Camp
Uncle Sam Says
ENLIST TODAY[65]

While limited participation of children in the war effort was acceptable, particularly in agricultural pursuits, efforts to prohibit child labor in industry continued during the war on the grounds that "the safeguarding of children is an essential part of winning the war."[66] Thus when the

Keating Owen Child Labor law, which had come into effect on 1 September 1917, was subsequently declared unconstitutional by the Supreme Court in 1918, child labor prohibition was still written into federal contracts and discouraged in public statements by government officials. Despite the shortages of labor and demands to relax restrictions, child labor seemed to decline during the war. The percentage of children in the work force of manufacturing industries dropped from 1.7 percent in 1914 to 1.3 percent in 1919, and whereas in 1910 25 percent of boys and about 12 percent of girls between the ages of ten and fifteen were working, by 1920 the figures were around 12 and 5 percent respectively. The overall number of children employed dropped from 1.9 million in 1910 to little over 1 million ten years later.[67]

Despite the apparently downward trend in child labor, the pattern was again by no means uniform. Certainly employers continued to use children as workers, and in some places this practice increased. One survey of employment in New York state, for example, found that although the number of children in factories declined between 1913 and 1917 (from 15,926 to 14,650), the number *illegally* employed actually rose (from 1,057 to 1,655). Even after the passage of the child labor law government surveys found increases in the number of children employed. In Cincinnati, one of several cities studied by the Children's Bureau, "figures showed a marked increase in child labor," and employers who had not previously used children were now doing so. The bureau attributed this development "primarily to the high cost of living, high wages, and the great demand for labor."[68] An inspection of factories and canneries in Virginia between 1917 and 1918 found 755 children between fourteen and sixteen years, 319 under fourteen, and 130 under twelve; a report to the U.S. Employment Service concerning the Tennessee Postal Service cited the case of twelve-year-old John Parrish, who worked from 8:00 A.M. to 6:00 P.M., seven days a week, completing sixty-three hours' labor—this in spite of the laws of Tennessee and government directives. This impulse to use children did not cease: with the end of the war and the failure of the second child labor law (1919), there was an increase in child labor in the twenties, with one estimate putting the number of children at work in 1924 at two million. Not until the 1930s was child labor to be effectively limited by law.[69]

Closely related to the concern for child labor during the Progressive era and the war was the question of education. Again, the war served to highlight existing issues and was used to push the claims of interested parties. One source suggested that "American education in 1918 underwent more fundamental changes than in any previous year on record. The war brought problems and it also brought opportunities." The impact of the war, the writer said, established "the idea of education as a national concern"—or, according to the commissioner of education, Philander P. Claxton, "the war has turned a searchlight on the Nation's interest in the education of its citizens."[70]

There were three aspects of the wartime focus on education. First, there was a reaction to children leaving school early as a consequence of wartime employment coupled with a desire to maintain standards of education. Second, there was an obvious response to the findings of the draft boards with regard to educational standards, and third, an increased awareness of the role of education as an instrument of Americanization. The first of these was occasioned by an obvious drop in student numbers. High school enrollments for 1916–17 were down overall, but particularly among older pupils. While the decrease in first-year numbers was 6 percent, that for third-year classes was 658 percent. The number of *all* school pupils rose by 1.5 percent in 1917–18 instead of the anticipated 2.5 percent.[71]

Government officials and administrators did as much as they could to counter this pattern. A Bureau of Education circular argued strongly "that the war should in no way be used as an excuse for giving the children of the country any less education" and went on to say, "Boys and girls should be urged, as a patriotic duty, to remain in school to the completion of the high school course." This was reiterated by the president when, in a letter to Secretary of the Interior Lane, he too said, "That . . . there should be no falling off in attendance in elementary schools, high schools, or colleges is a matter of the very greatest importance affecting both our strength in war and our national welfare and efficiency when the war is over."[72] When the war did end the Bureau of Education pursued this theme and mounted the "Back to School Drive" already mentioned. The arguments were strengthened then by the claim that "Children Back in School Means Soldiers Back in Jobs." How successful this was is hard to determine, but the number of children between five and seventeen attending school was higher in 1920 than before the war. The 21.5 million school enrollments represented 78 percent of the age group, and according to one source, "Recovery from abnormal war conditions . . . proceeded rapidly during 1919."[73]

The importance of education to the nation's well-being was stressed by draft revelations. Many Americans were as shocked to discover the high rates of illiteracy as they were the poor state of the nation's health. Illiteracy had been a matter of concern among reformers and educationalists before the war, but the fact that 25 percent of draft registrants were illiterate created much more widespread alarm. One report described illiteracy as a "national liability," and this was emphasized by Lane when he pointed out that "we are drafting into our Army men who cannot understand the orders that are given them to read . . . our manpower is deficient because our education is deficient."[74]

A number of separate states reacted to these revelations by introducing intensive educational programs for illiterates—in Alabama, for instance, fifteen hundred dollars was spent teaching thirty-five hundred men to read and write; in California, too, there were statewide educational programs. More significantly, the army itself provided education at a variety of different levels. While educational centers were established at some camps in America, 167,000 illiterates went to France, where they were "gradually segregated in development battalions." At the war's end, while waiting to return the Expeditionary Force home after the Armistice, one hundred thousand men were taught basic literacy skills, and the army also established a university at Beaume, attended by twelve thousand soldiers. Another eight thousand went to French universities, and over two thousand attended colleges in Britain—one of the latter was, of course, Scott Fitzgerald's *Great Gatsby,* who boasted of being educated at Oxford—an "Oggsford man" according to Wolfsheim.[75] At the other end of the scale the army also provided a considerable amount of vocational training, having found that the draft did not secure the required numbers in appropriate trades. Army recruiting posters made a point of this, saying, "Learn and Earn—There's a Trade and an Education in the Ordnance Department," or asking, "Do You Want To Be a Mechanic—The Motor Transport Corps Will Train You." Indeed, some 130,000 mechanics were trained in the army, and altogether by 1919 369,000 men received training, including 7,400 Negro soldiers, who "were trained at 12 colored schools in 24 occupations."[76]

As was so often the case, such developments were not totally new, but were very much in line with Progressive ideas. In February 1917 the passage of the Smith-Hughes Act had provided federal aid for vocational education, and the war clearly encouraged further growth in this area. Between 1917 and 1918 the government provided $1.6 million for this purpose, matched by state funds. In June 1918 the Federal Board of Vocational Education established the Vocational Rehabilitation Division in order to train and place disabled servicemen in civilian occupations. By 1919 ten thousand men were approved for training and five thousand were in training. In 1921 the program was transferred to the Veterans' Administration and was finally discontinued in 1928.[77]

While army training could obviously provide certain vocational skills, military training and related educational programs also contributed to the assimilation and "Americanization" of servicemen from foreign backgrounds. Armed service enabled immigrants to demonstrate their loyalty and master the English language at the same time. Furthermore, the draft figures on illiteracy and the inability to speak English gave an added urgency to what had already been a prewar concern. The fact that 5.5 million people, 7.7 per cent of the population, were illiterate in 1910, and that 2.95 million could not speak English, had encouraged demands for improved national education on the grounds of social harmony and efficiency. It had also strengthened the call to limit immigration by means of a literacy test, and legislation to introduce such a measure had been passed by Congress on two occasions prior to the war, only to be vetoed by Presidents Taft and Wilson. These issues were to be raised again during the war, as "the whole question of Americanization began to assume the proportion of a national crusade."[78]

The main thrust of this crusade was, of course, to create a sense of national identity and unity mainly through demonstrations and celebrations of patriotism. Thus the North American Civic League for Immigrants, one of the most influential of the prewar Americanization organizations, which by 1914 had become the Committee for Immigrants in America, encouraged the celebration of Americanization Day on 4 July 1915 as a national civic event. The Committee on Public Information was also to organize subsequent celebrations of Flag Day. In the process of organizing such events, both the CPI and the Committee for Immigrants became involved in educational programs, and the Committee for Immigrants actually became responsible for aspects of federal policy in education. Americanizers had always seen education as an essential mechanism for the transmission of culture and values; the war provided the opportunity for them to put this into practice.

As early as 1914 the Committee for Immigrants had approached Secretary of the Interior Lane with regard to developing educational programs for immigrants, and following the sympathetic response of Lane and the Commissioner of Education, Philander Claxton, the committee had financed the creation of the Division of Immigrant Education in the Bureau of Education. Led by the militant Americanizer, former Settlement House worker, and New York attorney Frances Kellor, the division was to be a major force in publicizing the need for Americanization. These efforts grew during the war—the Committee for Immigrants now became the National Americanization Committee with Kellor as its secretary, and together with the Division of Immigrant Education, encouraged the growth of Americanization bureaus at state level. In April 1918 an Americanization conference was held in Washington, D.C., attended by representatives from nineteen states, the Council of National Defense, other branches of government, chambers of commerce, and other interested parties. However, the end product of all this activity was in many ways limited, and not necessarily beneficial to education in its broadest sense. Americanization inevitably tended to take on a conservative and repressive aspect. Secretary Lane's speech at the April conference pointing out the effects of educational deficiencies on the war effort was followed by proposals insisting on the teaching of English, demands for an end to all teaching of German, and even a suggestion that all foreign languages should be banned from American schools.[79] .

The emphasis on loyalty continued elsewhere, and the main consequence of the Americanization drive was an increase in propaganda and "educational" material ranging from the Americanization Committee's pay envelope series—"Why Become an American Citizen," "What American Citizenship Means to You" (Better Work, Better Home), and "How to Become an American Citizen"—through to 96,958 circulars, newsletters, and syllabi from the Bureau of Education, and 9,265 "America First" posters. Much of this work overlapped with that of the Committee on Public Information, which even produced a journal for school teachers, the *National School Service*, which made "the war an integral part of the school day."[80] Perhaps the most important material produced by the Bureau of Education was the pamphlet series, "Lessons in Community and National Life." Over three million copies of the pamphlets were sold, but there was considerable criticism of the content for its apparently partisan nature. It was partly for such reasons that the plans to produce "a strong federal program of legislation" came to naught. Although the number of citizenship classes increased, and various states established educational programs in order to "unite the different factions; cement friendships and discourage enmities; bring Americans and immigrants together," the basic effect of the Americanization campaign was to foster the hysteria and xenophobia that gripped the country. The fact was that immigrants were viewed with suspicion, seen as "pliant tools of the enemies of this country"—"I.W.W. plotters and pacifists."[81] At the end of the war Frances Kellor became involved in new programs "to save America from Bolshevism," including welfare capitalism, and the National Americanization Committee was wound up in 1919.[82]

If the lasting effects of wartime Americanization were hard to quantify, they did nonetheless place an emphasis on education and schooling in an ethnically diverse population. Coupled with the other aspects of wartime concern for education, this was of some significance. As Philander Claxton said

With the entrance of the United States into the conflict, and the necessary mobilization of the military, industrial, and intellectual resources of the Nation, education as a national concern has assumed a significance hitherto unrealized and the task of the Bureau of Education as the national agency for education has become greater and more definite than at any time since its creation half a century ago.[83]

The commissioner supported his statement by pointing to the wide variety of activities undertaken by the bureau, but it clearly suited his purposes to make such claims in order to gain recognition for his agency and to strengthen the case for the creation of a separate department with cabinet rank. Throughout the war he was to attempt to increase the role of the bureau in an effort to organize and centralize a national educational policy, but the results were mixed. The bureau briefly acted as a clearinghouse to find and place teachers to fill the thirty-seven thousand vacancies that existed in 1918, and the Registration and Placement Service was able to register twenty thousand teachers and nominate fifteen thousand for posts, but this was nowhere near enough, and the scheme collapsed for lack of congressional, and financial, support. Other proposals were less successful. Claxton's offer to administer the literacy program for the army was turned down as unnecessary given its own programs; a bill for a national literacy drive failed for lack of support—President Wilson could not back such a measure, as he was "not at liberty to urge any legislation which has not some immediate connection with the conduct of the war"; and although in 1920 there were "More than 70 Educational Bills Pending Before Congress"—"the result of the world war"—Congress was by then in little mood to contemplate growth in federal government or its authority, and nothing came of them. The proposal to establish a Department of Education, presented in the Towner—Sterling Bill, was defeated on grounds of cost and opposition to federal interference in the affairs of the states.[84]

The remarks made by Claxton and others about the war's impact on education reflected rhetoric and wishful thinking rather than reality. Despite all claims to the contrary, wartime produced few concrete gains—as one commentator remarked in 1919, "Little has yet been done nationally to put into effect the lessons learned or emphasized during the war."[85] Still there were some positive features: vocational education advanced, and physical education became required in the school systems of twenty-three states between 1915 and 1921. More significantly, illiteracy *did* decline during the war years—by 1920 the rate was 6 percent, and the number unable to speak English had dropped from 22 percent to 11 percent.[86] Of course, this was due as much to the passage of time and the decline of immigration, but the latter at least was an incidental (or unguided) consequence of the war. The literacy test, eventually passed over the president's veto in 1917, also may have had some effect and could fairly be seen as a wartime measure.

Similarly, the number of children in school increased dramatically in the 1920s as secondary education became almost as universal as primary education had been in the nineteenth century. Again, this was not the result of the war so much as increased affluence and a growing awareness of the "technical requirements of industrial America," but the war had certainly added to both of these. Higher education, too, expanded after the war. In 1919 and 1920 registration in universities increased by half as returning soldiers poured back into college, aided in some cases by bonus payments or grants from their individual states. By 1926 over three-quarters of a million students attended colleges in America, four or five times the numbers in European countries.[87]

If the First World War did not fundamentally effect education, nor did it alter the American family. However, by raising issues such as education and child welfare as matters of national concern, and by opening or increasing employment opportunities for women, the war did reveal how much the family's functions had changed in industrial society. In accelerating the separation of home and work and by encouraging the allocation of certain responsibilities such as health, education, and welfare outside the family, the war hastened the trend toward modernization. Although none of these concerns ceased to be individual responsibilities, they were now recognized as matters of national importance, vital to the well-being of the community as a whole. In raising such matters the war contributed to the sense and awareness of change—and thus contributed too to the reaction—that was evident in the 1920s; it also helped to ensure that when individuals were unable to fulfill their obligations in these areas on a large scale in the 1930s, they would look to government for assistance.

Notes

1. The "traditional" viewpoint is best exemplified in Frederick Lewis Allen, *Only Yesterday: An Informal History* (New York, 1957); and see also W. E. Leuchtenburg, *Perils of Prosperity* (Chicago, 1964). The "revisionist" view is expressed by William H. Chafe, *The American Woman* (New York, 1972). The two most detailed recent works are Barbara J. Steinson, *American Women's Activism in World War I* (New York and London, 1982); and Maurine W. Greenwald, *Women, War and Work: The Impact of World War I* (Westport, Conn., and London, 1980).
2. Joseph Hill, *Women in Gainful Occupations 1870 to 1920*, Dept. of Commerce, Bureau of the Census, Census Monograph IX (Washington, D.C., 1929); Alice Kessler-Harris, *Out to Work: A History of Wage-Earning Women in the United States* (New York and Oxford, 1982), 86–116, 140–45.
3. Kessler-Harris, *Out to Work.*
4. W. Lord, *The Good Years: From 1900 to the First World War* (London, 1960), 278–79; Eleanor Flexner, *Century of Struggle: The Women's Rights Movement in the United States* (Cambridge, Mass., 1959), 250–60.
5. Catt in J. Stanley Lemons, *The Woman Citizen: Social Feminism in the 1920s* (Urbana, Chicago, and London, 1973), 4.

6. Steinson, *American Women's Activism*, 220, 237–29; *New York Times*, 22 April 1917; Catt to Clara Sears Taylor, 28 December 1917, Council of National Defense Committee on Women's Defense Work, NARG 62, 13B-A1, Box 578.
7. Steinson, *American Women's Activism*, 182–86, 306–7; Bessie R. James, *For God, For Country, For Home: The National League for Woman's Service* (New York and London, 1920); National League for Woman's Service, *Annual Report for the Year 1918* (New York, 1918). "National Woman's League" file, in Dept. of Labor, Chief Clerk's File, NARG 174, Series 1, 20/476; and Dept. of Labor, Secretary of Labor, NARG 174, Series 4, 20/17.
8. Steinson, *American Women's Activism*, 309; Blanche Cook, introduction to Marie Louise Degen, *The History of the Woman's Peace Party* (Baltimore, Md., 1939), 11.
9. Steinson, *American Women's Activism*, 311–13; Catt to Josephus Daniels, 10 April 1940, Daniels Papers, Box 71, LC.
10. "Resolutions Adopted at the National Conference of the Woman's Committee, May 13, 14, and 15 1918, and by the Woman's Committee of the Council of National Defense, May 23 1918," Council of National Defense, NARG 62, Directors Office, Publicity Material 2–0–4, Box 138.
11. U.S. Council of National Defense, *First Annual Report* (Washington, D.C., 1917), 46; Georgia Council of Defense, Woman's Committee, *Final Report of Woman's Committee, April 1917–July 1919* (Atlanta, 1919); Women's Committee of State of California Council of Defense, *Report June 1 1917 to January 1 1919* (Los Angeles, 1919); Marguerite Edith Jenison, *The War-Time Organization of Illinois* (Springfield, Ill, 1923), 56–57.
12. Nevada Davis Hitchcock, "The Mobilization of Women," *Annals* 77, no. 167 (July 1918): 28; Darrell H. Smith, *The United States Employment Service: Its History, Activities, and Organization* (Baltimore, 1923), 17.
13. George Theofiles, *American Posters of World War I* (New York, n.d), 151, 152, 165.
14. U.S. Dept. of Labor, Woman in Industry Service, *First Annual Report of the Woman in Industry Service* (Washington, D.C., 1919), 5.
15. Greenwald, *Women, War, and Work*, xx; Albert E. Van Dusen, *Connecticut* (New York, 1961), 273; "Women Helping to Win War by Working in Places of Men," *Washington Star*, 14 February 1918; Hill, *Women in Gainful Occupations*, 11; "Cincinnati," USHC, NARG 3, Box 350.
16. Hill, *Women in Gainful Occupations*, 32–33.
17. Benedict Crowell and Robert F. Wilson, *How America Went to War: The Armies of Industry* (New Haven, Conn., 1921), 259, 530–31; Maurice J. Clark, *The Costs of the World War to the American People* (New Haven, Conn., 1931), 34, 45.
18. Josephus Daniels, *The Wilson Era Years of War and After* (Westport, Conn., 1974), 211–12; National Manpower Council, *Womanpower* (New York, 1957), 285.
19. Mark Sullivan, *Our Times, vol. 5, Over Here 1914–1918* (New York and London, 1933), 458; Pauline Goldmark, "Women in the Railroad Service," Academy of Political Science, Columbia University Proceedings, *War Labor Policies and Reconstruction* 8, no. 2 (February 1919): 16–19;

Greenwald, *Women, War, and Work,* 87–139; Hill, *Women in Gainful Occupations,* 81.

20. Greenwald, *Women, War, and Work,* 139–85; U.S. Dept of Labor, Women's Bureau, Bulletin 11, *Women Streetcar Conductors and Ticket Agents* (Washington, D.C., 1921). See also NWLPB, NARG 1, Box 27, "Findings in Employees Vs Cleveland Traction."

21. Hill, *Women in Gainful Occupations,* 81; Greenwald, *Women, War, and Work;* Florence Kelley, quoted in National Conference of Social Work, *Proceedings 45th Annual Session, Kansas City, May 15–22, 1918* (Chicago, 1919), 425, and see John Ryan, *Social Reconstruction: A General Review,* in J. T. Ellis, ed., *Documents of American Catholic History* (Milwaukee, 1956), 619; U.S. Dept. of Labor, National War Labor Board, *Report of the Secretary of the NWLB* (Washington, D.C., 1920), 70–71; Valerie Jean Conner, *The National War Labor Board: Stability, Social Justice and the Voluntary State in World War I* (Chapel Hill, N.C., 1983), 150–56.

22. *Cleveland Press,* 29 August 1918.

23. Memo on Sterling Motor Co., Agnes Peterson to M. Van Kleeck, 7 November 1918, Dept. of Labor, Women in Industry Service, NARG 86, Box 4; Surveys, USHC, Surveys and Statistics Division, NARG 3, Series 75, Boxes 338–54; "Women, War, and Wages," *Saturday Evening Post,* 20 January, 1917, 25.

24. Greenwald, *Women, War, and Work,* 65–67, 70–78; Mary Anderson, *Women at Work: The Autobiography of Mary Anderson as told to Mary N. Winslow* (Westport, Conn., 1951), 86–91; "Government Standards," *Official Bulletin,* 21 November 1918, in "Employment of Women" file, WLPB, NARG 1, Series 2, Box 17.

25. M. Van Kleeck, "Women's Invasion of Industry and Changes in Protective Standards," Academy of Political Science, *Proceedings, War Labor Policies and Reconstruction,* 9–10; Anderson, *Women at Work,* 91.

26. U.S. Dept. of Labor, "Women in Industry Service"; Anderson, *Women at Work,* 97, 100–101; Alice Henry, *Women and the Labor Department* (New York, 1923), 173–78.

27. Anderson, *Women at Work,* 102–3; WLPB, "Women in Industry Service," 12 December 1913.

28. Valley Cotton Oil Company, Memphis, Tennessee, to Theodore Hoepfnes, State Factory Inspector, 15 October, 1918, in Women's Bureau, NARG 86; Mrs. Myrtle Altenburg to Wisconsin State Railway Commission, 27 August 1918, U.S. Railway Admin., NARG 14, both in National Archives Teaching Unit, "World War I—The Home Front."

29. Memo to Mrs. Gertrude Beeks Easley, Secretary Executive Committee, Committee on Labor to Matthew Woll, 25 September 1918, "Nightwork for Women," Council of National Defense, Committee on Labor, NARG 62, 10A-C3, Box 364; "To The Governors of All States: Regulations Controlling Nightwork of Women. . .," Labor Department, Women in Industry Service, NARG 86, Miscellaneous Folder, Box 4; Memo, M. Van Kleeck to Major Rosensohn and Major Tully, 22 November 1918, Box 5, and see files Box 3.

30. Conner, *The National War Labor Board,* 144, 156–57.

31. "Report of Cursory Survey of the Work Women Are Doing at the

Atlantic Refining Company, Philadelphia," October 1918, by U.S. Public Health Service, WIS, NARG 86, Box 3; "An Investigation of the Work in the State of New York in Which Women Have Replaced Men since the War," by Medical Inspector of Factories, 18 July 1918, Council of National Defense, Committee on Labor, NARG 62, 10A–C3, Box 366.

32. "Ice Plants in Philadelphia," WIS, NARG 86, Box 3.

33. "Maxwell Motor Company," report of visit 15 October 1918, WIS, NARG 86, Box 4.

34. Greenwald, *Women, War, and Work,* 93–100; "Exhibit C: Chester, Pennsylvania," USHC, Surveys and Statistics Division, NARG 3, Series 75, Box 374.

35. Memo Edith Dudley, Bridgeport Ordnance Office, to Clara M. Tead, 14 November 1918, WIS, NARG 86, Box 3; U.S. Dept. of Labor, Women's Bureau, Bulletin 2, *Labor Laws for Women in Industry in Indiana,* 31 December 1918; Bulletin 10, *Hours and Conditions of Work for Women in Industry in Virginia,* 1920.

36. *New York Times,* 6 October 1918; Greenwald, *Women, War, and Work,* 93; Conner, *The National War Labor Board* 145; Memo Van Kleek to Major Tully, Bridgeport, 25 September 1918; and "Report from Charlotte Hine to Van Kleeck—Grand Rapids, Michigan, 25 September 1918, WIS, NARG 86, Box 43; "Atlanta," USHC, Surveys and Statistics Division, NARG 3, Series 75, Box 339.

37. USHC, "Exhibit C: Chester."

38. Woll, "American Labor Readjustment Proposals," Academy of Political Science, *Proceedings, War Labor Policies and Reconstruction,* 51.

39. Chafe, *The American Woman,* 51–52; Hill, *Woman in Gainful Occupations,* 16; Woman's Bureau, Bulletin 12, *The New Position of Women in American Industry* (Washington, D.C., 1920), 30–31; Greenwald, *Women, War, and Work,* xxi.

40. Industrial Safety Congress of New York State, *Proceedings of Third Industrial Safety Congress, Syracuse, 1918,* 21.

41. Carrie Catt, "Women and War," typescript, n.d., Box 5, 1, Catt Papers, NYPL.

42. Jane Addams, *The Second Twenty Years At Hull House* (New York, 1930), 103.

43. Francis C. Wickware, ed., *The American Yearbook, A Record of Events and Progress, 1917,* (New York and London, 1918), 180–81; "The War Teaches a Believer in Woman Suffrage to Oppose the Extension of the Right to Vote," *New York Times,* 3 May 1917: 14; Mrs. Alice Hay Wadsworth in *New York Times,* 2 July 1917.

44. *Saturday Evening Post,* 29 December 1917; Steinson, *American Women's Activism,* 322.

45. "Reply to Delegation from New York State Woman Suffrage Party at the White House, 25 October 1917," in *Papers 44,* 440–42; Wilson to Catt 18 October 1917, *44,* 372 (Wilson Papers Reel 210 LC); and Ray Stannard Baker, *Woodrow Wilson: Life and Letters* (New York, 1968), VII, 306.

46. Albert Bushnell Hart, *Selected Addresses and Public Papers of Woodrow Wilson* (New York, 1918), 154–57.

47. Wilson to Catt, 8 May 1917, Catt Papers, Box 1, F. 23, LC.

48. Statement by Dr. Anna Howard Shaw, U.S. Congress, House of Repre-

sentatives, Committee on Woman Suffrage, *Hearings January 3–7 1918* (Washington, D.C., 1918/19); Catt, *Hearings on S.J. Res: 2. Proposing An Amendment to the Constitution of the United States Conferring upon Women the Right of Suffrage, April 20 1917* (Washington, D.C., 1917), 32–37, 52–54.

49. Creel to Wilson, 25 September, 1918, Creel Papers, vol. 2, LC.
50. "Equal Suffrage: Address of the President of the United States Delivered in the Senate of the United States on September 30, 1918," 65th Congress, 2d Session, Senate Document 284 (Washington, D.C.), 6th Annual Address to Congress, 2 December 1918, in Albert Shaw, ed., *Messages and Papers of Woodrow Wilson* (New York, 1924) I, 536.
51. Carrie Chapman Catt and Nettie Rogers Shuler, *Woman Suffrage and Politics: The Inner Story of the Suffrage Movement* (New York, 1923), 496, 462.
52. Preston Slosson, *The Great Crusade and After 1914–1928* (New York, 1930), 160; Maud Wood Parker, quoted in J. R. Burns, "Continuity and Change; A Comparative Study of the Afro-Americans and the Woman Suffragists as Minority Groups in American Society, 1900–1929," M. Phil. dissertation, Sheffield University, 1978, II, 305.

Family, Children, Education and the State

53. Hill, *Women in Gainful Occupations,* 81.
54. Esther Lovejoy, "Democracy and Health," in Frederick A. Cleveland and Joseph Schafer, eds., *Democracy in Reconstruction* (Boston, New York, and Chicago, 1919), 173; Lathrop to Armstrong, Children's Bureau, NARG 102, Box 51, 6153.
55. R. S. Lynd and H. M. Lynd, *Middletown: A Study in Modern American Culture* (New York, 1929), 121; O'Neill, *Divorce in the Progressive Era* (New Haven and London, 1967), 19–20, 255; U.S. Dept. of Commerce, Bureau of the Census, *Historical Statistics of the United States 1759–1945* (Washington, D.C., 1949), 49; President's Research Committee on Social Trends, *Recent Social Trends in the United States* (New York and London, 1933), 39.
56. "Abstract of Reports on Juvenile Delinquency since the War from Ten Cities in the United States," 16 August 1918, Children's Bureau, NARG 102, Box 53, 7-1-0; U.S. Dept. of Labor, Children's Bureau, *Sixth Annual Report of the Chief, 1918* (Washington, D.C., 1918), 17–19.
57. U.S. Secretary of Labor, *Sixth Annual Report, 1918* (Washington, D.C., 1918), 188; letter, Charles L. Chute, Secretary, New York State Probation Commission to Lathrop, 26 June 1918, Children's Bureau, NARG 102, Box 53, 7-1-3-2.
58. Children's Bureau, *Sixth Annual Report,* 18, 19.
59. "Abstract of Reports on Juvenile Delinquency," 6; Henrietta S. Additon, "Work Among Delinquent Women and Girls," *Annals,* 79, no. 168 (September 1918): 155.
60. Ibid.
61. John Ihlder, "How War Came to Chester," *The Survey,* 1 June 1918: 246.
62. Paula Fass, *The Damned and the Beautiful: American Youth in the 1920s* (Oxford and New York, 1979), 18–20, 380–81.

63. William G. Rose, *Cleveland: The Making of a City* (Cleveland and New York, 1950), 764; U.S. Dept. of Labor, *Seventh Annual Report of the Secretary . . . Fiscal Year June 30 1919* (Washington, D.C., 1919).
64. Darrell H. Smith, *The U.S. Employment Service: Its History, Activities and Organization* (Baltimore, 1923), 16; Illinois State Council Defense, *Final Report* (Chicago, 1919), 205; Hall to Assistant Secretary of Labor, "History of The Public Service Reserve," WLPB, I, *2*, Box 29; *The Farmer's Wife: A Woman's Farm Journal* 2, no. 9 (February 1919).
65. U.S. Dept. of Labor, Children's Bureau, *Seventh Annual Report* (Washington, D.C., 1919), 9; Memo from Mrs. Matthew Page Gaffney 12 December 1918, Children's Bureau, NARG 102, Box 69, 8-2-1-11.
66. Children's Bureau, *Sixth Annual Report*, 8.
67. Rowland Berthoff, *An Unsettled People: Social Order and Disorder in American History* (New York and London, 1917), 399; U.S. Dept. of Commerce, Bureau of the Census, *Earnings of Factory Workers 1899–1927: An Analysis of Payroll Statistics* (Washington, D.C., 1929), 10.
68. Industrial Safety Congress of New York State, *Proceedings of the First Industrial Safety Congress* (Albany, 1917), 288–89; press release, 1 February 1919, Children's Bureau, Box 69, 8-2-1-11.
69. Memo, Miss Matthews, Acting Director Child Labor Division to Assistant Sescretary of Labor, 12 August 1919, Dept. of Labor, Office of Secretary, NARG 174, Box 205, file 6/14B. Letter to Nathan A. Smyth, 1 November 1918, WLPB, Committee on Conditions of Living, NARG 1, Series 2, Box 17, "Employment Service"; Slosson, *The Great Crusade and After*, 175.
70. Philander P. Claxton, *Education for the Establishment of Democracy in the World* (Washington, D.C., 1919), 20; Francis Wickware, ed., *The American Year Book 1918*, 786.
71. Lewis Paul Todd, *Wartime Relations of the Federal Government and the Public Schools* (New York, 1945), 172–73; Wickware, *The American Year Book, 1917* (New York and London, 1918) 751.
72. Wilson to Lane, 31 July 1918, Bureau of Education, NARG 12, 107; Dept. of Interior, Bureau of Education, "Government Policies Involving the Schools in War Time," *Teachers Leaflet*, no. 3 (April 1918).
73. Francis Wickware, *The American Year Book 1919* (New York and London, 1920), 796; John G. Clark, et al., *Three Generations in Twentieth Century America*, 76–77; U.S. Dept. of Labor, Children's Bureau, *Seventh Annual Report 1919* (Washington, D.C., 1919), 9.
74. U.S. Dept. of Interior, Bureau of Education, *Americanization as a War Measure: Report of a Conference Called by the Secretary and Held in Washington, April 3, 1918* (Washington, D.C., 1918), 18; Fred C. Butler, U.S. Director of Americanization, "Illiteracy as a National Liability," n.d., Bureau of Education, NARG 12, File 106.
75. Alabama Council of Defense, *Report of the Alabama Council of Defense Covering Its Activities from May 17, 1917 To December 31, 1918* (Montgomery, Ala., 1919), 16–17; Women's Committee of State Council of Defense of California, *Report: From June 1, 1917 to January 1, 1919* (Los Angeles, 1919), 46–47; Clarence H. Cramer, *Newton D. Baker: A Biography* (Cleveland and New York, 1961), 199–200; Wickware, *American Year Book 1919*, 812–13; Newton D. Baker, "The Army as an

Americanization Agency," n.d., Baker Papers, "Speeches and Writings," Box 244, "1915–18," LC.
76. Theofiles, *American Posters*, 217; U.S. War Dept., Committee on Education and Special Training, *Final Report of the National Army Training Detachments* . . . (Washington, D.C., 1919); Samuel P. Capen, "The Educational Lessons of War," in Cleveland and Schafer, *Democracy in Reconstruction*, 223–32.
77. James Munroe to Baker, 8 September 1919, Baker Papers, Reel 9, LC; Wickware, *Year Book 1917*, 744.
78. U.S. Department of Commerce, Bureau of the Census, *Abstract of the Fourteenth Census of the United States, 1920* (Washington, D.C., 1923), 427; Edward George Hartmann, *The Movement to Americanize the Immigrant* (New York, 1948), 105.
79. John F. McClymer, *War and Welfare: Social Engineering in America, 1890–1925* (Westport, Conn., and London, 1980), 110–12; Bureau of Education, *Americanization as a War Measure*.
80. Hartmann, *The Movement to Americanize*, 159; George T. Blakey, *Historians on the Homefront: American Propagandists for the Great War* (Lexington, Kentucky, 1970), 122–24; Stephen Vaughn, *Holding Fast the Inner Lines: Democracy, Nationalism and the CPI* (Chapel Hill, N.C. 1980), 98–89; "Recent Activities of the Division of Immigrant Education," 17 January 1917, Bureau of Education, NARG 12, File 420, Box 18; File 106, "Americanization War Work."
81. Letter to nonsubscribers, 17 October 1917, National Americanization Committee, Bureau of Education NARG 12, File 420, Box 18; "Americanization as a War Measure: Program for Secretary Lane," February 1918; Memo, "Immediate Work—June 30, 1918," Bureau of Education, File 106. Correspondence Relating to "Lessons in Community and National Life," Historical File 1914–20, File 106.
82. Gerd Korman, *Industrialization, Immigrants and Americanizers: The View from Milwaukee, 1866–1921* (Madison, Wis., 1967), 165; Hartmann, *The Movement to Americanize*, 120–22.
83. U.S. Commissioner of Education, *Report for the Year Ended June 30, 1917* (Washington, D.C., 1917), 1.
84. Bureau of Education, NARG 12, File 106, Box "School Board Service Station: Teacher Registration and Placement Service," Claxton to Lane, 26 March 1918; Wilson to Lane, 14 May 1918, in Box 18, File 420; *School Life* 4, no. 4 (15 February 1920). On Smith Towner and other bills, see *New York Sun*, 18 May 1919, *Washington Star*, 6 January 1919, and U.S. Congress, Senate Committee on Education and Labor, *Joint Hearings on Department of Public Welfare, May 1921* (Washington, D.C., 1921); and discussion in Walsh Papers, Box 269, LC.
85. Wickware, *Year Book 1919*, 796.
86. Bureau of Census, *Fourteenth Census 1920* (1922), II, 1043.
87. Fass, *The Damned and the Beautiful*, 123–24; Slosson, *The Great Crusade and After*, 320–22, 329.

7

Black Americans and the First World War

If the theory that military participation brings rewards and recognition for minority groups had any validity, then black Americans would have been free and equal long before the twentieth century dawned. Sadly, however, the countervailing forces of racism and prejudice ensured that blacks remained second-class citizens, victims of segregation and discrimination, even though they had fought in all America's wars from the revolutionary conflict through to the Spanish–American war of 1896. In many ways the First World War was to be no exception to this depressing pattern: while black involvement in all aspects of the war effort was to become considerable, it was resisted by whites, and wartime race relations were to be marked by an intensification of violence. Nonetheless, fundamental changes of a more positive nature were taking place in the black situation, and, indeed, race violence was often a response to, and reflection of, the changes that had occurred. By the end of the war observers could write of "the new Negro problem" and of the "New Negro," and historians since have seen the origins of modern Afro-American history in this period— "the war had completed the destruction of the old status quo."[1]

Whatever the subsequent views, the omens for change in race relations in prewar America were not good. Unlike white American women, who could point to considerable advances before 1914, black Americans could only look back on the previous twenty years with a sense of despair.

Whereas white women already had long-established, powerful national organizations with some access and influence in government and a growing social and economic status, blacks could actually point to a decline in their position between 1880 and 1914. So much was this so that the period has justifiably been seen as the "nadir" of black American history.[2]

Concentrated in the former Confederate states, the vast majority of the black population, almost 90 percent of the nine million or so in the United States in 1900, were former slaves, free only slightly more than fifty years, and lacking in education, power, organization or leadership. The years after Reconstruction brought "redemption" for the white South, but condemnation for blacks, who fell under the control and domination of their former owners. In the system of sharecropping and tenant farming, which evolved after the Civil War, the landless black freedmen were virtually trapped in a pattern of permanent indebtedness and poverty. From the 1880s on their inferior status was confirmed as southern states and cities passed legislation segregating the races in places of public accommodation from streetcars and railways, theaters and restaurants, through to schools and colleges. While such "Jim Crow" legislation was upheld by the Supreme Court in successive rulings in the 1890s culminating in the famous "separate but equal" doctrine of *Plessy v. Ferguson,* various constitutional devices were also introduced in the South to deprive blacks of the vote. Poll taxes, literacy tests, property qualifications, and the notorious grandfather clauses (preventing from voting those whose grandfathers had been slaves) all had the same effect—by 1910 the civil rights guaranteed to blacks under the Fifteenth Amendment were circumvented in all southern states, and black voting was almost negligible: in Louisiana, for example, the number of blacks registered to vote in 1896 was over 130,000; by 1904 this was a mere 1,342.[3]

The legal discrimination against blacks in the South was reinforced with violence and intimidation. The sense of fear evident in black writing is hardly surprising given the general, and haphazard, occurrence of brutal repression. Lynchings involving shooting, burnings, maiming, and torture were a regular phenomenon: in the 1880s and 1890s there were an average of 150 such murders a year; in 1892 alone 235 were recorded, and between 1900 and 1914 over 1,000 blacks died at the hands of mobs.[4] Not surprisingly, many blacks fled.

Economic hardship and the constant threat to life and limb encouraged a regular black exodus from the South, and approximately two hundred thousand moved elsewhere between 1890 and 1910. One consequence was the growth of black populations in a few northern cities, and in a few such cases the black ghetto was already in existence before the war came. However, the rate of migration remained slow, and the black northern population was small and confined to major centers—Washington, D.C., Baltimore, Philadelphia, Chicago, and New York. The restraining force was of course the limited opportunity that existed in the North while European immigrants flooded the country. Northern industrialists prefered to recruit whites from across the Atlantic rather than blacks on their own doorstep. Besides, even in the North blacks met with discrimination and segregation. Some northern cities forbade the settlement of blacks, and in others the black presence was met with a violent response such as the riot that broke out in Lincoln's hometown of Springfield, Illinois, in 1908, which left two dead and seventy injured.

Black Americans were hardly in a position to resist this oppression. Without a strong urban base and with little economic strength or even group awareness, the constituents of a powerful organization did not exist. Black leadership was dominated by Booker T. Washington, a former slave who had risen to become head of Tuskegee Institute in Alabama. His public acceptance of racial separation and the denial of civil rights to blacks, even though he might contest them in private, led critics then and since to see him as an "accommodationist" Uncle Tom figure, although it is difficult to see what alternative he had if he wished to remain (alive) and have influence in the South. However, in saying what many whites wished to hear, Washington was able to build up his college with white financial assistance, and in so doing secure the position of leading Negro spokesman for himself. This position was being challenged toward the end of the nineteenth century by voices representing the growing northern black population, notably Monroe Trotter, editor of the *Boston Guardian*, and W. E. B. DuBois, an academic and scholar who was the first black to be awarded a Ph.D. from Harvard.

It was DuBois who wrote in 1903 that the "problem of the Twentieth Century is the problem of the color line," and it was in an attempt to resolve that problem that he, along with Trotter and other blacks, met together at Niagara in 1905 to call for an end to racial discrimination in America. In 1909 this small group of black spokesmen joined a conference of white Progressives, shocked by the Springfield riots, to form the National Association for the Advancement of Colored People (NAACP). Among the white participants in what was to eventually become the most important civil rights movement until the 1950s were some distinguished people: the writer William English Walling; New York social worker Mary Ovington; Oswald Garrison Villard, publisher and grandson of the abolitionist Wiliam Lloyd Garrison; novelist William Dean Howells; John Dewey; and, of course, Jane Addams. DuBois, initially the only black officer in the association, was responsible for publicity and became the editor of the official journal, the *Crisis*. Circulation of the monthly publication had reached over thirty thousand by 1914, and NAACP membership was around nine thousand. Other concerned whites, led notably by Frances Kellor, responded to the growing black presence in northern cities by creating the National Urban League (NUL) in 1911, but this remained primarily a New York City–based organization concerned with social work rather than the reform of race relations.[5]

Despite the fact that some observers might echo DuBois and see race as " 'the most fundamental of all American social and political problems,' " neither the NAACP nor the NUL could rank as significant when compared with other movements, and the plight of the Afro-American was far from being a central concern for most Progressives. Neither of the two reform presidents did anything for blacks. Theodore Roosevelt did at first seem sympathetic and even entertained Booker T. Washington to tea at the White House. It was a mistake he did not repeat. Following the angry outcry, no further invitations were extended, and subsequently the president spoke of the inferiority of the Afro-American. In 1906, when black soldiers in Brownsville, Texas, rioted after endless harassment and provocation, Roosevelt ordered the dismissal of 167 men from the service without honor although none were definitely proved to have been party to, nor have knowledge of, the incident. The record was not to be cleared until 1972.[6]

If blacks were disappointed with Roosevelt, they were further dismayed by the performance of Woodrow Wilson, whose New Freedom did not extend to Afro-Americans. Indeed, with the return of the Democratic party to the presidency they actually suffered setbacks, as segregation was introduced to government offices in Washington, D.C., and as traditional black federal and diplomatic appointments were withdrawn. Wilson was not a likely candidate to argue in favor of black rights. He was a southerner who believed in states' rights, the separation of the races, and, as president of Princeton, had discouraged blacks from applying to the college. Not only was he dependent upon southern support in Congress in order to pass his legislative program, but he also appointed a predominantly southern cabinet, which he left largely to do as it saw fit with regard to racial practices, and he often entertained his advisers with "darky" stories. A meeting in 1914 with black leaders on the subject of continued discrimination in federal government was a particularly stormy affair. Reminded of statements made in a similar meeting the year before, Wilson responded coolly. The leader of the delegation, Monroe Trotter, demanded to be heard, insisting that he and his fellows were there as "full-fledged American citizens." Confronted in this manner, the president terminated the discussion and suggested that any future delegation should be headed by a new spokesman. In the event, no further meetings were to take place on this subject, as the president became increasingly preoccupied with events in Europe. While not prepared to act personally, the president did, nonetheless, welcome efforts to advance "the economic success and comfort of the negroes and put them in a position where they can work out *their own* success and self respect" [italics mine]. As Kelly Miller, dean of Howard University, the black college in Washington, D.C., was to observe, as far as race went Wilson reversed the old motto: for him "charity began abroad rather than at home."[7]

That the Progressive era should have yielded so little for blacks is hardly remarkable given the climate of opinion on racial matters. Behind much of the reform ferment lay an attempt to preserve the white Anglo-Saxon Protestant tradition, and many reformers believed not just in the superiority of the white race, but also of western Europeans over those from the south and east—"the dark pigmented things" was Jack London's view of the new immigrants—and, as we have seen, many of the problems of the cities and of labor were attributed to new arrivals. Of course, Americans were not exceptional in their attitudes. Many Europeans accepted social Darwinist ideas, and the belief in the superiority of *their* race was evident in the "New Imperialism" of the 1890s. Indeed, many of the American ideas on race originated in Europe, and writers such as Gobineau, Galton, Le Bon, and others were influential in the United States. Such influences could be traced in Charles Carroll's *The Negro Is a Beast* (1900), William Calhoun's *The Caucasian and the Negro* (1902), Robert Shufeldt's *The Negro a Menace to American Civilization* (1907), and the writings of Thomas Dixon, most notably his *Leopard's Spots* (1902) and his celebration of the Ku Klux Klan, *The Clansman* (1905), which provided the basis for D. W. Griffith's distorted movie version of Reconstruction, *The Birth of a Nation* (1915). Griffith's portrayal of black Americans as ignorant, violent, and depraved was indicative of the general climate of racial opinion and helps to explain how the Negro could be treated so harshly with so little protest. Not surprisingly, race and race hatred were not themes that Griffith dealt with in his great study of human conflict through the ages, *Intolerance* (1916), although this was clearly an aspect of American life at the time.[8] Such attitudes were hardly to be affected by the experience of war—indeed, one of the most potent books on race, Madison Grant's *Passing of the Great Race, or The Racial Basis of European History,* was published in 1916 (and could be referred to by Tom Buchanan in Fitzgerald's *Great Gatsby* in 1925). Nonetheless, the war was to have some effect: if only, as one observer said, " 'to disturb the equilibrium of the races.' "[9]

When America entered the war in 1917 blacks' response was generally supportive despite their second-class treatment in society and the history of disappointment in the past. Afro-Americans were to contribute over $250,000 in war loans, and the black leadership was almost solidly committed to supporting the war effort regardless of the Negro's disadvantaged position in American life. Thus the leading black paper, the *Chicago*

Defender, could "call every able-bodied man among us now to rally to his country's need in this time of trial" (17 November 1917). Later that same month (24 November), the paper's editorial stated: "It is our duty to keep a stiff upper lip and make the most out of the situation. Victory must and will be ours, so let us all pull together." Even as it became apparent that war might change very little, the *Defender* refused to "rock the boat" but instead repeatedly urged its readers to set aside grievances—"and we have many of them"—on the grounds that

if we again demonstrate our loyalty and devotion to our country in face of the injustice referred to, those injustices will disappear and the grounds for complaint will no longer exist. [6 April, 4 May 1918]

The colored soldier who fights side by side with the white American . . . will hardly be begrudged a fair chance when the victorious armies return. [19 May 1918]

The optimism and expectation of the *Defender* were echoed by DuBois in the *Crisis.* In successive editorials the black leader urged his people to participate, "to seize the opportunity to emphasize their American citizenship" because "out of this war will rise, too, an American Negro with the right to live without insult." In July 1918 DuBois wrote a now-famous editorial that called upon blacks to "forget our special grievances and close ranks shoulder to shoulder with our own white citizens and the allied nations that are fighting for democracy."[10]

Not all blacks were prepared to go this far, and there was an outburst of protest, particularly when it became known that DuBois was considering the offer of a commission in the Army Military Intelligence Bureau as adviser on racial affairs. One of DuBois's fellow founders of the Niagara movement, who found it hard even to believe that DuBois had written the offending article, suggested that the war was "the most opportune time for us to keep our special grievances to the fore." At an NAACP meeting in Washington, DuBois was referred to as "traitor" and "Benedict Arnold."[11] This was not an isolated view by 1918, and the general reaction among blacks to the *Crisis* editorial was such that the offer of the commission was pursued neither by DuBois nor the government. By the summer of that year the government was becoming increasingly aware of the growing discontent among the black population.

Although the editors of black newspapers and journals could perceive the issues at stake, the significance of the war was not always apparent to ordinary blacks any more than it was always to whites, especially those in remote rural parts of the country. It was even harder for blacks given the treatment they received at home: for some it was difficult to distinguish between "the Huns of Alsace and the Huns of Alabama." As one black remarked, "The Germans ain't done nothin' to me, and if they have, I forgive 'em."[12] The feeling that this was a white man's war was articulated by two young black Socialists, A. Philip Randolph and Chandler Owen, who, as editors of the *Messenger,* rejected the notion of participation in the war effort in return for recognition. "Since when," they asked, "has the subject race come out of a war with its rights and privileges accorded for such participation?"[13] Such views soon attracted the attention of the Justice Department, and both men were arrested in the summer of 1918 in Cleveland. For once racial prejudice worked in favor of the defendants: the judge could not believe that the two men were other than the dupes of white radicals, and he dismissed the charges. In August Owen was drafted and spent the remainder of the war in a camp in the South; Randolph avoided a similar fate because the war ended just as his call-up was due.[14]

It is impossible to determine what influence Randolph and Owen had or how representative their attitudes were. However, black Americans were sufficiently disenchanted for a number of members of government to express concern. Earlier reports, in 1917, had suggested that German propaganda was aimed very much at blacks, but this was generally accepted to be exaggerated or ineffective. However, by June 1918 George Creel could write to the president that "the colored population of the country . . . has been torn by rumor and ugly whispering ever since we entered the war." The following month Secretary of War Baker wrote that he was "disturbed," and his "anxiety was growing at the situation in this country among the negroes." According to Baker, Military Intelligence indicated "more unrest among them [blacks] than has existed before for years." Even DuBois was writing in August of "unrest and bitterness." The seriousness of the situation was well described by Joel Spingarn, chairman of the directors of the NAACP, acting in his capacity as army intelligence officer:

> The co-operation of this large element of our population in all civilian and military activities is of vital importance; the alienation, or worse, of eleven million people would be a serious menace to the successful prosecution of the war.[15]

The chief response of the government to this problem was to follow the suggestion of Creel and Baker and hold a conference of black newspaper editors in Washington, D.C. This in itself was remarkable, as one paper noted:

> Never before in the history of the country were colored men invited to Washington by the government to discuss problems and questions which so urgently demand adjustment and answering.[16]

Creel reckoned the meeting to be a success although the president declined to meet with the editors. The black spokesmen issued a statement that unanimously affirmed their support for the war effort and a "readiness to make every sacrifice to win this war." However, the editors also pointed to "justifiable grievances" as a source of bitterness and called specifically for better conditions of public travel, the use of blacks where needed without discrimination, and the immediate suppression of lynching.[17]

The continued incidence of lynching and racial violence was clearly a major cause of black discontent. Numerous complaints were made against such brutal occurrences, including those from representatives of the NAACP to the president and to his secretary. Even Newton Baker pointed to lynching as a chief cause of black unrest, and suggested that some presidential action might have "a wholesome effect." However, John Shillady, secretary of the NAACP, was informed that "the Federal Government has absolutely no jurisdiction over matters of this kind, nor are they connected with the war in any such way as to justify the action of the Federal Government under the war power." In a meeting with blacks in February 1918, in which they presented a petition, the president was very much moved, but he still declined to speak out against lynching. By the summer he could no longer deny the necessity of some action, and on 26 July he issued a general condemnation of mob violence, which did not, however, make any specific mention of race. In the true spirit of states' rights the president urged governors of states and members of every community "to make an end of this disgraceful evil." No direct federal action was taken.[18]

Lynching was only the most obvious cause of black discontent, but other provocations were not hard to see. From the very beginning of the war blacks were met with the persistence of discrimination, as their participation in the war effort was resisted or severely curtailed. Black volunteers for military service were accepted only as long as there remained places in the four black regular army regiments established after the Civil War; once those vacancies were filled Afro-Americans were turned away. When Selective Service was first debated, black military service was opposed altogether by some southerners. Senator Vardaman (Mississippi) said that if the act was passed "millions of Negroes who will come under the measure will be armed, [and] I know of no greater menace to the South than this."[19] However, once the act was passed 2.29 million blacks registered, and some 370,000 were called into service. In fact, discrimination often worked in reverse: nearly 31 percent of registered blacks were drafted compared with 26 percent of whites. Thus in Fulton County, Georgia, 526 out of 815 whites were granted exemptions, but only 6 out of 212 blacks.[20]

Once accepted by the military, blacks found limitations to their range of service. In the navy the ten thousand black sailors could work only as messmen, cooks, or heavers of coal; they were barred entirely from the marines and the Coast Guard, and from the Army Aviation Corps. Of the almost 400,000 black men in the army 380,000 were in services of supply as stevedores, drivers, engineers, cooks, laundrymen, and the like. Over 200,000 blacks served in France, but only 42,000 of these were in combat roles.

No matter what the branch of service, blacks were segregated from their white counterparts, denied the opportunity to fight "shoulder to shoulder." Newton Baker made it clear that "there is no intention on the part of the War Department to undertake at this time to settle the so-called race question," and little was done by his department to protect black soldiers from discrimination and insult.[21] Many training camps were situated in the South, where military practices conformed absolutely to local requirements, and the black soldiers, including those from the North, had to accept the Jim Crow laws and suffer harassment from white civilians. When, in one instance, a black sergeant at Camp Funston, Kansas, insisted upon what was acknowledged to be his legal right and protested against discrimination in a theater, he was held to be in the wrong by his commanding officer and disciplined. In a general bulletin issued to black soldiers as a consequence of this incident, they were urged, "Don't go where your presence is not desired."[22]

Such strictures were hard to obey given that there were few places in the South where blacks *were* welcomed. On 23 August 1917 in Houston, Texas, this situation finally came to a head when black soldiers responded to constant racial humiliation and, following a fracas involving the police, rioted. Sixteen whites, including four policemen, and four black soldiers died in the violence. In November sixty-four black soldiers were court-martialed for murder and mutiny, and fifty-nine received sentences ranging from death to long prison terms. Thirteen were speedily executed on 11 December without any appeal, review of sentence, or publicity. When news of this finally became known, the public protest was such to ensure a review of the later trial verdicts, and ten out of a further sixteen men sentenced to death had their sentences commuted to life imprisonment in "recognition of the splendid loyalty of the race." Military policy was also amended to provide for the suspension of capital punishment until both the judge advocate and secretary of war had examined the records.[23]

It was fortunate that there were no repetitions of the events of Houston elsewhere in the South given the prevalent white attitudes. Even within the camps blacks were often maligned and ill treated by their officers, many of whom were white southerners chosen deliberately because they "would understand the Negro temperament." The number of black officers was minuscule, and the best-known and most senior of these, Charles Young, only the third black graduate of West Point, was retired as colonel in June 1917 apparently on medical grounds but coincidentally at the point when he was due for promotion to brigadier general. White officers made it clear that they would not serve under Young, and although he demonstrated his fitness by riding from Ohio to the capital, the retirement order was not rescinded until 6 November 1918. By that time, of course, the war was over and black pride had received just one more setback. However, protests again had some effect: a segregated black officer training camp was established, and there were to be some twelve hundred black officers at the war's end.[24]

Despite the various barriers in their way, black troops served with some valor and distinction in Europe. But even in the trenches they found discrimination. The first black combat regiments were assigned to the French command on the grounds that they had experiences with their own colonial forces. *"Les enfants perdus,"* as the black soldiers became known, were well regarded by the French, and three regiments of the 93d Infantry Division were awarded the Croix de Guerre, as were more than one hundred individual black soldiers. So sympathetic were the French that in August 1918 their liaison officer with the Americans warned his compatriots against dealing with blacks "on the same plane as with white Americans." This "indulgence and this familiarity are," he said, "matters of grievous concern to the Americans." The officer further suggested that blacks should not be praised too highly, and "pronounced intimacy" should be avoided.[25]

The Frenchman was right to say that white Americans resented blacks, but some were prepared to acknowledge the contribution and bravery of their black countrymen. One commentator said, in language that speaks volumes, "You will have to hand it to these coons as they certainly did some fighting." Other observers, while complimentary, were also patronizing and demonstrated how little the war had altered racial stereotypes. Thus black soldiers were "splendid hikers," "with great powers of endurance," but who suffered from "extraordinary nervousness," and who were afraid of the dark and lacking in will and initiative. "In fighting qualities," this observer noted, "the average of the colored race is not as high as that of the white."[26]

Such views predominated in military circles. Examples of black heroism were forgotten, failure was remembered—even when the black soldiers involved in defeats were exonerated by official investigations. Similarly, rumors of general inefficiency, cowardice, and outbreaks of rape persisted long after the war and despite evidence to the contrary. In sum, military service was restricted, and blacks were given few opportunities to demonstrate their equality. Placed in limited roles, badly treated, and often poorly led, blacks were hardly likely to excel, and so the prejudices of whites could be confirmed. Successes in the face of overwhelming obstacles were forgotten or ignored. Worse still, the black soldier was often to find himself the target of white anger and the victim of violent attacks when he returned home. In 1919 at least ten black soldiers, some still in uniform, were lynched. Little wonder the blues singer could sing:

> When Uncle Sam called me,
> I knowed I'd be called the real McCoy,
> When I got in the Army,
> They just called me soldier boy.

and then ask:

> I wonder when, I wonder when,
> I wonder when will I get to be called a man.[27]

The violent treatment of black soldiers was not just an attempt to put them back "in their place," but part of a general response to the changes that had affected race relations during the war, for if there had been little change in racial patterns in the military, there had been much more on the domestic front. These changes were not, however, a consequence of government actions but once again were the spontaneous response to wartime demands and pressures. The most dramatic and far-reaching of these was the "Great Migration" of blacks from the South to the North.

As already noted, there had been a slow but steady trickle of blacks out of the South in the prewar years, but this was almost insignificant when compared with the numbers involved after 1914. Where previously the average number of blacks leaving the South per decade between 1870 and 1910 had been about 67,000, estimates for the war period range from 150,000 to over 2 million. The most reliable figures, however, suggest a total somewhere between 300 to 500,000, with the greatest number moving after 1916, i.e., in a four-year period. Whatever the exact figure—and it is impossible to be exact because of the absence of firm records, the problem of blacks returning to the South, and the reliance on census figures by decade—between 1910 and 1920 the black population in the North rose by almost 700,000 and in the West by 48,000, while in the South it declined by 733,000. This was in contrast to the movement of white population, which showed a decline in northern population and an increase of almost three million in the West.[28]

The magnitude of the "Great Migration" was clearly remarkable— some northern cities witnessed a thousand new arrivals every month; in others a thousand were said to be arriving *every week*—but another striking feature besides sheer numbers was the greater distance traveled by the wartime migrants. Whereas previously most southern black migrants had moved from border states, now they also came from the Deep South—the largest single loss occurred in Mississippi (seventy-five thousand). Equally significant was the fact that the northern black population was becoming more widely dispersed, not just concentrated in a handful of centers, but now in a number of towns and cities in Pennsylvania, Illinois, Ohio, New York, and Michigan. The greatest single number still went to Chicago (sixty-five thousand), an increase of 150 percent, but in Detroit the black population grew by over 600 percent with an increase of thirty-five thousand. Smaller cities, too, experienced enormous proportional increases: in Cleveland, for example, the black population grew by 307 percent, from 8,448 to 34,451; in Akron, the percentage increase was almost 750 percent.[29]

The causes of this movement are well known and have been fully documented in a number of sources.[30] The expansion of northern industry, coupled with the simultaneous drop in European immigration, provided the final "pull" to the "push" of poverty, inequality, and violence long present in the South. Additional disasters such as flooding and the ravages of the destructive boll weevil provided new incentives to depart at the same time as letters from earlier migrants spoke of greater economic opportunity, better education, and more freedom in the North. The black newspaper the *Chicago Defender* was also enormously influential. Throughout this period the paper urged blacks to leave the South, and in the spring of 1917 launched a "Great Northern Drive." When reports spread of blacks freezing to death in the inhospitable climate of the North, the *Defender* countered with details of similar deaths in the South and asked,

> If YOU CAN FREEZE TO DEATH in the North and be free, why
> FREEZE in the South and be a slave . . .
> The Defender Says Come.[31]

The *Chicago Defender* was not the only voice that said come—labor agents from northern industries also provided encouragement, offering good wages, courteous treatment, and assistance in shipping families and household goods. Such activity was reported as widespread throughout the southern states, and there were suggestions that black communities in some areas moved en masse in response to inducements of this sort.[32] Many migrants attracted by such promises were to be disappointed—there was a suggestion that blacks were deliberately misled in order to cheapen labor generally in the North—but most of the new arrivals were at least able to find some sort of employment. They were often assisted by the *Chicago Defender* and the National Urban League, both of which acted as clearinghouses for job information. From 1918 the Urban League office in Chicago was in fact being run by the U.S. Employment Service and in Detroit the League was funded by the Employers' Association from 1916. With or without such assistance "some 255,000 blacks found new jobs in the wake of the war emergency," and the number employed in industry as a whole rose between 1910 and 1920 by almost 400,000. As several writers noted, "the war gave [blacks] their first great industrial opportunity," and "the first black industrial working class came into existence" in what was seen as this "dawn of a day of new opportunity."[33]

The improvement in the black situation was not due merely to an increase in the number of jobs open to them: the range and quality of employment also expanded during the war years. In Chicago in 1910 over 50 percent of black workers had been engaged in domestic and personal service, and in Cleveland one-third worked in similar capacities before the war; by 1920 only 28 percent of black Chicagoans were in domestic service, and in Cleveland the proportion was down to 12 percent. In Detroit, too, blacks who had formerly been porters and elevator boys were now carmakers, engineers, and crane operators.[34] In some areas the increase in employment was particularly pronounced: the Westinghouse Company employed only twenty-five blacks in 1916; by 1918 it employed fifteen hundred. The number of black shipyard workers rose from about thirty-seven thousand to over one hundred thousand, and in the U.S. Shipyards blacks entered "the skilled and semi-skilled occupations . . . in large numbers."[35] Black women made advances too, as over 40 percent moved from domestic work into factory occupations, often replacing white women in textile, clothing, food, and tobacco industries as the number of black women in mechanized and manufacturing production rose from over 67,000 in 1910 to almost 105,000 in 1920.[36]

For both black men and women the wartime conditions of employment in the North were much better than those in the South, as indeed the letters from migrants suggested. Such letters spoke of daily wages of from six to eight dollars a day, often the equivalent of a week's earnings in the South. In Chicago, where the average rate of pay was fifty cents an hour compared with seventy-five cents *a day* in the South, one survey found that "almost without exception the Negroes interviewed declared that their economic situation had improved in Chicago." Thus while a waiter might earn only ten dollars a week, those blacks in the stockyards could earn almost fifty dollars.[37] Although blacks went mainly into the lower-paid jobs, and there was, besides, often discrimination in rates of pay so that blacks were paid less for doing the same work as whites, this was not always the case. An investigation of the situation of Negroes in basic industries in Illinois, Ohio, and Pennsylvania at the end of the war compared earnings of blacks and whites in 194 occupations and found that while one-third of the blacks earned less than whites, one-third earned the same, and one-third earned more. However, even government boards discriminated—the U.S. Shipbuilding Labor Adjustment Board, for example, approved wage rates from ten to twenty cents lower than white rates for black workers. Nonetheless, the *Chicago Defender* could still announce, "The opportunity we have longed for is here; it is ours now to grasp it. The war has given us a place upon which to stand."[38]

Despite such optimism, the wartime economic advances had drawbacks other than those just of lower wage rates. The majority of gains were in unskilled areas and concentrated in a few industries such as iron, steel, meat packing, shipbuilding, and so on. In 1910 blacks constituted 6.4 percent of the unskilled laborers in the steelworks, but by 1920 this had increased to 17 percent. Black employment in the automobile industry increased as technological change brought a decline in the proportion of skilled work from 75 percent to 10 percent. A new stereotype of blacks performing the hot, heavy, dirty, and dangerous industrial tasks had arisen, and this was to continue in the postwar period. Black women were less fortunate in that their employment gains, such as they were, proved to be largely temporary. In the aftermath of the war black women were displaced again by white females (mainly foreign workers), and in 1930 "the occupational status of Negro women was not much different from what it had been in 1870."[39]

If the migration did not lead to equal employment opportunities, nor did it necessarily result in better living conditions. For blacks the wartime shortages in housing were compounded by the racial prejudice that restricted their choices and confined them to existing black areas. In Detroit, for example, there was not a single vacant house or tenement in the black area by 1919, and as Robert C. Weaver, a later leading authority on black housing, was to write, it was during the war years and after that "the idea of Negro ghettos in northern cities became fixed." Thus while it was true that segregation was evident prior to the war, the concentration of black urban dwellers in limited areas increased markedly during the conflict, with 10 percent increases in segregation registered in cities such as Chicago, Cleveland, and Buffalo. According to Kenneth Kusmer, "the sudden influx of migrants . . . caused the black ghetto in cities like Cleveland to consolidate much sooner than would otherwise have been the case."[40]

The combination of overcrowding, inferior housing, and low economic status led to conditions that could only be described as deplorable. In Chicago, where blacks were mainly crammed into the South Side, "the core of the black belt was a festering slum." The Chicago Commission found that the ordinary conveniences, considered necessities by the average white citizen, are often lacking. Bathrooms are often missing. Gas lighting is common, and electric lighting is a rarity. . . .

The commission found housing in black areas to be generally in poorer repair than in other districts and described over 30 percent of homes in one black district as "absolutely delapidated." Another observer had earlier described an area of the city in which almost every house was inhabited by black families:

two thirds of them are in unsanitary condition and in fact, uninhabitable; nevertheless, groups of colored people are residing there. In some instances three or four families are occupying space which, according to the law of sanitation, should be occupied by one family only.

This reporter went on to say that he had found people in dives and brothels "living on a bare pittance of ten or fifteen cents a day."[41] This did not sound much like the Promised Land.

It is difficult to gauge accurately the effects of such conditions. Comparisons with housing in the South are almost impossible to make on any precise basis. Certainly, for many blacks the situation in the North *was* an improvement, particularly for those who had left behind one-roomed or two-roomed wooden shacks with earthen floors. Some figures suggest a marked decrease in, for example, the number of deaths due to tuberculosis, with a drop from over 401 deaths per 100,000 of the population to 262 between 1914 and 1920 (the white figures were 133.4 in 1914 and 100 in 1920). However, other sources point to a deterioration. In Cleveland there was a "marked increase in infant mortality, pneumonia, tuberculosis, and venereal disease," and in Harlem in the early 1920s the death rate among blacks was over 50 percent in excess of the rest of the city. Whether these facts reflected on the already poor health of the in-migrants or on the effects of the city slums was impossible to tell, but whatever the cause, black Americans continued to find city life "debilitating."[42]

Although it may be difficult to assess the "Great Migration" in terms of losses or gains, it clearly marked a major change in American social structure. This change, however, was not always welcomed by whites, either in the South or North. Initially encouraged as a possible solution to the South's "race problem," the rapid exodus of blacks soon brought mounting opposition from all parts of the country. White southerners were soon, as a representative from Louisiana wrote, "becoming very much exercised" for fear the migration would prevent crops from being harvested, and the sudden loss of the traditional labor force appeared to be a growing reality. Such fears led to the harassment or outlawing of labor agents (who were generally described in critical terms by white southerners who viewed them as agitators), and attempts to prevent the sale or circulation of the *Chicago Defender*. The Louisiana congressman also told of one group of two hundred Negroes who were "prevailed upon" by the local sheriff to remain in the South, and similar occurrences undoubtedly took place in other states.[43]

In the North, too, the arrival of large numbers of blacks was viewed with increasing alarm. While the *New York Times* could write of the "Harmful Rush of Negro Workers to the North" and point to both the loss of labor in the South and overcrowding in the North, other headlines spoke of "half a million darkies" "swarming" to the North and suggested that they were "incited by German spies."[44] The governor of Minnesota, complaining of the importation of black labor by the Great Northern Railway, said: "The government must stop the movement of Negros [*sic*] into this section at once. I shudder to think of the consequences if this is not done."[45] Such statements were motivated by fear of racial violence, fear brought about by events elsewhere. Just a few days before the governor's letter, on 2 July 1917, the nation had been horrified by the outbreak of a major race riot in East St. Louis during which whites attacked blacks with a ferocious intensity. Although the official figures put the death rate at forty-seven (eight white, thirty-nine black), other estimates suggested as many as two to four hundred deaths.[46] The fact that many American towns and cities seemed to share the ingredients that resulted in conflict on this scale clearly caused alarm.

To most observers, the causes of the riot in East St. Louis were obvious. The *New York Times* put it down to "ill feeling engendered by the importation of negro labor from the South," and the report by the Labor Committee of the State Council of Defense of Illinois concurred: "the riots," it concluded, "were due to the excessive and abnormal number of negroes . . . in East St. Louis." This influx, estimated at between six thousand and fifteen thousand, caused resentment as blacks moved "into sections of the city regarded as exclusively the precincts of the white people." In addition, the migrants were felt to threaten labor standards, and it was strongly suggested that there had been a deliberate campaign to bring blacks to East St. Louis in order to reduce labor's bargaining power by creating a surplus work force.[47]

Some of these conclusions have been questioned by the leading modern authority on the riot, Elliott M. Rudwick. Rudwick points out that the city was a terminus rather than final destination and suggests that most blacks were passing through. His estimate of the increase in black population was five thousand rather than fifteen thousand, and he points to a legacy of racial bitterness in existence as a result of political discord arising from elections in which race had been an issue. Labor violence was also a background factor, and stories of a "Negro residential invasion" added to this to cause a series of racial clashes that brought the first outbreak of rioting. Although quelled by troops, this conflict flared up again and led to the larger outburst on 2 July. Thus the major cause of the riot was a general instability, which found expression in a race fear that had little connection with reality.[48]

The racism that lay behind the East St. Louis riot appalled black Americans. On 28 July the NAACP staged a silent protest in which several thousand blacks marched down Fifth Avenue, New York. Among the banners was one that asked, "Mr. President, why not make America safe for Democracy?" The president, however, declined several requests to meet black delegations due to pressures of time and a feeling that such meetings could do little good. He did, though, ask Attorney General Gregory to see whether the government could "exercise any jurisdiction in this tragical matter," but federal agents found no evidence to justify federal action. National and local authorities were also powerless to prevent the smaller-scale riots that broke out in two more war-impacted cities, Chester and Philadelphia, later that same month.[49]

But although East St. Louis, Chester, and Philadelphia shared problems of overcrowding and job competition, racial violence was not just a by-product of defense industries, nor was it confined to northern centers: as James Weldon Johnson was to write in 1919, "An increased hatred of race was an integral part of wartime intolerance."[50] Intimidation of black Americans continued throughout the war as a means of maintaining the racial status quo, particularly in the South, where black lives continued to be taken for the most trivial of reasons. In August 1916, for example, five blacks, including two women, were lynched in Gainesville, Florida, following an argument over a pig. The *Labor Year Book* for 1919 listed forty-five lynchings in 1917 in which blacks died for "crimes" ranging from "alleged" attacks on white women through to "writing an insolent letter to a white woman," or for "disputing a white man's word."[51]

Such actions, particularly at a moment when American was "fighting for democracy," contributed to the mood of disillusionment evident among Afro-Americans by 1918. Following a tour of southern states Robert Russa Moton, Booker T. Washington's successor at Tuskegee, wrote to President Wilson and said, "There is more genuine restlessness, and perhaps dissatisfaction, on the part of the colored people than I have ever before known," and he called for some definite action from the government. Joel Spingarn of the NAACP also spoke of the black bitterness during the House Judiciary Committee hearings on an antilynching bill. Arguing that lynching interfered with the prosecution of the war, Spingarn urged the passage of the bill as a war measure. However, no such

bill could be passed, and although the President spoke out against lynchings as unjustified acts of lawlessness, his words seemed to have little or
no effect: just a few days later the white IWW organizer Frank Little was
lynched, and in 1918 at least another sixty-four blacks died as a consequence of mob violence.[52]

If little could be done to change white attitudes, the government did
attempt to improve the black mood. One such act was the conference of
black newspaper editors already described, but steps were also taken to
incorporate blacks directly in the war effort. Following the riot in East St.
Louis, Secretary of War Newton D. Baker appointed Booker T. Washington's former secretary, Emmett J. Scott, as special assistant to advise
on racial matters. On 1 May 1918 George E. Haynes, professor of economics at Fisk University, was made director of Negro economics within the
Department of Labor in order to assist with the mobilization of black
manpower for industry. The secretary of Labor also created the Negro
Division within the U.S. Employment Service headed by Giles B. Jackson
of the Richmond National Civic Improvement Association (despite objec-
tions from a number of black spokesmen, for reasons never too clear).
Other blacks served in different capacities in the Food Administration and
in the Committee on Public Information.[53]

Altogether these appointments marked a considerable departure from
the Wilson administration's previous lily-white policy. However, they were
entirely war-oriented, intended to increase black contributions to the war
effort rather than bring long-term changes in race relations. The morale-
boosting role was an important function too, and Emmett Scott's chief task
was to provide liaison between the government and black leaders, to tour
training camps, and to investigate complaints. He did initiate action
against discriminatory draft boards in the South, but otherwise had little
real effect, as he "became a faithful and often uncritical servant of the war
effort."[54] Haynes, too, concentrated on public relations and enlisting
black support for the war effort. Various Negro workers' advisory committees were established, and state conferences on Negro labor were held in
Florida, Georgia, Illinois, Kentucky, Mississippi, North Carolina, and
Ohio.[55] Again, however, reform was not the object, and discrimination and
segregation continued even within federal offices. Once the war had
ended, concern for black workers disappeared, and although some blacks
remained within the Department of Labor, the Division of Negro Economics ceased to exist, and Haynes returned to academic life. Scott also left
government service and became secretary and business manager of
Howard University.

Black participation in the war effort was not always enthusiastic.
Something of the enforced element and the patronizing attitudes of whites

are revealed in the description of activities in Sumter County, South Carolina, where the secretary of the County Council of Defense could write:

> We organized or induced colored people over the county to organize Red Cross chapters and to subscribe to the Red Cross, to buy Liberty Loan bonds, and to educate colored people that this is as much their war as the whiteman's war.
>
> We got the darkies doing just what we were and still are doing. . . .
>
> Our colored people are loyal, patriotic, and as proud of the United States as the white people are. They know now that the Sumter County white people are their best friends.[56]

Other sympathetic whites could also still speak of blacks in stereotyped terms such as "uncle," "Hottentot," and "pickaninny," or describe soldiers as "boys who do not grow up even under shell fire." An Army Signal Corps film, *Training of Colored Troops,* is full of such images. The dramatized story of a black soldier from induction to training, it concentrates on comic aspects and includes shots of a watermelon-eating competition and blacks dancing to their band. The soldier at the center of this story is, of course, joining the engineers.[57]

Some white attitudes were affected by the experiences of war, but these were to be very much in the minority. During a postwar debate on antilynching measures, the senator for Mississippi, Selden P. Spencer, could ask:

> If the colored man is deemed worthy to carry a rifle in the defense of his country and to risk his life for the honor of his nation, who shall say that he is unworthy to cast a ballot in the government of that nation whose life he has helped preserve?[58]

Despite such appeals, the legislation came to naught, killed off by southern filibusters in Congress. Still, some white southerners came together under the leadership of Will Alexander to form the Commission on Interracial Cooperation in 1919, but this—the chief voice of southern moderation until World War II—was to have little tangible effect.

For the majority of white Americans the fact of black participation in the war, whether at home or abroad, was either ignored or resented. Significantly Frederick Paxson's three-volume study of *American Democracy and the World War,* has the very barest mention of blacks, with no reference at all to their role in the armed forces or industry, nor any comment on wartime racial violence. This was all the more remarkable given the almost endemic nature of violence as whites attempted to reestablish by force the racial patterns of the prewar era. Any hopes that blacks had held of gaining recognition in return for their service were to be sadly crushed when, rather than the subjects of white gratitude, they found themselves instead the victims of the postwar xenophobia and hysteria that swept the country in 1919.

In the year after the war's end over eighty blacks were lynched, and eleven were burned at the stake. In addition, twenty-five race riots of differing intensity broke out in towns and cities as far apart as Charleston, South Carolina; Longview, Texas; Knoxville, Tennessee; Omaha, Nebraska; Elaine, Arkansas; Washington, D.C.; and Chicago. In addition, George Haynes could report near-riot situations in Sumter, South Carolina (despite the comments from the county council of defense already quoted); Columbia, South Carolina; Birmingham, Alabama; New York City; Jacksonville, Florida; Montgomery, Alabama; and Atlanta, Georgia.[59] Although the common underlying feature was the wartime disturbance of race relations, each riot had its own characteristics. The outbreaks in Knoxville and Omaha were "jailhouse" riots in which white mobs enforced "race law" against blacks; in Longview whites reacted against critical reports in the *Chicago Defender* by attacking the black thought to be responsible for the reports and then blacks in general. In Charleston the violence was a consequence of a clash between black and white sailors, and in Washington, D.C., the riot was very much dominated by white servicemen, orchestrated by the local press, in response to the black migration and apparent prosperity enjoyed by blacks in the city. Servicemen were, in fact, conspicuous in a number of the riots, no doubt reflecting on their feelings of resentment at having had to serve, and in Chicago they were also involved in the worst riot, in which at least thirty-eight people, twenty-three black and fifteen white, died, and over five hundred were injured.[60]

The riot in Chicago began on the lakeshore following a clash between black and white youths and an incident in which a black swimmer was stoned. The violence quickly spread throughout the city as white gangs chased and hunted blacks through the streets, halting streetcars and pulling out black passengers, and beating and stoning them—in some horrifically photographed incidents, to death.[61] The background to the Chicago riot was, of course, the enormous increase in black population and the resultant friction over jobs and housing as whites resisted the expansion of the ghetto and the employment of black workers. Some twenty-four bombings of black homes occurred between 1917 and 1919, and a number of racial gang fights and shootings preceded the riot. Labor conflict also contributed, and the fact that in some areas 90 percent of the white labor force was unionized, while 75 percent of black workers were not, created divisions and ill feelings.

The reactions to the riot after the event were, though, predictable—

rather than there being calls for an end to the discrimination and prejudice that affected the blacks in Chicago, the blacks themselves were held to be responsible. Thus the number of blacks indicted after the riot was twice that of whites, even though blacks were clearly the victims rather than the aggressors in most cases. The solution to the racial problem was seen to be to restrict further in-migration and to reinforce patterns of racial segregation. Well might a young black veteran who had been chased by a mob during the riot ask:

> Had the ten months I spent in France been all in vain? Were all those white crosses over the dead bodies of those dark-skinned boys lying in Flanders field for naught? Was democracy a hollow sentiment? What had I done to deserve such treatment?[62]

The sense of black disillusionment after the war was enormous. However, it was evident that the old passive attitude of meek acceptance had gone. In February 1919 the *Chicago Defender* found it hard to believe that men who had fought in Europe would "tamely and meekly submit to a program of lynching, burning, and social ostracism," and commenting upon the white casualties in Chicago, pointed out that blacks were "no longer content to turn the left cheek when smitten upon the right."[63] Black soldiers wrote, "If we have fought to make safe democracy for the white races, we will soon fight to make it safe for ourselves and our posterity"; and, "I done my part and I'm going to fight right here till Uncle Sam does his." These comments were echoed in the *Crisis,* which stated openly, "When the mob moves we propose to meet it with bricks and clubs and guns," and DuBois now urged blacks to "marshal every ounce of our brain and brawn," and warned, "We *return,* we *return from fighting,* we *return fighting.*"[64]

This was no idle threat nor empty rhetoric. In August 1919 Robert Moton could describe "the apparent revolutionary attitude of many Negroes," while George Haynes reported "widespread dissatisfaction bordering on bitterness" as a consequence of the reports heard from returning black soldiers of their treatment in the forces. Haynes recorded stories of blacks arming themselves in St. Louis, and in Washington, D.C., where eleven whites were among the sixteen dead, blacks clearly *did* fight back. In Elaine, Arkansas, while the reported version of an armed black insurrection was discredited by later investigations, black resistance to white violence was certainly evident.[65]

For DuBois, "A new, radical Negro spirit" had been born in France: the "New Negro" who said, "I ain't looking for trouble, but if it comes my way I ain't dodging," had arrived.[66] But the spirit of resistance was not limited just to black servicemen. The mood of anger and resentment was widely felt even in the South, and a heightened race consciousness and a "new activism" were major consequences of the war and evident in a number of ways. Together with the actual shift in black population, which "made race one of the social issues of the day" on a national rather than merely southern basis, this new black mood signaled "a definite change in American race relations."[67] While disillusionment led some Afro-Americans to support the black nationalism and separatism of Marcus Garvey and the Universal Negro Improvement Association in the 1920s, it also spurred others on to fight for acceptance and full integration into American society. NAACP membership had reached ten thousand by 1918 and was over sixty-two thousand by 1919, and the circulation of the *Crisis* exceeded 560,000. However, the postwar reaction also brought a questioning of earlier views. DuBois, for example, later suggested that perhaps "passive resistance by 12 million to war activity might have saved the world for black and white" and confessed, "I did not realize the full horror of war and its wide impotence as a method of social reform."[68] Even Emmett Scott was to express similar feelings when he addressed black veterans in 1933:

> As one who recalls the assurances of 1917 and 1918, I confess personally a deep sense of disappointment, of poignant pain, that a great country in a time of need should promise so much and afterward perform so little.[69]

Clearly, the experiences of the First World War were not to be forgotten, and they were remembered in 1941 by men like A. Philip Randolph, Rayford Logan, and others who vowed not to make the same mistakes again. Accommodation was discredited and never again would black Americans accept discrimination in defense industries, nor, given their place in the industrial work force, would their country be so able to ignore them. And neither would Afro-Americans provide, unquestioningly,

> Black men, going to be killed like cattle,
> To die while fighting, a white man's battle.[70]

Notes

1. David Gordon Nielson, *Black Ethos: Northern Urban Negro Life and Thought, 1890–1930* (Westport, Conn., and London, 1977), 101–2, 139; Allan H. Spear, *Black Chicago: The Making of a Negro Ghetto, 1890–1920* (Chicago, 1967), 129; *New York Times,* 5 October 1919.
2. Rayford W. Logan, *The Betrayal of the Negro from Rutherford B. Hayes to Woodrow Wilson* (New York and London, 1965), chapter 5.

3. C. Vann Woodward, *The Strange Career of Jim Crow* (London and New York, 1966), 84–85.
4. Logan, *Betrayal,* 348–49; John Hope Franklin, *From Slavery to Freedom: A History of Negro Americans* (New York, 1969), 439–40.
5. Langston Hughes, *Fight for Freedom: The Story of the NAACP* (New York, 1962), 197–98; Nancy J. Weiss, *The National Urban League 1910–1940* (New York, 1974); Nancy J. Weiss and Avarh E. Strickland, *History of the Chicago Urban League* (Urbana, Ill. and London, 1966), 1–12.
6. Mary Frances Berry and John W. Blassingame, *Long Memory: The Black Experience in America* (New York and Oxford, 1982), 310–12.
7. Kelly Miller, *The Everlasting Stain* (Washington, D.C., 1924), 10; Nancy J. Weiss, "The Negro and the New Freedom: Fighting Wilsonian Segregation," *Political Science Quarterly* 84, no. 1 (March 1969): 61–79; *Papers, 28,* and *31,* 298–305 for meetings with Trotter, and letter to Moton, 6 November 1914, *31,* 270.
8. Logan, *Betrayal,* 354; I. A. Newby, *Jim Crow's Defense: Anti-Negro Thought in America, 1900–1930* (Baton Rouge, La., 1965), 54–55, 67–69.
9. Robert E. Park quoted in Arthur I. Waskow, *From Race Riot to Sit-In: 1919 and the 1960s* (Garden City, N.Y., 1967), 40.
10. The *Crisis,* May, June, July 1918.
11. Byron Gunner, President National Equal Rights League, to DuBois, 30 July 1918, in H. Aptheker, ed., *The Correspondence of W. E. B. DuBois: Vol I: Selections 1877–1934* (Boston, 1973), 228; and see report of initial NAACP meeting, *Chicago Defender,* 20 July 1918.
12. Nielson, *Black Ethos,* 131–32.
13. Quoted in Jervis Anderson, *A. Philip Randolph: A Biographical Portrait* (New York, 1973), 112.
14. Anderson, *A. Philip Randolph,* 108–9.
15. Spingarn, quoted in J. L. Scheiber and H. N. Scheiber, "The Wilson Administration and the Wartime Mobilization of Black Americans, 1917–18," *Labor History* 10, no. 3 (1969): 440; Creel to Wilson, 17 June 1918, Creel Papers, vol. 2; Baker to Wilson, 1 July 1918, Baker Papers, Reel 6; DuBois, *Crisis* (August 1918); *Papers, 48,* 341–42, 475–76.
16. *Washington Bee,* 13 July 1918.
17. *Crisis,* August 1918; Creel to Wilson, 5 July 1918, *Papers, 48,* 528–30.
18. "Lynching is unpatriotic," 26 July 1918, *Papers, 49,* 97–98; See correspondence John R. Shillady to Tumulty and Wilson, 13, 18 February 1918, Baker to Wilson 1 July 1918, Wilson to Baker, 19 February 1918, in *Papers, 46,* 380–81, 383, and *48,* 475–76 (Wilson Papers CF543 Reel 285).
19. Vardaman, quoted in Scheiber and Scheiber, "The Wilson Administration," 441.
20. Jack D. Foner, *Blacks and the Military in American History* (New York, 1974), 111–12; Arthur E. Barbeau and Florette Henri, *The Unknown Soldiers: Black American Troops in World War I* (Philadelphia, 1974), 36.
21. Emmett J. Scott, *Scott's Official History of the American Negro in the World War* (Chicago, 1919), 59–60.
22. "Bulletin No. 35," 25 March 1918, Camp Funston, in Morris J. MacGregor and Bernard C. Nalty, *Blacks in the United States Armed Forces: Basic Documents, Vol. IV, Segregation Entrenched, 1917–1940* (Wilmington, Del., 1977), 277.
23. Baker to Wilson, 23 August 1918, and Wilson to Baker, 24 August,

Papers, 49, 324–28, 400–403; Baker Papers Reel 6.

24. Correspondence on Young Case, Wilson-Baker, 25, 26 June, 7 July 1917, in Baker Papers, Reel 3; Chester D. Heywood, *Negro Combat Troops in the World War: The Story of the 371st Infantry* (New York, 1928), 46.

25. "Secret Information Concerning Black American Troops," French Military Mission, 7 August 1918, in DuBois, "Documents of the War," *Crisis*, May 1919: 16–21.

26. Lt. Allen G. Thurman on 371st Infantry in Florette Henri, *Black Migration: Movement North 1900–1920* (Garden City, N.Y., 1975), 299; John Richards, "Some Experiences with Colored Soldiers," *Atlantic Monthly* 124 (1919), in D. Trask, ed., *World War I At Home: Readings on American Life 1914–1920* (New York, 1970), 140–45; Colonel Ballou to Assistant Commandant, General Staff College, 14 March 1920, in MacGregor and Nalty, *Blacks in the United States Armed Forces*, 323; Irwin S. Cobb, "Young Black Joe," *Saturday Evening Post*, 24 August 1918.

27. Big Bill Broonzy, "I Wonder When I'll Get to Be Called a Man," *Big Bill Broonzy Sings Country Blues*, FA 2326, 1957.

28. Emmett J. Scott, *Negro Migration During the War* (New York, 1920), 3; U.S. Dept of Commerce, Bureau of Census, *Historical Statistics of the United States 1789–1945* (Washington, D.C., 1949), 30–31.

29. Olivier Zunz, *The Changing Face of Inequality: Urbanization, Industrial Development, and Immigrants in Detroit, 1880–1920* (Chicago and London, 1982), 288; Chicago Commission on Race Relations, *The Negro in Chicago: A Study of Race Relations and a Race Riot* (Chicago, 1922); 79–80; Kenneth L. Kusmer, *A Ghetto Takes Shape: Black Cleveland, 1870–1930* (Urbana, Ill., Chicago, and London, 1978), 160; Nielson, *Black Ethos*, 47, 65–66.

30. Allan Spear, *Black Chicago*, 130–38; Henri, *Black Migration*.

31. *Chicago Defender*, 24 February 1917. See also U.S. Dept. of Labor, Division of Negro Economics, *Negro Migrations in 1916–17* (Washington, D.C., 1919), 22–30.

32. "Resolution," Executive Chamber of Commerce, Richmond, n.d.; John T. Watkins, Representative 4th Louisiana District, to W. B. Wilson, 14 July 1917, in Dept. of Labor, Chief Clerk's files, Box 17, 8/102–8/102C. RG 174.

33. Charles H. Wesley, *Negro Labor in the United States, 1850–1925: A Study in American Economic History* (New York, 1927), 282; Scott Nearing, *Black America* (New York, 1929), 82; Philip S. Foner, *Organized Labor and the Black Worker, 1619–1973* (New York, 1974), 131; Joyce Shaw Peterson, "Black Automobile Workers in Detroit, 1910–1930," *Journal of Negro History* 64, no. 3 (Summer 1979), 178.

34. Spear, *Black Chicago*, 151; Kusmer, *A Ghetto Takes Shape*, 190; Zunz, *The Changing Face of Inequality*, 321.

35. Wesley, *Negro Labor*, 295–96; Dept. of Labor, Division of Negro Economics, *The Negro at Work During the World War and During Reconstruction; Second Study on Negro Labor* (Washington, D.C., 1921), 59–62.

36. U.S. Dept. of Labor, Women's Bureau, *Negro Women in Industry*, Bulletin 20 (Washington, D.C., 1920), 5–10; E. Franklin Frazier, *The Negro in the United States* (New York, 1969), 598.

37. Chicago Commission, *The Negro in Chicago,* 163–65; Carl Sandburg, *The Chicago Race Riots, July 1919* (New York, 1919), 29.
38. *Chicago Defender,* 29 December 1917; Chicago Commission, *The Negro,* 365; U.S. Dept. of Labor, *The Negro at Work,* 40–44; *American Labor Year Book, 1919–20* (New York, 1920), 60, 64.
39. Spear, *Black Chicago,* 151–55; Kusmer, *A Ghetto Takes Shape,* 195; U.S. Dept. of Labor, *Negro Women in Industry.* Peterson, "Black Automobile Workers in Detroit, 179.
40. Robert C. Weaver, *The Negro Ghetto* (New York, 1948), 4; Nielson, *Black Ethos,* 47; Kusmer, *A Ghetto Takes Shape;* Peterson, "Black Automobile Workers in Detroit," 187.
41. R. T. Sims to E. N. Nockels, Secretary, Chicago Federation of Labor, 19 January 1917, Dept. of Labor, Office of Secretary, Box 205, 13/65, NARG 174; Chicago Commission, *The Negro,* 152–53.
42. David Trask, ed., *World War I at Home* (New York, 1970), 10; Spear, *Black Chicago,* 24; Gilbert Osofsky, *Harlem: The Making of a Ghetto* (New York, 1968), 141; Florence Murray, ed., *The Negro Handbook 1942* (New York, 1942), 75–76.
43. J. T. Watkins to W. B. Wilson and other letters in file; Chicago Commission, *The Negro in Chicago,* 103–5; St. Clair Drake and Horace R. Cayton, *Black Metropolis: A Study of Negro Life in a Northern City* (Chicago, 1944), 59–61.
44. *New York Times,* 3 June 1917; New York *Tribune,* 14 March 1919; Drake and Cayton, *Black Metropolis;* Spear, *Black Chicago,* 202–3.
45. Governor John Lind, to W. B. Wilson, 7 July 1917, Dept. of Labor, Chief Clerk's Files, Box 17 8/102–8/102C, NARG 174.
46. *Crisis,* September 1917; Elliott M. Rudwick, *Race Riot at East St. Louis, July 2, 1917* (Carbondale, Ill., 1964), 50.
47. "Report of Labor Committee of State Council of Defense of Illinois upon the Inquiry into the Recent Race Riots at East St. Louis," 30 July 1917, Dept. of Labor, Office of Secretary, Box 205, file 13/65, NARG 174; *New York Times,* 3 July 1917.
48. Rudwick, *Race Riot,* 158–66.
49. *New York Times,* 28 July 1917; Wilson's responses are contained in correspondence in *Papers, 43,* 107, 116, 146, 284.
50. J. W. Johnson, "The Riots," *Crisis,* September 1919.
51. *Labor Year Book, 1919–20,* 301–5.
52. Spingarn, H. R., Committee on the Judiciary, *Hearings: To Protect Citizens Against Lynching, June 6, 1918* (Washington, D.C., 1918); Moton to Wilson, 15 June 1918, Wilson Papers, CF543, Reel 285.
53. Correspondence dealing with appointments in Dept. of Labor, Chief Clerk's file, Box 17, 8/102A–8/102C; Scott, *Scott's Official History,* 362.
54. Scheiber and Scheiber, "The Wilson Administration," 446.
55. "Functions and Work of the Division of Negro Economics,"31 December 1918, in Chief Clerk's files 8/102a–8/102b; U.S. Secretary of Labor, *Sixth Annual Report, . . . June 30, 1918* (Washington, D.C., 1918), 110–11.
56. E. I. Reardon to George F. Porter, Chief, Section on Co-operation with States, Council of National Defense, 10 October 1917, CND, Box 587, NARG 62.
57. "Training of Colored Troops," Signal Corps Films, NA, Film Library

(NA 111H–1211–PPSA–1); Kingsley Moses, "The Negro Comes North" in Trask, ed., *World War I at Home,* 130–35.
58. "Speech of Hon. Selden P. Spencer of Missouri in Senate, Saturday, May 22, 1920," in Dept. of Labor, Division of Negro Economics, Box B.
59. "Negro labor situation in Chicago, Ill., and other localities following recent race disturbances at Chicago," 27 August, 1919; and letters on 20 May 1919 and June 1919, all in Chief Clerk's files, Box 18, 8/102e; William M. Tuttle, *Race Riot: Chicago in the Red Summer of 1919* (New York, 1977), 22–23.
60. Waskow, *From Race Riot to Sit-In,* 12–50; DuBois, "The Insurgent Negro," 7, in DuBois Papers, Box 19, "Writings 1920–29; NAACP, "Why Should Congress Investigate Race Riots and Lynching," August 1919, NAACP Admin FC 338; *Washington Evening Star,* 21 July 1919.
61. Chicago Commission, *The Negro In Chicago.*
62. Ibid., 483.
63. *Chicago Defender,* 22 February and 2 August 1919.
64. Chicago Commission, *The Negro in Chicago,* 481; William M. Tuttle, "Views of a Negro During the Red Summer of 1919," *Journal of Negro History* 51, no. 3 (July 1966); William A. Hewlett to DuBois, 26 August 1919, in Aptheker, *Correspondence,* 234–35; *Crisis,* May, September 1919.
65. Waskow, *From Race Riot to Sit-In,* 21–38, 143–74; Moton to Woodrow Wilson, 8 August 1919, Wilson Papers CF543, Reel 286; Haynes, "Negro labor situation in Chicago, Ill, . . . ," Division of Negro Economics, Box 18, 8/102e; Washington *Evening Star,* 21 July 1919; U.S. Dept. of Labor, *The Negro at Work,* 30.
66. Chicago Commission, *The Negro in Chicago,* 481, 488; W. E. B. DuBois, "An Essay Toward a History of the Black Man in the Great War," *Crisis,* June 1919: 72.
67. Spear, *Black Chicago,* 129; Nielson, *Black Ethos,* 139; Scott, *Scott's Official History,* 459; Theodore Hemingway, "Prelude to Change: Black Carolinians in the War Years, 1914–1920," *Journal of Negro History* 65, no. 3 (Summer 1980), 220.
68. DuBois, quoted in Roi Ottley, *New World A-Coming* (New York, 1943), 318; Hughes, *Fight for Freedom,* 197–98; Tuttle, *Race Riot,* 212.
69. Foner, *Blacks and the Military,* 127.
70. W. E. B. DuBois, "A Black Veteran Dreams," DuBois Papers, Box 61. For World War II and black reactions, see N. A. Wynn, *The Afro-American and the Second World War* (New York, 1976).

8

The Aftermath of War

Reconstruction, Red Scare, and the 1920s

The race riots that shook America in 1919 were not isolated events but part of a general outbreak of social disturbance, which affected the whole country as the wartime dislocations continued and as doubts and uncertainties about the postwar world surfaced. Across the nation anxieties and tensions exploded in violence and hysteria following the sudden, and unexpected, coming of peace. Labor unrest, strikes, radical demonstrations, and a wave of bombings in turn produced repression and intolerance culminating in the "Red Scare" and an outburst of xenophobia on an unprecedented scale. The final outcome was a mood of disillusion and conservatism and a general attempt to return to something called "normalcy." This story has already been well told in a number of studies.[1] However, it is important to see these events in the light of both the pre-war and war years, and in the wider context of world affairs. America was not alone in suffering postwar difficulties and disturbances. Defeat and the collapse of empires in central and eastern Europe created enormous problems and was to leave a legacy of instability that was in the long run to help produce a second world war. But even the victorious powers felt the adverse effects of the war, and emerged economically weaker and torn by new political and social forces produced by the war experience. The young American Progressive Raymond Fosdick described the postwar chaos in Europe as a consequence of "the forces this war has let loose. We seem to be faced with a disease which is perhaps too deep to be healed by a peace treaty."[2] The other factor of some influence, and itself a product of the war, was the Bolshevik Revolution of 1917, which sent shock waves around the world and provided inspiration for some groups and revulsion among others. America was no longer immune from such forces, and despite attempts to return to isolation events in Europe now had direct and indirect repercussions in the United States. Jane Addams to some extent summed up the postwar situation when she wrote that "we were living in the midst of post-war psychology and that . . . these years were concurrent with the development of a revolution in Russia which filled the entire civilized world with a paralyzing fear."[3]

In many ways the problem in America was that the people were not prepared for peace. The country was still in the process of mobilization, and the war effort had hardly reached its peak when the war ended. Most people, including those in government, had expected the war to go on for two or three years more: Secretary of the Interior Franklin Lane expected the conflict to last until 1920, Postmaster General Sidney Burleson thought 1921, and some observers predicted it would continue into the mid-1920s.[4] Certainly, little thought had been given to the question of postwar reconstruction, and, indeed, such planning was specifically ruled out as premature by some government members. According to Bernard Baruch in October 1918, "This is no time to let thoughts of peace interfere with work for war."[5] Thus, the declaration of an armistice on 11 November 1918, while producing jubilation and celebration in the streets, created new problems to be resolved in a very short space of time. A Reconstruction Research Division was established with presidential approval by the Council of National Defense in June 1918 in order to coordinate studies of reconstruction (itself an implicit suggestion that there was plenty of time), but this was really concerned with the collection and dissemination of information, mainly within government agencies, and it had barely started when the war ended.[6]

While the government may not have been thinking or planning for the postwar period, American citizens in different groups and organizations had been—or at least had developed certain expectations, which they voiced in various forms. As early as January 1918, President Wilson's secretary, Joseph Tumulty, could write that "the mass of people, underfed and dissatisfied, are clamoring for a fuller recognition of their rights to life and liberty." Tumulty went on to suggest that the Democratic party needed a program of "policies which will make life more easy, more comfortable, and more prosperous for the average man," and he quoted with approval the British Labour party's platform as an example to be followed. Other Americans were also impressed by the Labour party's proposals, published as *Labour and the New Social Order,* including minimum-wages legislation, full employment programs, public ownership, the redistribution of wealth through taxation, and public education. The entire February issue of *The New Republic* was devoted to *Labour and the New Social Order,* and the writers of the liberal journal saw reconstruction as an opportunity "to complete the unfinished business of the Progressive Era."[7]

The "Progressive publicists" were not alone in their expectations. Many reformers hoped that the gains of war could be continued and extended in peacetime. At the Annual Session of the National Conference of Social Work in May 1918, President Robert A. Wood asked, "Why not continue on into the years of peace this close, vast wholesome organism of service, of fellowship, of creative power?" A later survey of reconstruction programs suggested that "every section of this study has given additional proof that out of a common effort during the war has been born a new spirit and a new vision." The *American Federationist* could write optimistically that the "war has opened the door of opportunity through which the more sound and progressive policies may enter."[8] Such hopes found expression in a whole range of conferences and proposals. One collection of writings ranged over a variety of social concerns and called for accident compensation, social insurance, vocational rehabilitation, labor bureaus, the eight-hour day, public works schemes, and the centralized coordination of health services; the *American Labor Legislation Review* also listed workmen's compensation, health insurance, and a public employment service among its "Foundations for Reconstruction"; the AF of L called for better wages, shorter hours, the eight-hour day, equal pay, the abolition of child labor, and government ownership of public utilities.[9]

Among the many other groups suggesting reconstruction plans were the New York Academy of Political Science, the American Public Health Association, the Reconstruction Congress of American Industries, and the Conference of Social Agencies and Reconstruction. Perhaps the best-known and most striking proposals were those of the National Catholic War Council's "Bishop's Program of Social Reconstruction," published in February 1919. This document, largely the work of John Ryan, "the most influential Catholic in the field of American social reform," again quoted the example of the British Labour party, and listed eleven proposals: public works; the continuation of the U.S. Employment Service; equal pay for women; the maintenance of the National War Labor Board; the maintenance of wage rates; reduction of the cost of living; a legal minimum wage; social insurance against illness, invalidity, unemployment, and old age; vocational training; an end to child labor; and labor participation in industrial management.[10]

Such schemes were indicative of the more positive thinking evident in the United States. Not everyone shared this outlook. At the end of November 1918 Newton Baker, no conservative himself, wrote to the president concerning "a general expectation that you will outline a policy of reconstruction," but the secretary of war counseled that new lines of action were not in fact necessary. What was needed, he suggested, was readjustment, not reconstruction. The president indicated his own agreement with this assessment, and in his address to Congress on 2 December 1918, prior to departing for Europe, he spelled out his approach to reconstruction. Remarking that the American people "do not want to be coached and led," the president disavowed any specific government direction in reconstruction, offering instead government mediation where necessary. He did not think that any of the general proposals he had seen would be acceptable to "our spirited businessmen and self-reliant laborers," and furthermore pointed out that the return to a peace footing was proceeding so rapidly that it would "outrun any inquiry that may be instituted and any aid that may be offered. It will not be easy to direct it any better than it will direct itself." The only specific suggestions the president offered were the recommendation to grant women the vote and the development of public works.[11]

Such views were hardly surprising from the prewar advocate of the New Freedom, and the winding down of government agencies, occurring without any order or control, was a result of the desire to free business and the economy from direction and regulation as quickly as possible—even more unremarkable given that most of the bodies were, of course, made up of businessmen. Some agencies went very quickly: Bernard Baruch resigned on 28 November 1918, and the War Industries Board had virtually ceased operation by the end of the year; the Fuel Administration had ended by about March 1919, and the last remnants of the Food Administration finally disappeared early in 1920. Much debate centered on the Railway Administration, and various suggestions were made ranging from the immediate return to private ownership, the continuation of government management for a trial period, or even permanent government ownership. In the event, lacking clear direction from the Wilson administration, in 1920 Congress provided for the return to private ownership but with greater government regulation and more power for the Interstate Commerce Commission.[12]

While the whole American war machine seemed, at least to Franklin Lane, to go "to pieces in a night," the Wilson administration itself faced setbacks with the end of the war.[13] First, of course, there was the preoccupation with foreign affairs. Wilson sailed to Europe on board the *George Washington* on 4 December 1918 and returned to the United States on 24 February 1919. After a second visit to Paris, from March until July, the president returned to present the Treaty of Versailles to Congress. Much of his time thereafter was to be devoted to the defense of the treaty and the proposed League of Nations, and early in September he embarked upon his tour of the country to put the case for ratification to the American people. In the course of this whirlwind campaign, the President suffered a stroke, which left him "in varying degrees an invalid," "a broken ruined man" for his remaining time in office, jealously protected by his wife.[14]

With presidential leadership lacking, the way was open for strong cabinet government. It was not forthcoming. Some cabinet members were leaving office, and others were preparing for the presidential campaign of 1920 with a view to running as candidates themselves. Many must have felt, like William Gibbs McAdoo, the need to rest after the exertions of government and "to get back to private life to retrieve my personal fortunes."[15] The consequence was that no one really took responsibility for domestic affairs between 1918 and 1920, a problem compounded by the fact that the president had made his leadership an issue in the congressional elections of 1918 when he asked the electorate to return Democratic majorities. In part reacting against such direction, in part influenced by issues such as prices and the cost of living, and in part returning to the old prewar patterns of congressional politics, the electorate did just the reverse and returned Republican majorities to both House and Senate. With government so divided it was to be a lame duck until 1920.[16]

In the absence of strong government many of the expectations and hopes for a better society collapsed in the chaos of decontrol and the recriminations over the failure to ratify the peace treaty. Many Progressives were to be sadly disillusioned by their experiences in this period. Raymond Fosdick, the young man who had encouraged singing among the troops as they prepared for war and who had held such high hopes of the future that would emerge from the battle, now saw victory parades as funeral marches. The "botched" peace settlement represented "the chance we've missed to make this world a fit place to live in instead of a place to fight in." Similarly, men like Walter Lippmann who had been even closer to the center of the war administration and had participated in the advisory body to the American peace delegation, thought the Treaty of Versailles a disaster, "an instrument of punishment." William Allen White could write of "these damned vultures" who had "taken the heart out of the peace; taken the joy out of the great enterprise of the war, and have made it a sordid malicious miserable thing like all the wars in the world. We had such high hopes of this adventure."[17] In May 1919, *The New Republic* proclaimed "THIS IS NOT PEACE," and in Christmas the journal published extracts from John Maynard Keynes's overwhelmingly critical assessment, *The Economic Consequences of the Peace,* which included among its savage views of the participants in Paris the description of Woodrow Wilson as a "blind and deaf Quixote."[18]

But if the seeds for later historical revisionism were sown in Paris, the postwar disillusionment was also the product of events at home. Rather than the fulfillment of wartime expectations, postwar society was to be divided by mounting social conflict and a growing sense of fragmentation. "Never," wrote Ray Stannard Baker, "did the crust of civilization seem so thin." Later he wrote, "There is so much unrest. So much unreason, so much violence: so little sense!"[19] Of course, this must appear to modern man, faced with constant change, to be a perennial cry repeated by every new generation—and one still uttered today. However, the war had probably created a greater and wider sense of instability than was normally the case. The combination of international chaos with political division, riots and labor troubles at home, created an enormous sense of unease. A number of witnesses attributed this directly to the war's impact. As one writer observed, the war left "an extremely heightened susceptibility to mass excitement," and according to Newton Baker the end of it was followed by a "relaxation of the nervous tension of mankind" and "the breaking down of all the restraints of normal society."[20] While such abstract emotional factors were certainly a part of the events of 1919–20, more fundamental considerations lay behind such forces. Doubts about employment, prices, wages, and standards of living were the underlying causes of conflict.

Some of the problems facing the work force during the winding down of war industries and of servicemen as they returned from overseas were foreseen. President Wilson pointed out in his address of 2 December that private initiatives alone could not "provide immediate employment for all the men of our returning armies," and he proposed that "the development of public works of every sort be promptly resumed, in order that opportunities should be created for unskilled labor in particular." The president supported Secretary Lane's program of land reclamation submitted to Congress that day, calling upon states to provide land and the federal government to provide capital up to $100 million to reclaim land, initiate irrigation projects, build homes, and provide employment for one hundred thousand. Despite over forty thousand requests for information from servicemen and the consideration given to this and other public works schemes, nothing came of any of them. There was, in fact, little backing for Lane's proposal, but quite a lot of opposition. Farmers particularly feared that such action would reduce land values and the prices of farm produce; politicians resisted the financial costs and what were, increasingly, seen as un-American ideas. Not surprisingly more "radical" schemes such as that proposed by the former Immigration Commissioner Frederic C. Howe to provide paid furloughs, absorption into schools through government aid, large-scale work programs, transportation development, and land settlement, had even less chance of success (although these were clearly forerunners of the later G.I. Bill). In the end little was to be provided for veterans other than a sixty-dollar bonus for all with honorable discharges. Some states, such as Wisconsin, provided educational grants for ex-servicemen, and others offered free tuition.[21] War workers were left to fend for themselves in reconstruction.

The plight of displaced workers was made worse by the fact the military demobilization itself was rapid and relatively lacking in controls. Initially, it had been intended that soldiers would be released according to their skills and employment opportunities. However, in the end the desire to wind the war effort down as quickly as possible and to "get the boys home" prevailed. Demobilization was carried out simply by units at a rate of almost fifteen thousand troops a day. So rapid was this process that the American Expeditionary Force was virtually disbanded in six months, and by August 1919 only forty thousand remained of the two million troops who had been in Europe. Without any special provision to aid the transition back into peacetime, and with industry suffering dislocations during reconversion, the outcome was obvious: in 1920 4 percent of the labor force, 1.8 million, were unemployed; by 1921 it was 11.9 percent, or 5 million people.[22]

The one agency that might possibly have helped to prevent this situation was the U.S. Employment Service (USES), but this was to go the way of other agencies that had grown during the war. The USES had sprung up from practically nothing in January 1918 to a nationwide service with 750 offices by the war's end, but opposition was so strong that appropriations were cut in 1919. The agency was able to maintain some 490 offices for a while with the aid of donations and voluntary assistance in staffing, but the end of all appropriations led to the closure of all but fifty offices in 1920, even though surveys showed that the USES had placed more than 900,000 out of 1.3 million discharged servicemen by the end of 1919. Indeed, despite all the problems of demobilization, one general survey found only about twenty thousand ex-servicemen out of work.[23]

Decontrol affected not only employment but also prices. So severe was the postwar inflation that further action by government was felt to be necessary, and the Lever Act was extended to enable the government to act against hoarding. This led to the seizure of large quantities of farm produce—10 million eggs in Detroit, 100,000 pounds of beans in Kansas City!—but it was soon discovered that this had little effect where prices were determined on a world market, as was the case with sugar.[24] Attempts to fix domestic industrial prices led in February 1919 to the formation of the Industrial Board in the Department of Commerce headed by George N. Peek, formerly vice-president of the Deere Plow Company and acting vice-chairman of the War Industries Board. Drawing other personnel from the WIB, Peek used WIB methods, but found them little use without the WIB's ultimate authority. Thus, representatives were called upon to agree to prices determined on the basis of national demands and enforced purely by reliance upon appeals to patriotism. However, this attempt to stabilize prices was a miserable failure—having secured agreement with the steel industry, Peek then met opposition from the government's new railroad administrator, Walker Hines, who objected that the prices fixed were too high. The debate was carried out in public through April 1919 until both participants appealed to the president for adjudication. He found in favor of the railroad administrator, and the Industrial Board, robbed of all authority, virtually ceased to function. The final straw came when the attorney general ruled that price fixing was illegal and had only been sanctioned during the war by the Food and Fuel Act.

The consequence of all this was a soaring cost of living, which in turn put pressure on wages. However, the war had also served to raise the expectations of labor just as much as everyone else, and rising prices and falling employment were bound to cause resentment. Full employment and high earnings had increased appetites during the war but, "It was not just what was put in their pockets but what was put into their heads that counted—a war for democracy." Having won recognition and grown in strength during the war, organized labor was determined to maintain those gains in peacetime. At the beginning of 1918 one labor commentator could observe that "when this war is over the masses of the people are to occupy a much more favorable position," and before the end of the war even industrialists were acknowledging that there would be change; John D. Rockefeller, Jr., could speak of "Labor and Capital as partners," and Charles M. Schwab, head of Bethlehem Steel, could talk of "a new age," "a world for the workers."[26]

However, once the war had ended the spirit of unity and cooperation vanished. Employers now seemed determined to return to the prewar situation and to recover their control in the industrial sector. Speaker after speaker at the twenty-fourth annual convention of the National Association of Manufacturers in New York in 1919 affirmed their commitment to the open shop and the end of wartime regulation. Under the title of the "American Plan" these objectives became the basis of the drive "to liquidate labor's wartime achievements."[27] Given such mutually conflicting aims, labor and management were bound to clash. The result was a wave of industrial disputes and strikes in 1919 that affected over thirty-six hundred establishments and involved four million workers or 20 percent of the work force.[28]

To some extent, of course, these strikes were a continuation of conflicts that had arisen during the war as a consequence of the changing labor situation, wage-price levels, and conditions of work generally, but now the situation was further exacerbated by the additional problems of reconversion, the withdrawal of government mediation, and competing postwar aims. The postwar strikes began even before the ink had dried on the armistice agreement with the disputes in the cotton and textile industries in November 1918. Further industrial action occurred in the communications industry, printing, the railways, shipbuilding, steel, coal, and even the acting profession.[29] The most serious disputes took place in 1919, and not only did they affect essential areas of the economy, but to many observers they threatened the fabric of society itself.

The image of society under challenge began in February 1919 in Seattle, a town that had grown rapidly during the war as a consequence of the shipbuilding and lumber industries and where the population had risen by 194 percent between 1910 and 1920. The dispute began among the shipyard workers and had its origins in a pay settlement of 1917, which had left a legacy of discontent, but in 1919 the shipyard workers had AFL support, and the strike became a general one involving sixty thousand workers. Although dramatic, it was to be short-lived. Divisions within labor and the strong stand taken against them by Mayor Ole Hanson brought the dispute to a conclusion after a week. Fears aroused by events in Seattle were, however, to be encouraged by developments elsewhere later in the year.[30]

In August 1918 the AFL formed the National Committee for Organizing Steel Workers, hoping to capitalize upon its wartime strength in an industry that had resisted unionization successfully before the war, and pressed for union recognition, the eight-hour day, and a wage raise. These demands were presented to Judge Elbert Gary, head of U.S. Steel, in August 1919. Not only did Gary reject the union's claims, but he refused to negotiate even when requested to do so by the president's intermediaries. The strike, involving 350,000 workers nationwide, lasted from September 1919 until January 1920, but the use of troops and strikebreakers ensured the continued working of most plants, some almost at full capacity, and forced the surrender of the unions. In the course of the dispute at least eighteen strikers died in associated outbreaks of violence.[31]

If the violence and bitterness of the steel strike was to cause national concern, even greater alarm arose as a consequence of events in Boston in September 1919. Violence and looting broke out in the Massachusetts capital when policemen struck in support of colleagues sacked for joining a union. Mayor Peters used the militia to break the strike, supported, after a delay, by Governor Calvin Coolidge, who mobilized the entire state guard and became a national figure upon remarking that "there is no right to strike against the public safety by anybody, anywhere, anytime." His action paved the way for his selection as Republican party vice-presidential candidate in 1920.[32]

The last major strike of the year, lasting from November 1919 until December, was that of the bituminous coal miners. The United Mine Workers union had concluded an agreement with the government in 1917, pledging not to strike until 1920 in return for a pay award. However, while anthracite workers received pay increases, their colleagues in other areas did not, and in 1919 the union presented a demand for a 60 percent wage increase, a six-hour day, and a five-day week. When the coal owners refused to negotiate until the expiration of the 1917 agreement, strike action followed and continued despite both injunctions and the orders from union officials to return to work. In the end the miners won an immediate 14 percent raise and arbitration, which brought further increases in pay but no change in the hours of work.[33]

These various disputes were serious enough to merit some government action, and in the face of the growing labor disorder, particularly in the steel industry, the president announced the calling of an Industrial Conference. Pointing to the dislocation of war, Wilson said in his statement of 3 September that

> the necessity of devising at once methods by which we can speedily recover from this condition and obviate the wastefulness caused by the continued interruption of many of our important industrial enterprises by strikes and lockouts emphasizes the need for a meeting of minds. . . .[34]

The conference, consisting of sixty-one participants representing labor, employers, and the public, met from 6 to 23 October 1919. It achieved nothing. Resolutions were presented on all sides, and public representatives, including such well-known figures as Ida Tarbell and Lillian Wald, made recommendations for the suspension of disputes for three months and an arbitration board. However, for the labor group the steel strike was *the* central issue and with it the right of workers to organize and to take part in collective bargaining through their chosen representatives.

Samuel Gompers spoke in favor of the labor resolution and made the position of labor quite clear:

> Out of this war from which we have so triumphantly emerged—that war for which so many sacrifices have been made—the men and women of America are determined that we shall never again go back to prewar conditions and concepts. . . .

But if Gompers expected rewards for labor's loyal participation in the war, he was to be disappointed. Elbert Gary restated his position: "I believe in conciliation, co-operation, and arbitration *whenever practicable without sacrificing principle*" [italics mine]. The principle, of course, was union recognition. In the face of these unyielding positions, and unable to resolve the central dispute of the day, labor withdrew, and the First Industral Conference ended.[35]

The second, smaller Industrial Conference took place during December, and then from January to March 1920. This meeting consisted of seventeen prominent individuals chaired by Herbert Hoover. Again, this body, like its predecessor, was concerned with the general principles upon which to settle disputes rather than dealing with particular strikes or identifying their causes. The conference report, largely the work of Hoover himself, was influenced by wartime precedent and also showed something of the transition from Progressive ideas through war experience to voluntarism and the guiding principles of the twenties. The report endorsed the forty-eight-hour week, minimum wages, equal pay, the end to child labor, and improved housing programs, but time and time again stressed state and local community responsibilities. The federal government should provide liaison and information, but little overt direction or regulation. Thus, the idea of compulsory arbitration was abandoned. Similarly, while collective bargaining was supported, this did not necessarily imply union recognition. Collective bargaining could be shop-based, through employee representation schemes *within* individual factories or industries. The number of such shop committees did in fact triple between 1919 and 1922 as the moves toward welfare capitalism increased, but in most other areas the committee's proposals were not acted upon.[36] In reality it was no longer possible to achieve the president's desired "meeting of minds." Without the patriotic motivation of war or direct pressure from government itself, cooperation and progress in labor relations were unlikely. This was especially the case given the mounting antilabor sentiment, which merged with antiradicalism to create the Red Scare of 1919–20.

The Red Scare grew out of a number of events and circumstances. According to the *Saturday Evening Post* in 1924, it was "nothing but the last symptoms of war fever," and clearly the mounting hysteria in 1919 was a continuation of the wartime mood of intolerance, if only with a different point of emphasis.[37] The wartime insecurities could, in turn, be traced back to the anxieties of the prewar era. However, the particular form of the Red Scare was produced by the combination of factors that came together in the immediate aftermath of the war.

In addition to strikes, race riots, and economic problems, the postwar period in America was marked by a concern for radical movements. This was brought about firstly by the conclusion of several of the wartime trials under the Espionage Act, highlighting the antiwar, and therefore supposedly disloyal, position of different groups and individuals. In January 1919 Victor Berger was found guilty of conspiracy but was released on bail pending review; less fortunate were the forty-six Wobblies convicted of disloyalty following their trial in Sacramento. Throughout the following month further attention was drawn to the Industrial Workers of the World when newspaper headlines announced more arrests and a "Plot to Kill President."[38] Although neither weapons nor bombs were found, the IWW was increasingly associated not just with strikes, but also with the Bolshevik Revolution and the threat of international communism. The connections were easy to make: the Wobblies had opposed the war, strikes had disrupted the war effort and aided the Germans; the Germans had assisted the Bolsheviks; the Bolsheviks had abandoned their allies, made a separate peace, and now called for worldwide revolution. The point was made more sharply by the fact that at the end of 1918 American troops were actively involved in Russia and were aiding, directly or indirectly, the anti-Bolshevik forces. In these circumstances it was easy to switch from attacking the "Hun" to attacking "Reds," particularly if they were seen as one and the same thing.

In March 1919, the month of the formation of the Third International, the *Washington Post* announced that various groups were combining to bring "bloody revolution and the establishment of Bolshevik Republic" in America; the *New York Times* could report that the IWW members "are agitating for the overthrow of the United States government and its replacement by a system such as now prevails in Russia." This agitation, it was claimed, was being carried out through "spending huge sums of money" and via the foreign-language press and trade unions—some 8,334 of which were said to be influenced by the IWW.[39]

Strikes were thus characterized not as the product of legitimate economic grievances, but as the work of ideologically motivated, and foreign, groups: Wobblies, Socialists, Bolsheviks, and anarchists—the finer points of ideological difference were ignored. In Seattle Mayor Hanson described the strikers as revolutionary and warned that the city threatened to become the Petrograd of America unless firm action was taken. During the steel strike union leader William Z. Foster was castigated for his *former* membership of the IWW, and his previous syndicalist writings were widely quoted as evidence of the revolutionary nature of the strike. The Senate committee investigating that dispute and reporting in November 1919 suggested:

Behind this strike there is massed a considerable element of I.W.W.'s, anarchists and revolutionists and Russian Soviets; some radicals are attempting to elevate themselves to power within the ranks of organized labor.[40]

Such reports were given greater credence by men normally sympathetic to labor such as Secretary of Labor William B. Wilson, who, in March 1919, had said:

> the strikes that took place in Seattle, at Butte, at Paterson, at Lawrence, and at a number of other places were not industrial, economic disputes. . . . A deliberate attempt was made to create a social and political revolution that would establish a Soviet form of government in the United States.[41]

Given the extent of labor and other violence, and the sense of fragmentation described by Ray Stannard Baker and others, such dramatic claims were not difficult for people to believe. However, if further proof was needed it came in a series of bombings. On 28 April 1919 Mayor Hanson received a suspicious package in the mail, which, on further inspection, turned out to be a bomb. Similar packages were detected in the New York City mailing office, and more were found in other parts of the country. All told thirty-six bombs had been mailed: only one exploded. The unfortunate victim was not the senator for whom it was intended (Thomas Hardwick of Georgia), but his maidservant, who had her hands blown off.

These atrocities were reported in the press on 1 May—the traditional day for left-wing and labor celebrations. Rather than celebrations, however, the marches turned into riots as the demonstrators were attacked by antiradical crowds in towns and cities across the country ranging from New York, Boston, Chicago, Detroit, and Cleveland. In Cleveland a full-scale battle, involving army tanks as well as the police and civilians, broke out, and two people were killed.[42]

Conspicuous among the participants in these attacks on radicals were ex-servicemen, and while undoubtedly inflamed by the unpatriotic implications of left-wing marches and motivated by their own heightened sense of loyalty following armed service, such actions were not necessarily just expressions of antiradicalism any more than their role in race riots was simply racist. The involvement of soldiers and sailors, groups one might have expected to behave with discipline and restraint, was indicative of their feelings of resentment and alienation. Scott Fitzgerald captured this sense very well when he described soldiers in New York City in his short story "May Day," "wanting fearfully to be noticed and finding the great city thoroughly fed up with soldiers." The two soldiers he described were left "uncertain, resentful, and somewhat ill at ease," and after much drinking, and incidents heightening their feeling of isolation, they joined in an attack on "Bolsheviks." Such events did not happen just in fiction; the *New York Sun* reported on 3 May:

> Their fighting blood aroused . . . discharged soldiers and sailors loitering about the streets and parks continued yesterday to make life miserable for everyone who looked or acted like Bolsheviki.

While the Rand School, a Socialist institute—and probably the subject of the attack in Fitzgerald's story—remained under guard, the veterans attacked people with red neckties, and "one elderly man was said to have been chased through the park for wearing a beard of the orthodox Bolshevik type."[43]

Other outbursts by servicemen elsewhere at the time confirmed the absence of real ideological motivation and demonstrated a propensity to attack any group regarded as "slackers" or "disloyal," or even disrespectful of national symbols. When the 102d Infantry returned to New Haven, Connecticut, on 24 May 1919, they were subjected to insults and catcalls from watching students; three days later the soldiers laid siege to the campus. According to the historian who described the "siege of Yale," this was in part a continuation of town-gown conflicts and in part "rooted in the pent-up emotions of people who had just passed through the trying experience of a World War." In other words, traditional targets of criticism and abuse now became the objects for the release of newly created tensions.[44]

While the attack on students may not have been very serious, it was again indicative of the general mood, and other incidents were much more alarming, and again involved veterans as well as civilians. On 6 May 1919 a man in Washington, D.C., failed to stand for the playing of the national anthem during a victory loan pageant; a sailor shot him three times and was cheered for doing so! On Armistice Day, 11 November 1919, members of the American Legion in Centralia, Washington, charged the newly reopened IWW office, and were fired upon. Four legionnaires fell dead. Subsequently one of the twelve Wobblies arrested, Wesley Everest, himself a former soldier, was seized by a mob, castrated, and beaten before finally being hanged from a railway bridge.[45]

Such was the general mood of the time that these acts of violence and murder rarely resulted in punishment but were instead condoned by judges and juries, and encouraged by the press. In November 1919, for instance, the *Seattle Post-Intelligencer* could call upon "Real Americans" to

> rise as one man in the righteous wrath of outraged patriotism. We must smash every un-American and anti-American organization in the land. We must put to death the leaders of this gigantic conspiracy of murder, pillage, and revolution.[46]

In states such as Washington and Arizona, western states not long established but affected by wartime changes and considerable labor conflict, the violence and reaction seemed more pronounced, and again it was these that led the call for tough action. By 1920, some twenty-eight states, most of them in the West, had passed sedition, syndicalist, or red-flag legislation, and as had been the case during the war their governors and legislatures demanded federal action.[47]

Various official and semiofficial bodies joined the popular groundswell against radicalism, and just as in a later period of American history hearings were to be held to confirm peoples' worst fears, so too they were in 1919. From February to March the Senate Judiciary Subcommittee, chaired by Lee Overman, sat to investigate German wartime propaganda, but in the course of the hearings extended its brief to include Bolshevism. Its sensational report not only condemned the liquor trade as vicious, unpatriotic, and pro-German, but also established that the radical element in America, like beer, was German in origin. Not only did it give substance to fears of revolutionary plots, it also implicated well-known reformers and radicals such as Jane Addams and Robert Baldwin when it listed people regarded as potentially dangerous.[48] Further support for these allegations came from the Joint Committee of the New York State legislature investigating seditious activities, which, under Clayton R. Lusk, held hearings throughout 1919. The Lusk Committee went even further than the Overman Committee, conducting raids on left-wing offices in the spring and summer before producing a report in 1920, which became "the Bible of the super patriots for the next decade." Like the Senate committee, the Lusk Committee too claimed that Bolshevism was German in origin, that there were plans to "sovietize" the United States, and that people like Jane Addams were dangerous.[49]

In the course of the Senate hearings racial disorder was also associated with radicalism, and in a report called "Radicalism and Sedition among the Negroes," which gave "a substantial appreciation of the dangerous spirit of defiance and vengeance at work among the Negro leaders," the U.S. attorney general wrote:

> Practically all of the radical organizations in this country have looked upon the Negroes as particularly fertile ground for the spreading of their doctrines. These radical organizations have endeavored to enlist Negroes on their side, and in many respects have been successful.

A number of black journals and magazines were singled out for criticism, the "most able and most dangerous of all" being Randolph's *Messenger*—no amount of quotation could capture its "evil scope"—but the *Crisis* had also "frequently been objectionable."[50]

Claims such as those made about blacks, reformers, unions, and others were legitimized in these official hearings and often were based upon intelligence reports or Justice Department evidence, but the role of the Wilson administration itself is a matter of disagreement among historians. While some writers see the government as leading the hysteria, others arrive at less critical conclusions. Certainly, in the course of his speaking tour Wilson himself linked internal unrest with international disorder and spoke critically of strikes. In cabinet meetings too, he expressed fears concerning domestic security. However, most writers find Wilson guilty of the sin of omission rather than commission—too involved in foreign affairs or too ill to take an active part, he was responsible neither for starting nor stopping the Red Scare. As had been the case with the wartime suppression of civil liberties, the president left his subordinates a free hand and probably believed that their actions were justified.[51] In 1919 the central figure as far as government involvement in the campaign against radicals was concerned was A. Mitchell Palmer, the man who had succeeded Thomas Gregory as attorney general in 1918.

For one writer, Palmer "deliberately fanned the flames of fear and prejudice," largely, it is argued, for personal political gain. However, Palmer's biographer, while accepting that he was politically ambitious and had an eye on the presidential nomination in 1920, points out that the attorney general was criticized at the time for inactivity and for delay in responding to the revolutionary threat, rather than for being overzealous. Indeed, even his critics remark upon Palmer's reform background, his early restraint, and his support for the commutation of sentences for those imprisoned under the Espionage Act. The turning point in his attitudes came following the bombings in the spring and more especially those in June when one of eight bombs exploded outside his own home. The only victim was the bomber, who, although blown to pieces, left sufficient evidence to implicate anarchists. The attorney general was unhurt but shaken, and in a letter to Newton Baker wrote that he was now

> more determined than ever that, if humanly possible, the Department of Justice under my administration shall be the means of putting an end for ever to these lawless attempts to intimidate and injure, if not destroy, organized government in this country.[52]

Palmer began his campaign by establishing the Intelligence Division in the Justice Department in order to collect information on radical activities. Headed by the young J. Edgar Hoover, the division found plenty of material, most of it expressing hopes rather than intentions, but among which there was said to be evidence of a day of terror scheduled for 4 July 1919. Police forces were alerted, but nothing happened. However, Palmer was now prepared to crack down hard upon would-be revolutionaries.

Like most Americans, the attorney general associated radical ideas with foreigners—radical ideas *were* alien, un-American, foreign. A number of commentators and writers had long suggested that the cure to America's problems was to remove the alien immigrant community. During the war the *Saturday Evening Post* (among others) ran a series of articles on Americanization and immigration. One of these, entitled "The Overflowing Melting Pot," warned that the new order in Russia was "unsocial and selfish," and that America must not be "Russianized" if she were to have any influence in the world. An editorial in May 1918 could write of the "Scum of the Melting Pot" and argue that America's free policy of immigration had led to the entrance of "foreign agitators," "pikers, grafters, liars, and demagogues." A week later the journal included an article, "Our Imported Troubles and Trouble Makers," which singled out the IWW as among those foreign groups capitalizing upon the unrest of war.[53] Similar views were expressed by ordinary Americans; one, signing himself simply "An American," wrote from Montana to Bernard Baruch that

> our domestic troubles can be traced in large part to aliens who are not in sympathy with our constituted forms of government. They, together with foreign-born advisors, who persist in communing with these imps of hades, should be deported at the rate of not less than five thousand a month until we are purged of this contaminating influence. . . .[54]

Such thinking lay behind the immigration law passed in October 1918, and it was this that Attorney General Palmer was to use in 1919 and 1920.

The new law not only excluded immigrants who held revolutionary views, but also enabled the government to deport aliens already resident in the United States subsequently found to have, or to have adopted since their entry, revolutionary attitudes. Armed with this power, the Justice Department launched the first of a series of raids on the anniversary of the Russian Revolution in November. Some six hundred individuals were arrested in eleven different cities, and on 21 December 249 were deported on the USS *Buford*. A further 600 people were deported early in 1920 following raids at the beginning of January in which almost six thousand people were detained. Little real evidence of revolutionary intent was found—the total arms haul was three pistols—but this hardly mattered in 1920. Among the first deportees were Emma Goldman and Alexander Berkman, longtime residents in the United States and two of the most prominent anarchist speakers and organizers—but neither involved in revolutionary plots in 1919, and hardly a threat to society. Like so many others, Goldman and Berkman were the victims of a general climate of intolerance that provided the opportunity to expel elements long regarded as undesirable.[55]

The Palmer raids and deportations marked the height of the Red

Scare. Indeed, in going so far the attorney general produced a reaction against his policies. In November 1919 one of Newton Baker's correspondents could suggest that "there is a general feeling that Palmer is going much too far now," and the same writer later remarked upon the attorney general's "panicky temper."[56] Criticism and doubts mounted when in 1920, for the second time, Palmer announced that 1 May had been set as a day of violent protest by left-wing groups. Again, police and troops were mobilized, but the day passed without event. Now the mood of fear had dissipated, and the attorney general was seen in terms of the boy who cried wolf.[57]

By spring 1920 the sense of wartime and postwar emergency was passing, and Americans were becoming concerned about attacks on civil liberties. Reservations were expressed about deportations, and further concern was voiced when five New York Socialists, duly elected to the New York Assembly, were refused their seats. Victor Berger was also rejected by Congress (with relish) on several consecutive occasions despite being returned each time by the electorate. He finally took his seat in 1922. When several distinguished lawyers, including Felix Frankfurter, Frank P. Walsh, and Zechariah Chafee, published a report questioning the legality of the Palmer raids, the methods used, and the treatment of those detained, the tide of opinion had completely turned. When a bomb exploded in the heart of Wall Street, on 16 September 1920, killing thirty-three people and injuring two hundred, suggestions of revolutionary plots were dismissed as ludicrous, and the response was in general muted.[58]

Despite passing as quickly as it had come, the Red Scare was not without significance or effect. The intolerant mood enabled the final suppression and breakup of the Industrial Workers of the World and of the Socialist Party of America—although the latter was breaking up of its own accord on the rocks of ideological schism. Certainly the conflicts in the postwar period encouraged a generally conservative and less sympathetic attitude toward unions—in 1918 Joseph Tumulty could suggest to the president that the government had been overgenerous to labor, and others felt that labor was becoming too powerful. *The New Republic* reiterated a prewar view when it suggested that the middle classes were in danger of being crushed between the forces of capital *and* labor. One scholar has in fact suggested that members of the middle classes participated in strike-breaking and the Red Scare because of a deteriorating relative economic position.[59] Certain attitudes persisted: George Babbitt, Sinclair Lewis's epitome of middle-class, small-town values, could still claim that agitators were bought with German gold, and that all agitators who tried to force men to join unions should be hanged.

To some extent the Red Scare encouraged the swift passage and ratification of the Prohibition amendment, and so indirectly affected much of the 1920s. More direct was the continuation of anti-immigrant sentiment and the passage of the immigration acts of 1921 and 1924 establishing controls and quotas that would have been much approved by some sections of the community in 1900. The trial of Italian anarchists Sacco and Vanzetti following their arrest for murder in 1920 and their eventual execution in 1927 demonstrated that antiradical sentiment had not entirely vanished. Racial and religious intolerance also persisted, as evidenced by the phenomenal growth of the Ku Klux Klan in the early 1920s under the leadership first of William Simmons, and then Hiram Wesley Evans. By 1924 the Klan was estimated to have a membership of between two and four million, and had spread out of the South and into northern states and cities. In so far as the Klan represented an attack on the modernism and change of the 1920s it was very much a part of the postwar decade, but reformed in 1915, in its defense of "Americanism" and white Anglo-Saxon Protestantism, and in its "suspicion of everything foreign," its roots were in the war years and earlier.[60]

What the war had done in America was to increase and sharpen many existing tensions and conflicts and provide a focus for the fear and paranoia evident for some time. These tensions continued to find expression in the postwar period when, in the absence of a clear, managed program of reconstruction, and with the withdrawal of government mediation, a free-for-all took place between labor and capital. The violence of this conflict, set against the backdrop of the Russian Revolution and international disorder, led to a sense of insecurity and a continuation of the wartime hysteria. Anti-German feeling now became anti-Bolshevik, and as both were foreign, immigrants provided the convenient scapegoat. As Stanley Coben has argued, "the Red Scare . . . was brought on largely by a number of severe social and economic dislocations which threatened the national equilibrium."

> These sudden difficulties, moreover, served to exaggerate the disruptive effects already produced by the social and intellectual ravages of the World War and the preceding reform era, and by the arrival before the war, of millions of new immigrants.[61]

If the origins of the Red Scare lay in the prewar years, they clearly did not immediately disappear in the postwar era. However, the level of hysteria did decline, and the hunt for revolutionaries ceased. It is possible to see the events of 1919 as a release mechanism that allowed tensions built up during the war to escape. A number of commentators suggested that the war had created a tension that had not been expunged—Scott Fitzgerald, of course, went as far as to suggest that the mood of the entire postwar decade, his Jazz Age, had something to do "with all the nervous energy stored up and unexpended in the war." No doubt the author, and subsequent writers, were echoing Woodrow Wilson's remarks in 1919 that "the nervous tension of our people has not yet relaxed to normal."[62] However, when the relaxation did come it was a consequence of more mundane factors than those suggested here.

The passing of the Red Scare and other social disorders of 1919 probably had as much to do with the beginning of economic recovery and the fall in unemployment as any psychological factors. Despite the absence of an organized government program, the process of reconversion from war to peace-time production proceeded fairly rapidly. Indeed, American postwar economic recovery compared very favorably with that of other participants in the war. Germany was beset with economic problems until the midtwenties, and Britain suffered severe economic dislocations throughout the decade, so much so that unemployment in the United Kingdom never fell below one million—about 9 percent of the labor force. America's good fortune was brought about by the application of new technology in industry (mass-production techniques and electrification), the development of new consumer industries (electrical goods, plastics, automobiles), combined with the pent-up demand resulting from wartime earnings and savings, and, of course, the fact that it had not suffered the same degree of disruption and destruction as other nations.

In cities like Bridgeport, Connecticut, war problems eased as some of the excess population departed at the end of the war and as new industries appeared. In 1920 the Remington Arms plant was sold to General Electric. By 1922 the company was using 35 percent of the floor space but expected to use it all by 1925. In nearby New Haven the Winchester Arms Company switched to the production of sporting goods and camping equipment, both growth areas during the twenties. While electrical and leisure products were important, it was the enormous expansion of the motor industry that indicated the extent of the consumer boom and symbolized the mood of the decade. In 1915 there were 2.5 million automobiles registered in America; in 1920 it was 9 million, and by 1929 it was a colossal 25.5 million. Whereas in 1909 two million horsedrawn carriages were made to only eighty thousand cars, in 1923 four million cars were made to only ten thousand carriages. Not surprisingly, servicing automobiles, along with the electrical industry, became central concerns in cities like Bridgeport, and by 1923 employment was back to wartime levels.[63]

Already by 1920 the American people were beginning to concentrate on the pursuit of material concerns rather than worrying about either ideological foes at home or idealistic principles abroad. Old heroes were disappearing or becoming outdated—Theodore Roosevelt died in 1919, Wilson lingered on until 1924, William Jennings Bryan suffered humiliation in the Scopes Monkey Trial and died in 1925—and new ones such as Henry Ford and the stars of the silent movies were emerging. While some prewar concerns survived through the war years and beyond, the American mood as a whole was changing. It was summed up by Sinclair Lewis's eponymous hero, George F. Babbitt, when he said:

> What the country needs—just at this present juncture—is neither a college president nor a lot of monkeying with foreign affairs, but a good—sound—economical—business—administration, that will give us a chance to have something like a decent turnover.[64]

Of course, this was the view of the small-town, middle-class businessman, but it was widely held.

Nowhere were the new mood and changed political circumstance more evident than in the presidential campaigns and election of 1920. With President Wilson ill and to some extent discredited, the Democratic party faced an uphill struggle. Wilson's refusal to nominate a successor or to say whether or not he would consider running for an unprecedented third term also created internal difficulties. His son-in-law, William Gibbs McAdoo, for instance, was regarded by many as the "heir apparent" but would not officially admit to his candidacy until the convention itself, out of family loyalty, and insisted on denying his intention to run although it was clear he was a strong contender. A. Mitchell Palmer had built up support during the Red Scare and entered the race in February 1920. With Wilson out of the running, the fight was between these two although there was a total of sixteen names put forward at the convention. With McAdoo and Palmer tying, the third contender, Governor James M. Cox of Ohio, gained in strength, and finally, following Palmer's withdrawal, secured the nomination with Franklin Roosevelt as his running mate.

Although the Democrats eventually rallied to their chosen candidate, there was little doubt that the party was divided on a number of issues, Prohibition and the League of Nations particularly, and it was to remain so throughout the twenties. The Republican party on the other hand, was very much more unified, having shed, or reintegrated, the Bull Moose element since 1916. Lacking any strong personalities with obvious claims to leadership, the party managers produced a candidate who was to capture perfectly the sentiments of the convention and of the electorate— Warren Harding of Ohio. Promising healing not heroism, normalcy not nostrums, with Calvin Coolidge as his running mate, Harding was elected with a greater majority than any previous candidate.[65]

In his inaugural address the new president reaffirmed his confidence in American institutions but rejected the world role in which the country had lately been cast: "Confident of our ability to work out our own destiny, and jealousy guarding our right to do so, we seek no part in directing the destinies of the Old World. We do not mean to be entangled."[66] In adjusting from war to peace, the president said the nation "must strive for normalcy to reach stability," and disavowed "wild experiment" which would "only add to the confusion." Noting the economic changes already taking place, he promised administrative efficiency, a lightened tax burden, sound commercial practices, adequate credit facilities, a sympathetic concern for agriculture, and "an end to Government experiment in business." It was, in other words, a program of which George F. Babbitt would have been proud—and one delivered in much the same language. Much of the program was to be put into effect. The secretary of the Treasury, Andrew Mellon, reduced taxation, particularly on business, throughout the decade, and the government actively encouraged rationalization and cooperation—the war had demonstrated, and the Supreme Court had confirmed in its 1918 ruling on U.S. Steel, that bigness itself was not necessarily a bad thing. Backed by government, businessmen again seemed to be acceptable especially as they revealed a new concern for their workers in various welfare schemes and worker representation plans. Faced with the closed shop and welfare capitalism, trade union strength declined from 5 million in 1921 to 3.5 million in 1929. Concern for the working man generally ceased to be a public issue.

This view of the twenties as a conservative era in sharp contrast to the Progressive years places the war as the great divide. However, the break was neither as sudden nor as pronounced as this simple picture suggests. At an obvious level, it is worth bearing in mind how many of the features or symbols of the twenties were evident prior to the war—Ford's model T and moving assembly line, movies, and even the "flapper" were all part of prewar America, to name just a few. What happened in the twenties was that these became much more widespread and noticeable phenomena as America became recognizably a modern society.[67]

Undoubtedly the twenties did witness a more general prosperity, and the material products of a technological consumer society were available in greater abundance than ever before—manufacturing output increased by 50 percent during the decade, and by 1927 two-thirds of all homes had electric power, and many had electric irons, vacuum cleaners, and especially radios. However, the image of the twenties owes more to Scott Fitzgerald than to reality; it was not all "a thousand parties and no work." Even the view of the Harding administration as "conservative" is an oversimplification, and one not now generally accepted by historians. The new president adopted a fairly liberal and sympathetic attitude to groups who had been dealt with quite harshly by the previous administration. It was Harding who agreed to the early release of Eugene Debs on Christmas Day 1921, after Wilson had repeatedly refused to do so.[68]

Harding also continued some wartime programs—the War Finance Corporation, which had carried on through 1919–20 to aid exporters, was maintained froom 1921 to 1929 to help farmers through agricultural exports. In his address to Congress in April 1921, the president made a number of proposals that had their origins in wartime or earlier. Among his recommendations was one for a single department of public welfare to coordinate programs for "education, public health, sanitation, conditions of workers in industry, child welfare, proper amusement and recreation, and the elimination of social vice." While little came of this or of his suggestion for a biracial committee to study race relations, the growth of federal responsibilty for highways and communication was accepted. The Federal Highway Act of 1921 increased spending from $19.5 million in 1920 to $75 million in 1921 and $88 million in 1923—providing a sizable injection of money into the economy.[69]

These policies and programs do something to restore the reputation of Harding and to modify the harsher historical judgments made of him. Despite such modifications he remains an uninspiring figure, forever tainted by the corruption of his administration. However, one figure was free from all the scandals and was more representative of the administration's "liberalism" and provided a link with the past. This was Herbert Hoover, who, as secretary of commerce under both Harding and Coolidge, was to make a significant contribution to the 1920s before becoming president in his own right.

At the end of the war, Hoover, the former food administrator and advisor in Paris, had a considerable public reputation, and he was seen as a Progressive by many people—"a thorough going liberal spirit," "sane, progressive, competent"—and before he declared himself a Republican there were attempts to nominate him as the Democratic candidate in 1920.[70] (In Michigan Hoover actually won the Democratic primary even though the voters then knew his party affiliation.) As secretary of commerce he was to try to adapt his wartime experiences to peacetime needs, to use the same appeals to achieve a "liberal managerial order" without creating a welfare or regulatory state. In his belief in "voluntarism," "the collectivity of free individual initiative," he showed an optimism that owed much to an earlier generation and even had overtones of Wilson's New Freedom. He hoped that by bringing people together he could enable cooperation to develop freely from the perception of a larger community and national interest. Government would merely provide information and the forum in which self-regulation could take place. Thus the Department of Commerce helped organize some 250 major conferences on numerous issues.[71]

Seeing even unemployment as a problem similar to that of organizing foodstuffs in wartime, it was Hoover who encouraged the calling of a conference on unemployment in September 1921. Like the Food administration, the conference proposed local committees and organizations to establish work-sharing schemes. Few tangible results emerged, and employment increased anyway as a result of the upturn in the economy rather than any government initiative. However, one can see here the basis for Hoover's later response to the problems of the depression. Nonetheless, the attitude to labor was not wholly unsympathetic, and it was Hoover who finally persuaded U.S. Steel to adopt the eight-hour day in 1923.[72]

As an engineer turned politician, Hoover placed great emphasis on efficiency and the reduction of waste. These were Progressive concerns too, but the emphasis prior to 1914 had been upon social efficiency; after 1920 it was perhaps more on economic matters. Hoover actively encouraged mergers, rationalization, and the reduction of wasteful competition, and through various agreements with trade associations, and some twelve hundred conferences, the Department of Commerce was able to secure further agreements on standardization in major areas. According to his biographer, under Hoover the department became the "epitome of 'progressive' government," combining ideas on scientific management, organized cooperation, and private initiatives under government aegis.[73]

But progressivism survived outside the Department of Commerce and beyond the confines of either of the main parties. Prior to the 1920 election attempts were made to unite the Progressives in the forty-eight states of the union in the Committee of Forty-Eight, led by Amos Pinchot. Conventions in 1919 and 1920 were, however, unsuccessful in agreeing upon candidates or establishing unity with labor representatives. Always a diverse movement, progressivism was even more so after the war. However, it survived at state and individual levels—in Pennsylvania, for instance, Gifford Pinchot was to be reform governor from 1923 to 1927—and in Congress Progressive representatives and senators remained active as watchdogs of the public interest, exposing the Teapot Dome scandals and preventing the privatization of the nitrate plant at Muscle Shoals. In 1924 a number of individuals, including Dewey, Pinchot, and Addams, joined by discontented farmers and unions, formed the Progressive party with Robert M. La Follette as their presidential candidate. Although ill and poorly financed, the old war-horse from Wisconsin polled almost 5 million votes, 16 percent of the total. This compared favorably with Roosevelt's 4.1 million votes in 1912, although then that represented 27 percent of the electorate.[74]

Clearly, then, progressivism did not totally disappear in the twenties, but no one could claim it was the force it once had been. The decline of the reform impulse had a number of explanations. Obviously the war had diverted much attention from domestic to foreign affairs; it had also brought some progressive aims to fruition in increased government direction of economic and social life. Vital prewar issues, such as female suffrage, Prohibition, and immigration control, had been resolved, and certain minimum standards with regard to hours of employment and child and female labor now had a much wider acceptance. As Newton Baker pointed out when asked, in 1926, "Where Are the Pre-War Radicals?" many pre-war objectives had been accomplished, others tried and rejected.[75]

While the movement had suffered fragmentation—divided between Republicans and Democrats, wets and Prohibitionists, isolationists and internationalists, rural and urban—the Russian Revolution and the mood of conservatism it brought in America dampened support for radicalism. Too many ideas were now seen as stamped "made in Russia."

Of course, it would have been surprising, even without all the effects of these various events, if radicalism had continued unabated. As Walter Weyl remarked, "As young radicals grow older they marry pleasant wives, beget interesting children and begin to build homes in the country, and their zeal cools."[76] The fact that the older reformers were not replaced by a new generation reflected both on their successes and failures and upon the changing times and circumstances. The materialism of the age made reform seem unnecessary to some, and discouraged others. Harold Ickes, the Chicago reformer, asked "Why try to reform a world that has set its iniquities to jazz?" Jane Addams commented on the postwar "political and social sag" and the "outstanding emphasis upon sex."[77]

While economic and cultural changes added to the disillusionment of people like Ickes, it also brought greater employment for the educated young in managerial and service industries. As a consequence, the prewar amateur was replaced by a professional working in an organization with specific, rather than broad, general concerns. An example is the growth of the American Civil Liberties Union directly from war experience, but perhaps more noticeable was the replacement of Settlement House workers with social workers, now qualified in the "science" of psychology. Even the clientele changed as new immigrant groups and blacks replaced those who had moved into the suburbs. Jane Addams, the old leader of the movement, now concentrated on working for peace and was awarded the Nobel Peace Prize in 1931 in recognition for her services. But while she was recognized abroad, at home the woman many had formerly seen as a saint was now denounced as "the most dangerous woman in America" and as a Communist. Periods of reaction were not compatible with concerns for social justice.[78]

If Settlement House workers and reformers were not conspicuous in the twenties, many reappeared in the 1930s, and some, like Ickes, Harry Hopkins, and Frances Perkins, served in the New Deal. In responding positively to the crisis of the depression politicians established continuities by turning not just to earlier memories of reform, but also to the precedents for national action provided by the World War—a war which, with the readjustments and dislocations that followed, had helped to create a different America. The unrest after, and indeed during, the war was both a reaction to and reflection of those changes. The very intensity of wartime hysteria and Red Scare revealed the extent to which America had departed from prewar norms.

Notes

1. Burl Noggle, *Into the Twenties: The United States from Armistice to Normalcy* (Urbana, Ill., Chicago, and London, 1974); Robert K. Murray, *Red Scare: A Study in National Hysteria, 1919–1920* (New York, Toronto, and London, 1964); W. E. Leuchtenburg, *The Perils of Prosperity, 1914–1932* (Chicago and London, 1958); Stanley Coben, "A Study in Nativism: The American Red Scare of 1919–20," *Political Science Quarterly* 79, no. 1 (March 1964): 52–75.
2. Raymond B. Fosdick, *Chronicle of a Generation: An Autobiography* (New York, 1958), 198–99.
3. Jane Addams, *The Second Twenty Years at Hull House* (New York, 1930), 153.
4. Lane, *The Letters of Franklin Lane: Personal and Political* (Boston and New York, 1922), 270; Josephus Daniels, *The Cabinet Diaries of Josephus Daniels 1913–1921* (Lincoln, Neb., 1963), 279, 341.
5. *New York Times* 24 October 1918; E. Jay Howenstine, *The Economics of Demobilization* (Washington, D.C., 1944), 87–88.
6. Noggle, *Into the Twenties*, 52–53.
7. John Morton Blum, *Joe Tumulty and the Wilson Era* (Boston, 1951), 150; John A. Thompson, "The First World War and the American Progressive Publicists," Ph.D. dissertation, Cambridge University, 1969, 442.
8. National Conference of Social Work, *Proceedings, 45th Annual Session, Kansas City, Missouri, May 15–22* (1918), 9; Estella T. Weeks, *Reconstruction Programs: A Comparative Study of Their Content and of the Viewpoints of the Issuing Organizations* (New York, 1919), 69, and *American Federationist,* quoted, 11.
9. Academy of Political Science, Columbia University, *Proceedings: War Labor Policies and Reconstruction* 8, no. 2 (February 1919); "Foundations for Reconstruction," *American Labor Legislation Review* 3, no. 4 (December 1918); Philip Taft, *The A.F. of L. in the Time of Gompers* (New York, 1970), 369–72.
10. Noggle, *Into the Twenties*, 39–40; National Catholic War Council, *Administrative Committee, Bishops' Program of Social Reconstruction: A General Review of the Problems and Survey of Remedies for Social Reconstruction,* 20th anniversary edition, presented to Senate, 6 June 1939; John Tracy Ellis, *Documents of American Catholic History* (Milwaukee, 1956), 611.
11. Baker to Wilson, 30 November, 1918, Reel 6, Baker Papers, LC; Wilson, address to Congress, 2 December 1918, in Alfred Bushnell Hart, *Selected Addresses and Public Papers of Woodrow Wilson* (New York, 1918), 289–303.

12. Frederic Paxson, *American Democracy and the World War: Postwar Years, 1918–1923* (Berkeley, Calif., 1948), 93–94, 130–31.
13. Lane, *The Letters of Franklin K. Lane*, 307.
14. Paxson, *Postwar Years*, 116; Ray Stannard Baker, Diaries and Notebooks, Box 6, vol. 32, 1 December 1920, LC.
15. McAdoo to Wilson, 14 November 1918, McAdoo Papers, 525, LC.
16. See correspondence on 1918 elections, McAdoo Papers, 213; Paxson, *Postwar Years,* 4–6; Seward L. Livermore, *Woodrow Wilson and the War Congress, 1916–1918* (Middletown, Conn., 1966), 206–24.
17. Fosdick, *Chronicle,* 212; White to Ray Stannard Baker, 3 June 1919, Lippmann to Baker, 15 May 1919, vol. 24, Box 5, Baker Papers.
18. Ronald Steel, *Walter Lippmann and the American Century* (Boston and Toronto, 1980), 158–59, 164–65.
19. Vol. 26, 1919–20, vol. 27, 1920, Box 6, Baker Papers.
20. Baker, "Speech to Ohio Federation of Women's Clubs, Hotel Statler, October 15, 1919," Newton D. Baker Papers, Box 245, LC; J. R. Commons, et al., *History of Labor in the United States 1896–1932* (New York, 1935), 435.
21. Howenstine, *Economics of Demobilization,* 85, 134, 158.
22. Noggle, *Into the Twenties,* 9–15; Howenstein, *Economics of Demobilization,* 179.
23. Benedict Crowell and Robert Forrest Wilson, *How America Went to War: Demobilization: Our Industrial and Military Demobilization After the Armistice* (New Haven, Conn., 1921), 105–6.
24. Stanley Coben, *A. Mitchell Palmer: Politician* (New York, 1972), 162–66.
25. George N. Peek, *History of the Industrial Board of the Department of Commerce* (Moline, Ill., 1923).
26. Ray Stannard Baker, *The New Industrial Unrest: Reasons and Remedies* (Garden City, N.Y., 1920), 53; John B. Andrews, "Labor Laws in the Crucible: Measures Necessary for Effectiveness During and After the War," 18 January 1918, and John D. Rockefeller, Jr., "Brotherhood of Men and Nations," 13 June 1918, in Box 573, 574, Council of National Defense, Committee on Women's Defense Work, NARG 62; Schwab quoted in Charles W. Wood, *The Great Change: New America as Seen by Leaders in American Government, Industry and Education Who Are Remaking Our Civilization* (New York, 1918), 121.
27. Commons, *History of Labor,* 511; Taft, *The A.F. of L.,* 401.
28. Murray, *Red Scare,* 9; Commons, *History of Labor,* 445.
29. Taft, *The A.F. of L.,* 385–400.
30. Robert L. Friedham, *The Seattle General Strike* (Seattle, 1964).
31. Correspondence on steel strike, Cary T. Grayson to Bernard Baruch, 5 September, and Baruch to Grayson, 9 September 1919, Wilson Papers, CF4341, Reel 366, LC; David Brody, *Labor in Crisis: The Steel Strike of 1919* (Philadelphia and New York, 1965), 103–4, 113–29; Colston E. Warne, ed., *The Steel Strike of 1919* (Lexington, Mass., 1968).
32. Murray, *Red Scare,* 129–31.
33. Arthur S. Link and William B. Catton, *American Epoch: A History of the United States Since the 1890s* (New York, 1967), I, 237.
34. Wilson Papers, CF5085, Reel 378.
35. Industrial Conference, *Preliminary Statement of Industrial Conference*

Called by the President (Washington, D.C., 1919); Industrial Conference, *Proceedings of the First Industrial Conference,* Dept. of Labor (Washington, D.C., 1920), 58, 220–21.

36. Gary Dean Best, *The Politics of American Individualism: Herbert Hoover in Transition, 1918–1921* (Westport, Conn., 1975), 39–49; Industrial Conference, *Report of Industrial Conference Called by the President* (Washington, D.C., 1920); Woodrow Wilson Papers, 5085A, Reel 378.

37. John Higham, *Strangers in the Land: Patterns of American Nativism, 1860–1925* (New York, 1973), 233.

38. *New York Times,* 13 February 1919; *New York World,* 24 February 1919.

39. *New York Times,* 12 March 1919; *Washington Post,* 11 March 1919; *Philadelphia Public Ledger,* 11 March 1919.

40. David Brody, *Labor in Crisis,* 136–37; Francis G. Wickware, ed., *American Labor Year Book, 1919* (New York and London, 1920), 26.

41. *New York Times,* 4 March 1919.

42. *New York World,* 1, 2 May 1919; Coben, *A. Mitchell Palmer,* 204.

43. Fitzgerald, "May Day," in *The Stories of F. Scott Fitzgerald, Volume 1: The Diamond As Big As the Ritz* (Harmondsworth, Middlesex, 1980), 40, 43; *New York Sun,* 3 May 1919.

44. Rollin G. Osterweiss, *Three Centuries of New Haven* (New Haven, Conn., 1953), 409.

45. Murray, *Red Scare,* 183–84.

46. Quoted in Alexander Bing, *Wartime Strikes and Their Settlement* (New York, 1921), 250.

47. H. C. Peterson and Gilbert C. Fite, *Opponents of War, 1917–18* (Washington, D.C., and London, 1968), 288.

48. U.S. Congress, Senate Sub-Committee on the Judiciary, *Brewing and Liquor Interests and German and Bolshevik Propaganda,* 66th Cong., 1st sess., Doc. 62 (Washington, D.C., 1919), I, 505–6, 1084–88.

49. New York State Legislature, Joint Committee Investigating Seditious Activities, *Revolutionary Radicalism: Its History Purpose and Tactics* (Albany, N.Y., 1920), 20–26; Allen F. Davis, *American Heroine: The Life and Legend of Jane Addams* (New York, 1973), 252–54.

50. A. Mitchell Palmer, Attorney General, *Radicalism and Sedition among Negroes as Reflected in Their Publications,* Exhibit no. 10, Senate Documents, vol. 12, 66th Cong., 1st sess., 1919.

51. Harry N. Scheiber, *The Wilson Administration and Civil Liberties, 1917–1921* (Ithaca, N.Y., 1960), 49–60; Paul L. Murphy, *World War I and the Origins of Civil Liberties in the United States* (New York and London, 1979), 253–56.

52. Scheiber, *The Wilson Administration,* 52; Coben, *A. Mitchell Palmer,* 62–63, 197, 202–14; Palmer to Baker, 9 June 1919, Reel 8, Baker Papers.

53. *Saturday Evening Post,* 2 March 1918, 4 May 1918, 11 May 1918.

54. Telegram to Baruch, 20 October 1919, 13/143, Box 206, Dept. of Labor, Office of Secretary, NARG 174.

55. Murray, *Red Scare,* 196–97, 210–17; Alice Wexler, *Emma Goldman: An Intimate Life* (London, 1984), 266–74.

56. George Peabody to Baker, 18, 25 November 1919, Reel 8, Baker Papers.

57. Coben, *A. Mitchell Palmer,* 236; Murray, *Red Scare,* 252–53.

58. Murray, *Red Scare,* 255, 258–62.

59. Tumulty to Wilson, in Blum, *Joe Tumulty and the Wilson Era*, 148, 240; Coben, A. *Mitchell Palmer*, 172; Jurgen Kocka, *White Collar Workers in America 1890–1940: A Social-Political History in International Perspective* (London and Beverly Hills, 1980), 159–60.

60. Paul L. Murphy, "Sources and Nature of Intolerance in the 1920s," *Journal of American History* 51, no. 1 (June 1964):60–77; Kenneth J. Jackson, *The Ku Klux Klan in the City, 1915–1930* (New York, 1967), 11, 18.

61. Coben, "A Study in Nativism," 59.

62. Wilson, letter announcing calling of Industrial Conference, 3 September 1919, CF 5085, Reel 378, Wilson Papers; Baker, "Speech to Ohio Federation of Women's Clubs"; F. Scott Fitzgerald, "Echoes of the Jazz Age," in *The Crack-up* (Harmondsworth, Middlesex, 1976), 9; Malcolm Cowley, *A Second Flowering: Works and Days of the Lost Generation* (London, 1973), 13.

63. John M. Cooper, Jr., ed., *Causes and Consequences of World War I* (New York, 1972), 264, 265; Herbert F. Janick, *A Diverse People: Connecticut to the Present* (Chester, Conn., 1975), 12, 21–23; Preston William Slosson, *The Great Crusade and After, 1914–1928* (New York, 1930), 219.

64. Sinclair Lewis, *Babbitt* (1922; London, 1974), 27.

65. See Coben, A. *Mitchell Palmer*, 260–61, Paxson, *Postwar Years*, 151–59, and Leuchtenburg, *Perils of Prosperity*, 86–89, for convention and election details.

66. Warren Harding, Inaugural Address, *Congressional Record*, 67th Congress, 51, no. 1 (4 March 1921): 4–6.

67. See chapter 1; see also Henry F. May, *The End of American Innocence: A Study of the First Years of Our Own Time, 1912–1917* (London, 1960), 334–39, on prewar trends.

68. For the story of Debs's release, see Ray Ginger, *The Bending Cross: A Biography of Eugene Victor Debs* (New York, 1969), 405–13.

69. J. Leonard Bates, *The United States 1898–1928: Progressivism and a Society in Transition* (New York, 1976), 280–81; Eugene P. Trani and David L. Wilson, *The Presidency of Warren G. Harding* (Lawrence, Kan., 1977), 58, 87.

70. Ray Stannard Baker, vol. 26, 1919–20, Box 6, Baker Papers; Lane, *The Letters of Franklin Lane*, 334.

71. Trani and Wilson, *The Presidency of Warren G. Harding*, 90, 92; Joan Hoff Wilson, *Herbert Hoover: Forgotten Progressive* (Boston and Toronto, 1975), 91; David Burner, *Herbert Hoover: A Public Life* (New York, 1979), 159.

72. Wilson, *Herbert Hoover*, 91–92; Trani and Wilson, *The Presidency of Warren G. Harding*, 95–96.

73. Ellis W. Hawley, "Reappraising the Great Engineer," *Reviews in American History* 7, no. 4 (December 1979): 565–70; Best, *The Politics of American Individualism*, 93-94; Burner, *Herbert Hoover*, 161.

74. Kenneth C. MacKay, *The Progressive Movement of 1924* (New York, 1947); Amos R. E. Pinchot, *History of the Progressive Party 1912–1916* (New York, 1958), 71–74; Richard Lowitt, *George W. Norris: The Persistence of a Progressive, 1913–1933* (Urbana, Ill., Chicago, and New York, 1971), 198–99.

75. "Where Are the Pre-War Radicals?" *The Survey* 55 (1 February 1926): 556–66.
76. Weyl, *Tired Radicals and Other Papers*, quoted in John Tipple, *Crisis of the American Dream: A History of American Social Thought, 1920–1940* (New York, 1968), 290.
77. Harold Ickes, *The New Democracy* (New York, 1934), 218; Addams, *The Second Twenty Years at Hull House*, 192, 196.
78. Clark A. Chambers, *Seedtime of Reform: American Social Service and Social Action, 1918–1933* (Minneapolis, 1963), 119–23; Allen F. Davis, *Spearheads for Reform: The Social Settlements and the Progressive Movement, 1890–1914* (New York, 1967), 232–35.

Epilogue

From Progressivism to Prosperity:
The First World War in Perspective

In "Soldier's Home," Ernest Hemingway's short story of postwar alienation, the young veteran Harold Krebs returns to find "nothing was
changed in the town except that the young girls had grown up." In fact,
however, the problem was not that America remained the same, but that it
was radically different from the society remembered by both servicemen
and civilians. The war *seemed* to act as a great divide, separating what was
thought of as a peaceful prewar era from a troubled postwar world. Much
of the decade of the twenties was to be preoccupied with attempts to
return to a "normalcy" located somewhere in prewar memory, a memory
impossible to re-create. Thus George F. Babbitt goes back to the countryside in search of relief and solace, only to find "Paradise" corrupted by
the modern age. Even more famously Jay Gatsby was determined "to fix
everything just the way it was before" in pursuit of his dream. The broader
manifestation of these literary themes were the Prohibitionists, fundamen-
talists, and Klansmen who all tried to assert "traditional" American
values in the face of overwhelming change. As historian Frederic Paxson
wrote, "Nostalgia glorified the old way of life until it seemed more attractive than it ever really was."[1] In the process war experiences were to be
modified and amended to suit the changing temper of the times; they were
also to be remembered as guidelines for future action.

If, as Donald McCoy suggests, the twenties was a decade in which

America was "struggling to escape and preserve the past and to find and evade the future,"[2] then the war often occupied a central role in the dialogue between past and present. Given the enormity of the event the war was the more obvious point at which to separate past from present—the phrase *before the war* indicating the good old days of a bygone era. But the war was also seen as the initiator of change, the moment at which to locate changes that had probably begun at some less clearly defined or even less identifiable moment in time. The temptation to attribute everything to the war was overwhelming. For Robert M. La Follette, the war had "changed our country, our government, our life." Fellow Progressive George Norris went further. According to his biographer, commenting on the changing morality of the twenties, "Norris placed the blame on World War I. It had helped change human nature and affected the moral fiber of individuals." As the author of *The Great Change* said, describing the "New America," "That so much world history could be crowded into so few years has made everybody gasp."[3]

Such judgments have rightly been modified by historians. The most fundamental cause of change in America, as in western Europe, was not a single, defined event sandwiched neatly between two dates but the ongoing process of industrialization. Since the Civil War at least, the development of American industry had been affecting economic, social, and political life, and it was to go on doing so as the nation reached in the 1920s what Rostow called the stage of high mass consumption. All the characteristics of a modern industrial society—the relative decline in the role of agriculture, the rise in importance of manufacturing, the widespread use of technology in large-scale factory production, rapid urbanization, new class tensions, and the growth of the state—were evident before America entered the war. However, this is not to deny the significance of the war. Through the demands and pressures of the conflict, processes already in existence were modified, amended, and accelerated. It was precisely because the war compressed and highlighted the innovations and shifts in American life that people associated that one moment with all the changes now evident. As is always the case in history, however, the outcome of this event was the unique combination of long-term processes compounded by the particular short-term circumstances.

The major alterations in the economy continued with greater velocity during the war. The farm population in 1910 was just over 32 million, by 1920 it was 31.6 million, and during the war alone the farm labor force declined by 10 percent. However, farm production, acreage, and income all rose as a consequence of the artificial and temporary increase in demand brought by the war. Encouraged by the wartime boom, farmers increased their mortgages, but when prices fell with the return of world competition and the decline in the European market, their problems began. Farm income rose from $4.5 billion in 1914 to $9.6 in 1918 but dropped to $3.7 billion in 1921. By 1925 this figure had only risen to $6.8 billion, and, crippled with large debts, many farmers went bust. For those who survived, the postwar years were not to be easy, and government aid was to be limited. Although helped by the continuation of the War Finance Corporation and protective tariffs, a bill proposing much greater assistance through a federal farm corporation (the McNary-Haugen Bill), was twice vetoed by Calvin Coolidge, who remarked that "farmers have never made much money. I don't believe we can do much about that."[4]

While agriculture already suffered a depression, manufacturing experienced a boom during the twenties. Output had clearly increased during the war, as had capital investment—the number of establishments rose by over thirty-six thousand, and the total work force in manufacturing increased by two million. During the twenties there was not only further growth, with a 50 percent increase in output, but also greater innovation and rationalization. In 1914, 30 percent of industry was electrified; by 1929 this had risen to 70 percent. New machines revolutionized construction, new techniques advanced iron, steel, and glass production, new methods speeded the output of motor vehicles, and new materials such as rayon, bakelite, and cellophane affected a wide spread of products. In the process of growth, business amalgamation also increased. In the course of twelve hundred mergers between 1919 and 1928 six thousand independent concerns disappeared. The postwar decade saw the rise of new national conglomerates—Kodak Eastman, General Motors, A & P. Antitrust activity almost disappeared as attitudes toward business changed between 1917 and 1920.[5]

New methods in industry were not without their drawbacks. An estimated three million workers were displaced by new technology and machines during the twenties. However, if some elements of the labor force were victims of progress, in general the picture is one of improvement. Overall, the pattern of the decade was one of full employment and an increase in purchasing power. A comparison of 1914–25 earnings figures with those of 1899–1914, yields the percentage increases in real earnings shown here (see table). One estimate put the overall increase in buying power for workers in all branches of manufacturing between 1914 and 1927 at 35 percent and pointed to the greatest gains being made at the end of the decade. In Europe, by comparison, wages were half those of Americans, and barely keeping up with the cost of living.[6]

Besides wages, the other major improvement for labor was in hours worked. In one study it was found that whereas 73 percent of workers had been employed for ten hours, six days a week in 1914, by 1919 only 33 percent worked such hours, and this trend continued through the decade.[7] The war marked a definite change in terms of working hours, and the eight-hour day, so long a major object of union agitation, received government backing during the war and became increasingly the norm in the twenties. Labor relations also seemed to improve—or at least after 1919 the violent confrontations diminished, if only for the time being. That fact was, however, as much due to the decline in labor's support in this period, and when unions grew again, the clashes between capital and labor would resume.

Percentages of Increases in
Real Earnings

	1914–25	1899–1914
Auto workers	65%	7%
Lumber	53%	3%
Iron and steel	39%	5%
Chemicals	27%	0%
Cotton	29%	0%

Source: U.S. Department of Commerce, Bureau of the Census, *Earnings of Factory Workers, 1899–1927: An Analysis of Payroll Statistics,* Census Monograph X, (Washington, D.C., 1929), 76.

That these were the lean years for organized labor cannot be denied. The inherent weaknesses of the American labor movement—its ethnic and racial divisions, the conservatism of its leadership, its craft orientation—had not disappeared.[8] Union strength had grown only during the abnormal circumstances of the war, and with government support. Without either, and following the Red Scare, its decline was probably inevitable. This decline was encouraged too by the improved earnings and hours, and by the changed attitudes of employers. As one labor organizer despairingly remarked, "as long as men have enough money to buy a second-hand Ford and tires and gasoline, they'll be out on the road and paying no attention to union meetings." At the same time, on the employers' side, the war had demonstrated the benefits of a more conciliatory attitude and the necessity to safeguard workers' welfare. As a result, welfare capitalism reached its height in the midtwenties; a survey of the fifteen hundred largest companies in 1926 found that almost 50 percent had comprehensive programs, and 80 percent had at least some form of welfare provision:

workers lived in company houses, were treated by company doctors, attended company schools, played on company teams, purchased company stock, and were represented by company unions.

Even Judge Gary of U.S. Steel could see the logic of such schemes: "It is the way men ought to be treated, and . . . it pays to treat men that way."[9]

The rewards were greater productivity—and a decline in union activity and less likelihood of government interference.

This picture of the twenties as a period of economic progress and industrial harmony must, of course, be qualified. Many grievances lay latent, to surface in the thirties. Large numbers of people remained poor despite all the evident prosperity, and many groups seemed as trapped in poverty after the war as before. Some things never seemed to change. Welfare capitalism was perhaps the exception rather than the rule, and certainly hardly affected an industry like coal mining. The number of miners killed in 1914 was 2,454; in 1926 the toll was 2,518. Sharecroppers and cotton workers in the South and small farmers elsewhere barely felt the prosperity of the twenties, and although the great robber barons of the prewar era no longer seemed as dominant, the distribution of wealth had barely changed. While 10 million still lived in poverty, the number of millionaires had risen from forty-five hundred in 1914 to eleven thousand in 1926.[10]

One important shift in the occupational and income structure had taken place. During the decade white-collar and professional workers increased in number by over 3.5 million and moved into second place behind the number of workers in manufacturing, ahead of those in agriculture, and constituted almost 30 percent of the labor force.[11] In part this was a reflection of the growth in service industries, in part a result of the growth in scale of industry itself. The twenties witnessed the rise of the manager, the business organizer, and the advertising and public relations expert. With this trend the middle-class involvement in industry increased, not just through work, but also through the ownership of stocks and shares. One estimate put the number of stockholders in 1922 at 14.4 million, and suggested that 3.4 million of these had come following American entry into the war, which, through Liberty bonds, "had increased the habit of investment among the general public." Linked to this increase in investment was the increase too of credit. By 1927 some 15 percent of all goods were bought on credit, and undoubtedly this was a reflection of middle-class prosperity. Little wonder, then, that one historian could suggest that during the twenties "almost all war-related causes of white collar discontent evaporated."[12]

Another notable area of growth probably reflecting the improved situation of the middle classes was in education. If the war had emphasized the importance of education to the nation, postwar prosperity rather than political action made its expansion possible. Between 1919 and 1928 the number of individuals in all levels of education rose by over six million; the percentage of fourteen- to seventeen-year-olds in school jumped from 32 percent in 1920 to 51 percent in 1930, and the university population rose by half a million. Not surprisingly, the twenties was to be marked by an emphasis on youth. To some extent the war itself had emphasized the younger generation, but prosperity and educational opportunities enhanced this trend.[13]

Linked to both the growth in school attendance and the special attention given to the young was the decline in child labor. Again, this major prewar issue had been a matter of concern during the war, and despite the demands to utilize all available labor and the failure of the child labor law, the trend had continued downward, and did so still in the postwar years. Whereas in 1910 25 percent of boys aged ten to fifteen worked, in 1930 only 6 percent did so. The figures for girls the same age were 12 and 3 percent respectively.[14] The issue of child labor remained a significant concern in the decade and was to result in legislative action in the 1930s.

Child care also continued to develop in the twenties following the encouragement provided in the war years. The Sheppard-Towner Maternity and Infancy Care Act of 1921 was a major achievement that marked at least one significant survival of progressivism into the twenties and led to the creation of three thousand child and maternal health centers between 1921 and 1929. Whether as a consequence of better child care at an early age or of the greater amounts spent on health provision generally, infant mortality dropped from eighty-five deaths per thousand births in 1920 to sixty-four per thousand in 1928.[15]

If the war did much to point up the need for education and health care, it also had a considerable impact on housing. Housing problems were a matter of considerable concern before 1914, but they became an issue of greater urgency, of national importance, during the war because of the connection with war production and efficiency. New departures were adopted to meet wartime exigencies, but those initiatives were not sustained in peacetime, and the housing shortage was to be a major postwar problem. The number of dwelling units built dropped from 400,000 in 1914 to a mere 174,000 in 1918 and was only back at prewar levels in 1919. A survey of fifty-three cities found shortages ranging from "evident" to "critical" and "deplorable."[16] One response was the government campaign in 1919 to persuade people, "Own Your Own Home," but little could come of this without some kind of federal home loan program, and this was not forthcoming. However, some states provided veterans with loans—by 1928 California, for instance, had spent $24 million on five thousand homes for ex-servicemen. Perhaps the government program to encourage home ownership had some effect in publicizing possibilities for there was something of a building boom after 1921, and over three million families moved to new homes between 1923 and 1929. Nonetheless, between nine and ten million more remained in slums, and for many experts the failure to solve this problem by private means emphasized the need for federal action.[17]

The problems of housing were exacerbated by the movement of people into towns and cities during the war. As everyone knows, it was in 1920 that America became classed as predominantly urban for the first time. Of course, this development began years before (if not with the first settlements, at least in the 1830s!), but it had accelerated during the war. The most obvious aspect of the wartime change was the movement of black Americans from the South to the North—a change that would not have occurred at that time, on such a scale, but for the war. With the limitations on immigration and the continuation of industrial growth, the migration of blacks maintained momentum in the twenties as a further 600,000 moved to northern centers. By 1930 the black population of Chicago was almost 250,000, and that of Detroit was just over 120,000.[18]

Although more than 75 percent of the black population continued to live in the South in 1930, the presence of a sizable number in the North, concentrated as it was in a few urban centers, was of considerable significance. While this demographic change brought new problems, it also brought a number of benefits. The North did provide greater employment opportunities and allow more political and social freedom. One important consequence of the changing economic status of blacks was an increased involvement in trade unions, and in 1925 A. Philip Randolph began to mobilize black railroad workers in the Brotherhood of Sleeping Car Porters. Eventually the BSCP was to provide Randolph with a platform for action within the AFL and a base from which he could organize other black workers in, for instance, the National Negro Congress and the later March on Washington Movement.

The increased political power of blacks in the North also had some effect. In Chicago black voters had considerable influence, and in 1928 Oscar DePriest, a black city councilman, was to be the first black elected to Congress since the turn of the century. At the national level, the failure to achieve any recognition from the Republican administrations in the twenties led to the beginning of a move toward the Democratic party.

Such political advances as there were did little to effect any real change in the black position in either North or South. True, race violence seemed to diminish in the twenties, but prejudice and discrimination prevailed. NAACP files indicate that opposition to blacks in urban centers in the North did not decline, and limitations on the purchase of housing by blacks probably increased. In St. Louis, for instance, in August 1919 a priest reminded his white congregation of the Protective Association, which was intended to prevent "the Negro Invasion"; in 1921 a black woman in New York forwarded a letter warning the black occupants of 154

Gates Avenue that unless they moved by a certain date they would be killed. Meanwhile, in 1922 the mayor of Johnstown, Pennsylvania, ordered all blacks with less than seven years' residence to leave. In the south, race relations were still marked by brutality, and blacks' inferior place was reinforced by lynching—over two hundred cases between the end of the war and 1926.[19]

If black life in the twenties consisted of the continuation of segregation and discrimination in the South and increased ghettoization in the North, the difference was now in the black response. Paradoxically, the ghetto helped to further the sense of black community and identity. A growing black middle class was evident in the increase of newspaper circulation, the growth of organizations like the NAACP and National Urban League, and the famous outpouring of black culture known as the Harlem Renaissance. It is true that the renaissance was short-lived, but it was indicative nonetheless of what Alain Locke described as the "New Negro"—a black now self-assertive and proud of his identity. Langston Hughes rightly said that "the ordinary Negroes hadn't heard of the Negro Renaissance. And if they had, it hadn't raised their wages any,"[20] but ordinary blacks were experiencing similar feelings to those of their more literary fellows. Their attitudes found expression in Marcus Garvey's Universal Negro Improvement Association (UNIA), an essentially urban movement of the black masses established in America in 1916 that rose to prominence in the twenties.

The UNIA, through its journal *The Negro World*—"the voice of the awakened Negro," articulated a sense of racial community and pride and established a series of black organizations to direct a return to Africa. This latter idea had little appeal for the majority of black Americans, but the manner in which Garvey spoke for blacks did. It is impossible to know how many followers Garvey had—certainly not the six million he claimed, nor the twenty thousand that W. E. B. DuBois suggested. Probably the membership of the organization was in the region of forty to fifty thousand, but its support was undoubtedly greater. Sadly, Garvey was more of a spokesman than leader and organizer, and corrupt practices in the UNIA led to his being jailed for fraud in 1925, and in 1927 he was deported (as a West Indian he was an alien).[21]

Vestiges of Garveyism remained in the American ghettos and influenced later movements such as the Black Muslims. Other black organizations like the NAACP survived through the decade. The NAACP became more and more a black organization, and during the twenties it began the long legal struggle against segregation in education and increased its efforts to outlaw lynching. The voice of black protest would grow through the decade, revealing "a growing consciousness of the desire for some of the real, substantial, things of American democracy."[22]

The history of the women's movement was almost the reverse of that of blacks. While one can agree that the "war coming at a time when the feminist movement was making an immense surge forward, led to a vast broadening of the activities in which women took part," it is hard to see the years 1914–18 as a turning point in anything other than the question of suffrage.[23] Although there was an increase in female employment and a shift within the female labor force from one type of work to other, more diverse, and better-paid areas, much of this was to prove temporary. The greatest progress had already taken place in the decades before the war, and latest research suggests that those areas where wartime progress was sustained were precisely those of prewar change. The largest single growth sector was in clerical work, where the number of females employed increased five times as much as the overall nonagricultural female labor force, and more than twice as fast as the increase in the male clerical work force. In addition to clerical work, an enormous increase occurred in social welfare work, in which two-thirds of all workers in 1920 were female.[24]

While the total number of women employed outside the home continued to grow in the twenties, rising by over 2 million to over 10 million, a 27 percent increase, the proportion of women in the labor force as a whole hardly changed. But one noteworthy point was the fact that 3.1 million married women worked in 1930 compared with 1.9 million in 1920. One of the women interviewed by the Lynds commented on this, and more besides, when she said, "I began work during the war *when everyone else did* [italics mine]; we had to meet payments on our house and everything was getting so high. The mister objected at first, but now he don't mind."[25]

Whatever the limitations on women's wartime economic advances, they did strengthen the claim to political representation. The passage of the Nineteenth Amendment, the culmination of years of struggle, was accelerated by women's contribution to the war effort and the publicity given to it. Having won the vote, however, much of the coherence of the women's movement disappeared. In fact it might be claimed that in creating an illusion of political and economic progress the war actually encouraged a decline in activism, just as the notion of a "New Woman" in the twenties, an image rather than a reality, persuaded many that further action was unnecessary. That women's organizations lost direction after the passage of the amendment is hardly surprising, but as J. Stanley Lemons has demonstrated, women continued to be active in a number of different and less obvious spheres, including child welfare and protection, and consumer affairs. Indeed, according to Lemons, "The impetus gained in the war brought feminism into its best years."[26]

Lemons's point, exaggerated though it may be, is further substantiated by Susan Ware's study of women in the New Deal. Time and time again the women who appear in New Deal agencies were those who had entered public service during the war, continued in some form of social or political work during the 1920s, and found new opportunities in the 1930s. Women who had worked in the Committee of Public Information, Women's Committee, or Red Cross might through work in the Children's Bureau, Democratic party, or National Consumer's League, end up in the Department of Labor, Treasury, or National Recovery Administration in the thirties. They could, of course, end up like Frances Perkins as secretary of labor, and the first woman cabinet member.[27]

Women were not the only ones to provide links between the war and a later generation of reform. When faced with a crisis of enormous proportions in the 1930s the American people turned again to the experience of war in order to combat the problems of economic collapse. As W. E. Leuchtenburg has pointed out, politicians resorted both to the images of war as a metaphor to encourage national mobilization and sacrifice, and to war agencies themselves as models for new government action. As Bernard Baruch said, "What was done in those war years was never to be completely forgotten." Woodrow Wilson indicated something of the direction of the war's lessons in 1918 when he said it "has taught us many things we did not previously know about national economy and efficiency at the same time stimulating the opportunities for individual achievement and development."[28] President Hoover applied some of those lessons in his way during the twenties and in his responses to the depression, but Wilson's comments were to be most fully borne out by Franklin Roosevelt and the New Deal.

The most obvious link between the war and the New Deal was in terms of personalities—men who had come to the fore in the war emergency and who were now included in or associated with the New Deal included Felix Frankfurter, Baruch, George Peek, Hugh Johnson, Leon Henderson, Harold Ickes, even George Creel, and a whole host of administrators. The best-known of all was the president himself, assistant secretary of the Navy during the war, and involved particularly in labor matters. More significant even than these links was the fact that "there was scarcely a New Deal act or agency that did not owe something to the experience of World War I."[29] From the TVA, NRA, and AAA through to the National Labor Relations Act and Federal Housing Act precedents for economic and social reform were found in wartime mobilization from agencies such as the War Industries Board, Food Administration, War Labor Board, War Labor Policies Board, and United States Housing Corporation. Of course, the analogy between depression and war was to outlive its usefulness, and New Deal agencies were to develop in response to the particular problems of the thirties well beyond the scope envisaged during the war. While some New Deal agencies in their turn disappeared, others remained, and in doing so provided not just a legacy of the depression years but of an earlier era and of a different crisis. When America became involved in yet another world war many of those lessons were to be recalled again, some to be emulated, others to be avoided.

Although the effects of the First World War were not as great in America as those in Europe—and in terms of human losses, were insignificant by comparison—they were still profound nonetheless. The war radically altered America's economic relationships with the rest of the world and affected its internal economic institutions. The pressures of war brought political departures which, although short-lived, provided the basis for conservative governmental policies in the twenties and yet provided inspiration for reform measures in the thirties. The emotional and psychological effects of the war colored domestic politics and resulted in an increased intolerance and the suppression of various groups and movements. At the same time, the war brought spontaneous shifts in population distribution and work patterns, increasing tensions and anxieties in certain areas. Although these forces often led to violent responses, the changes could not be denied. Whatever happened in the future, the place and role of women would never be quite the same, nor would the pattern of race relations. Labor affairs too were not the same after the war, and precedents for future union action were established if not immediately put into effect. While all these changes contributed, with foreign affairs, to the sense of social unrest, the war paradoxically enhanced the homogeneity of the country by emphasizing the role of the federal government, nationalism, and "Americanization." In the new relationships that developed between different groups, and between individuals and the state, the war accelerated the process of modernization and, in helping to reconcile the different forces of change, brought about the transition from progressivism to prosperity.

Notes

1. Paxson, *American Democracy and the World War: Postwar Years; Normalcy, 1918–1923* (Berkeley, Calif., 1948), 2; "Soldier's Home," in *Our Time* (New York, 1925), 91; Sinclair Lewis, *Babbitt* (1922; rep. St. Albans, England, 1973), 234–38; F. Scott Fitzgerald, *The Great Gatsby* (1926; rep. Harmondsworth, Middlesex, 1968 ed).
2. Donald R. McCoy, *Coming of Age: The United States During the 1920s and 1930s* (Harmondsworth, Middlesex, 1973), 11.
3. Charles W. Wood, *The Great Change: New America* . . . (New York, 1918), 9, and A. Bushnell Hart, "The New United States," quoted in "Introduction"; Robert La Follette, in Belle Case and Fola La Follette,

Robert M. La Follette, June 14, 1855–June 18, 1925 (New York, 1953), 935; Richard Lowitt, *George W. Norris; The Persistence of a Progressive, 1913–1933* (Urbana, Chicago, and New York, 1971), 324.

4. Coolidge quoted in James T. Patterson, *America in the Twentieth Century: A History* (New York, 1983), 158; U.S. Department of Commerce, Bureau of the Census, *Historical Statistics of the United States, 1789–1945* (Washington, D.C., 1949), 99.

5. President's Committee on Social Trends, *Recent Social Trends in the United States* (New York and London, 1933), Volume 1, 241; Preston W. Slosson, *The Great Crusade and After 1914–1928* (New York, 1930), 184; W. E. Leuchtenburg, *Perils of Prosperity, 1914–1932* (Chicago and London, 1958), 179.

6. U.S. Dept. of Commerce, Bureau of the Census, *Earnings of Factory Workers, 1899–1927: An Analysis of Payroll Statistics* (Washington, D.C., 1929), 76; Slosson, *The Great Crusade,* 170–71.

7. R. S. and H. M. Lynd, *Middletown: A Study in Modern American Culture* (New York, 1929), 53; Leuchtenburg, *Perils of Prosperity,* 178.

8. Irving Bernstein, *The Lean Years: A History of the American Worker, 1920–1933* (Boston, 1960).

9. R.S. and H. M. Lynd, *Middletown,* 254; Stuart D. Brandeis, *American Welfare Capitalism, 1880–1940* (Chicago and London 1976), 28–32; David Brody, "The Rise and Decline of Welfare Capitalism," in John Braeman, et al., eds., *Change and Continuity in Twentieth Century America: The 1920s* (Ohio, 1968), 154–55.

10. Slosson, *The Great Crusade,* 169; *Historical Statistics,* 153.

11. Patterson, *America in the Twentieth Century,* 143.

12. Slosson, *The Great Crusade,* 177, 181; Jurgen Kocka, *White Collar Workers in America 1890–1940: A Social-political History in International Perspective,* (London and Beverly Hills, 1980), 165.

13. *Recent Social Trends,* 329–31; McCoy, *Coming of Age,* 133.

14. *Recent Social Trends,* 303.

15. *Historical Statistics,* 46; Louis J. Covotsos, "Child Welfare and Social Progress: A History of the United States Children's Bureau," Ph.D. dissertation, Chicago, 1976, 145–46; Walter Trattner, *From Poor Law to Welfare State: A History of Social Welfare in America* (New York and London, 1979), 184; J. Stanley Lemons, "The Sheppard-Towner Act: Progressivism in the 1920s," *Journal of American History* 55, no. 4 (March 1969): 776–85.

16. U.S. Housing Corporation, Surveys and Statistics Division, "Housing General File," Box 9, NARG 3.

17. U.S. Housing Corp., Commission on Living Conditions, Box 10, NARG 3, and Council of National Defense, Reconstruction Research Division, Housing File, 16–D1, Box 1002; Lubove, *Community Planning in the 1920s: The Contribution of the Regional Planning Association of America* (Pittsburgh, 1963), 18, 23–25.

18. Robert C. Weaver, *The Negro Ghetto* (New York, 1948), 84.

19. NAACP Papers, Admin File, C276, "Housing," and 336, "Lynchings." The *Crisis* also recorded lynchings throughout the decade.

20. Hughes quoted in David G. Nielson, *Black Ethos: Northern Urban Negro Life and Thought, 1890–1930* (Westport, Conn., & London, 1977), 34.

21. On Garvey and the UNIA, see David Cronon, *Black Moses: The story of Marcus Garvey* (Madison, Wis., 1955) and Judith Stein, *The World of Marcus Garvey: Race and Class in Modern Society* (Baton Rouge, La., and London, 1986).

22. George E. Haynes, "Effect of War Conditions on Negro Labor," Academy of Political Science, Columbia University, *Proceedings: War Labor Policies and Reconstruction* 8, no. 2 (February 1919): 174.

23. Mark Sullivan, *Our Times: Over Here 1914–1918* (New York and London, 1933), 458.

24. Bernstein, *The Lean Years*, 55–56; Elyce J. Rotella, *From Home to Office: U.S. Women at Work, 1870–1930* (Ann Arbor, 1981), 4, 125; Alice Kessler-Harris, *Out to Work: A History of Wage-Earning Women* (New York and Oxford, 1982), 116, 219.

25. Lynd and Lynd, *Middletown*, 28–29.

26. J. Stanley Lemons, *The Woman Citizen: Social Feminism in the 1920s* (Urbana, Chicago and London, 1973), 63.

27. Susan Ware, *Beyond Suffrage: Women in the New Deal* (Cambridge and London, 1981), 5–6, 32, 143–55.

28. Baruch quoted in William Appleman Williams, *The Contours of American History* (Chicago, 1966), 425; Wilson to Tumulty, 11 May 1918, copy in Burleson papers, vol. 20.

29. W. E. Leuchtenburg, "The New Deal and the Analogue of War," in John Braeman, et al., *Change and Continuity in Twentieth-century America* (Ohio, 1964).

Bibliography

Abbreviations

LC   Library of Congress
NA   National Archives (Thus NARG = National Archives Record
       Group)
NYPL   New York Public Library

1. *Private Papers*

Newton D. Baker, NYPL
Newton D. Baker, LC
Ray Stannard Baker, LC
Albert Sidney Burleson, LC
Carrie Chapman Catt, NYPL
George Creel, LC
Josephus Daniels, LC
W. E. B. DuBois, Fisk University, Nashville
Felix Frankfurter, LC
William Gibbs McAdoo, LC
Mark Sullivan, LC
Lillian Wald, NYPL
Thomas James Walsh, LC
Woodrow Wilson, LC

2. *Government Records*

Bureau of Education, Records of the Office of the Commissioner, NARG 12
Historical File, 1914–1920

Children's Bureau, NARG 102
Historical File, 1914–1920

Connecticut State Council of Defense, Papers, 4 Boxes, LC

Council of National Defense, NARG 62
Director's Office
Newspaper clippings, entry 2-E1
Publicity material 2-D4
Committee on Labor, Chairman's Office 10A-C3
Committee on Women's Defense Work 13A-D1
Reconstruction Research Division 16-B1 and 16-D1

Dept. of Labor, NARG 174
Fragments of Presidents Mediation Commission
Chief Clerk's Files, Papers of Hugh Kerwin
Sec. of Labor, William B. Wilson

Dept. of Labor, NARG 257
Bureau of Labor Statistics, "Schedules of Cost of Living"

U.S. Housing Corporation, NARG 3
Series 1 Office of the President, Records Relating to the Need for Industrial Housing
Series 75 Surveys & Statistics Division, Industrial Housing Surveys
Series 6 General Records of the Commission on Living Conditions

War Labor Policies Board, NARG 1
Series 2 "Correspondence of the Chairman & Executive Secretary"
Series 6 Daily Digest
Series 8 Papers Relating to Presidents Mediation Commission

Women in Industry Service, NARG 86
(Women's Bureau)
Dept of Labor: Labor Relations File, Acc. no. 167

3. *Official Publications*

Alabama Council of Defense. *Report of the Alabama Council of Defense Covering Its Activities From May 17, 1917 to December 31, 1918.*
Alabama State Council of Defense. *Proceedings . . .* Montgomery, Ala., 1917.
Arizona Council of Defense. *The Arizona Council of Defense: Its Pur-*

poses and a Brief Statement of Its Work, Accomplished and Under Way. Phoenix, Ariz., 1917.

Chicago Commission on Race Relations. *The Negro in Chicago: A Study of Race Relations and a Race Riot,* 1922.

Committee on Public Information. *Complete Report of the Chairman of the Committee on Public Information 1917: 1918: 1919,* Washington, D.C., 1920.

Georgia Council of Defense, Woman's Committee. *Final Report of Woman's Committee, Georgia Division, April 1917–July 1919.*

Illinois State Council of Defense. *Final Report of the State Council of Defense of Illinois, 1917–1918–1919.* Chicago, 1919.

Industrial Conference. *Report of Industrial Conference Called by The President.* Washington, D.C., March 6, 1920.

Industrial Safety Congress of New York State.
Proceedings of the First Industrial Safety Congress, Albany, 1917.
Proceedings of the Second Industrial Safety Congress, Albany, 1918.
Proceedings of the Third Industrial Safety Congress, Albany, 1919.

Milwaukee County Council of Defense. *Report on Twenty Months of Wartime Service in Milwaukee, May 1st to January 1st 1919.* N.p., 1919.

Missouri Council of Defense, *Final Report.* N.p., 1919.

National Conference of Social Work.
1. *Proceedings of 44th Annual Session, Pittsburgh, Pa., June 6–13, 1917.* Chicago, 1918.
2. *Proceedings of 45th Annual Session, Kansas City, Missouri, May 15–22, 1918.* Chicago, 1919.

New York State Legislature. Joint Committee Investigating Seditious Activities. *Revolutionary Radicalism: Its History, Purpose and Tactics With An Exposition And Discussion Of The Steps Being Taken and Required To Curb It.* Part I, 2 vols., Albany, N.Y., 1920; Part II, 2 vols., Albany, N.Y., 1920.

New York State. Reconstruction Commission. *Housing Conditions: Report of the Housing Committee of the Reconstruction Commission of the State of New York, March 26, 1920.* Albany, N.Y., 1920.

New York State. Reconstruction Commission. *Report of Governor Smith's Reconstruction Commission on Business Readjustments and Unemployment, April 14, 1919.* Albany, N.Y., 1919; *Report of Governor Smith's Reconstruction Commission on a Permanent Unemployment Program, June 17, 1919.* Albany, N.Y., 1919.

Ohio State Council of Defense. *A History of the Activities of the Ohio Branch, Council of National Defense.* Columbus, Ohio, 1919.

President's Committee on Social Trends. *Recent Social Trends in the United States.* 2 vols. New York and London, 1933.

President's Mediation Commission. *Report To The President of the United States.* Washington, D.C., 1918.

Rochester, Anna. "Child Labor in Warring Countries: A Brief Review Of Foreign Reports." Dept. of Labor, Children's Bureau. Industrial Series no. 4. Bureau Publications no. 27, 1917.

U.S. Commissioner of Education. *Report For the Year Ended June 30, 1917.* Vol 1. Dept. of Interior, 1917.

U.S. Congress. House. Committee on Labor. *Hearings: To Employ Con-*

vict *Labor for the Production of War Supplies.* 65th Cong., 2d sess., H.R. 7353, 18 January 1918.

U.S. Congress. House. Committee on Woman Suffrage. *Extending the Right of Suffrage to Women: Hearing, January 3–7 1918,* 1918.

U.S. Congress. Senate. Committee on Education and Labor. *Hearings on the Report of the Industrial Conference* (8 May–1 June 1920, 66th Cong., 2d sess.), 1920.

U.S. Congress. Senate. Committee on Education and Labor. *Joint Hearings on Department of Public Welfare May 1921,* 1921.

U.S. Congress. Senate. Committee on Public Buildings and Grounds. *Report on United States Housing Corporation.* 66th Cong., 2d sess., Rpt. 336. 18 December 1918.

U.S. Congress. Senate. Committee on Woman Suffrage. *Report.* 63d Cong., 1st sess., Rpt. 64, 13 June 1913; *Hearings on S.J. Res 2 Proposing An Amendment To The Constitution of the United States Conferring Upon Women The Right of Suffrage, April 20, 1917, 1917.*

U.S. Congress. Senate. Sub-Committee On The Judiciary. *Brewing and Liquor Interests and German and Bolshevik Propaganda.* 66th Cong., 1st sess., Doc. 62, 3 vols., 1919.

U.S. Council of National Defense
First Annual Report, Washington, D.C., 1917
Second Annual Report, Washington, D.C., 1918
Third Annual Report, Washington, D.C., 1919

U.S. Council of National Defense. General Munitions Board. *Munitions Industry: Minutes of the General Munitions Board, from April 4 to August 9, 1917.* 74th Cong., 2d sess., Senate Committee Print no. 6. Washington, D.C., 1936.

U.S. Dept. of Commerce. Bureau of the Census. *Fourteenth Census of the United States, 1920: Population.* Vol. 1, Washington, D.C., 1921; Vol 2, Washington, D.C., 1922.

U.S. Dept. of Commerce. Bureau of the Census. *Earnings of Factory Workers, 1899 to 1927: An Analysis of Pay-Roll Statistics.* Census Monographs X. Washington, D.C., 1929; *Mortgages on Homes: A Report on the Results of the Inquiry as to the Mortgage Debt on Homes other than Farm Homes at the Fourteenth Census, 1920.* Census Monographs II. Washington, D.C., 1923.

U.S. Dept. of the Interior. Bureau of Education. *Americanization As a War Measure: Report of a Conference Called by the Secretary of the Interior and Held in Washington, April 3, 1918,* Bulletin no. 18, Washington, D.C., 1918.

U.S. Dept. of Labor. Bureau of Industrial Housing and Transportation. *Report of the United States Housing Corporation: War Emergency Construction.* Washington, D.C., 1920. 2 vols.

U.S. Dept. of Labor. Children's Bureau. *Sixth Annual Report of the Chief, Children's Bureau, 1918.* Washington, D.C., 1918. *Seventh Annual Report of the Chief, Children's Bureau, 1919.* Washington, D.C., 1919.

U.S. Dept. of Labor. Division of Negro Economics. *The Negro at Work during the World War and during Reconstruction.* Washington, D.C., 1921; reprint, New York, 1969.

U.S. Dept. of Labor. National Industrial Conference. *Proceedings of the*

First Industrial Conference (Called by the President) October 6 to 23 1919. Washington, D.C., 1920.

U.S. Dept. of Labor. National War Labor Board. *Report of the Secretary of the National War Labor Board.* Washington, D.C., 1920.

U.S. Dept. of Labor. Secretary of Labor. *Sixth Annual Report: For the Fiscal Year Ended June 30, 1918.* Washington, D.C., 1918. *Seventh Annual Report: For the Fiscal Year Ended June 30 1919,* Washington, D.C. 1919.

U.S. Dept. of Labor. Woman in Industry Service. *First Annual Report of the Director of the Woman in Industry Service, 1919.* Washington, D.C., 1919.

U.S. Dept. of Labor. Women's Bureau. *Second Annual Report of the Director, 1920.* Washington, D.C., 1920.

U.S. Dept. of Labor. Women's Bureau. *Labor Laws for Women in Industry in Indiana.* Bulletin 2, December 1918. *Women in Government Service.* Bulletin 8, 1920. *Hours and Conditions of Work for Women in Industry in Virginia.* Bulletin 10, 1920. *Women Street Car Conductors and Ticket Agents.* Bulletin 11, 1921. *The New Position of Women in American Industry.* Bulletin 12, 1920. *Negro Women in Industry,* Bulletin 20, 1920.

U.S. Federal Trade Commission. *World War Activities of the Federal Trade Commission, 1917–1918.* Washington, D.C., 1941.

U.S. Fuel Administration. *Fuel Facts.* Washington, D.C., August 1918.

U.S. Provost Marshal General. *Report to the Secretary of War on the First Draft under the Selective Service Act, 1917.* Washington, D.C., 1918.

U.S. Provost Marshal. *Final Report of the Provost Marshal General . . . on the Operations of the Selective Service System to July 15, 1919.* Washington, D.C., 1920.

U.S. Selective Service System. *Conscientious Objection.* Special Monograph no. 11. 2 vols. Washington, D.C., 1950.

U.S. War Dept. Committee on Education and Special Training. *Final Report of the National Army Training Detachments Later Known as Vocational Section S.A.T.C.* Washington, D.C., 1919.

U.S. War Dept. Office of the Secretary. *A Report of the Activities of the War Department in the Field of Industrial Relations during the War.* Washington, D.C., 1919.

U.S. War Department. Office of the Surgeon General. *Physical Examination of the First Million Draft Recruits: Methods and Results.* Bulletin 11. Washington, D.C., March 1919.

U.S. War Industries Board. *American Industry in the War: A Report of the War Industries Board (March 1921).* By Bernard Baruch. New York: Prentice-Hall, 1941.

Women's Committee of the State Council of Defense of California. *Reconstruction Program.* Los Angeles, December 1918.

4. Memoirs, Diaries, Autobiographies

Addams, Jane. *Twenty Years at Hull House.* New York, 1960.
———. *The Second Twenty Years at Hull House, September 1909 to*

September 1929: With a Record of a Growing World Consciousness. New York, 1930.

Anderson, Mary. *Woman At Work: The Autobiography of Mary Anderson as told to Mary N. Winslow.* Westport, Conn., 1951.

Baker, Newton D. *Frontiers of Freedom.* New York, 1918.

Baker, Ray Stannard. *Woodrow Wilson: Life and Letters.* Vol. 7. *War Leader April 6, 1917–Feb. 2, 1918.* New York, 1968.

Baruch, Bernard. *The Public Years.* New York, 1960.

Creel, George, *Rebel At Large: Recollections of Fifty Crowded Years.* New York, 1947.

Daniels, Josephus. *The Cabinet Diaries of Josephus Daniels 1913–1921.* Lincoln, Neb., 1963.

Daniels, Josephus. *The Wilson Era: Years of War & After 1917–23.* Westport, Conn., 1974.

Eastman, Max. *Love and Revolution: My Journey through an Epoch.* New York, 1964.

Fosdick, Raymond B. *Chronicle of a Generation: An Autobiography.* New York, 1958.

Goldman, Emma. *Living My Life.* New York, 1970.

Hoover, Herbert. *The Memoirs of Herbert Hoover: Years of Adventure 1874–1920.* London 1952.

Howe, Frederic C. *The Confessions of a Reformer.* New York, 1925.

Ickes, Harold L. *The Autobiography of a Curmudgeon.* New York, 1943.

Jordan, David Starr. *The Days of Man: Being Memories of a Naturalist, Teacher and Minor Prophet of Democracy.* New York, 1922.

Lane, Franklin K. *The Letters of Franklin K. Lane: Personal and Political.* Boston and New York, 1922.

McAdoo, William G. *Crowded Years: The Reminiscences of William G. McAdoo.* Boston and New York, 1931.

Martin, Franklin H. *The Joy of Living: An Autobiography.* Vol. 2, Garden City, N.Y., 1933.

———. *Digest of the Proceedings of the Council of National Defense During the World War.* 73rd U.S. Cong., Senate, 2d sess., Doc. 193. Washington, D.C., 1934.

Milner, Lucille B. *Education of an American Liberal: An Autobiography.* New York, 1954.

Norris, George W. *Fighting Liberal: The Autobiography of George W. Norris.* New York, 1945.

Steffens, Lincoln. *The Letters of Lincoln Steffens: Vol. I 1889–1919.* New York, 1938.

Villard, Oswald Garrison. *Fighting Years: Memoirs of a Liberal Editor.* New York, 1939.

White, William Allen. *The Autobiography of William Allen White,* New York 1946.

Woodrow Wilson. *War and Peace 1917–1924.* Vol. 1 (The Public Papers of Woodrow Wilson, edited by Ray Stannard Baker and William E. Dodd). New York and London, 1927.

———. *Selected Addresses and Public Papers of Woodrow Wilson.* Edited by Albert Bushnell Hart. New York, 1918.

———. *The Papers of Woodrow Wilson.* Edited by Arthur S. Link et al., Princeton. Vol. 30. *May 6–Sept. 5, 1914,* 1979. Vol. 31. *Sept. 6–*

December 31, 1914, 1979. Vol. 41. *January 24–April 6, 1917*, 1983. Vol. 42. *April 7–June 24, 1917*, 1983. Vol. 43. *June 25–August 20, 1917*, 1983. Vol. 44. *August 21–November 10, 1917*, 1983.Vol. 45. *November 11, 1917–January 15, 1918*, 1984. Vol. 46. *January 16–March 12, 1918*, 1984. Vol. 47. *March 13–May 12, 1918*, 1984. Vol. 48. *May 13–July 17, 1918*, 1985. Vol. 49. *July 18–September 13, 1918*, 1985.

Messages & Papers of Woodrow Wilson. Edited by Albert Shaw. Vol. 1. Review of Reviews Corporation. New York, 1924.

5. *Other Published Materials*

Abbott, Grace. *From Relief to Social Security: The Development of the New Public Welfare Services and Their Administration.* Chicago, 1941.

Academy of Political Science. Columbia University. *War Labor Policies and Reconstruction Proceedings.* Vol. 3, no. 2. February 1919.

American Civil Liberties Union. *War-time Prosecutions and Mob Violence.* National Civil Liberties Board. New York, March 1919.

American Council on Education. *The American Council on Education: History and Activities 1938–9.* Washington, D.C., 1939.

American Federation of Labor. *Report of the Proceedings of the Thirty-Seventh Annual Convention, Buffalo, New York, November 12–24, 1917.* Washington, D.C., 1917.

American Legion Auxiliary. *Indiana. Indiana Women In the World War,* Typescript, 1936, 1938.

Annals of the American Academy of Political and Social Science. Vol. 56, November 1914.

Annals of the American Academy of Political & Social Science
Financing the War. Vol. 75, no. 164, January 1918.
War Adjustments in Railroad Regulation. Vol. 76 no. 165. March 1918.
Mobilizing America's Resources for the War. Vol. 78 no. 167. July 1918.
War Relief Work. Vol. 79, no. 168. September 1918.

Baker, Ray Stannard. *The New Industrial Unrest: Reasons and Remedies.* Garden City, N.Y., 1920.

Bennett, Ira E. *Editorials from the "Washington Post" 1917–1920.* Washington, D.C., 1921.

Bing, Alexander M. *Wartime Strikes and Their Adjustment.* New York, 1921.

Bullard, Washington Irving. *Women's Work in War Time* (pamphlet). Boston, 1917.

Burchard, Edward L. *Organization of the Community Councils of Defense by the Federal Government.* Washington, D.C., 1942 (?).

Catt, Carrie Chapman and Nettie Rogers Shuler. *Woman Suffrage and Politics: The Inner Story of the Suffrage Movement.* New York, 1923.

Chafee, Zechariah. *Freedom of Speech.* London, 1920.

Clark, Maurice John. *The Costs of the World War to the American People.* New York, 1942.

Clarkson, Grosvenor B. *Industrial America in the World War: The Strategy Behind the Line 1917–1918.* Boston & New York, 1923.

————. *A Tribute and a Look into the Future: A Statement of the Work of the State and Territorial Councils of Defense.* Washington, D.C., 1919.

Claxton, Philander P. *Education for the Establishment of Democracy in the World.* Washington, D.C., 1919.

Cleveland, Frederick A. and Joseph Schafer, eds. *Democracy in Reconstruction.* Boston, New York, and Chicago, 1919.

Commons, J. R., Selig Perlman, and Philip Taft. *History of Labor in the United States 1896–1932 Vol. IV: Labor Movements.* New York, 1935.

Coombs, Whitney. *The Wages of Unskilled Labor in Manufacturing Industries in the United States, 1890–1924.* New York, 1926.

Crowell, Benedict and Robert F. Wilson. *How America Went to War: The Armies of Industry.* New Haven, 1921.

Crowell, Benedict and Robert Forrest Wilson. *How America Went to War: Demobilization; Our Industrial and Military Demobilization after the Armistice 1918–1920.* New Haven, Conn., 1921.

Daggett, Mabel Potter. *Women Wanted.* New York, 1918.

D'Annele, Irene. *Woman Hood.* ca. 1927.

Degen, Marie Louise. *The History of the Woman's Peace Party.* New York and London, 1972.

Fisher, Irving. "The Need for Health Insurance," *American Labor Legislation Review.* Vol. 7, 1 (1917). "Health & War," *American Labor Legislation Review.* 8, 1, (1918).

Hapgood, Norman, ed. *Professional Patriots: An Exposure of the Personalities, Methods & Objectives Involved in the Organized Effort to Exploit Patriotic Impulses in These United States during & after the Late War.* New York, 1927.

Hart, Albert Bushnell and William M. Schuyler, eds. *The American Year Book: A Record of Events and Progress Year 1925.* New York, 1926.

Hart, Hastings H. *The War Program of the State of South Carolina: A Report Prepared at the Request of Governor Richard I. Manning, The State Council of Defense, & the State Board of Charities of Corrections.* New York, 1918. *Social Problems of Alabama: A Study of the Social Institutions and Agencies of the State of Alabama as Related to its War Activities.* Montgomery, Ala., 1918. *Child Welfare in the District of Columbia: A Study of Agencies and Institutions for the Care of Dependent & Delinquent Children.* New York, 1924.

Henry, Alice. *Women and the Labor Movement.* New York, 1923.

Hitchcock, Curtice N. "The War Housing Program and Its Future." *Journal of Political Economy* 27, 4 (April 1919).

Holbrook, Franklin F., ed. *St. Paul and Ramsey County in the War of 1917–1918.* St. Paul, Minn., 1929.

Holbrook, Franklin F. and Livia Appel. *Minnesota in the War With Germany.* Vol. 1. St. Paul, Minn., 1928; Vol. 2. St. Paul, Minn., 1932.

Hough, Emerson. *The Web: The Authorized History of the American Protective League, A Revelation of Patriotism.* Chicago, 1919.

Ickes, Harold L., *The New Democracy.* New York, 1934.

James, Bessie R. *For God, For Country, For Home: The National League for Women's Service.* New York and London, 1920.

Jenison, Marguerite Edith. *The War-time Organization of Illinois (Illinois in the World War, vol. 5).* Springfield, Ill., 1923. *War Documents and Addresses (Illinois in the World War, vol. 6).* Springfield, Ill., 1923.

Kerney, James, *The Political Education of Woodrow Wilson.* New York and London, 1926.

Kolbe, Parke Rexford. *The Colleges in War Time and After: A Contemporary Account of the Effect of the War upon Higher Education in America.* New York and London, 1919.

Leland, Waldo G. and Newton D. Mereness. *Introduction to the Official Sources for the Economic & Social History of the World War.* New Haven, Conn., 1926.

Lovejoy, Owen R. "Children and Reconstruction." An Address. Educational Municipal Court. Philadelphia, 20 February 1920.

MacKay, Kenneth Campbell. *The Progressive Movement of 1924.* New York, 1947.

March, Peyton C. *The Nation at War.* Garden City, N.Y., 1932.

Mock, James R. and Cedric Larson. *Words That Won the War: The Story of the Committee on Public Information 1917–1919.* New York, 1939. Reprint, 1968.

Mullendore, William C. *History of the United States Food Administration 1917–1919.* Stanford, Calif., 1941.

National Association of Manufacturers of the U.S.A. *Industrial War Service Bulletin,* 1–12 June to December 1918 (later the *Washington Office Bulletin*).

National Association of Manufacturers of the U.S.A. *Proceedings of the Twenty-third Annual Convention, New York City.* New York, 1926. *Proceedings of the Twenty-fourth Annual Convention,* New York City, May 19–21, 1919. New York, 1927.

National Catholic War Council. *Handbook of the National Catholic War Council.* Washington, D.C., 1918.

National Catholic War Council. Administrative Committee. *Bishops' Program of Social Reconstruction: A General Review of the Problems & Survey of Remedies for Social Reconstruction.* 20th Anniversary Edition presented to Senate. 76th Cong., 1st sess., Doc. 79, 6 June 1939 (originally published 1919).

National Catholic War Council. Committee on Special War Activities. *Reconstruction Pamphlets.*
No. 1. "Social Reconstruction: A General View . . . (January 1919).
No. 2. "Land Colonization" (March 1919).
No. 3. "Unemployment" (May 1919).
No. 6. "Fundamentals of Citizenship" (June 1919).
No. 7. "Outlines of a Social Service Program" (June 1919).
No. 8. "Girls Welfare" (August 1919).

National Housing Association. *A Symposium on War Housing* (Philadelphia, 25 February 1918). New York, 1918.

National League for Woman's Service. *Annual Report For the Year 1918.* New York, ca. 1912.

National Women's Trade Union League of America, *Proceedings of Sixth Biennial Convention, Kansas City, Missouri, June 4th–9th 1917. Proceedings of Seventh Biennial Convention Philadelphia, June 2nd–7th 1919.*

Nearing, Scott. *Black America.* 1929. New York, 1969.

Palmer, Frederick. *Newton D. Baker: America at War.* 2 Vols. New York, 1931.

Peck, Mary Gray. *Carrie Chapman Catt: A Biography.* New York, 1975.
Peek, George N. *History of the Industrial Board of the Department of Commerce.* ca. 1923.
Pinchot, Amos. *History of the Progressive Party 1912–1916.* Washington Square, 1958.
Pixley, Rutherford B. *Wisconsin in the World War.* Milwaukee, 1919.
Ryan, John A. *Social Reconstruction.* New York, 1920.
———. *Social Doctrine in Action: A Personal History.* New York and London, 1941.
Scherer, James A. B. *The Nation at War.* New York, 1918.
Scott, Emmett J. *Scott's Official History of the American Negro in the World War.* Chicago, 1919.
Slosson, Preston William. *The Great Crusade and After, 1914–28.* New York, 1930.
Smith, Darrell Hevenor. *The United States Employment Service: Its History, Activities, and Organization.* Baltimore, Md., 1923.
Southern Sociological Congress, 1916–1918. *Democracy in Earnest.* Nashville, Tenn., 1919.
Sullivan, Mark. *Our Times: The United States 1900–1925, Vol. III: Prewar America.* New York and London, 1930. *Vol. V: Over Here 1914–1918.* New York and London, 1933.
Thomas, Norman. *The Conscientious Objector in America.* New York, 1923.
Tobey, James A. *The Children's Bureau: Its History, Activities, and Organization.* Baltimore, Md., 1925.
Tobin, Harold J. and Percy W. Bidwell. *Mobilizing Civilian America.* New York, 1940.
Trachtenberg, Alexander L., ed. Dept. of Labor Research. Rand School of Social Science. *The American Labor Year Book 1916.* New York, 1916. *The American Labor Year Book 1917–18.* New York, 1918. *The American Labor Year Book 1919–20.* New York, 1920.
Walling, William English. *American Labor and American Democracy.* 2 vols. New York and London, 1926.
Watkins, Gordon S. *Labor Problems and Labor Administration in the United States during the World War.* University of Illinois Studies in the Social Sciences. Vol. 8, no. 3. Urbana, Ill. (September 1919). Part 2, vol. 8, no. 4. Urbana, Ill. (December 1919).
Weber, Gustavus A. *The Women's Bureau: Its History, Activities and Organization.* 1923. Brookings Institute Service Mono.of the U.S. Govt., no. 22., 1979.
Weeks, Estella T. *Reconstruction Programs: A Comparative Study of Their Content and of Its Viewpoints of the Issuing Organization.* New York, 1919.
Weyl, Walter. *The New Democracy.* New York, 1914.
Whitaker, Charles Harris et al. *The Housing Problem in War and in Peace* (Journal of American Institute of Architects). Washington, D.C., 1918.
Wickware, Francis G., ed. *The American Yearbook: A Record of Events and Progress 1917.* New York and London, 1918. *The American Yearbook: A Record of Events and Progress 1918.* New York and London, 1919. *The American Yearbook: A Record of Events and Progress 1919.* New York and London, 1920.

Williams, Paul B. *United States Lawn Tennis Association and the World War.* New York, 1921.

Willoughby, William Franklin. *Government Organization in War Time and After: A Survey of the Federal Civil Agencies Created for the Prosecution of the War.* New York and London, 1920.

Wilson, Woodrow. "Equal Suffrage": Address of the President Delivered in the Senate on September 30, 1918. 65th Cong., 2d sess., S. Doc. 284, Washington, D.C., 1918.

Wilson, Woodrow. "Labor and the War." Address to the American Federation of Labor. Buffalo, N.Y., 12 November 1917. Washington, D.C., 1917.

Wolman, Leo. *The Growth of American Trade Unions 1880-1923.* New York, 1924.

Wood, Charles W. *The Great Change: New America as seen by Leaders in American Government, Industry and Education Who are Remaking Our Civilization.* New York, 1918.

Woods, Robert A. and Albert J. Kennedy. *The Settlement Horizon: A National Estimate.* New York, 1922. Reprint, New York, 1970.

Young, Ernest W. *The Wilson Administration and the Great War.* Boston, 1922.

6. Newspapers and Journals

American Labor Legislation Review
Annals of the American Academy of Political and Social Science
Chicago Defender
Crisis (NAACP)
Housing Betterment (National Housing Association)
The Nation
The New Republic
New York Times
New York World
Quarterly Journal of Economics
Saturday Evening Post
The Survey
Washington Post
Washington Star

7. Annotated Bibliography of Selected Secondary Sources

Introduction

The major modern study of America's war experiences is David Kennedy's stimulating *Over Here: The First World War and American Society* (New York and Oxford, 1980). This is detailed and comprehensive on political and economic change, but rather plays down social consequences and stresses the negative effects of the war in a rather traditional fashion. It includes an interesting discussion of the American serviceman's experiences. Three other recent works give something of the flavor of the period, but are less academic in approach: Allen Churchill, *Over Here! An Informal Recreation of the*

Homefront in World War I (New York, 1968); Edward Robb Ellis, *Echoes of Distant Thunder: Life in the United States, 1914–1918* (New York, 1975); and Steven Jantzen, *Hooray For Peace, Hurrah For War: The United States During World War I* (New York and Ontario, 1978).

Collections of contemporary documents and readings are illuminating, but limited in that they concentrate on ideas and attitudes and have little on social and economic matters. Particularly useful are David Trask, ed., *World War I at Home: Readings on American Life, 1914–1920* (New York, 1970) and Stanley Coben, ed., *Reform, War, and Reaction: 1912–1932* (New York, Evanston, Ill., and London, 1972). John M. Cooper, ed., *Causes and Consequences of World War I* (New York, 1972) is a collection of articles, several on American aspects; Keith L. Nelson, ed., *The Impact of War on American Life: The Twentieth Century Experience* (New York, 1971) covers a much wider period, but uses extracts from contemporary observers and historical works to examine the economic, political, social, and cultural consequences of war. Otis Graham, Jr., *The Great Campaigns: Reform and War in America 1900–1928* (Englewood Cliffs, N.J., 1971) combines an excellent survey of the whole period and its major themes with a selection of key documents.

Chapter 1.
The Progressive Era

The major studies of the pre-war period are still George E. Mowry, *The Era of Theodore Roosevelt, 1900–1912* (New York, 1962) and Arthur S. Link, *Woodrow Wilson and the Progressive Era 1910–1917* (New York, 1963). David Shannon, *Twentieth Century America: Volume I, The Progressive Era* (Chicago, 1974), and Arthur S. Link and William B. Catton, *American Epoch: A History of the United States Since the 1890s, Volume I, 1897–1920* (New York, 1967) are both detailed orthodox accounts. John G. Clark, et al., *Three Generations in Twentieth Century America: Family, Community, and Nation* (Homewood, Ill., 1977) uses the history of particular individuals and their families, set in the context of general social developments, to produce a book full of detail and insight covering much more than the period under discussion.

Books placing the main emphasis on change occurring before the American entry into the war are Harold U. Faulkner, *The Decline of Laissez Faire, 1897–1917* (Evanston, Ill., and London, 1951), Henry F. May, *The End of American Innocence: A Study of the First Years of Our Own Time, 1912–1917* (Chicago, 1964), and Robert H. Wiebe, *The Search For Order 1877–1920* (New York, 1967). Arthur E. Ekirch, Jr., *Progressivism in America: A Study of the Era from Theodore Roosevelt to Woodrow Wilson* (New York, 1974) is also a useful general survey.

Valuable studies of the reform movement and particular concerns include Paul Boyer, *Urban Masses and Moral Order in America, 1820–1920* (Cambridge, Mass., and London, 1978), Allen F. Davis, *Spearheads for Reform: The Social Settlements and the Progressive Movement, 1890–1914* (New York, 1967), and James Leiby, *A History of Social Welfare and Social Work in the United States* (New York, 1978). James Weinstein, *The Corporate Ideal in the Liberal State, 1900–1918* (Boston, 1968) and Daniel Nelson, *Managers and Workers: Origins of the New Factory System in the United States, 1880–1920* (Madison and London, 1975) point to the reform tendency within business circles. Biographical studies are enormously valuable in the appreciation of the range and variety in progressivism. Particularly useful are Clarke A. Chambers, *Paul U. Kellogg and the Survey: Voices for Social Welfare and Social Justice* (Minneapolis, 1971) and Allen F. Davis, *American Heroine: The Life and Legend of Jane Addams* (New York, 1973).

Chapter 2.
From Peace to War, 1914–17

American peace movements are the subject of a number of studies. C. Roland Marchand's *The American Peace Movement and Social Reform, 1898–1918* (Princeton, 1972) is a scholarly examination of progressive peace organizations, while Charles DeBenedetti's *Origins of the Modern American Peace Movement, 1915–29* (Millwood, N.Y., 1978) takes the story further and examines the developments during and after World War I. Benedetti's *The Peace Reform in American History* (Bloomington, Ind., and London, 1980) is also a good general survey of the subject, as is Charles Chatfield, *For Peace and Justice: Pacifism in America, 1914–1941* (Knoxville, 1971).

The Woman's Peace party is central to Barbara J. Steinson's *American Women's Activism in World War I* (New York and London, 1982), and progressive responses to war are also the subject of John F. McClymer's *War and Welfare: Social Engineering in America 1890–1925* (Westport, Conn., and London, 1980). On Progressives and the war, see also Charles Forcey, *The Crossroads of Liberalism: Croly, Weyl, Lippmann and the Progressive Era, 1901–1928* (London, 1972), Ronald Steel, *Walter Lippmann and the Twentieth Century* (Boston and Toronto, 1980), and John A. Thompson, "The First World War and the American Progressive Publicists" (Ph.D. dissertation, Cambridge, 1969).

America's entry into war has been examined in many studies, and the many issues are considered in Daniel W. Smith, *The Great Departure* (New York, 1965).

Chapter 3.
Mobilizing the Population for War

After Mock and Larson's *Words That Won The War* (1939), the most recent account of the Committee on Public Information is Stephen Vaughn's useful *Holding Fast the Inner Lines: Democracy, Nationalism and the Committee on Public Information* (Chapel Hill, N.C., 1980), which places the CPI in the context of progressive ideology. George T. Blakey, *Historians on the Homefront: American Propagandists for the Great War* (Lexington, Ky., 1970) examines the contribution of academics.

Opposition to the war, and the government's response, is detailed in H. C. Peterson and Gilbert C. Fite, *Opponents of War, 1917–1918* (Seattle and London, 1971). The Socialist party during the war is examined in David Shannon, *The Socialist Party of America* (New York, 1955), James R. Green, *Grass-Roots Socialism: Radical Movements in the South-West, 1895–1943* (Baton Rouge, La., and London, 1978), and Norman Bindler, "American Socialism and the First World War" (Ph.D. dissertation, New York University, 1970). On the I.W.W., the classic text is still Melvyn Dubofsky's *We Shall Be*

All: A History of the I.W.W. (Chicago, 1969), while the Non-Partisan League is dealt with in Robert L. Morlan, *Political Prairie Fire: The Non-Partisan League, 1915–22* (Minneapolis, 1950).

The reactions of the Wilson administration have been subject of much examination, mostly critical. The latest, and perhaps most severe, attack comes in Paul L. Murphy, *World War I and the Origins of Civil Liberties in the United States* (New York and London, 1979). Other studies of value include Harold H. Hyman, *To Try Men's Souls: Loyalty Tests in American History* (Berkeley and Los Angeles, 1958), Joan M. Jensen, *The Price of Vigilance* (Chicago and New York, 1968), Donald Johnson, *The Challenge To American Freedoms: World War I and the Rise of the American Civil Liberties Union* (Lexington, Ky., 1963), and Harry N. Scheiber, *The Wilson Administration and Civil Liberties 1917–1921* (Ithaca, N.Y., 1960).

Chapter 4.
Organizing for War

The major work on wartime government organizations has been done by Robert D. Cuff. His major study, *The War Industries Board: Business-Government Relations During World War I* (Baltimore and London, 1973), is supplemented by his many articles, such as "Herbert Hoover, the Ideology of Voluntarism and War Organization During the Great War," *Journal of American History* (September 1977), Harry Garfield, "The Fuel Administration, and the Search for a Co-operative Order During World War I," *American Quarterly* (Spring 1978). The wartime organization at state and local levels is the subject of William J. Breen, *Uncle Sam At Home, Civilian Mobilization, Wartime Federalism, and the Council of National Defense, 1917–1918* (Westport, Conn., and London, 1984).

Financial policy is detailed in Charles Gilbert, *American Financing of World War I* (Westport, Conn., and London, 1970), and political events are thoroughly examined in Seward W. Livermore, *Politics is Adjourned, Woodrow Wilson and the War Congress, 1916–18,* (Middletown, Conn., 1966).

Biographies are useful on government activities: the most recent is Jordon A. Schwarz, *The Speculator: Bernard M. Baruch In Washington, 1917–1965* (Chapel Hill, N.C., 1981). Various studies of Herbert Hoover provide useful insights: David Burner, *Herbert Hoover: A Public Life* (New York, 1979), Joan Hoff Wilson, *Herbert Hoover: Forgotten Progressive* (Boston and Toronto, 1975), and Craig Lloyd, *Aggressive Introvert: A Study of Herbert Hoover and Public Relations Management, 1912–1932* (Columbus, Ohio, 1972); Daniel R. Beaver's *Newton D. Baker and the American War Effort 1917–1919* (Lincoln, Neb., 1966) is indispensable. The war is seen in the larger context of central government growth in a number of studies of different emphases: Richard L. Watson, *The Development of National Power: The United States 1900–1919* (Boston, 1976), Ronald Radosh and Murray N. Rothbard, *A New History of Leviathan: Essays on the Rise of the American Corporate State* (New York, 1972); both tend to follow the line established by Gabriel Kolko in *The Triumph of Conservatism: A Reinterpretation of American History* (Glencoe, Ill., 1963). Rather more general and less obviously revisionist are Stephen Skowronek, *Building a New American State: The Expansion of National Administrative Capacities, 1877–1920* (Cambridge, London, and New York, 1982) and Barry D. Karl, *The Uneasy State: The United States from 1915 to 1945* (Chicago, 1983).

Chapter 5.
Labor and the War

Modern studies of labor in wartime are scarce and there is little to match the contemporary accounts of Bing and Watkins. Melvyn Dubofsky has an excellent chapter in *Industrialism and the American Worker, 1865–1920* (Arlington Heights, Ill., 1975) as does David Brody in *Workers in Industrial America: Essays on the Twentieth Century Struggle* (New York and Oxford, 1980). Frank L. Grubbs, *The Struggle for Labor Loyalty: Gompers, the A.F. of L., and the Pacifists, 1917–1920* (Durham, N.C., 1968), is a short monograph that concentrates primarily on the pro-war activities of the AFL and its leader. Also useful is Marc Karson, *Labor Unions and Politics, 1900–1918* (Carbondale, Ill., 1958). The labor troubles in Arizona are described in James W. Byrkit, *Forging the Copper Collar: Arizona's Labor-Management War of 1901–1921* (Tucson, Ariz., 1982), although the fact of the war is hardly mentioned. The best up-to-date account of government-labor relations is Valerie Jean Conner, *The National War Labor Board: Stability, Social Justice, and the Voluntary State in World War I* (Chapel Hill, N.C., 1983). Also useful is Michael E. Parrish, *Felix Frankfurter and His Times: The Reform Years* (New York and London, 1982).

The social and economic consequences of the war are hardly discussed anywhere in detail. A number of local studies contain useful material: John Bodnar et al., *Lives of Their Own: Blacks, Italians and Poles in Pittsburgh, 1900–1960* (Urbana, Ill., Chicago, and London, 1982); Herbert F. Janick, *A Diverse People: Connecticut to the Present* (Chester, Conn., 1975); James B. Lane, *City of the Century: A History of Gary, Indiana* (Bloomington, Ind., and London, 1978); M. Proctor and B. Matuszeski, *Gritty Cities: A Second Look at Allentown, Bethlehem, Bridgeport, . . .* (Philadelphia, 1978); William Ganson Rose, *Cleveland: The Making of a City* (Cleveland and New York, 1950); Olivier Zunz, *The Changing Face of Inequality: Urbanization, Industrial Development, and Immigrants in Detroit, 1880–1920* (Chicago and London, 1982).

On housing and social conditions the most useful source is Roy Lubove, particularly his *Community Planning in the 1920s: The Contribution of the Regional Planning Association of America* (Pittsburgh, 1963) and "Houses and 'A Few Well-Placed Fruit Trees': An Object Lesson in Federal Housing," *Social Research* 27, 4 (Winter 1960). Cecelia Bucki, "Dilution and Craft Tradition: Bridgeport, Connecticut, Munitions Workers 1915–19," *Social Science History* 4 (Winter 1980), is good on labor-relations in the war-boom community.

Chapter 6.
War, Women, and the Family

Useful general surveys of women's history in America are William H. Chafe, *The American Woman* (New York, 1972), Carl N. Degler, *At Odds: Women and the Family in America* (Oxford, New York, and Toronto, 1980), William L. O'Neill, *Everyone Was Brave: The Rise and Fall of Feminism in America* (Chicago, 1969).

On the campaign for equal suffrage see Eleanor Flexner, *Century of Struggle: The Women's Rights Movement in the United States* (Cambridge,

Mass., 1959), and Aileen S. Kraditor, *The Ideas of the Woman Suffrage Movement 1890–1920* (Garden City, N.Y., 1971).

Women's changing economic status has been the subject of several excellent studies: Alice Kessler-Harris, *Out To Work: A History of Wage-Earning Women in the United States* (New York and Oxford, 1982), Elyce J. Rotella, *From Home to Office: U.S. Women at Work, 1870–1930* (Ann Arbor, 1981), and Margaret Gibbons Wilson, *The American Woman in Transition: The Urban Influence, 1870–1920* (Westport, Conn., and London, 1979).

The two major studies of the war years are Steinson's *American Women's Activism* (op.cit.) and Maurine W. Greenwald's excellent but necessarily selective *Women, War and Work: The Impact of World War I* (Westport, Conn., and London, 1980).

On children in America most studies concentrate on the activities of the Children's Bureau. Good introductions to the period are provided in Susan Tiffin, *In Whose Best Interest? Child Welfare Reform in the Progressive Era* (Westport, Conn., and London, 1982) and Walter Trattner, *Crusade for the Children: A History of the National Child Labor Committee and Child Labor Reform* (Chicago, 1970). On the Children's Bureau see especially Nancy P. Weiss, "Save the Children: A History of the Children's Bureau, 1903–1918" (Ph.D. dissertation, UCLA, 1974) and Louis J. Covotsos, "Child Labor and Social Progress: A History of the United States Children's Bureau, 1912–1935" (Ph.D. dissertation, University of Chicago, 1976). J. Stanley Lemons, "The Sheppard-Towner Act: Progressivism in the 1920s," *Journal of American History* 55 (March 1969), examines the important postwar legislation affecting maternal and infant care.

Chapter 7.
Black Americans and the First World War

The history of black Americans is now comprehensively documented, but surprisingly the First World War has not received as much attention as it might warrant. Black migration and urbanization is the focus of Allan H. Spear, *Black Chicago: The Making of a Negro Ghetto, 1890–1920* (Chicago, 1967) and Gilbert Osofsky, *Harlem: The Making of a Ghetto* (New York, 1968), but neither pays particular attention to the effects of the war. Kenneth L. Kusmer, *A Ghetto Takes Shape: Black Cleveland, 1870–1930* (Urbana, Ill., Chicago, and London, 1978) is full of insight and useful comparisons, while David Gordon Nielson, *Black Ethos: Northern Urban Negro Life and Thought, 1890–1930* (Westport, Conn., and London, 1977), is a superb general study that includes much social and cultural material. An interesting comparison between blacks and women is made in James R. Burns, "Continuity and Change: A Comparative Study of the Afro-Americans and the Women Suffragists as Minority Groups in American Society, 1900–1929" (M. Phil. thesis, Sheffield, England, 1978).

The black military experience is described briefly in Jack D. Foner, *Blacks and the Military in American History* (New York, 1974) and in Arthur E. Barbeau and Florette Henri, *The Unknown Soldiers: Black American Troops in World War I* (Philadelphia, 1974). Useful documents can be found in the valuable collection compiled by Morris J. MacGregor and Bernard C. Nalty, *Blacks in the United States Armed Forces: Basic Documents, Vol. IV: Segregation Entrenched 1917–1940* (Wilmington, Del., 1977).

The black migration and its consequences are discussed in Florette Henri, *Black Migration: Movement North 1900–1920* (Garden City, N.Y., 1975), Elliott M. Rudwick, *Race Riot at East St. Louis, July 2, 1917* (Carbondale, Ill., 1964), William M. Tuttle, Jr., *Race Riot: Chicago in the Red Summer of 1919* (New York, 1977), and Arthur I. Waskow, *From Race Riot to Sit-In: 1919 and the 1960s* (Garden City, N.Y., 1967).

The histories of black organizations and leaders reveal something of the forces affecting black life. Langston Hughes, *Fight For Freedom: The Story of the NAACP* (New York, 1962) has much information. Nancy J. Weiss, *The National Urban League 1910–1940* (New York, 1974) is a more academic book. Herbert Aptheker, ed., *The Correspondence of W. E. B. DuBois: Vol. I: Selections 1877–1934* (Boston, 1973) provides interesting insights. On black "militants," see Theodore Kornweible, Jr., *No Crystal Stair: Black Life and the Messenger, 1917–1928* (Westport, Conn., and London, 1975). Jervis Anderson, *A. Philip Randolph: A Biographical Portrait* (New York, 1973) also deals with the early career of the black leader.

Chapter 8.
The Aftermath of War

The only study of reconstruction is Burl Noggle's *Into The Twenties: The United States from Armistice to Normalcy* (Urbana, Ill., Chicago, and London, 1974), but this has gaps in social and economic areas. For labor and other disorders see Robert K. Murray, *Red Scare: A Study in National Hysteria 1919–1920* (New York, Toronto, and London, 1964) and W. E. Leuchtenburg, *The Perils of Prosperity, 1914–1932* (Chicago and London, 1958). Also on the Red Scare one must read John Higham, *Strangers in the Land: Patterns of American Nativism, 1860–1920* (New York, 1973) and Stanley Coben's seminal "A Study in Nativism: The American Red Scare of 1919–20," *Political Science Quarterly* 79 (March 1964). Coben's study, *A. Mitchell Palmer: Politician* (New York, 1972), has much general information and is judicious in its conclusions. Julian F. Jaffe, *Crusade Against Radicalism: New York During the Red Scare, 1914–1924* (New York and London, 1972) provides much material on the Empire State and the activities of the Lusk Committee.

On postwar labor problems Robert L. Friedham's *The Seattle General Strike* (Seattle, 1964) is a detailed narrative. More analysis of labor troubles can be found in David Brody, *Labor in Crisis: The Steel Strike of 1919* (Philadelphia and New York, 1965). The most important single study of labor in the postwar period remains Irving Bernstein's *The Lean Years: A History of the American Worker 1920–1933* (Boston, 1960).

A reevaluation of the Harding administration can be found in Eugene P. Trani and David L. Wilson, *The Presidency of Warren G. Harding* (Lawrence, Kans., 1977). In addition to the works already cited on Herbert Hoover, the postwar period is covered by Gary Dean Best, *The Politics of Individualism: Herbert Hoover in Transition, 1918–1921* (Westport, Conn., 1975).

The issue of progressivism in the twenties is fully explored in a number of articles: Arthur S. Link, "What Happened to the Progressive Movement in the 1920s," *American Historical Review* 64 (July 1959), Allen F. Davis, "Welfare, Reform and World War," *American Quarterly* 19 (Fall 1967), and Sidney Kaplan, "Social Engineers as Saviours: Effects of World War I on Some

American Liberals," *Journal of the History of Ideas* 17 (June 1956). The postwar history of progressive organizations can be found in Kenneth C. MacKay, *The Progressive Movement of 1924* (New York, 1947), Amos Pinchot, *History of the Progressive Party* (New York, 1958), and in various biographies, such as Richard Lowitt, *George W. Norris: The Persistence of a Progressive, 1913–1933* (Urbana, Ill., Chicago, and London, 1971) and Belle Case LaFollette and Fola LaFollette, *Robert M. LaFollette, June 14, 1855–June 18, 1925* (New York, 1953).

J. Stanley Lemons, *The Woman Citizen: Social Feminism in the 1920s,* (Urbana, Ill., Chicago, and London, 1973) examines an important aspect of progressivism's survival, and Susan Ware, *Beyond Suffrage: Women in the New Deal* (Cambridge, Mass., and London, 1981) follows through into the later period.

On the twenties generally Donald R. McCoy, *Coming of Age: The United States During the 1920s and 1930s* (Harmondsworth, Middlesex, 1973) and J. Leonard Bates, *The United States 1898–1938: Progressivism and a Society in Transition* (New York, 1976) are both well-balanced, detailed surveys of the period. John Tipple, ed., *Crisis of the American Dream: A History of American Social Thought, 1920–1940* (New York, 1968) is an interesting collection of contemporary extracts and comments, while John Braeman et al., eds., *Change and Continuity in Twentieth Century America: The 1920s* (New York, 1966) is a valuable collection of articles reexamining the postwar period. Paul A. Carter, *Another Part of the Twenties* (New York, 1977) is a thoughtful consideration of the decade.

Index

257